American Development Control:

Parallels and Paradoxes from an English Perspective

Richard Wakeford

London: HMSO

This report is the outcome of a year's study
in the United States in 1987–88 by the author,
who is an administrator in the British Government's Department of the Environment. His
study leave was sponsored by that Department under the Nuffield and Leverhulme
Travelling Fellowships programme administered by the Cabinet Office. All the views
expressed in this report are the responsibility
of the author, and are not necessarily those
of the Department. But the Department sees
this work as a worthwhile contribution to the
subject of land use planning and therefore
supports its publication by HMSO.

HMSO

HMSO publications are available from:

HMSO Publications Centre
(Mail and telephone orders only)
PO Box 276, London, SW8 5DT
Telephone orders 01-873 9090
General enquiries 01-873 0011
(queuing system in operation for both numbers)

HMSO Bookshops
49 High Holborn, London, WC1V 6HB   01-873 0011 (Counter service only)
258 Broad Street, Birmingham, B1 2HE   021-643 3740
Southey House, 33 Wine Street, Bristol, BS1 2BQ   (0272) 264306
9-21 Princess Street, Manchester, M60 8AS   061-834 7201
80 Chichester Street, Belfast, BT1 4JY   (0232) 238451
71 Lothian Road, Edinburgh, EH3 9AZ   031-228 4181

HMSO's Accredited Agents
(see Yellow Pages)

and through good booksellers

From 6 May 1990 the London telephone numbers above carry the prefix '071'
instead of '01'.

ISBN 0 11 752269 4

Contents

Preface

This is a paper about land use planning in the United States. It examines development control in that country from a reasonably basic perspective, and points up some of the parallels with the British planning system. I have never intended that it should be comprehensive in its coverage. The idea is simply to explain, primarily to a British audience, the basic development control methods used and how we might learn from successes and mistakes of initiatives tried. One feature of American public administration is the extent of 'home rule', or local independence, that makes the 50 states a kind of giant test bed.

My original aim was to set down the development control mechanisms of the United States in a factual way, complementing the studies of the control of development in four European countries, carried out by the Joint Centre for Land Development Studies at the University of Reading*. However, I had not been long in the United States before I realised that planning and development control methods reflect the history, character and national identity of the country concerned. Despite our almost common language, the American attitudes to land are very much at odds with those in long and densely populated England.

So, this paper starts by considering how the character of the United States and its people has led to current patterns of development, and how a different approach to local government and a national Constitution have constrained the evolution of development control methods. It then describes the widespread techniques of zoning and subdivision control, and who operates them. In the apparent absence of any data, I sought information about the efficiency and extent of control from a number of local governments and have set this out in the text. The information supplied was clearly not prepared on the basis of common definitions, but it is sufficient to quantify some of the parallels and differences between the American and British control systems.

Finally, this paper examines some aspects of American practice that have something to say to us in England. There are chapters on the co-ordination of control systems by states, on what it can cost developers to buy development rights, on the extent to which mechanisms such as incentive zoning approach the flexibility of discretionary control, and on using the planning system to deliver affordable housing.

This paper has its roots in a report I was required to write as the price for a year's travelling fellowship sponsored by the British government – a Nuffield and Leverhulme Travelling Fellowship. The rules required me to submit a report to the Permanent Secretary of the sponsoring Ministry, the Department of the Environment. I decided that if I was so certain that what I had elected to do with my year was worthwhile, then I should be prepared to share my findings with a wider audience.

---

* The reports of these studies were published by Her Majesty's Stationery Office in April 1989 (ISBN 0 11 752079).

My perspective is neither that of a professional planner, nor that of an academic specialising in the urban field. But, thanks to the patient help of many individuals involved in development control in America, I believe that I have gained a reasonable appreciation of these matters. Nor do I write, as so many have written about the American planning process, with any legal qualification. But, by the nature of my work as an administrator in the English Department of the Environment, I do recognise the importance of the law and legal processes in the planning field. Nor can I apply any special economics perspectives, though at various points the concept of economic efficiency is an important element in analysing planning mechanisms. My approach has been to meld aspects of all these fields, and to put together a document that might be read by those in England – of whatever professional approach – wanting to expand their horizons and find out more about how American planning processes operate. I have also been encouraged to think that some Americans too might be interested to see how one interested visitor has perceived their planning process. I hope that, whichever side of the Atlantic this paper is read, it will stimulate objective thoughts about the way we trample and tiptoe in the field of property rights.

Before whetting the reader's appetite with an introductory chapter, I should acknowledge the tremendous degree to which I have relied on the help and support of others. There are so many that I cannot mention them all here. But in particular, I should say that the year was based on an idea from John Pearson, and materialised through the tremendous support of John Delafons in the Department of the Environment and of the Woodrow Wilson School of Public and International Affairs at Princeton University (they did not really think I would materialise – O ye of little faith!). That I was able to learn something about American planning so quickly was due in no small measure to the unstinting efforts of David Callies, to the determination of Ingrid Reed that I should involve myself in real planning policy in central New Jersey, to the welcome of the Lincoln Institute of Land Policy, and to the American Planning Association's superbly organised convention in San Antonio, Texas. Countless thanks are also due to those who made me welcome in so many cities, especially to Dick Roddewig in Chicago and Will Fleissig in Denver. And to Steve Decter of West Windsor, New Jersey, and Henry Richmond of the 1000 Friends of Oregon, who had the courage to accept a complete stranger to work briefly in their organisations.

I must thank two other special people at Princeton University; Ann de Marchi-Corwin for repeated injections of positive enthusiasm, and Professor Chester Rapkin just for being there. For insight, I must acknowledge Dick Babcock especially; and above all from start to finish I am greatly indebted to Professor Malcolm Grant of University College, London who provided me with key introductions and then proceeded to bully me mercilessly until this report was finally written and published.

Whilst I readily acknowledge all these sources of inspiration and help, I take full and personal responsibility for the views expressed in this report. In particular, the content should not be taken as having been endorsed in any way by the British Department of the Environment.

1   Introduction

Parallels and perpendiculars

One of the more popular books about American land use planning is Dick Babcock's 'Zoning Game Revisited'. It contains a foreword written by Sir Desmond Heap, doyen of the English land use lawyers and a respected commentator on both English and American planning systems. Sir Desmond suggests that the characteristics of the systems are so wildly different that there is a yawning gulf between them. He ends up by declaring agreement with the Babcock sentiment that the United States process of land use control remains unfair, and is patently in need of reform.

While accepting that there are major differences, I believe that land use planning practices in Britain and the United States are as close as they have ever been. The evolution of land use planning structures in the different countries from different starting points has brought about some interesting contrasts. For example, in Britain recent legislation enables zones to be established in which development rights can be granted for particular sizes of buildings and types of uses in advance of any specific application. Such zoning is one well established form of development control found almost everywhere in the United States.

At the same time, state-wide planning initiatives are increasingly bringing to America the equivalents of structure or regional plans, designating areas for growth and areas for strict control of growth, covering regions containing many local government units. This comes at a time when development plans in Britain seem likely to become more locally based.

And, on both sides of the Atlantic, there is debate over the ethics of elected or appointed officials bargaining away development restrictions in return for other benefits offered by the developer to the community.

Such parallels indicate that this is a good time for comparative study. In reality the processes seem even closer than books imply. The process that can be readily observed in local government council chambers all across the United States resembles that in English local authority committee rooms. Admittedly the legal basis for the discussions – the framework of the negotiating process – is completely different. That is why the complex cases told so entertainingly by Babcock seem so alien to the British observer. But the actors are essentially the same. There are *developers* seeking to overcome what they perceive as the major hurdle of local authority consent, *neighbours* defending their communities and property values against the uncertainties of change, and *interest groups* calling for 'growth management' or the protection of open space or historic buildings. In the middle is the *local government* concerned. Many of the parties will be advised or represented by professionals, reflecting the increasing legal complexity of the devices employed in recent years, and the increasing likelihood of having to resort to some kind of appeal, in both Britain and America.

The thrust of deregulation in Britain, combined with what some comment-ators have represented as increasing central Government dominance over local government, are leading to processes resembling the original American simplicity of uncomplicated zoning to implement locally independent master plans. Meanwhile, in the United States, particularly in the more densely developed areas, there is a gradual drift towards slower, more complicated methods of 'growth management', employing mechanisms of discretionary review and consultation which the British have used for many years, but which the British Government is currently aiming to streamline.

A comparative overview of recent changes in planning practice

In its essentials the British system remains firmly founded in the Town and Country Planning Act 1947. That Act established the current definition of development subject to local authority control; it limited severely what could be undertaken without planning permission. Compared with United States practice the extent of control may seem excessive (but in the United States zoning shapes many very minor developments by determining certain overall constraints; just because the development proposed is not a subject for discretionary control, that does not mean that it is not regulated).

The 1971 Act[1], which consolidated the earlier legislation, brings under control the carrying out of any building, engineering, mining, or other operations in, on, over or under land, or the making of any material change in the use of any buildings or land. But it goes on to make clear that some works and uses are not to constitute development. In addition, a general permission for a very wide range of minor developments is granted by central government order; this General Development Order permission is very much akin to the American method of permitting development by local zoning ordinance. Provided that you do not breach the envelope or regulation in the ordinance, you will generally be entitled to a permit. But there are two main differences.

Firstly, in Britain the boundary between what is permitted and what is not is determined nationally by central Government, which decides what types of development may proceed without local government intervention. Until recently there were only two degrees of sensitivity – normal areas and conservation areas. By contrast, in the United States the individual local government units determine their own standards, subject only to the constraints of the Constitution and the enabling act in force in the state concerned, and these standards are different for each zone created.

Second, despite the harsh bite of development control in some suburban American jurisdictions, the degree of control measured by the number of discretionary planning actions per head of population is comparatively less in the United States. In other words, more is permitted without local government intervention than in Britain. The British General Development Order permits only minor developments.

That is not to say that local government influence over development is less in the United States than in Britain. In the United States, it is generally clear from the zoning ordinance what development and uses of land are permitted by right. But whether that is necessarily what a developer would want to achieve is another matter. It is difficult to assess how many developments go ahead in a way that is less than ideal, because of the zoning requirement and the difficulty of obtaining a variance for the ideal solution. By contrast, in Britain, a developer is free to put in an application

Figure 1.1 San Francisco; where the City has recently moved to prohibit demolition of single family housing, where there is a strict quota on the downtown office floor space that may be approved each year, and where even developments permitted by the zoning ordinance may nevertheless be called in for review by the Planning Commission to ensure neighbourhood compatibility of what is proposed. An illustration of American development control extending far beyond that in most of Britain.

for whatever shape of development he cares to design. That application must be considered on its merits by the local planning authority and only refused if there are sound and compelling reasons. One such reason for refusal may be the provisions of the local government prepared development plan. But that is not a prescriptive document; it is simply one of the material considerations that may impinge on the presumption in favour of development. So, in Britain the outcome of an application might be far less certain, but the design details of the development are not automatically constrained by universally applied setback or lot coverage requirements.

The fundamental principle in Britain that development should always be permitted unless there are sound and clear cut reasons for refusal or conditional consent has been the subject of reminders to local authorities from central Government. Those reminders are backed up by the British quasi-judicial appeals system, which allows a Minister of the Crown to consider afresh and allow an application for development refused earlier by a local authority. The presumption in favour of development has been strengthened through a reinforcement of the policy on the award of costs where refusals result in appeals not justified by substantial reasons. And the requirement for local authorities to give reasons for their decisions has added to the discipline.

The movement in the United States seems to be in the opposite direction – towards less certainty for the developer. What the zoning ordinance permits seems less and less likely to be what the developer would himself want to pursue. The current demands for mixed use, or planned unit, developments are less and less likely to accord with the basic zoning in force for any particular site. Zoning ordinances are being amended to permit less, in order to accommodate extra floorspace bonuses for particular types of development, or schemes to transfer development rights from area to area, or simply to ensure that local governments have a discretion to review development. Conditional uses, and overlay zoning have become widely used devices. The result is more and more haggling in the planning boards, often at late night hearings, rather than the certainty which once seemed an important characteristic of zoning.

While Americans seem to be introducing uncertainty, in Britain the Government has been looking for less regulation. I have mentioned that zoning is now on the menu. The latest planning legislation – the Housing and Planning Act 1986 – introduced the concept of simplified planning zones. These zones represent a new technique for facilitating development in designated areas, where the planning authority is entitled to grant a general permission in advance for types of development defined in the plan for the zone. There is then no need for a planning application or the consequent application fee. This is simpler even than the American model, where permits are often needed for permitted development, if only to certify that the development conforms with the zoning ordinance.

Another likely change in the British planning process is a change in the local government tier responsible for the preparation of the development plan. This is the only document the legislation specifically requires to be taken into account in reaching development control decisions. Subject to the passage of legislation, development plans will be prepared by the district and borough councils everywhere. This will complete the transition from the earlier two tier development planning system with district and borough plans prepared to conform with county prepared structure plans approved by the Secretary of State. The future county role will be limited to preparing strategies on specified subjects – transportation in particular. By contrast, in the United States there is a distinct trend towards the production of plans and procedures covering more than a local government area. The aim is to overcome the disadvantages of local government fragmentation and parochial decision taking. In New Jersey, for example, a state planning commission has been hard at work. A final state development and redevelopment plan should emerge, after a process called 'cross acceptance' – a super-consultative process involving adjustment of both local master plans and preliminary state plan until they conform – with the counties playing a intermediate arbitration role. Preparation of New Jersey's plan looks like taking at least 5 years from start to finish, and it is not clear just how much impact the plan will have on local decisions. Despite the slow progress, the direction is clearly towards a hierarchy of planning documents and control systems; this increased regulation is found in other states too, and contrasts with the thrust of deregulation in Britain during the same period.

A further area of common interest concerns 'exactions', where a developer is required to make contributions in cash or in kind, as the price for his permit. These demands are justified by reference to the extra demands on infrastructure that new development creates – perhaps a new school, or sewers or roads that the existing community would not otherwise require. In Britain the Government's aim is to secure adherence to its guidance on 'planning gain' (the British term) and keep such exactions to a minimum. This position contrasts with the development of mechanisms in the States designed to maximise such contributions within the limitations of the Constitution. States are enacting enabling legislation, and the US Supreme Court, by its recent forays into the field, has encouraged more local governments to devise ordinances up to the limit of what seems to be permitted. Both the British and the American actions represent financial innovation at the local level partly as a reaction to increasing constraints over local government spending.

Figure 1.2 Route 1 in New Jersey. The state transportation department has prepared a package of legislation that will allow much greater state control over the creation of accesses to such main roads from new development. The aim is to tackle congestion and safety. In England the role of highway authorities in examining planning applications has been reduced from one of direction–being able to require conditions, or even refusal–to an advisory role, a deregulation initiative.

Figure 1.3 A thriving warehouse in the path of waterfront development in Jersey City, New Jersey. In Portland, Oregon (and Chicago, Boston, New York City . . .), measures have recently been adopted to protect manufacturing districts from an insurgence of office and residential conversions. By contrast, in Britain the 1987 Use Classes Order removed planning control nationwide over changes of use between light industrial and office uses. US cities are able to translate their social concerns into ordinances, while the British planning system is concentrated more on physical use and development.

Many recent changes in Britain have been initiated under the theme of deregulation. A similar driving force seems unlikely to emerge in the United States, where there are many thousands of planning systems, directed within 50 different legal structures, and with no apparent influence from the centre. President Reagan's deregulatory Federal government chose not to attempt to influence any local land use planning process. State governments, which are seen as responsible for the economic health of their electorates, seem largely unconcerned about the efficiency of municipalities in their areas, or indeed about the efficiency of their own review processes. At the local level, the system is frequently dominated by volunteers whose main aim is to reach the best decision for their locality – the local people who have trusted them to act wisely – even if that means increased bureaucracy and permit requirements. One manifestation of this is the increasing scale and scope of local ordinances; many municipalities find it politically expedient to create an ordinance in response to every local problem. An extreme example of this is to be found in one Idaho locality's control over fence construction materials, introduced to stem a spate of corrugated iron fences. During my time in New Jersey I often read of how only certified builders would be allowed to operate in townships, because residents had suffered from 'cowboy operators'. In another example, an ordinance requiring clear street numbers to be placed on every building was introduced because the fire company could not easily locate new buildings. The degree to which such ordinances are enforced varies widely. Achievement of Oregon's much vaunted state-wide planning goals is said by some to be endangered by the unwillingness of the rural county administrations to implement plans forced upon them by the state requiring the refusal of piecemeal development of non-farm dwellings on farm land, an unpopular requirement among local farmers.

In short, increasing environmental awareness at the local level is driving the American development control system towards the much more refined control that the density of population and mixture and intensity of uses in Britain have long justified. In Britain meanwhile, experiments such as simplified planning zones may represent a trend to a system as straightforward as the American system once was. The British government is able to pursue this theme because there are so many fewer planning authorities, each with a substantial full time development control staff, and because it has a direct part to play in the administration of the planning system through its approval of development plans, its ability to call-in applications, its role in deciding appeals, and through advice in circulars designed to influence local decisions.

The aspect where the two systems are fundamentally different and will remain so is their legal foundation. In England and Wales the planning system founded in the 1947 Act is intended to regulate the development and use of land *in the public interest*. The planning system is not intended to protect the private interests of one person against the activities of another, although sometimes it is operated to that effect. And yet the protection of private property rights and values is one premise upon which Euclidean[2] zoning in the United States is founded – that the value of the property of one individual must be safeguarded against nearby development that would devalue it, and incidentally reduce the local tax base. Of course public and private interests inevitably converge, but they surface in differences, for example in the lack of any *right* for the third party to be heard in the British planning process, and in the lack of any easy appeal (short of expensive legal action in the courts) against the *grant* of planning permission by a local authority. So, it is fascinating in the United States to see the effects of the procedural due process requirement of the Constitution – interested parties speaking up for their own property, and having their views taken into account. Equally, it is agonising to observe how different local governments believe that the constitutional requirement not to 'take' land binds their hands and prevents them introducing the regulation sound planning seems to demand. Planning administration takes on many different characteristics in many different places according to the interpretation adopted or the risks taken in regulation. Always the contrast is with Britain where there is very rarely any inherent development value to be 'taken' in advance of a planning permission being granted, because the development rights remain effectively nationalised since the 1947 Act.

Despite the differences, much of what transpires is so similar as to demonstrate that our processes are closer than might be inferred from Sir Desmond's words in Babcock's book. If we were to represent the British and American development control systems as ships on the ocean, each in search of some ideal or promised land, they might be seen to be on parallel courses but travelling in opposite directions. One is going towards the destination of more complexity, while the other has set course for the original American embarkation point. As they pass, there seems no better time to compare notes on our respective problems and to take stock. This paper is intended to aid such a process and to provide a snapshot of the American system of development control in the late 1980s. It is written to encourage those on both sides of the Atlantic to develop policies and administration with a slightly wider perspective.

About this paper

In this context of comparison, this paper sets out to describe American land use planning systems – and there are many of them – in a discursive way. First, it establishes the framework in which development control operates – the vast amount of space, the continuing frontier spirit, and the pattern of communities and the resultant political structure. The role of the Constitution is also an important part of this framework. Second, it explains the menu of zoning and sub-division controls, twin components of the development control process, and some of the other development control mechanisms employed. These chapters are followed by appraisals of how these menu items are combined to create the current scope of control, of the resultant operational efficiency, and of the different organisations by which people operate the controls for their areas.

The remaining chapters are devoted to discussion of four crucial policy concerns currently shared by both Britain and America. The first area explored is the action of some states and other agencies to bring a wider perspective to land use planning decisions. The foremost example is the state of Oregon but others have followed similar courses. The focus has been to seek to shift to developers the full costs on society of its locational demands, to overcome the distortions of local government diffusion and fiscal uncertainty, and generally to create devices to protect wide areas against the adverse effects of intensive development in environmentally sensitive areas. The British reader may find it difficult to appreciate just how rapidly a wide landscape in America can change as it becomes the focus of development pressure. There is no order to the patchwork of housing subdivisions, office parks and shopping malls. It is to try to focus and redirect some of that development energy that states and other regional bodies have begun to act.

Secondly, Chapter 9 explores the extent to which it is proper to exact payments from developers, in cash or in kind, either by discretionary or mandatory means, in return for a development permit. In America, such exactions or impact fees are increasingly required and the interest in them could be seen from the high attendance at the relevant sessions of the 1988 American Planning Association conference (at which the agenda was dominated by such issues). In Britain too, developers have been increasingly concerned about the contributions they have been asked to make as part of planning agreements with local authorities. Perhaps a formally authorised system of bargaining for development rights, or at least requiring developers to pay the costs their developments impose on society could deliver more economically efficient decisions about land use.

Chapter 10 examines of the tensions between as-of-right and discretionary permitting systems, drawing on the specific experiences of New York City with zoning bonuses and special districts. This issue may be characterised as cities and communities using the zoning system to create an artificial currency, which can then be used to pay for the sort of amenities more traditionally provided from local taxes. There is widespread uncertainty about the 'proper' levels of provision in zoning ordinances. Should the basic ordinance reflect the maximum amount of development that the community and its planners judge ought to take place (in which case any derogation would clearly cause unwanted environmental damage to set against any public benefit produced by the bonus scheme)? Or, at the other extreme, should the zoning be reduced to the minimum possible without compensation being payable to the landowner, so that development can be strictly controlled and publicly held development rights bid for? The gap between the two approaches is frequently very wide – and depends on such factors as the tautness and timing of the original introduction of zoning to a given community. No such zoning quandary faces British local government, where most development rights rest with the controlling body, to be dispensed in response to applications, and where the development value in land generally accrues from speculative factors which local government actions may change without compensation being payable. Even in this discretionary system, however, each development control decision must surely be taken against a subconscious vision of the maximum possible development for a given site; and there may well be a temptation to go beyond that limitation in return for some extraneous benefit through 'planning gain' contributed by the developer.

This theme is continued in Chapter 11 which describes perhaps the most ambitious of examples of trading zoning rights for public benefits. New Jersey developers can obtain authority for much denser housing development, provided that they either set aside and deed-restrict 20 per cent of the units for households with low and moderate incomes, or make payments into a fund to secure such provision elsewhere. Planning for low income housing in the United States, unlike the general position in Britain, can involve the use of land use planning mechanisms to determine the characteristics, by reference to income, of those entitled to own what is ultimately built. The British exception is in low cost housing to meet local needs in rural areas, additional to the normal housing provision in the development plan.

In summing up, in Chapter 12, perhaps the pervasive theme is the difficulty of attempting to shape development at little public cost within a constitutional framework where there is greater expectation of being able to develop land, and a greater risk that a local government going too far (or its insurers) will have to bear an enormous financial burden. Sometimes the development value created by the same local government at an earlier stage needs to be bought out, by fair means or foul. Many of the innovative devices in land use planning in the United States are designed to create a currency which may be spent on local socially desirable objectives. Transfer of development rights schemes to preserve historic buildings or open countryside, density bonus provisions in zoning ordinances on condition that subsidised housing is incorporated in the development, and impact fees securing developers' cash for parks, schools or sewers, are all initiatives designed to secure public goals without the public paying the full cash price. It is a salutary thought to consider how the British planning process might change if there was even a partial shift of development rights back to the landowner. Yet such a trend might seem possible with the simplified planning zone possibilities, the changes in the Use Classes Order, and the designation of planning free areas such as enterprise zones. Add to that scenario the prospect with district level development plans of more fragmented local government, dependent under the new poll tax on its local tax base for more of its local income, and some of the American devices do not seem quite so irrelevant.

NOTES TO CHAPTER 1

1. The Town and Country Planning Act 1971.

2. The term zoning is sometimes qualified by reference to the landmark Supreme Court case, *Village of Euclid v Amber Realty Co*, (272 US 365 (1926)) in which the owner of 68 acres of land appealed a zoning ordinance which reduced the value of that land from $10,000 to $2,500. The Village's zoning ordinance restricted use of the property for apartment houses, churches, schools or any other public or semi-public buildings. The Court declared that the ordinance was valid, and that it was legitimate to segregate different uses, and even different building types which might inhibit construction of other types of building.

2 The Nation in Perspective: Land and People

Introduction

Colonial Williamsburg could be said to be the ultimate historical theme park. Each year millions come to see this partly restored, partly reconstructed colonial city, established in the 1690s, and reborn this century due to the vision of the Reverend Goodwin and the support of John D Rockefeller. What visitors see is one of the first planned cities in America. The street plan was drawn up by the colonial governor, and development control mechanisms then shaped the settlement[1]. The size of building that could be erected depended on the importance of the street. On the main street, linking the Capitol Building with the College of William and Mary, houses had to come within 6 feet of the street and no nearer, and the lots had to be enclosed within 6 months from construction of the building so as to define the boundary between the public and private domain. What the visitor sees at Williamsburg is not typical of most American small towns today, even given that there are common principles of streets laid out and zoning ordinances prescribing the development that is to be permitted by reference to height and set-back.

Yet many Americans subscribe to the vision of a town of the scale of Williamsburg as their ideal community. Dislike of conditions in the cities, places created through economic necessity, and the desire for security in a select and confined community, if possible with a rural feel, has led to successive waves of suburbanisation. Conditions in cities have been responsible too for fuelling the drive towards the frontiers. Today, a combination of the traditional frontier spirit and ever lengthening suburban tentacles are leading to renewed growth in what has been termed America's 'New heartland'[2]. The contrast between the small town ideal and the visual appearance of most suburban areas has also led two prominent community architects to propose new planning rules for 'traditional neighborhoods'[3]. These proposed rules would require houses to be set back by no more than a precisely specified amount from the street, just as in colonial Williamsburg. Implementation of similar rules in a new village developed on the Gulf coast of Florida, has won Seaside international acclaim. It features in H.R.H. the Prince of Wales' personal view of architecture – 'A Vision of Britain' – in which extracts of the Urban Code are reproduced.

In cities too some are urging a return to development control systems of the past. Witnesses in New York City contributing to an examination of development amenities, the requirements made of developers to ameliorate community problems where normal planning limits would be breached, urged a return to the original 1916 type of simple zoning ordinance. Such a system would make clear precisely what was permitted and what was not. Others argue that the extraction of benefits is part of a bargaining process of increasing sophistication reflecting the market freedoms that have always characterised American society. In their view, the best outcome for the community will emerge from a negotiation between developer, local

10

government and local interest groups. That outcome does, however, require a careful balance of power among those parties.

The nature of land use planning mechanisms in play in any nation will reflect something of its history and character, its national identity and its constitution. In the United States constitutional freedoms, both actual and perceived, are a particularly important element. Moreover, the different constitutions and different court systems and attitudes in the different states lead to different applications of the planning process in the different states. What officials can achieve in Michigan is rather less than their counterparts of similar inventiveness in California. Before describing some of the mechanisms of American development control and their effects, and some of the issues of today, it is therefore important to identify the social framework. This chapter sets out to describe some of the demographic and political characteristics that have led to the urban structure of the United States today. The following chapter explains how that structure and certain of the basic constitutional freedoms continue to influence the pattern of the landscape.

The development urge and the frontier motivation

One US Congressman[4], not a land use specialist, summed up the American attitude to land use. 'America is addicted to growth,' he said, 'and to the concept that the supply of land is limitless. Economics has been so driving policy that the future is being imposed in a way that no-one would choose'. He suggested that the United States was alone among developed countries in allowing suburban sprawl to continue unchecked. He contrasted that observation with European planning which he perceived to be more concerned with the quality of life in urban neighbourhoods.

It would be difficult to gainsay the Congressman's observations in many of the denser parts of the United States. Land has always been seen as an asset to be exploited, often with little regard to the overall pattern of development that would result. His constituency is in Bergen County, part of New Jersey which has developed haphazardly, under the influence of nearby New York City. Concern about the shape of development there is largely a matter of hindsight. But not so far away, local government plans in the 'Skylands' part of the same state envisage that farmland, hills and forests will become vast tracts of residential or commercial development. The zoning has been prepared accordingly to allow huge developments of houses on one, two and five acre lots, and office parks that will convert large fields into neatly mown and watered sanitised landscapes. Farmers from these areas, appearing at the meetings of the State Planning Commission, regularly restated their expectation to be able to sell their land at high prices for development. They regard that as their inalienable right.

The amount of land

There is plenty of such land available even within the conurbation along the north east coast. One revealing journey is to drive the Taconic Parkway, a cars-only road leading north from New York City for some 200 miles. It was originally built to enable city dwellers to use their newly acquired cars as a recreational activity to escape to the open country. Now it is also a major commuter route. But within a half hour of Manhattan, there are already very few signs of human activity to be seen. The commuter settlements that are there lay hidden in the forests that surround the parkway, and towards the northern end appear great vistas of apparently empty, wooded landscapes. Yet this parkway is close to the relatively dense north east conurbation between Boston and Richmond Virginia – a string of cities that follow the fall line, the highest points navigable on rivers by the early settlers and the points where significant water power was available.

In the middle of the continent, the spaces are vast. The urge to tame that wilderness has traditionally run deep in the American culture, and continues to do so.

There is a vast amount of land available for exploitation, as the data in Figure 2.1 show.

Figure 2.1 Major uses of land in the United States and in the United Kingdom

Type of land use	United States (excl Alaska and Hawaii)	United Kingdom	England
Cropland	25%	22%	34%
Grassland and rough grazing	33%	55%	40%
Forests, woods, rural parks	36%	9%	7%
Urban land	**1.8%**	**12%**	**18%**
Wetlands, bare rock, desert, tundra	5%	—	—

Source: US figures adapted from Table 1 in *The Economics of Zoning Laws* by William Fischel, published by the Johns Hopkins University Press (1985). UK figures from Social Trends 1987, published by Her Majesty's Stationery Office, London.

Only 1.8 per cent of land in the United States is urban, compared with ten times that proportion in England. Moreover, that urbanised land is less intensively used in America, especially on the fringes of the metropolitan areas. The availability and sheer quantity of land, the encouragement of generous zoning provisions or even a total absence of zoning, and the traditional mobility of individuals and corporations (continuing the original immigrant spirit) foster a use and discard attitude with respect to land.

Another manifestation of the frontier mentality is what is known as the 'American dream'–the desire of a family to acquire a single family house of its own. That, the readiness to be mobile and the drive to live in an area with other families of the same or better social class, often meaning racial segregation, have combined to turn the United States into a largely suburban society. One contemporary historian, Kenneth Jackson[5], suggests that suburbia is the ultimate product of zoning, the separation of society into distinct categories with equality of all within the zones. The American suburban character, he suggests, has developed differently than that in Europe for four main reasons. First, with a few exceptions like Manhattan, the residential status of inner city living is low by comparison with the suburbs. This contrasts with the higher traditional status of housing in European city centres. Perhaps as part of this difference, there is also a different attitude to the use of land outside cities. In American suburbs, space in terms of lot size and its use as an ornament to the dwelling are important indicators of the wealth and status of the occupier. In Europe there is less land to use and thus less available for such ornamental purposes. Then there is the tradition of home ownership as the ideal way of securing shelter in American society and the relative ease until recently of achieving that ideal. And finally, the distance which Americans are prepared to travel to work is much greater than in European countries (some commuting distances into New York City are long indeed, even by comparison with the length of suburban tentacles following rail routes from London to the Home Counties). In short it can all be boiled down to space: plenty of it is available to be exploited by those wanting to escape the poorer areas. Those areas contain the poor or immigrants in turn attracted by the economic opportunity and affordability of those areas. Traditionally it has been the continuing exploitation of land on the fringes of cities and in the interior that has facilitated all this continuous movement.

The shaping of a nation

Most of the early American colonies were first settled in an agricultural pattern; that was inevitable as the distance to other food sources was immense. The first sizeable cities were the gateways on the east coast, trading locations where the resources of the hinterland were accumulated before export, where imported specialised products were stored and sold, and where the successive waves of settlers first became established, before moving on and making way for their successors. These settlements were compact, initially for the sake of safety from natives, but also because the traders and others in these new economic entities would generally have no alternative but to walk to their work. Examples of this type of compact development can still be seen in Charleston, South Carolina, in Savannah, Georgia, and in parts of central Philadelphia.

As the frontier was pushed back, forts were established inland, and on these more trading settlements were based. Rivers were the first routes into the interior of the nation. As the power of the rivers became harnessed, and canals were added to exploit the hinterland more efficiently, the next wave of cities developed. Then, the development of the railroads really drove the rapid expansion of the cities away from the east coast. The railroads were reacting to both government and public demand to open up both the fertile farmland and minerals west of the Appalachian mountains and the way to the west where the gold was. They were also motivated by real estate development profits. Many towns were established as a result of railroad land purchase and subdivision, and the sale of the lots in advance of the railroad construction helped to finance that construction.

The industrial revolution changed the pace of urban development in the United States just as it did in Europe. The early settlements developed in a spatially concentrated way because of the nature of the water or steam power used. Houses crowded around the factories so that people could walk to their place of work. Rapid development in the 1830s became intense in the 1860s with the demands of the Civil War. Agriculture was becoming sufficiently productive to support a greater urban population, and immigrants from Europe continued to arrive. Cities expanded rapidly, but continued to maintain a circular profile on the ground, unless otherwise constrained by physical features. Communities such as Paterson, New Jersey, and Lowell, Massachusetts still retain some of the character of that era.

In the last decades of the nineteenth century improvements in urban transport began to change this circular profile into shapes rather like starfish. Conditions in cities drove those who could afford it to want to move out. Transport became available to facilitate that objective. Many city dwellers were rural born, whether immigrants or people from the rural parts of America. They had a strong desire to escape urban conditions as far as possible, while still making a living out of the urban economy. Horse buses were initially so expensive that only the wealthiest could afford to move to large houses on the main thoroughfares leading out of the city centres. The installation of iron rails enabled more passengers to be carried more cheaply; the horse drawn trolley was born. After iron rails the next innovation was electric power. The effect of these innovations can be seen in the urban boundaries of cities like Boston. There the urban boundary expanded from 2 miles radius in the 1850s to 4 miles with the horse drawn railway. Electric power for these trolleys took the boundary out to 6 miles in the 1890s[6]. Development followed these trolley lines which, because of the heavy investment in infrastructure, were constructed only on the most important streets. These streets became lined with small shops – the first

Figure 2.2 Lowell, Massachusetts; One of the fastest developing mill towns in the 1840s, situated to exploit water power, and using vast amounts of immigrant labour.

commercial strips – while residential streets were built at right angles to the main street. Exactly the same phenomenon can be seen in the development pattern around the tram routes of London; but political boundaries within London have been revised so that the original development pattern has little relevance compared with some American cities in the east where today's political boundaries indicate the extent of development at the end of the last century.

At the same time rail routes used for the transportation of goods between cities became available for commuter services. The nature of the steam train was such that stops were spaced further apart than the trolleys; it took time and space to accelerate and decelerate. This meant a different pattern of land development superimposed on the starfish shapes generated by trolleys. Satellite towns became established. Here was good quality housing for the better off people who could afford the fares into town, but with that housing arranged quite densely on the developed land around the railway station. Large areas of this formerly agricultural land could most efficiently be covered with housing of the same design and cost. Railroad companies encouraged the sale of these houses to middle class families aspiring to healthier living. The segregation of the urban population by income and by ethnic origin had begun. The result was the classic pattern of spokes along the radial routes from cities, with denser development at points along the suburban railways. These various stages in the development of the city's 'footprint' are shown in simplified form in Figure 2.4 on pages 16–17.

14

Malone Park in West Orange, New Jersey is an example of an early suburb for the wealthiest escapees from the city. Built in the 1850s, the houses stand on lots of an acre or more along curvilinear roads with idyllic sounding names rather than numbers. There are spaces set aside as parks for common use. The common open space theme was picked up much later at the much studied planned suburb of Radburn, heavily influenced by Letchworth Garden Suburb in Hertfordshire, England. However, that theme was not copied widely, some say because in Radburn there was too much land in the public domain and not enough private space. Such private space is important in the American suburb as a component of the American dream, although it is less likely to be fenced than in the English counterpart.

The characteristic profile of the downtown areas as they appear today began to emerge around the turn of the century. At that time the introduction of lifts and steel construction methods facilitated much higher buildings, enabling the concentration of operations on one site for the large corporations that were beginning to dominate the American economy. The location of the downtown areas, where these taller buildings built to more modern standards were concentrated, was likely to be a little way away from their immediate predecessors in design, on cheaper land nearby. So, in parallel with the spread of residential development out to the edges of the cities there was also some shifting within the centres. That shift left room for businesses who could afford only lower rents, and close by were the houses of the poorest groups, who could not afford to move to any suburb, whether served by trolley or train.

Figure 2.3 Denver, Colorado; The shift of the central area can be seen, with the old warehouse district giving way to newer, taller buildings. Most recently, the old warehouse districts that characterise the older parts of the downtown areas of many cities are again attracting investment in shops, offices and hotels. The economic attraction of historic character is helping to regenerate such areas.

15

1. THE CITY UNTIL THE MID 19TH CENTURY

RIVER TO INTERIOR

FISHING PORT

OCEAN

original transhipment point 'fall line' where water power available: dense because able to walk to work.

roads beginning to serve agricultural settlements in the hinterland.

2. THE CITY IN THE MID 19TH CENTURY

RAILROAD

RAILROAD

ROAD

ROAD

city develops tentacles as roads are exploited first by horse bus then trolley

railroads penetrate deeper into the hinterland.

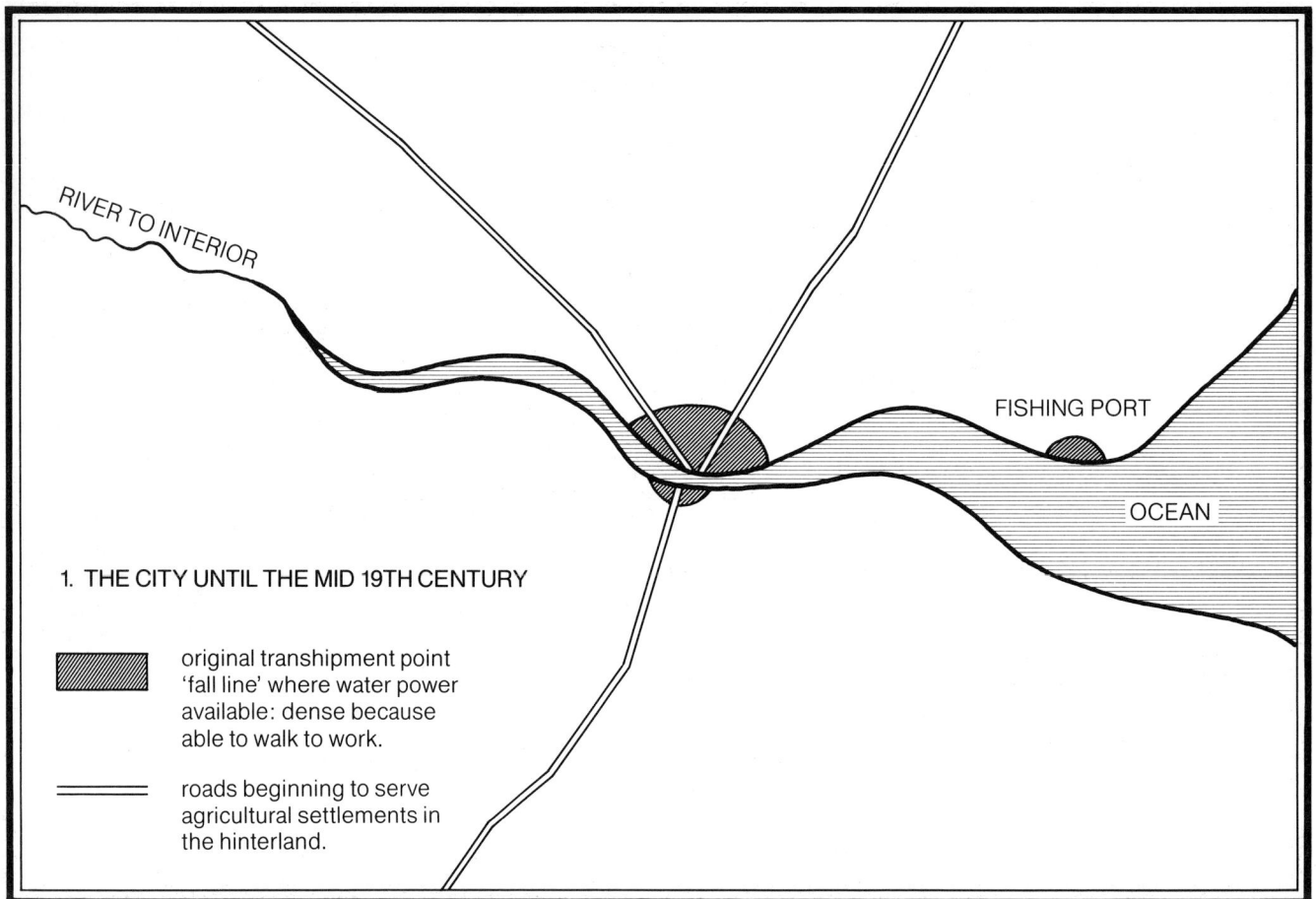

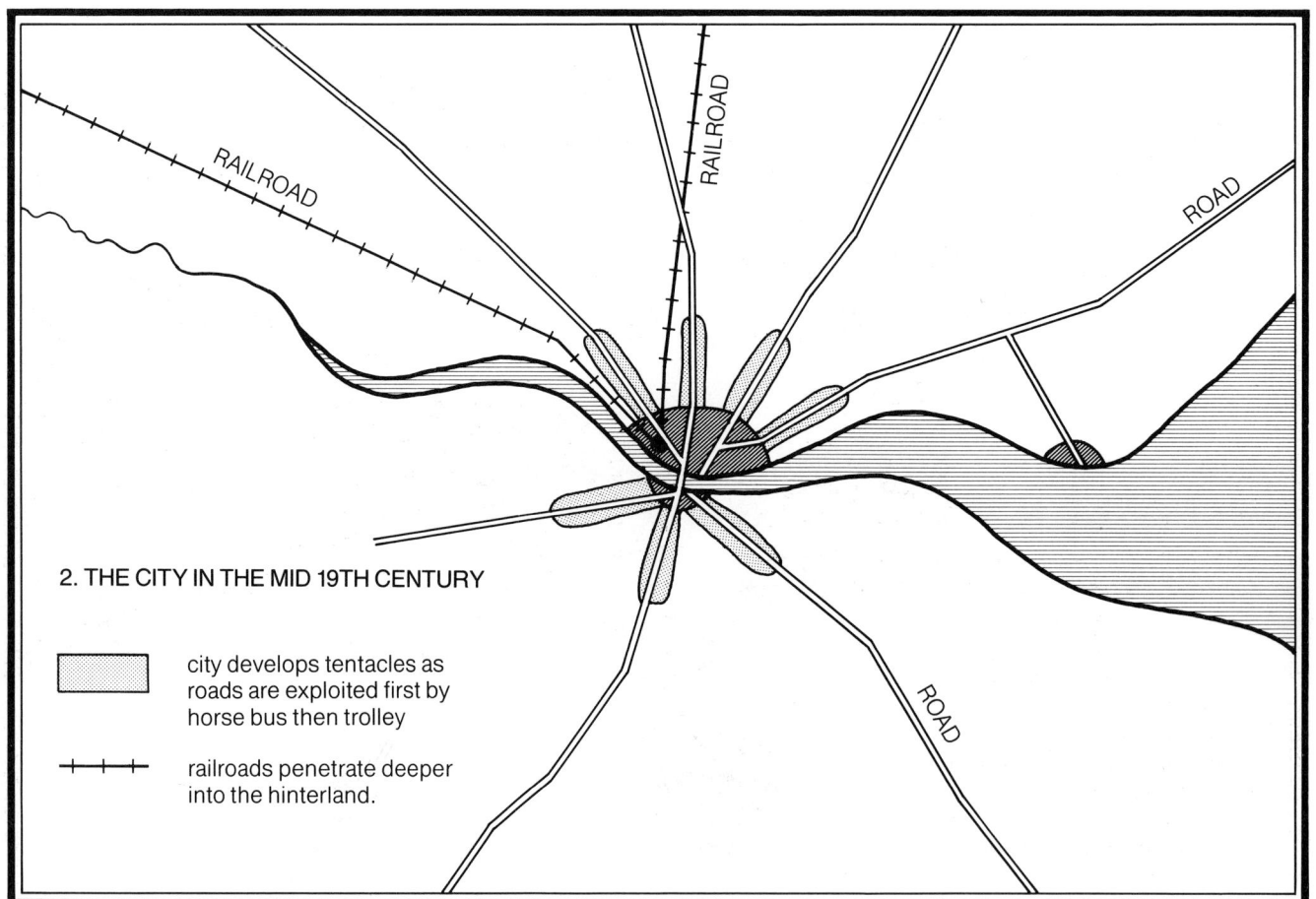

Figure 2.4 The effects of different transportation methods on the physical shape of the city

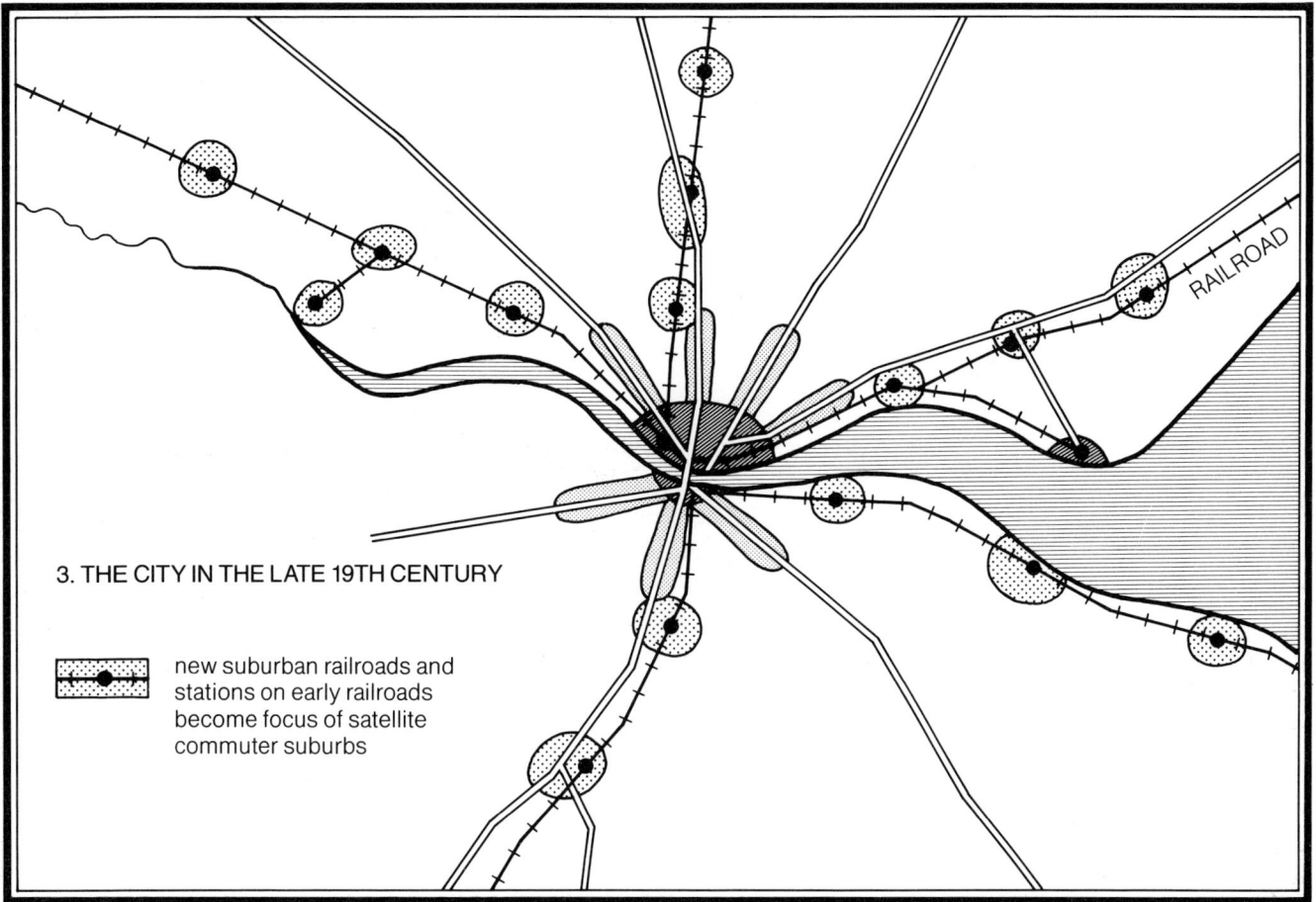

3. THE CITY IN THE LATE 19TH CENTURY

new suburban railroads and stations on early railroads become focus of satellite commuter suburbs

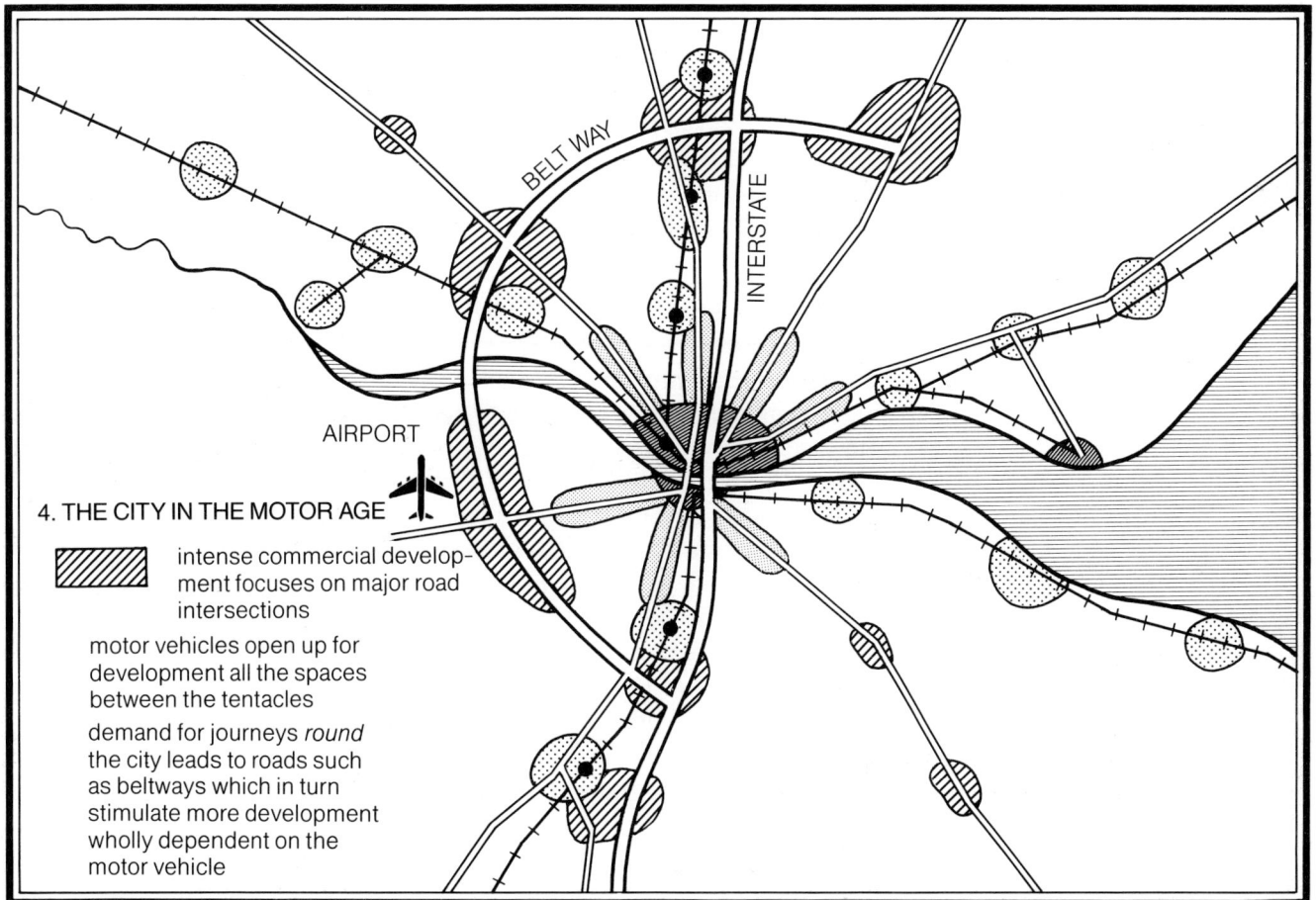

4. THE CITY IN THE MOTOR AGE

intense commercial development focuses on major road intersections

motor vehicles open up for development all the spaces between the tentacles

demand for journeys *round* the city leads to roads such as beltways which in turn stimulate more development wholly dependent on the motor vehicle

Then, on top of all this came the most profound impact of the motor car. No longer was development restricted to the spokes. All the spaces between the spokes could be filled in. Over the last 60 years, it is the motor car alone that has shaped America. Motor transport freed urban development from the traditional locational constraints. Industrial concerns could spread their processes over green field sites, rather than being constrained by operation on more than one floor in inner city sites. Mass production in suburban locations could be easily served by the motor lorry. But the most significant impact on development patterns was the spread of suburban housing, which continues unabated. The key elements enabling this rapid spread were:

i *The availability of cheap land;* this largely flows from the amount of land in the United States, and the relatively small population it needs to support. The existence well away from the cities of huge tracts of productive agricultural land that can be farmed very efficiently lowers the agricultural value of land around cities. Indeed, much of the woodland around the north-eastern cities is abandoned farmland that was important when it was difficult to transport fresh produce over long distances. But no longer is New Jersey – the 'Garden State' – the market garden of the cities of New York and Philadelphia. A wide range of choice of development sites flowed from the effective absence of artificial restrictions on the phasing of development. That wide choice of sites still keeps land prices comparatively low.

ii *Cheap construction methods;* the ready availability of timber resources from the earliest days has facilitated the development of cheap construction methods. There was a time when the nails in a house were more valuable than the timber, and after a fire the ashes were carefully sifted for nails to reuse. But, mass production of nails and standardisation of timber cutting on a two by four inch size enabled the development of what is known as 'balloon frame' house construction. Such construction methods enabled houses in the suburban expansion to be built cheaply, quickly, with minimum foundations, and employing only basic skills.

iii *Federal government encouragement;* after the depression of the early 1930s a scheme whereby the Federal Government subsidised home loans by guaranteeing mortgages began to lead to large scale development of single family housing for owner occupation. This process accelerated after the Second World War with the creation of new schemes to finance 'homes fit for heroes'. The Federal Housing Administration and Veterans' Administration insured long-term loans at low rates of interest. Income tax relief was introduced for home loan payments, and contributed to cheap financing of housing. Federal grants were available for the construction of sewers into unserviced areas, so that developers needed pay no premium for the cost of opening up the countryside. The 1950s saw the start of another Federal initiative encouraging the spread of the suburbs – the Interstate Highway programme. Specific grants from the Federal Government encouraged the rapid development of a comprehensive motorway network across the United States. Many city officials, anxious to sustain city centre economies in the light of increasing suburban competition, latched on to the Interstates as a way of bringing suburban people into the centres more efficiently. Alas, travel in the opposite direction was also made easier and developers could go much more widely afield and still remain within the sphere of influence of the city. The Interstates became conduits directing the spread of development out into the suburbs. The Interstate beltways – motorway rings around the cities – opened up more development land in the wedges between the developed radial routes, and continue to do so.

iv *Cheap finance;* locally based savings and loans associations became the traditional low cost means of financing suburban housing. The local office could take income from the steady salaries of the middle class suburbs and find housing for those of similar character and aspirations. By contrast the people of inner city areas had not the income to sustain the same savings, and the character of the areas abandoned by the middle class made institutions reluctant to lend in such areas. To participate in the American dream it was necessary to move to the suburbs.

v *Cheap transportation;* by comparison with many other countries, tax on motor fuel has been traditionally low in the United States, and new car purchase costs are also low. Motor insurance premiums are capped and subsidised by some states. The constraint on commuting, or on driving long distances to shopping or social facilities, is therefore not the financial cost of doing so, but the time it takes. The recent increase in freeway speed limits, from 55 to 65 mph, in rural areas of all but the eastern states may well have the effect of increasing development activity at greater distances from the cities.

In recent years the continuing shift from manufacturing to service industry has fuelled the spread. Office firms are much more mobile than traditional manufacturing industries, and are able to relocate in the suburbs without high investment costs. There they can find a pool of willing labour, including those who would rather work locally than commute into the city. Each relocation brings more supporting service jobs out from the city centre, and thus more people to live in the area. At the same time, those willing to commute find that they can live further out, in areas not yet infected by the outreach of the city, while still working within the economic sphere of the city. So the influence of the city continues to spread ever outward, albeit more thinly.

One consequence of this spread and the profligate and patchy use of land is dependence on the motor car. Suburban lot sizes, and the consequent distances between houses and shops and other community facilities, make it difficult to walk to shops or employment in most areas. It becomes necessary to drive for even the most trivial journeys. And once in a car a wide choice of shopping location is open to the consumer. No longer do shops need to be close to each other, close to houses, or close to places of work. They can be anywhere where there is adequate parking space and access from reasonable roads: in fact this can mean location anywhere *except* in the traditional town centre areas where a British consumer would look first for shops. Such dispersed investment in facilities would be almost impossible to reverse if some adverse outside factor were to affect the relationship between suburban dwellers and their cars. The most obvious threat is a substantial increase in oil price. Traditional public transport could not be a viable alternative given the dispersed nature of the suburbs and the complete lack of common travel patterns. Investments in light rail systems and cheap buses, such as in Portland Oregon, are comparatively rare and anticipated ridership for such projects has not materialised in most cities where the investment has been made.

There is a huge investment in infrastructure in the suburbs. There is also a political imperative of maintaining the value of the American homeowners' investment in the American dream. Given the scale of commitment to the suburbs, a crisis such as a severe oil shortage would seem likely to generate innovative working, shopping and leisure practices, rather than dismantling of the suburbs.

Physical characteristics of the American suburb

American suburbs are best seen from the air as one approaches cities such as Houston, Los Angeles, or Newark/New York. There are vast networks of single family dwellings, often cheaply built, set on relatively large lots, serviced by a maze of curvilinear streets. On the more major roads, often at junctions on the original country lanes, are small commercial centres in the shape of single storey 'strips' of shops and gas stations. On the more major routes, the Federal highways, there are larger shopping malls – known as 'regional centers'. The English equivalents are Brent Cross in north west London and the Metrocentre in Gateshead. In these there might be perhaps four 'anchor' department stores and between them along the interior corridors perhaps a further 100 stores on two levels. Such malls rarely include food stores or supermarkets: there seem few American equivalents to the English Sainsbury or Tesco out-of-town store. The hypermarket style of shop, with a wide range of goods at cheap prices on a very large shopping floor, is relatively new to the United States. Office parks also follow the major routes, where they can be more easily found; the area needed for car parks and landscaping to high standards demands that they often be located on the fringes of the urbanising area. Also on the outskirts of the suburbs are pieces of undeveloped land, sometimes farmed, but often wooded as a result of having been abandoned for some time. It takes a long time for all such pieces of land to come into the new economic use.

A drive through the suburbs reveals different views according to the roads used. The newest limited access roads or freeways are characterised by office parks, some modern factories, and the occasional regional shopping centre. The older through routes by-passed by the freeways have many more small scale developments – local strip shopping centres, petrol stations at many of the road junctions, frequent traffic lights where feeder roads join, and very many 'curb cuts' where individual small scale landowners have exercised their constitutional rights of access to the main road. Away from these roads are the residential zones, where driving can be a particularly frustrating experience, unless you have a street plan and a good sense of direction. Each house might have a road frontage of anything from 60 feet upwards, and plots might be ¼ acre. The newest suburbs have larger lot sizes, reflecting the pattern of development in an area as first the wealthiest move in. More dense development then fills in as those who aspire to live alongside the wealthiest demand more affordable housing. In some states such as California there is a recent trend towards larger homes on smaller lots, driven by such factors as higher infrastructure costs, higher home financing costs, and increasing delays in obtaining permit approvals.

These then are the suburbs. Driving on their fringes is the most extraordinary experience for anyone attuned to the tidier and incremental development patterns of England. Travelling along country lanes reveals the occasional residential subdivision in the middle of nowhere, with massive

Figure 2.5 San Luis Obispo, California; the newest suburban developments seem to comprise larger houses on smaller lots

homes of three bathrooms and three garages, standing in as yet unlandscaped fields but with the passing roadway improved by the developer, as a condition of his permit, to the sort of standards that will eventually apply all along the road. Or perhaps there is the start of the corporate office centre, long and low, and with more land reserved nearby for the expected later phases. It takes a long time to fill in the gaps, even at the pace of American development in the hottest areas.

The 'New Heartland'

The latest phase in the history of population and economic growth in the United States is described in compelling documentary fashion in a book[7] by John Herbers, a long time New York Times journalist. That newspaper is an avid spectator of how developments affect individual communities, with its frequent 'journal' columns, reports from small towns across the nation.

The book shows how, all across the nation, there is increasing settlement or resettlement of the agricultural and rural areas. This is the latest chapter in the long story which first started with the establishment of a new nation on a mainly agricultural basis. As we have seen, cities developed through economic demands for the centralisation of functions. The next stage was the attraction by cities of people from the land, as both agriculture and industry became more mechanised, and of people from other lands as the immigrants before them reported back their success in a new land. In time, successive transport innovations allowed successive waves of suburbanisation of the areas around the big cities. During this century these suburbs have expanded so much that more people now live there than in all the other areas put together. John Herbers has observed and describes the next stage in this evolution – the phenomenon of very low density development in the agricultural and wilderness areas, and around small free standing towns.

This phenomenon, he suggests, is taking place on a nationwide scale and is stimulated by a number of factors. There is a great desire by many to retire, or to take their businesses, to more attractive scenery or climate

21

Where City Meets Desert Somewhat Awkwardly

By RICHARD W. STEVENSON
Special to The New York Times

PALMDALE, Calif., Jan. 28 — This has long been Los Angeles County's last frontier, a sparsely settled oasis of clean air, light traffic and reasonable housing prices at the edge of the Mojave Desert.

It may not remain that way much longer. Palmdale, 60 miles northeast of downtown Los Angeles, is in the midst of a boom that has made it the fastest-growing city in California.

Its population has nearly tripled since 1982, to 42,000. It could double again in the next five years as more families pour in, primarily attracted by real estate prices half those in Los Angeles proper.

New homes are sprouting faster on Palmdale's 58 square miles than are the Joshua trees that dot the desert. New shopping centers stand gleaming where months ago only sagebrush grew. Never mind that it all sits almost literally atop the San Andreas Fault, as if daring nature. Never mind that most new residents face drives of an hour or more to reach jobs back in the Los Angeles area.

To many here, the rapid growth is simply evidence that Los Angeles is bursting its seams, spilling out through the suburban San Fernando Valley and over the San Gabriel Mountains into what some Angelenos still consider a dusty, isolated wasteland.

Palmdale and its neighboring towns in the Antelope Valley may be the last places in Southern California to face the issue of how or whether to rein in growth. Residents describe their town as the "next Orange County," referring to the area south of Los Angeles. Most mean it in a positive way, referring to Orange County's success in building a thriving economy and identity since 1960. But others see Orange County's congestion as an example of the perils of building too much, too fast.

Already pressures are mounting on Palmdale's city services. Students are crowded into temporary classrooms. Little League fields on private land are bulldozed for more housing developments. Traffic backs up on Palmdale Boulevard while the city arranges a more sophisticated system of synchronized stop lights. As homes push farther into the desert, patterns of mountain water runoff are disrupted, increasing the flood threat.

There is no doubt that the boom hit suddenly. "Growth here was inevitable," said Inez Neilson, a local realtor

Some see evidence that Los Angeles is bursting its seams.

and president of the Chamber of Commerce. "But the phenomenal growth we're having is not something we expected to happen." The city's five-year management plan, in fact, was recently scrapped halfway through because it did not reflect Palmdale's rapid change.

• • •

But over all, city officials contend, they have coped well. Palmdale recently won a $10 million Federal grant for a new sewage treatment plant. Police and fire budgets have doubled in three years, and three new schools are on the way. Perhaps most important, restrictions on housing development are being tightened; the minimum residential lot, previously 3,500 square feet, was doubled four years ago, and some consideration is being given to raising it to 8,000 square feet.

"There are a lot more checks and balances in place here than Orange County had 20 years ago," said Tracy Bibb, Palmdale's Mayor.

Palmdale has long been best known as the place where the space shuttle, the B-1B bomber and now the B-2 Stealth bomber are built. Even today huge hangars ringing the Air Force's airstrip at the edge of town continue to give Palmdale its identity and provide thousands of relatively high-paying engineering and assembly jobs.

Yet aerospace does not dominate the town as before. Most new residents, in fact, commute to jobs back over the mountains. "It' not just B-1 workers who go up there now," said Duane Paul, an economist with the Bank of America who has studied the region.

That is probably to the good, since the aerospace industry is notoriouly fickle, rising and falling with Congressional appropriations and the birth and death of new projects. Not only do many new residents have jobs elsewhere — some commute 80 miles or more — but additional employment in Palmdale comes from the stores, restaurants, motels, health care and other services following the

A view of a residential area of the city of Palmdale, Calif., on the edge of the Mojave Desert.

The New York Times/Feb. 3, 1988

Palmdale's population of 42,000 has nearly tripled since 1982.

migration into the desert. The city is also wooing non-aerospace industries.

Those like Mrs. Neilson who have lived here 30 years or more seem to have few regrets about the sweeping changes. "I've heard more complaints from people who have been here three or four or five years than from the old-timers," Mrs. Neilson said. "The new people want to shut the door right after they arrive."

THE NEW YORK TIMES **NATIONAL NEWS** *WEDNESDAY, FEBRUARY 3, 1988*

Figure 2.6 This extract from the New York Times is an example of its monitoring of the pattern and pace of physical and social development in the United States.

(whether sun or snow). This ambition for greener and more spacious surroundings can be seen as an extension of the same drive that led to the creation of the suburbs, but now people are finding that they can either cut off their links with the city, or stretch them to much longer distances. Other elements reflected in this movement are the frontier individualism ingrained in the American character, the willingness to move great distances to less known places in search of a better life, and the sentimental expectation that small towns in rural areas will provide the best framework for secure living.

The heartland movement seems to be largely the product of an affluent society. For although one attraction of the rural areas is the low price of land, a rather larger area of land has to be purchased in order to protect the open space surroundings that were the key motivation to move. The exchange may be of a suburban house for a small farm. Or the first step might be the purchase of some land with a mobile home to use as a second home, while retaining the main residence in the suburbs, before making the final break. This too requires the spare finance available in an affluent society. Alternatively the mobile home might be the only home available to those of lesser means wanting to set up in the relative wilderness. Particularly in the less densely populated states, hardly any town is without its mobile home sales park. (As an aside, the English reader needs to appreciate that these mobile homes are more than just large caravans, but rather a practical, quick and cheap method of house construction. Some are extremely expensive, being formed from two parts carried on separate trailers into a unit perhaps 80 feet by 30 feet. Perhaps they should be seen as a worthy successor to the house kits once available through mail order from Sears, the major retailing firm; everything except foundations would arrive on a railroad car at the nearest depot, and a small community could achieve a good standard of house without the cost of skilled labour.)

Other positive factors motivating the move to the new heartland are the desire for contact with nature in a rural environment and for easy access to outdoor recreation. In an affluent society with space available it is somewhat simpler to convert environmental ideals into reality. There is also a wish to live in a less regulated society. The individual enterprise culture of those moving into Arizona in recent years has contributed to a sharp shift to the right in that state's politics.

Negative forces leading people to move are easier to catalogue. Even in the suburbs there are perceived to be unacceptable levels of crime, in particular drug related crime. For some, racial intolerance is a reason to move on out. And the telling factor in many cases is a gradual deterioration of facilities and services. Investment in roads and bridges is simply not keeping pace with development on the one hand and the increasing number of cars on the other. Traffic congestion on the way to work may be acceptable to a moderate degree, but when there is also congestion at the weekends on the way to the shopping mall, people begin to question the reasons for living where they do. The situation will worsen as it becomes harder and harder to improve roads in the suburbs, because better roads are widely perceived as only leading to more growth. Delaying road construction is now pursued as a deliberate method of development control. Other development control methods also contribute to the spread of development. For example as the outer suburbs begin to erect barriers against new development likely to 'spoil' their areas, developers begin to leap-frog those areas and concentrate on places further out which still

Figure 2.7 Mobile homes provide a today's cheap successor to the kit built houses once available through Sears catalogues. Are these the slums of the future or a cost effective means of providing affordable housing (preferably in someone else's back yard)?

Figure 2.8 Kit built shops in Panguitch, Utah

welcome development, perhaps because it reduces the local taxes of those already there.

Movement to the suburbs and beyond to the new heartland could not be happening without cheap cars and cheap petrol. These have led Americans to become more spatially aware and to broaden their sense of place. It is not hard to find people who have made their move from Vermont to the Carolinas, because that is far enough to go to find a milder winter climate while remaining within motor car range of their roots. The same can be said in relation to Chicago and the Ozarks area of Missouri. In late April, there is a veritable migration north from Florida of people returning to their family homes in all the places of the chillier north. Family links can be retained, albeit at a stretched distance.

The motor car can also be the key to continuing links to employment, given the spread of offices and modern industry into the outer suburbs. It is possible to live 100 miles from the city centre and work in the offices or industrial plants that have located on the 50 mile ring to take advantage of the type of labour market there. The growth of service industries and of improved telecommunications also permit more work to be done without attending the office every day of the week. Once or twice a week journeys can be much longer while remaining tolerable. In all of this the construction of the Interstate highway network has served to make the country smaller and less remote.

Even when living in the more sparsely populated parts of the countryside, there is still a need for towns to act as a service hub. John Herbers identifies a number of smaller state capitals and university and other towns which perform that function. The towns themselves do not appear to be growing fast; that is because the new development is spread thinly over a wide sphere of influence in the more attractive and intimate landscapes nearby. In other words it is in the hills, where there are small farms to be taken over, rather than in the rich prairie lands. It is around lakes such as the Lake of the Ozarks. Here, the half mile long Bagnell Dam holds back what is nicknamed the Missouri Dragon, a lake with 1375 miles of shoreline twisting in a 129 mile valley. The lake's gently wooded shores are lined by year round residences, summer cottages, marinas, hotels and resorts. This example serves to demonstrate why in Britain there will be no significant parallel of the scale of population drift that Herbers describes. Certainly there are areas in the south Midlands and south west which are proving attractive to the long distance, twice a week, commuter, and to self employed and retired people. But the availability of developable land in open countryside such as can be found in south west Missouri is very much more restricted. In Britain, lake shores are simply not available for such linear development, despite the commercial approach to reservoir development that people perceive the privatised water companies might pursue. Building on land in Britain at anything near one unit per 5 acres would be regarded as wasteful indeed. On the other hand variations on the theme might be feasible – the development of 5 new units on each farm settlement might perhaps contribute to the need for new housing while enhancing the rural economy and preserving the landscape. Certainly the resultant populations of such hamlets would be no more than in the heyday of manual farming methods[8].

Effects of new development in rural areas

Development at such low densities as one unit per 5 or 10 acres makes it much less obvious that development has taken place at all, especially given that trees are often left *in situ* right up to the new residences. This ability to build in woods results largely from the construction methods employed; timber framed houses of the traditional American type are much more resilient against disturbance by nearby tree roots. So, the character of these rural developing areas is not necessarily changed by the new development. However, the new development is doing more than stem the long term decline of the economies of these areas. It is creating new pressures as the new types of inhabitant begin to demand the urban standards of local services to which they were accustomed. The local governments then have to ponder how they are to institute the new services, which are inevitably more costly in spread out areas, without raising the low taxes which all, including the newcomers, find politically attractive.

What kinds of land use problems will this latest phase in the population of the United States take, and what will be the role of development control in resolving those problems? Even though the physical effect on the landscape will not be the same as that accompanying suburbanisation, other effects of the development will be felt. In time the residents of the newly developed areas will adopt planning mechanisms to try to preserve the new environment they have discovered, or perhaps created. However, it is likely to be some time before such pressures arise. The areas affected are vast; mathematics alone demonstrates that there is ten times as much area in the land between 30 and 100 miles from the city as there is within a 30 mile radius. The extent of the space gets ever wider as the influence of the city becomes less important, and while the new development can harm the landscape in the most sensitive areas it does not represent a total assault. Of course, there will be questions about the number of septic tanks a locality can absorb, the locations for solid waste disposal, and the adequacy of water supply; plans will be needed to co-ordinate the provision of education, health, roads and other services to a growing but dispersed population, all without increasing local taxes significantly and in areas where traditionally little development control has been operated.

The resultant agenda for planners

But the main problems for planners in America over the coming decade will not arise in these rural areas as a result of the rural development. They are wider problems, and are mainly located in the urban and suburban areas. Just as development is taking place to facilitate the movement of people with the means to move, to the suburbs and beyond, the cities are losing population and thus political clout. They are frequently becoming locations of just a few specialised types of land use:

- downtown areas where office uses predominate, particularly offices in the financial sector, but where there are also supporting hotel, restaurant and limited retail uses

- tourist and cultural developments, based on the core historic districts where these have survived, but otherwise founded on galleries, museums, and other entertainment and supported again by hotel, restaurant and retail uses

- convention centers, perhaps best regarded as a mix of the above two

- airports

- housing for the poor

- industry and warehousing of the type that only survives in low quality and hence low cost premises

Specific grants such as the Urban Development Action Grants, and other devices to revitalise inner city areas seem to have stemmed some of the flow of investment out of the cities, but they have created islands of new development from which it remains to be seen whether wholesale economic growth will flow. The fact is that the cities of previous generations will not be recreated, since economic efficiency no longer needs them; the linkages between industries in close proximity simply do not exist.

Most commentators doubt that neighbourhood preservation, accompanied by limited repopulation by young upwardly mobile professionals, can take place on the scale needed to balance the substantial populations of poor and ethnic minority groups. Despite the length of time since urban renewal initiatives started, most downtown areas still seem to be ringed with a circle of decay – an incongruous juxtaposition of some of the most valuable office developments with untidy areas housing some of the poorest populations and the most marginal industry. The Bush presidency seems likely to deliver enterprise zones to help such problems, eight years after Reagan proposed their adoption. In the meantime, Britain has found the enterprise zone concept wanting because of the high hidden cost – about $50,000 per job created[9].

Urban areas continue to demand substantial investments to maintain their infrastructure. Developing suburbs also need new sewers and new roads. In these areas the cost of sewerage and water supply for each unit served is higher because of the distance between units. Similarly, the highways needed become more expensive, as the routes demanded are no longer simple radials from the city centres. School bus journeys become longer and more costly, and so on. Unit costs become even higher in the rural areas. Overall, therefore, the American nation is being transformed from a clear structure of cities, small towns, farms and wilderness into a community that is, to quote John Herbers, 'diffused, fragmented and without a center, but one that is charged with energy, individual initiative, and the capacity to organise around particular interests'. The physical structure of society seems to be headed towards a free form, widely spread metropolis where no one and no activity has to be anywhere.

Conclusions

In this chapter I set out to describe some of the demographic and political characteristics that have led to today's urban structure in the United States. First, there is the sheer area of land available for the population, and the mobile and development minded attitudes of that population. The American dream is the ambition of a family to have its own single family house – an ambition which has shaped much of American suburbia. Delivery of the American dream was facilitated by cheap land, cheap construction, cheap finance and Federal subsidies, and cheap transportation. The result is a suburban culture which even a major fuel crisis would not be able to destroy. On top of this there is a measurable trend in the last 20 years to repopulate some of the areas in America's heartland in decline since the agricultural depression of the 1930s. The aim is to escape urban problems such as drugs, perceived racial problems and road congestion, and to find the rural idyll.

The American way of spreading development over land would be quite unacceptable in England. But neither is the concept of ever-spreading suburbia particularly attractive. I conclude that there is more we could do in Britain to encourage small developments in even quite rural hamlets – provided that architects can find a way of making new developments part of an evolution of the old, using traditional materials and styles and within existing envelopes, rather than the scattered mobile homes of the American countryside.

In America, the rural and spread out development patterns are creating new problems for planners and local governments, problems of providing services to a dispersed population without significantly raising taxes. But the main problem for American planners will not be these; it will be the inner city and older suburban areas which the wealthier residents continue to abandon.

An important question is whether the American nation can afford to allow development to proceed in this ever outward way. Can vast tracts of derelict and underused land in the cities be abandoned because of the infrastructure needed to make re-use viable, while green field sites are developed in a way that is inevitably costly to service, both in terms of capital and continuing expenditure? Is development control evolving into a mechanism for forcing sensible decisions about the location of development? Do state-wide planning initiatives seem likely to encourage the most efficient and economic use of land on a wider scale? Would a proper reflection of infrastructure costs force up new house prices in the new suburbs and make rehabilitation of the older suburbs a better prospect? Or will use and dispose continue to be the name of the game? These are some of the questions considered in the later chapters. But progress towards any more orderly control mechanisms will be constrained by two other factors – the structure and financing of local government and their effect on growth, and the United States Constitution, itself a reflection of the character of the nation. In Chapter 3 we see how the local government structure and constitutional framework continue to influence these patterns of development.

NOTES TO CHAPTER 2

1. Colonial Williamsburg by Philip Kopper, published by Harry N Abrams Inc (1986).

2. John Herbers, in The New Heartland: America's Flight Beyond the Suburbs and How it is Changing Our Future, published by Times Books (1986).

3. Draft Ordinance for a Traditional Neighborhood District, written by Andres M Duany and Elizabeth Plater-Zyberk at the University of Miami School of Architecture at Coral Gables, Florida under a grant from the National Endowment for the Arts; 2 November 1987.

4. Congressman Robert Torcelli in an address to the Council on New Jersey Affairs in early 1988.

5. In his book Crabgrass Frontier.

6. Streetcar Suburbs: The Process of Growth in Boston, 1887–1900, by Sam Bass Warner, Harvard University Press (1962).

7. See note 2.

8. This idea might be closer than I realised when I first wrote this paragraph; the Times, on 25 January 1989, reported a rumour that the Secretary of State for the Environment was about to encourage a more positive, flexible approach to rural planning applications. In the formal announcement, on 3 February 1989, a clarification of the approach to the provision of low cost

housing in rural areas to meet local demand was announced in a written answer to a Parliamentary Question from Tim Boswell MP.

9. 'Not so EZ', in the Economist, January 28, 1989, p18. According to the Economist the beneficiaries will be, in order of significance, businesses that would have opened in the zone anyway; businesses transferring from nearby areas not quite so depressed, yet; businesses transferring from other areas; and last in order of significance, new businesses.

3 Local Government and the Constitution

Thomas Jefferson, one of the founders of the American nation, made a substantial contribution to its Constitution which so dominates American public life. His ideal was a nation of small towns inhabited by freeholders determining their own destiny. That ideal fitted well with the basic agrarian economy that continued to dominate the United States until the end of the nineteenth century. His aim was to limit the role of government, especially big government, in order to avoid problems such as the colonies had suffered under the British.

Since that time, American urban politics has gone through wholesale change, as the nation was transformed from an agricultural to an industrial economy. The cities grew and dominated, and in turn had their power constrained by the suburbs' influence in state legislatures. Tremendous numbers of immigrants sucked in over sustained periods came first to the poorer areas of the cities and, as they became prosperous and moved on to better areas, their place was taken by successive waves of new immigrants. The infamous political machines, in which the power to dispense appointments in the big cities was paramount, have given way to a more subtle form of transactional politics. In practice today, just as in Jefferson's time, all levels of government seem regarded with suspicion by the American people. If it is necessary for a public authority to administer some process, the people seem to demand that administration be structured in the most localised or fragmented way possible so as to limit the extent of power.

This theme manifests itself in the local police forces (every tier of government seems to have its own, even the smallest municipalities), in the fire service (a key service often provided outside the big cities by local volunteers substantially funded by local community events) and in the health service. In the field of education, there are 35,000 school districts in the United States, many with one or even no high school, but each run by local people. British notions of the appropriate size of government to deliver efficient services (for example in considering whether inner London boroughs are capable of running their own schools) contrast with this very local organisation of local government in much of the United States. Only in the big cities, and perhaps in the counties in which they are located, can be found substantial professional organisation of services. The localist approach has its roots in the volunteer spirit observed by Alexis de Tocqueville, one of the earliest observers of American public administration.

The big city administrations represent a kind of functional localism. Many special purpose agencies interact on the boundary between the public and private sectors. Often the co-ordination can only be achieved from the mayor's office. The agency chiefs are powerful within their own field, and reluctant to cede power to competitor agencies. Local groups and community boards often seem to have to fight hard to achieve local co-ordination of functions.

Overall, local government in the United States must be seen as having *evolved* over two centuries, influenced by the Constitution, but without too much central direction. This contrasts with the position in Britain with its frequent local government legislation and nationally *imposed* allocation of functions and of local government structures and boundaries. In trying to grasp why the administration of land use planning is so different in the United States than in Britain, it is important to understand the contexts of local government and the Constitution. This chapter sets out to try to convey some of the key features.

The pattern of local government

To an Englishman used to a logical structure of local government established to carry out the functions prescribed for it in central legislation, it is difficult to start to understand the operation of local government in the United States. Perhaps it is a salutary reminder that there are many alternative workable structures; there is no single ideal which government administrators might one day devise. This is especially the case when the responsibility for fixing problems is a local one. While I was in Oregon, one small rural city's electorate voted not to allow the city to raise taxes; as a result the city hall was closed and the police force disbanded. Although the county would provide emergency services, little other outside intervention could be expected; the people would have to work out their own political solution to the problem that they had precipitated.

The pattern of local government varies widely from state to state. A common concept is the 'incorporation' of an area. Within each state there are counties. Their tasks vary, but often extend to provision of only the basic services such as justice and law and order. Their income may be restricted to a property tax and not much more. Should the residents of a community within a county demand more for themselves by way of services than the county is prepared to provide, then they may well vote to form an *incorporated* local government unit. The larger the city, the more services that are likely to be provided locally and the fewer by the county. Because funding of the city's services will also depend on the size of the tax base, there is an incentive for it to try to expand the boundaries to take in adjoining urbanised areas. Equally, a developer who wishes to build at urban densities and tap into the necessary urban services, such as sewers, will wish to press for his land to be included in the city in order to facilitate the development. This process of city expansion is called 'annexation'. It featured prominently in big city expansion during the last century, and continues to be important in the western states today.

In fact, had it not been for a deliberate change in the political process, beginning around the turn of the century, the pattern of local government would have developed very differently. Until that time the major cities had proceeded by way of annexation to take powers over the adjoining land. But a number of factors combined to put a stop to that expansion. Some cities came up against natural boundaries such as the rivers on which they were first founded. Other inalienable boundaries were state and sometimes county boundaries (New York City is the exception to this rule, covering four counties within its boundaries). The political trend was for those outside the city boundaries to become increasingly able to persuade the states, which empowered annexation and saw the size of cities as a threat to their own power and influence, to make it more difficult for cities to expand. After all, the people in the suburbs had moved to escape the problems of the city and having to pay for them; it was only natural that those people should want to oppose the city coming to them. The result is that today, despite some 70 per cent of the population being urban residents, the majority of them live outside the central cities in areas often governed by very small units of local government.

In some eastern states, the pattern of local government has been set for some time, and annexation no longer features. For example, in New Jersey, which is predominantly in either the metropolitan areas of New York City or Philadelphia, there are 567 municipalities established to cover the entire area of the state. These are classified as cities, boroughs and townships, and state legislation governs the way certain of their functions are to be carried out. But not all municipalities carry out a uniform set of functions; some contract to buy services from a neighbouring local government, or perhaps from the county. Counties comprise the areas of sets of municipalities, and are responsible for a separate set of core functions, again enabled but not necessarily prescribed by state law. (This basic freedom to provide various services is accompanied by the power for any local government to regulate to protect the public health, safety and welfare of their citizens, known as the 'police power'. This wide discretion permits a great deal of variation between the style of regulation in individual localities.)

In Illinois, to take another example, the position is much more complicated. There is a grid like pattern of counties and component townships (such as was set up for much of the mid-west and west). But this grid pattern is overlaid by a separate pattern of incorporated municipalities, which may be located in more than one county. The position is confused further because some municipality powers extend beyond their boundaries (for example so that a city's service standards can be applied to any area likely to be annexed by that city). Moreover, some powers are shared between townships and municipalities. This means, for example, that a group pressing for public acquisition of open land for recreation must make a judgement whether state, county, township or municipality is most likely to be receptive to their cause.

Another feature of Illinois local government is the competition between nearby cities to annex land and collect the taxes that can be charged on new development. In the void between two municipalities a developer might negotiate with each local government unit to see which will permit more development; those local governments will themselves compete for the right kind of development in areas that they will annex – in other words development bringing in a high tax take, but without generating demands for costly extra services. So it is that spacious office parks and shopping malls come to be located on the urban fringes.

Local taxation

Reliance on the property tax as the most significant source of local income susceptible to local influence is another key factor in American local government, and one which can lead to claims of impropriety. In England for a long time the mechanism of the Rate Support Grant tended to adjust rateable resources per head of population so that there was little *income* incentive for most local authorities to encourage development of land. The poll tax and the uniform national business rate will continue that position. In America the attraction of development to enhance the local tax base is often crucial to the supply of services; cities sink or swim according to their planning decisions. In central Chicago, there is virtually no cap on the height of buildings that may be erected; this has much to do with the fact that new buildings downtown bring in tax dollars needed desperately to pay for urban services in the adjacent depressed inner urban areas of the city. The city aldermen (councillors) seem almost to compete to bring in most revenue. Local tax structures encourage certain types of development in preference to others. In New Jersey, offices might be preferred over housing development, because they bring in property tax resources without consequent costs. Single family houses on large lots will bring in people who do not place a great burden on local welfare services, while permitting old people's housing will not put pressure on school rolls. In Colorado, there is a greater reliance on local sales tax revenue, and in that state local governments compete to permit bigger and better out of town shopping malls, because of the revenue such developments bring. And downtown areas in places such as Denver have to invest heavily in infrastructure in order not to lose their sales tax revenue.

Areas that need protection for their sensitive qualities, protection which zoning is intended to facilitate by excluding industrial development where it would be inappropriate, are often exactly those where the only large sites are available for the commercial development 'needed' by an area. If not permitted there, the development and the accompanying tax base may well be lost to a neighbouring jurisdiction, anxious to reduce the tax per head of its own constituency. Such factors can only distort decision taking, unless proper values are put on all the benefits and disbenefits.

Limitations on local taxation such as that instituted by Proposition 13 in California in the late 1970s can also lead to distortions. They cause local governments to enter into financial arrangements with developers to secure future revenue flows. When an existing source of revenue is cut back, a municipality must look desperately for another. One obvious method is the sale of planning permissions, to the extent that such a practice can be dressed up to be legitimate. This might reveal itself in the local government taking a stake in a property development, and then smoothing the way to permissions that would not otherwise have been forthcoming. It is the same temptation that exists for British local governments engaging in planning gain arrangements.

State and federal government

On top of the local government structure are the tiers of state and federal government. They effect their influence over local government in three main ways – through legislative controls, through individual decisions of the courts or other permitting agencies, and through grant mechanisms. Legislative controls are important because all powers are generally assumed to rest with the state, unless the federal government has enacted laws reserving powers to itself; and in most states, local governments can act only in accordance with the powers granted by the state legislature, although the police power is broad in conferring administrative freedoms on local government. State and federal courts are important in that they develop the case law that accompanies the statute, and generally define the constraints imposed by the state and federal constitutions.

In addition, state and federal permit systems seem to be of increasing importance. As we shall see in the next chapter, state influence over land use decisions is most likely to be through the need for some supplementary permit for a specific aspect of the development. Federal agencies become involved in a similar way; the Federal Clean Air Act of 1970 and the National Environmental Policy Act of 1969 ensure thorough reviews of major projects involving federal funds. The Federal Clean Water Act has major influence over the location of development by controlling discharges

33

of pollutants into inland waters and encouraging proper planning for waste water management. The Federal Coastal Zone Management Act of 1972 encourages states to establish coastal zone management programmes by providing grant aid for those that do so in a way approved by Federal Government.

Finally there are the specific grant regimes. For example, a local government might be able to build whatever sort of bridge or road it wishes, but its decision would be heavily influenced by the availability of specific state and federal grants conditional on the achievement of certain standards. American citizens perceive the freedom to take the decision locally as important, even though in practice such freedom might be illusory. Federal grants became less important over the Reagan years, and the national economic situation currently seems unlikely to permit much influence on the planning system through federal grants for some time. The exception is the tax relief for restoration of historic buildings, which may have survived because it is income foregone. This is the attraction of enterprise zones, mentioned in Chapter 2 above; income foregone is politically easier to endorse than actual expenditure which must be accounted for.

Special districts and agencies

Another feature of American local government is the proliferation of special purpose agencies and boards. These may be run by either elected or appointed officials, and often have powers to raise income through a local tax precept. For example, in special improvement districts elected or appointed boards have the powers to carry out environmental improvements to the specified area – perhaps the city centre retail core, or an industrial area requiring new roads. The power to raise a special local property tax over that area is used to raise a bond to finance capital expenditure on local improvements. The loan is then paid off by those who benefit from the improvements, as they benefit. Such expenditure might be subject to a special vote of those who are to be taxed; so, it would be important for the responsible board to demonstrate the net economic gains that would flow from such improvements. (This type of structure could be of practical interest in Britain; it could allow local groups of traders to improve services or their environment beyond the extent local government is prepared to finance. It would allow a formal self-help alternative to businesses along main shopping streets not happy with the local infrastructure provided by local government.)

Other examples of special districts include school districts, agencies to provide local needs such as sewers, car parks, road improvements, or inner city redevelopment, and major bodies such as the Port Authority of New York, responsible for managing commerce and transport in a wide area of three states – New York, New Jersey and Connecticut – and seemingly distant from direct public accountability. There are many fewer such bodies in Britain, especially those of the kind that have the power to precept on the section of the community that benefits from the expenditure. However, these special agencies do not seem out of place in a system where political appointees play a greater role in government and where those who make the laws are often more formally separated from those appointed to implement them. Many state and local governments discharge their authority by specially appointed boards, which implement the policies set by the bodies that appoint them. (My view is that the legislative and executive branches of American local government are more separate than the equivalent arrangements in Britain, while the state legislature and the judiciary are closer.)

Figure 3.1 An example of the kind of area where infrastructure might be provided by precepts on local property owners

An interesting example of the activities of specialised agencies is to be found in Boca Raton, Florida. Here the development agency set up to revitalise the city centre has put together a redevelopment plan for the area with individual project plans for individual sites. It has then taken the proposals through all the necessary environmental review requirements, in effect obtaining a planning permission from its parent local government, to end up with a package that is capable of a quick start. In such circumstances it becomes difficult to work out where the responsibility for development control lies – with local government or development agency.[1]

Land use planning administration

The administration of land use planning and development control must fit into this localist fragmented structure supplemented by appointed authorities. As we have seen, local government has no constitutionally defined status, and must derive its powers in most instances from the state legislature. But very few states in practice find a political reason to carve a state role in the land use planning process beyond basic rule setting and specific environmental permits. An earlier federal role of providing funds for local expenditure on planning was discontinued by the Reagan administration, leaving the federal interest in local land use planning relatively limited.

To compare the position with that in Britain, there are well over 10,000 development control authorities for 250 million Americans, and only 400 for an English population of about 50 million. Decisions are generally the sole responsibility of the most local tier of government, there being no equivalent to the British right of appeal to the Secretary of State. There are very few instances where the state legislature or executive, let alone the federal government, has a role in intervening in individual decisions about zoning and subdivision of land. In addition, American decisions are often taken at one stage removed from the elected members, by boards appointed for the purpose, rather than by a subsection of the elected council.

In many areas, development control administration is operated from a very local base, similar in size to many British parish councils. Each controlling municipality will draw up its own ordinances, with professional assistance often brought in on a contract basis. The extent to which decisions are taken in accordance with statute and case law will often depend on the likelihood of a legal challenge. Where there are such small units of local government, local influences carry far more weight than in the British process, and it seems possible to ignore the law to a much greater extent. In areas where municipalities have not been established, it may fall to the county to operate development control, and the perceived failure of the county to act to the satisfaction of the inhabitants may itself lead to the formation of new local government units[2]. It is simply impossible to describe in general terms which bodies are responsible for which planning decisions – there are so many arrangements state by state, locality by locality, depending on whether the area has been incorporated as a municipality, or has been annexed by a city, or may be annexed by a city in the future, and on how council members or appointees are organised to take decisions.

The style of local government administration

Chapter 6 contains a fuller description of the various ways in which a local government administers its planning functions. However, there are some general themes in the way that local governments choose to organise themselves. First, the size of the elected body in terms of the numbers of councillors, is almost everywhere much smaller than in the British structure. Cleveland Ohio and Liverpool seem at first glance to have much in common as cities. They are two major ports now struggling to find a new role. Just as Liverpool's almost did, Cleveland's city council suffered financial bankruptcy, which was in fact a stimulus to a recent history of attracting new development and thus new income. Over this century, Cleveland has been administered under different structures of local government. Reformers, working generally against the abuses of the political machines, succeeded in installing a city manager – an appointed chief executive who would himself appoint department chiefs – in the early 1930s as a reaction to previous abuses of political power. That experiment was subsequently overturned and a large local council was instituted. That council grew in numbers as suburbs were annexed, with additional local representation (a safe seat for the unseated mayor) an important element in getting the annexation approved. Now, after later reforms and bankruptcy, the city has 17 elected members, which many people in that city still believe is too many. It contrasts with Liverpool's 99 elected councillors.

So it is with other cities. Minneapolis has a 13 member council, each member representing a ward. Denver also has 13 members, with 11 ward based and 2 elected by the city electorate at-large. Smaller cities often seem to have 7 or 9 members. Bloomington is the third largest city in the twin cities area of Minnesota, after Minneapolis and St Paul. Its council comprises 5 ward based members, 3 members elected at large, and the mayor (also elected at-large). The general view among those I interviewed during my year was that this kind of pattern is the most effective. Combining at-large and ward based members ensures a balance between city-wide and local objectives. However, it does make it more difficult for racial minorities to obtain representation than in a wholly ward based system, where each ward can cover a smaller area. Federal legislation to ensure fairer representation is already starting to erode the at-large elements of some councils.

Because city councils are comparatively lacking in numbers of members, compared with the British case, many of their functions have to be administered or supported through appointed boards. Members of these might be appointed by the mayor, by the council, or by the city manager, or various combinations of these parties, according to the type of city government in operation. The structures for the exercise of power are often categorised as the strong mayor, weak mayor, and city manager forms of local government. In each case the council is elected to legislate. A strong mayor would have the right to veto legislation, and moreover would appoint his own directors for each of the key city departments. A weak mayor would chair the city council meetings, but would otherwise be of equal status with the other elected members, each of whom would typically act as commissioner for a group of services and make appointments of key staff in those areas. Finally, in the city manager form of government, the mayor or council would appoint a chief executive along the lines of a business appointment, who would be responsible for all administration and staff appointments, while the council restricted itself to policy. This last form of local government is found in smaller cities.

The power within a particular administration is often delicately balanced, and quite deliberately so. Americans do not like to put too much trust in any particular individual or body. There will often be mechanisms of checks and balances requiring one board's decision to be subject to the mayor's approval, or the city council itself. There may even be a provision for a weighted majority of the council to overturn a mayoral decision. Given the complications of such structures within a local government, there is less need for a planning appeals system to some other tier of government such as the right of appeal to central government in England against a planning refusal by a local government. Local rights of appeal to another appointed board or person can appear to work without substantial risk of impropriety. If there is impropriety, then there are always the state courts.

Cycles of growth and resistance to growth

In a growing area it is often possible to plot a cycle of change, as the various influences grow and wane. A rural area may well plan to attract development, partly because the farming influence on the local government representatives tends to encourage decisions that will increase land values to the benefit of land owning farmers. Once the development starts, the important aim is to maximise the amount of commercial development or of housing development on very large and hence expensive lots, as that increases local tax income without increasing the demand for local services to the same extent. Reduction of local taxes is a significant political goal which demands careful selection of the land uses to attract. In time the newcomers to the area realise that the very features that first attracted them are being rapidly eroded. The net result on the administration of development control is to apply the brake; the outcome may be to divert the development tide to neighbouring municipalities.

Local government structure and finance are important determinants of the patchwork of development over the American landscape. As a result, states such as New Jersey and Vermont, under development pressure that is rapidly changing the environment that attracts that development, are considering the scope for local governments to *share* the revenue deriving from local development. These states are subject to the same cycles of growth and resistance to growth. Vermont suffered great reductions in its traditional agricultural population, before changing its economy to depend much more on leisure. New Jersey's success in attracting new development also brought with it pressure for control of that growth. But, despite the theoretical advantages of more orderly development control, revenue sharing arrangements are elusive in the United States; there are few examples.

In the big cities similar cycles of growth and resistance to growth can also be seen. In San Francisco preservationists and neighbourhood activists have succeeded in their campaign to impose a moratorium on the demolition of houses, or the construction of major additions. The background is a city that is 97 per cent developed and attracting increased population, mostly of Asian ethnic groups with traditionally large families. The pressure to demolish single family homes and construct much larger houses or multiple family homes is great, for the larger houses in the city are too costly for the families needing them. The purpose of the moratorium, timed just before a mayoral election, was to provide time for the planning officials to frame new zoning and open space rules, to control illegal conversions to multiple dwellings and to put into effect a slow growth referendum passed by the voters in 1987. This also meant strict limits on downtown office construction, and the preservation of traditional neighbourhoods and affordable housing by controls tougher than British development control. Such is the power of the population of San Francisco.

Initiative and referendum powers

California is well known for the exercise of power by its citizens through the initiative and referendum powers. Voters can themselves propose and enact local ordinances (the initiative power), including those relating to land use. They may also reject recently passed ordinances (the referendum power). Something like 10 per cent of the voters have to sign a petition in order to force a ballot on an initiative or referendum. But the power of voters is sufficient to force officials to be conscious of the danger of their own work being overturned. In San Francisco, 10 per cent of the voters are relatively easily reached on an issue which mobilises all the various neighbourhood associations.

The California Supreme Court noted that

> '. . . the initiative is essentially a legislative battering ram which may be used to tear through the exasperating tangle of the traditional legislative procedure and strike directly towards the desired end. Virtually every type of interest group has, on occasion, used this instrument. It is deficient as a means of legislation in that it permits very little balancing of interests or compromise, but it was designed primarily for use in situations where the ordinary machinery of legislation had utterly failed in this respect.'[3]

In California and other states then, there is this further complicating effect on the administration of land use planning by local government. The scope for legal challenge by initiative of decisions taken some time earlier has led some states such as Colorado to limit citizen challenges to a 90 day period starting from the zoning decision, to give the developer the certainty that he needs to see the development through.

Public pressure groups

A corollary of the distrust of government, even of very local government, is the strength of the civic movement in the United States. The multiplicity of small, directed, planning bodies created by local and state governments tends to merge into some of the more sophisticated non-profit organisations engaged on planning work. For example, a relatively common situation is the municipality wishing to identify ways of carrying forward some planning project. A first step might be to establish a committee of known interested citizens, leaders in the community, and perhaps others who might have the power to stifle the project later if not involved from the start. That committee might include elected members of the municipality to act as liaisons with the main township committee. The municipality's contract planner might be employed to provide professional input. Ultimately a report would go to the elected members to consider, and they might in turn instruct the planning board to act on it. But there would be little difference if the committee had not been sponsored by the municipality. The same people would probably serve, and a contract planner could probably be either 'volunteered' or funded from one of the many philanthropic funds that seem to be available, or from the community itself. Moreover, the report would probably be received and acted on in exactly the same way.

This greater respect for the work of non-profit organisations manifests itself in other ways. For example, the Middlesex Somerset Mercer Regional Council has proved to be one of the most influential bodies in central New Jersey, first in lobbying for a state plan where none existed, and then in influencing the content. It is supported by individual and corporate contributions, and has the advantage of being able to take a detached view of the regional planning needs of an area extending over parts of three counties (32 municipalities) sharing common characteristics and planning problems. Civitas is a not-for-profit citizens' organisation concerned with maintaining and improving the quality of life on the Upper East Side of New York City. It is a thoroughly professional organisation. Assisted by other non-profit bodies and partly funded by various foundations, it has prepared well argued reports proposing zoning changes, for example to stem the zoning bonus of extra height that developers can obtain in return for the provision of a public open space in a development. It even persuaded Paul Newman to narrate a film made to press its cause. It has also been active in the enforcement case where a tower block has been constructed 13 stories too high in contravention of the ordinances. Another example is a not-for-profit group formed to try to secure the most appropriate re-use of the historic Roebling factory complex in Trenton, New Jersey, where cables were manufactured for many of the world's suspension bridges. While the group has no formal power, standing or control over the site, it has been able to use city funds to appoint an executive director, and it has interviewed developers and helped to shape development proposals. The reason for its influence is simply that it comprises a number of local people who, with some professional help, will put to the city council views that will be respected on any zoning applications made. A similar balancing act is played in Cleveland Ohio by the Historic Warehouse District Development Corporation; I came across many others of a similar nature.

The role of bodies such as these should not be underestimated, as long as they clearly influence local government decision takers. There seem to be more of them, at least in the urban United States, than in Britain, and such bodies often develop into much more than just lobbying groups. (It is as if the county branches of the Council for the Protection of Rural England were suddenly to become brokers between local government and major developers.) The reasons are partly that American planning departments are not large enough to respond to public demand, or sufficiently endowed to apply public resources to the extent that the public would like in areas such as Cleveland's warehouse district. They therefore encourage others to participate, albeit on a voluntary basis. Second, the tax-exempt status of such groups encourages participation by those who are able to set their contributions, corporate or individual, against income tax. Third, there seem to be more and larger philanthropic funds to which American non-profit groups have access.

A wider role is played by bodies established to act as state-wide advocates and defenders of good planning. A prominent example of such a body is 1000 Friends of Oregon. This is a not-for-profit group set up at the initiative of Governor Tom McCall, a great champion of state-wide planning. The group's mission has been clear from the start; to act as a legally informed citizens advocacy group, able to put the positive point of view at times when the state and local government organisations might be tempted to concede to better funded developers. The group has a membership of between 2,000 and 3,000 (there were many more for a short period when the 1000 Friends were fighting a particularly controversial group, who wanted to settle in the desert area), a staff of 12, and a budget approaching $1m. It is widely respected, even by those who do not subscribe to its aims. Such citizens' advocacy bodies are inevitably heavily staffed by legal experts, as they frequently need to resort to the law to achieve their aims. The 1000 Friends of Oregon is a model for similar more recent organisations in other states. Everywhere, the work depends not only on individual contributions but on the foundations and funds.

Corruption

Yet, despite all this public interest, there still seems to be a fair amount of corruption reported, and it is hard to know why this should persist. Possibly it is easy to distort a diffuse decision making process, with different agencies having different roles, and with a greater proportion of appointed political officials coming and going. Perhaps another factor is the relatively small size of most elected bodies, by comparison with British experience. Or it could simply be that the people expect corruption, and it occurs; a certain amount of municipal graft is regarded as normal enterprise in an enterprise culture. To hear people talking about the role of aldermen, the elected ward councillors in Chicago is astounding. Even the planning department accept that the individual ward alderman's decision is paramount in the decision whether a development goes ahead. Situations like this might seem to make the planner's job rather frustrating. But on the other hand, this is the same country where one private citizen has established a fund to reward those who expose municipal corruption.

Constitutional Rights

Last but not least in this review of the background influences shaping American development control is the Constitution of the United States. Supplemented by the individual state constitutions, this is the most important formal constraint on the local government exercise of land use planning functions. The articles most relevant to land use planning are the Fifth and Fourteenth Amendments.

The Fifth Amendment requires that private property shall not be 'taken' for public use without just compensation. This is important because particular zoning actions of local governments may so limit the uses to which land may be put as to amount to a taking. The limitations which the risk of a taking imposes on zoning are discussed in more detail in Chapter 5. Generally, zoning regulations can go a long way before a taking requiring compensation is involved. This is because the courts have held that all potential economic uses have to have been extinguished before such a taking can arise. But the position is more complicated where there is what is known as a reasonable investment backed expectation, where a developer has paid a price that reflects a reasonable expectation that he will be able to proceed, and is then prevented from realising any return. Such a case can be extremely difficult to mount in the courts.

The Fourteenth Amendment entitles every citizen to 'due process' and 'equal protection'. Government action would fall foul of the Fourteenth Amendment if it were shown to deprive any person of liberty or property, without due process of the law. This means that every citizen can expect to be notified about any local government administrative action, such as the consideration of an application for a variance or special permit, that may affect his property or interests; moreover he is entitled to an opportunity to be heard before a decision that will affect his property or interests. It also means that citizens have a right to expect government regulation to be inherently reasonable and fair – it must advance a legitimate governmental purpose. Zoning ordinances must therefore not be arbitrary or capricious as they apply to particular parcels of property, although the courts have held that a presumption of validity applies; a reasonably debatable public purpose will be sufficient to sustain an ordinance against legal challenge. The equal protection element of the Fourteenth Amendment provides that no state, nor any local government within the state, may deny to any person equal protection of the laws. In land use planning this means that regulations must be fairly applied and administered as between different individuals.

Time and time again as I have enquired into the issues covered in this report, the constraints of the Constitution have become apparent. Each state seems to apply different standards of interpretation. There are differences in the application of the Constitution according to whether a legal case is brought in the state or federal court, and still wider possibilities of challenge based on the separate constitutions of each state. As a result it is often unclear when the constraint will apply to a particular case or type of local legislative device. Comparatively simple explanations of the basic concepts of the Constitution such as I have attempted in the two paragraphs above contrast with the volumes of legal texts which explain all the subtlety of the interpretation of the law in different states and in relation to different land use problems. Chapter 5 below contains a more detailed discussion of some recent US Supreme Court cases, which have gone a little way to underline the current limitations on public regulation possible under the Constitution.

Differences in interpretation and application impinge on local governments at the very local level. Each planning and zoning board will have its appointed attorney present to give advice, and organisations such as the American Planning Association do a good job of promulgating to those who subscribe (certainly not all planning authorities) advice on the latest legal cases. Nevertheless, there seems scope for confusion about the real application of court decisions to the local planning process. The costs of fighting a case in court are high, and the costs of losing may be higher if it is found that compensation must be paid. So it is often easier to err on the side of caution in exercising development control responsibilities. That generally means bending towards the wishes of the developer, since he is more likely than other groups to have sufficient financial muscle to go to law. In American law each party usually is responsible for its own costs, so even victories in court cost the local taxpayer. And losses may lead to a higher liability insurance premium for the local government involved.

It is a matter for debate whether planning processes are better served by appeals to the law on constitutional grounds, or quasi-judicial appeals to a government minister, as in Britain and occasionally in America[4]. This issue is discussed in more detail in Chapter 8 below, which describes some of the attempts by states to establish planning regulatory processes involving more than one tier of government. Neither the legal nor the administrative appeals process seem to give certainty of decision or a guarantee of consistency. If they did, there would be far fewer appeals.

Summary of Chapters 2 and 3

There is a whole range of areas where differences of approach between Britain and America have led to differences in the way land use planning mechanisms operate. At the most basic and readily apparent level, we saw in Chapter 2 the sheer amount of land available for use. The general presumption of the people who own that land is that it should be developed and exploited. Just as the frontier spirit that drove people west in the last century was one manifestation of that development culture, so also is the movement of the population today. Those who can afford it move to suburban areas where they can live with their social equals. Others move great distances, usually south and west, in the search for economic advancement or simply a better climate made habitable by the invention of air conditioning. All this movement is perhaps a simple extrapolation of the original motivation that brought colonists and immigrants to the continent in the first place.

Other elements that trace their roots to the colonists are the structure of local government and the safeguards of the Constitution. Evolution of local government structures is the key; arrangements are rarely determined by some central legislation. The key to all this is the police power, which provides a general authorisation to regulate the activities of citizens in order to promote public health, safety and welfare. Development control operates differently in different areas precisely because of the wide range of local government arrangements that have evolved. In particular the very small jurisdictions outside the cities are characterised by self contained, self sustaining attitudes. When areas dominated by such local governments come under prolonged development pressure it is difficult to change local attitudes to incorporate some broader awareness of the cumulative effect of purely local decisions. It was these attitudes to development and urban problems that first led suburbs to resist the expansion of cities, and led to today's polarisation between city and suburban jurisdictions.

Local tax arrangements are important too, because they distort land use decisions. The overlap between planning and economics is a recurrent feature in this report – whether it is because offices bring more property tax revenue for less service cost, or because sales tax is a significant local source of revenue, or because local tax limiting initiatives have led local governments to take initiatives of their own. Local tax reasons are often one factor in stimulating growth in an area; while growth and the concomitant services needed are often a reason for tighter development control methods.

Fragmentation of local government structure is also reflected in fragmentation of the functional agencies, appointed or elected to run particular functions. Development control may also be exercised by the state highway or county sewerage agencies. All this makes it much more difficult for a local government to control its own development patterns, despite the apparent local discretion. In addition there are so many different organisational structures that have evolved in different places, it is very difficult to generalise about American development control.

42

Fragmentation of agencies is matched by a large number of not-for-profit groups established to pursue particular planning objectives – either local or regional. These groups can play a major role in influencing development and protecting the public interest by forcing legislators to take more interest in the public agenda, and ultimately by resorting to the courts.

Last, but not least is the Constitution, and more important the way it has been applied by the courts and interpreted by local governments. To be certain, no-one would deny the beneficial values of unbiased decisions, adequate notice of hearings, the opportunity to be heard, decisions backed by reasons and facts, and the right to protection from confiscatory policies of local government. But different countries simply give different weight to different ways of securing those values. An action which in terms of the United States Constitution amounts to a taking of private property without compensation might be acceptable in Britain where development rights remain effectively nationalised. Some legitimate American interferences with property rights – for example restricting the occupation of houses to particular categories of people, by age or income – might fall foul of the British courts if applied through the planning process. The British land-owner would call it oppressive indeed if he had to seek local government permission before selling a field, or even a slice of garden, to a neighbour, as subdivision control requires in parts of the United States.

The next chapter goes on to describe some of the methods of development control that have been established against this background.

NOTES TO CHAPTER 3

1. I am grateful to Wendy Larsen and Charles Siemon for this information.

2. See for example the story of Sannibel, Florida told by Babcock and Siemon in The Zoning Game Revisited (1985).

3. In the case of Amador Valley Joint Union High School District v State Board of Equalization (22 Cal 3d 208,228 (1978)), a challenge against the most famous initiative of all – Proposition 13 – which limited the ability of local government to raise revenue through property taxes

4. For example, in Florida the Governor and his cabinet of elected officials have the power to review and overturn certain local decisions reached by elected representatives on developments of regional importance.

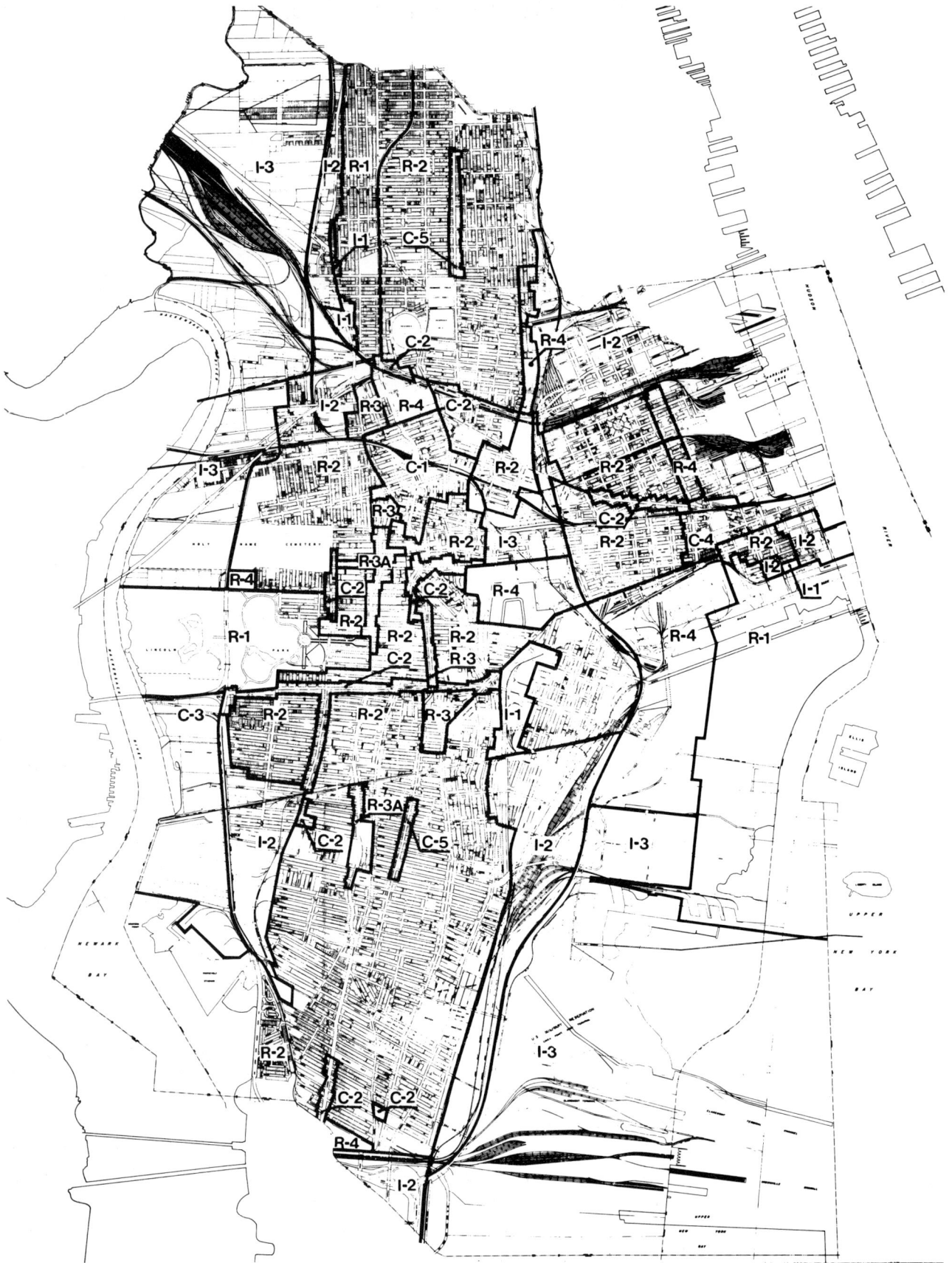

The zoning map for Jersey City, New Jersey

4   The Mechanisms of Development Control

Introduction

There is a commonly held preconception in Britain that the United States is a nation characterised by its go-getting style of management. With sufficient drive and a positive approach, little would seem to obstruct the conversion of an initial development concept into a profitable and successful project. Again, from afar, planning mechanisms that make clear in advance what uses of particular sites are acceptable would seem to contribute to the certainty of the process. In practice such preconceptions are misplaced. In most parts of the United States there is a whole range of detailed regulation that affects the development process. The developer is faced with a steeplechase of hurdles, of greater or lesser significance, that stand in the way of turning plans into reality. I was most surprised by the degree of bureaucracy, and the apparent acceptance of it by the private sector in the American market-based economy – one in which local governments are themselves in clear competition for new investment.

The extent of control of development has been steadily increasing in scale and complexity, especially since the 1960s and 1970s when a much greater environmental awareness started to pervade society on both sides of the Atlantic. The New Jersey Directory of State Programs for Regulating Construction[1] lists no fewer than 38 *state* permit processes. Over and above these are the more traditional local planning, land subdivision and other controls exercised by municipalities and counties. Still further permits may be required from Federal agencies, for example where wetlands are affected. Figure 4.1 gives an idea of the permits required by a large scale mixed use development with a significant housing element, situated in an environmentally sensitive area of New Jersey on a site requiring restoration because of the location of some sort of hazardous waste, but *not* in an area where a sewer ban is in force and *not* in the special areas of the state where there are regional planning entities and special permitting procedures apply. Neither is New Jersey one of the states requiring large scale private developments to go through a full blown environmental impact review. The figure shows controls that have evolved as incremental reactions of state government to specific problems. It does not demonstrate the potential for overlap between review processes and lack of co-ordination. Many states have reacted to criticisms of overlaps by establishing efficiency reviews of various sorts[2], but every government administrator knows how much easier it is to create separate new control systems than to merge existing ones with different basic requirements.

While there does not appear to be any definitive measurement of the increasing impact of development control systems, the trend is clear. The Urban Land Institute, an independent research and educational organisation in the field, commented[3] that it was only necessary to glance at the increasing bulk of legislation from all sides to see the increasing amount of bureaucracy

Figure 4.1 Range of state permits required by a large development in New Jersey[5]

Soil Erosion and Sediment Control Plan Certification	Projects that disturb more than 5000 square feet of surface area of land require a plan for soil erosion and sediment control, to be approved by the Department of Agriculture. The control extends to the demolition of structures and the creation of parking lots, among other things.
Plan Release	The State Uniform Construction Code Act requires Department of Community Affairs approval of construction plans for the category of most significant developments before the building starts, unless the function has been delegated to the municipality.
Planned Real Estate Development Registration	Any development which shares common facilities or areas, such as parking lots, gardens or sports facilities, must be registered before the developer disposes of any interest in it.
Coastal Area Facility Review	Separate review by the State of major residential (25 + dwellings), industrial, transportation, utility and energy related facilities in the coastal area–an irregular 3-mile wide strip along the Atlantic coast of the state. Effectively a double check of local government zoning decisions. Separate permits are required for waterfront developments within 500 feet of tidal or navigable waterways, and for developments affecting coastal wetlands.
Stream Encroachment Permit	Construction affecting the channel or flood plain of any stream requires a permit from the Department of Environmental Protection, or from the municipality where the responsibility has been delegated.
50 + Realty Improvements	This control ensures that proposed water supply and sewerage facilities for developments of more than 50 dwellings, not served by approved water or sewerage supplies, meet state standards.
Pollutant Discharge Elimination System	Permits are required for a range of discharges to surface water, groundwater or State lands.
Sewer System Permit	A Department of Environmental Protection control over any construction or modification of any part of a sewer system, including interceptors, collectors, force mains and pump stations.
Environmental Cleanup Plan Approval	Before disposing of land previously used for one of a range of industrial uses a cleanup plan must be submitted and carried out.
Health Care Facility Certificate of Need	No health care facility may be constructed or expanded, and no new health care services instituted without a certificate of need.
Access Driveway Permit	This is required before any new driveway is made on to a State highway; but access cannot be totally denied without constituting a taking (see previous chapter).
Drainage Permit	A Department of Transportation permit required before operations affecting drainage across State land or along a State highway.
Highway Occupancy Permit	This permit may authorise a wide range of miscellaneous works impinging on a State highway and its right of way.
Utility Opening Permit	Similar to the above, but authorising excavations to install utilities.

Note: Some of these permits have a requirement to obtain local government approval to the course of action proposed first, before making the application to the state agency.

attached to development control. A contributor to the Journal of the American Planning Association[4], comments:

> 'Two decades ago, American land-use regulation consisted nearly entirely of local zoning; it no longer does. Instead, it has become increasingly centralized, more and more likely to originate with regional, state and federal agencies rather than local ones. These changes in regulation have transformed American planning; its practice, its aims, its role in American government. . .'

In a draft management program prepared to illustrate the implementation of the New Jersey Development and Redevelopment Plan, the trend towards more control was also clear. There could soon be more controls in that state to add to those set out in Table 4.1. For example:

'Counties and other regional entities should establish review procedures for developments of significant regional impact . . .'

'An air quality assessment should be included as part of a community impact assessment to determine the extent to which future development and redevelopment will result in . . . an overall reduction in contaminant emissions, or . . . otherwise contribute to the attainment of air pollution standards' (a tax, or scale of contributions, is proposed according to the total emission of ozone precursors projected)

'Legislation [to] place under state review all development proposals within 1000 feet along the shoreline that is most vulnerable during storm activities'

'a strategy to limit development on critical slopes' (effectively more than 15 per cent)

'a stream corridors strategy is included in the State Plan to supplement existing laws'

'the State Plan employs the nitrate dilution model to determine the maximum density of development appropriate for the non-sewered area'[6]

The growth of specific environmental controls has tended to relegate the importance of the traditional land use controls of zoning and subdivision. The stimulus for the new range of controls has sometimes been the Federal government. For example, the environmental impact reviews that are required for any project supported by Federal funds have the effect of introducing a separate detailed investigation of projects such as grant aided historic building renovation. But the new controls usually come at the state or local level. The only likely return to the traditional land use control methods is as a result of increased state direction over local land use control, requiring improvements in the quality of local planning as has happened in the state of Oregon (see Chapter 8).

The scope of this report is mainly development control aimed at securing the most efficient and effective use of land. I have not attempted to address the incidence or effects of the new environmentally based controls, but concentrate on describing some of the commoner mechanisms of land use control and how they have developed. In the following chapters I then go on to describe how these controls are implemented in terms of the administrative mechanisms and efficiency. The final chapters consider some of the current issues where there is sufficient parallel, or potential parallel, with British policies and practices for deeper consideration to be of interest to practitioners on both sides of the Atlantic.

Zoning

Despite the emerging environmental varieties of development control, zoning is still the main instrument used by local government to influence the physical development of the land. It can be as simple or as complicated as the local community wants to make it. There are still some areas that choose to do without, but these are becoming rarer as the frontier of development pressure is rolled back into 'America's heartland'. The power of local governments to make zoning regulations derives from what is known as the police power, which I described in Chapter 3 above. There is a presumption in any legal case that such regulations will be reasonable.

This makes it more difficult for an individual to challenge particular regulations as a valid use of the police power, as he must prove that the regulations are *un*reasonable, rather than rely on the local government to demonstrate reasonableness.

The police power is used as a basis for a very wide range of local regulations. For example, it may be used to require residents to place large numbers on their houses, to make them easier for the fire brigade to identify. Or it may be used to restrict building contractors operating in a town to those who have paid a licence fee and are certified as sound and reliable (to protect residents from fly-by-night operators)[7]. It is used as a foundation for road traffic laws, for building regulations, for health codes and so on. Most important for this report, it is also the basis for zoning and all its variations over 70 years.

The principle of zoning is that a local government takes its area and divides it into zones on a map. Regulations set out for each zone which particular uses, or combinations of uses of land are to be allowed. They also prescribe standards or limitations on the physical shape of new development; such control generally extends to:

- maximum height of buildings;

- minimum required set-backs in the front, side and rear of the buildings;

- lot dimensions and coverage (often by reference to floor area ratio; the result of dividing the total floor area in the building by the land area on which the building stands) or volume of building; and,

- minimum car parking standards (crucial in an automobile-based society).

The map and ordinance can be amended at any time after following the appropriate procedures and those amendments apply once they have gone through the various adoption procedures. Many zoning ordinances are maintained in a loose leaf format in order to facilitate amendments. Such amendments might be prompted by an application from a developer wishing to develop in some other way than the zoning ordinance would permit, or by the broader planning work of the local government, or perhaps by some group of residents or pressure group.

The following extracts from a relatively straight-forward zoning ordinance demonstrate the key features. More complicated ordinances are much longer. That of New York City comprises 1000 pages of very small text in three loose leaf binders. That of San Francisco runs to 800 pages for the 47 square miles of that city. This one, from Jersey City, New Jersey, is rather shorter. It has a structure so that each zoning district has first a name and then an objective:

'R-3 and R3A MEDIUM DENSITY RESIDENTIAL

'The purpose of these districts is to introduce a limited number of higher density residential districts with commercial uses along major streets and streets with bus service except in the R-3A District where the pattern of commercial uses is less dominant. These districts also introduce a wide variety of public and quasi-public facilities. Building height is increased to accommodate the mixture of uses and higher densities.'

It then prescribes the principal uses that are permitted (definitions are provided separately):

'Detached dwelling units; dwelling with two dwelling units; row houses; townhouses; garden apartments; medium rise apartments; public and private schools; parks and playgrounds; houses of worship; government uses limited to offices, meeting, legislative and judicial functions.'

Next, the ordinance sets out the accessory, or incidental uses that are also permitted:

'1. Parking garages only when attached to or under the principal building or as a separate structure serving a college, university or hospital.

2. Off-street parking including a private garage.

3. Fences and walls.

4. Swimming pools.

5. Recreation area as part of residential developments.

6. Meeting rooms, cafeterias, recreation areas, gymnasiums, auditoriums, and similar uses normally associated with schools, houses of worship and other public buildings.

7. Retail sales and offices as part of ground floor of medium rise apartments at least six stories in height and provided said stores and offices face a street having regularly scheduled bus service or a street having a collector or arterial street classification in the city Master Plan, except that in the R-3A District, no such retail sales and offices shall be permitted.

8. Professional offices as a home occupation after site plan review and approval.'

And then there are a series of 'conditional uses', that is uses permitted only at the discretion of the Planning Board, which has to decide in the individual case whether the use will be detrimental to the health, safety and general welfare of the City.

'1. Utilities in accordance with all R-1 standards.

2. Meeting halls; dormitories, fraternity and sorority houses that are affiliated with an institution offering undergraduate or graduate level college instruction; community centers.

3. Hospitals.

4. Colleges and universities.

5. Day care centers, clubs, and clinics.

6. Mortuaries in accordance with all R-2 District regulations.

7. Narcotic and drug abuse treatment centers at hospitals where sanctioned by the hospital.'

The section then moves on to the construction of the buildings concerned. First, there is a series of maximum heights, according to the use to which the building is to be put:

'1. Detached dwelling units; dwellings with two dwelling units; row houses; townhouses; garden apartments; public and private schools; governmental uses; houses of worship; mortuary; meeting halls; dormitories, fraternity and sorority houses that are affiliated with an institution offering undergraduate level college instruction; clubs; day care centers; clinics; community centers; and utilities; **four stories or 40 feet.**

2. Medium rise apartment, hospitals, colleges and universities; **ten stories or 100 feet.**

3. A separate parking garage permitted as an accessory use shall not exceed **four stories or 40 feet in height.**'

There then follows a matrix determining the maximum site proportion the building may cover, the minimum lot sizes and yard dimensions, and the maximum dwelling unit density. This table is reproduced in Figure 4.2. Each use has its own off street car parking provision, not reproduced here; the requirements vary between different sizes of dwelling. For example, a one bedroom garden apartment would require 0.75 space per unit, while a one-bedroom medium rise apartment would require 0.66. A lower standard might apply where a developer is prepared to covenant the property so that only people over 62 years of age live there. Each 600 square feet of retail space would need a space, as would every two patient beds in a hospital, every 300 square feet of office space or every 800 square feet of day care

Figure 4.2 Area, yard and bulk requirements in a medium density residential zone of Jersey City, New Jersey.

	Max. Floor Area Ratio	Max. Bldg. Cover	Min. Lot Width	Min. Lot Depth	Min. Lot Area	Max D.U. Density Per Acre	Min. Yards for Principal Building Side			
							Front*	One	Side	Rear
Detached Dwelling	N.A.	60%	25'	100'	2,500	17.5	5'	2'	5'	15'
Dwelling w/2 Dwelling Units	N.A.	60%	25'	100'	2,500	35.0	5'	2'	5'	15'
Rowhouses &			16'/D.U.	100'	1,600		5'	0'	0'	10'
Townhouses	N.A.	50%	100'/Group	100'	10,000	23.33	5'	10'	20'	10'
Public/Private Schools	1.0	25%	150'	100'	15,000	N.A.	10'	***	***	***
Garden Apt.	N.A.	30%	150'	100'	15,000	35.0	10'	15'	25'	10'
Medium Rise Apt.	1.1	25%	200'	100'	20,000	60.0	10'	**	**	40'
Houses of Worship	N.A.	50%	100'	100'	10,000	N.A.	20'	10'	20'	10'
Government Uses	N.A.	50%	100'	100'	10,000	N.A.	20'	10'	20'	10'
Utilities	N.A.	30%	50'	100'	5,000	N.A.	10'	10'	20'	25'
Meeting Halls	N.A.	30%	50'	100'	5,000	N.A.	10'	10'	20'	25'
Dormitories Fraternity & Sorority Houses	N.A.	30%	50'	100'	5,000	N.A.	10'	10'	20'	25'
Hospitals	1.0	25%	150'	100'	15,000	N.A.	10'	***	***	***
Colleges & Universities	1.0	25%	150'	100'	15,000	N.A.	10'	***	***	***
Day Care Centers, Clubs, Clinics	N.A.	30%	50'	100'	5,000	N.A.	10'	10'	20'	25'
Mortuary	N.A.	50%	100'	100'	10,000	N.A.	20'	10'	20'	10'
Community Center	N.A.	30%	50'	100'	5,000	N.A.	10'	10'	20'	25'

*Setbacks may deviate from those listed here and adhere to the conditions noted in Article V for setbacks. **Each side yard 15 ft. or the equivalent of one-quarter (0.25) the building height, whichever is greater. ***Rear yard 25 ft. or the equivalent of one-half (0.5) the building height, whichever is greater; each side yard 10 ft. or the equivalent of one-half (0.5) the building height, whichever is greater.

center or clinic. Even mortuaries are provided for, at a rate of 6 spaces per viewing room! There are separate loading space requirements, and then maximum sign areas; one sign not exceeding 20 square feet for governmental uses, places of worship and mortuaries, down to one sign not to exceed 2 square feet for professional offices as home occupations.

The same ordinance contains a series of general requirements that must also be met. These relate to access to and grading of the site, and lighting of the completed development to standards set in foot candles. If lighting is not operational there could be a code violation warranting enforcement action, a degree of enforcement rather more stringent than in Britain and in a city not sufficiently resourced to carry out such enforcement. The size of parking spaces and aisles between them is also laid out. And the restrictions on signs and billboards are quite strict:

'Signs must be constructed of durable materials, maintained in good condition and not allowed to become dilapidated.'

'For Sale' signs may only be posted where the agent has an exclusive agreement with the vendor. 'Sold' signs may only be displayed for 14 days, and then only after serving notice on the planning department. No more than two 'For Sale' or 'Sold' signs may be posted by one person or agent between two road junctions or within 250 feet of a junction. (This sort of provision is intended to prevent estate agents stimulating fear of disintegration of a neighbourhood, and then using that fear to encourage those who can almost afford it to move out. If you don't move out now, the rumour goes, your house will be worth less, or even worthless next week. In several cities the racial mix of neighbourhoods has changed very rapidly following such 'initiatives' by real-estate agents.)

The ordinance I have explained here is not unusual. Indeed, I tried to pick a shorter section to minimise the demand on the reader. The fact is that zoning can quickly become complicated, as the tables on the next four pages summarising the City of Los Angeles zoning regulations demonstrate. It is rather like trying to review the English General Development Order to grant a general consent for relatively minor developments under the banner of simplifying the system: in practice, removing development from control tends to make the regulations more complicated.

Each city will have a different set of ordinances, reflecting concerns and actions of sets of politicians over a long period. There are some standardising influences such as textbooks of tried and tested definitions, and off-the-shelf ordinances. But generally, developers need to master the details of the ordinances for each American city or suburb in which they plan to operate. Where a proposed development does not fit, minor obstacles can sometimes be got around by applying for a variance (see the next chapter for more details); a major difficulty might lead the developer to propose an amendment to the zoning ordinance itself.

Zoning provisions can be very detailed in what they demand of developers by way of conditions. Where conditions are imposed in this way, it is as if a British development plan could mandate specific standard conditions. In other words the planning authority would have no discretion in considering whether to impose the condition. To escape the conditional requirements of the zoning ordinance, a developer must either obtain a variance from the zoning board of appeals, not a straightforward task unless a hardship unique to the applicant or the site can be proved, or else petition for a

Figure 4.3 GENERALIZED SUMMARY OF ZONING REGULATIONS: CITY OF LOS ANGELES†

Note: This summary is only intended to be a guide: definitive information should be obtained from the Department of Building and Safety.

ZONE	USE	MAXIMUM HEIGHT		REQUIRED YARDS			MINIMUM AREA		MINIMUM LOT WIDTH	PARKING REQUIRED
		STORIES	FEET	FRONT	SIDE	REAR	PER LOT	PER DWELLING UNIT		

Agricultural

ZONE	USE	STORIES	FEET	FRONT	SIDE	REAR	PER LOT	PER DWELLING UNIT	MIN LOT WIDTH	PARKING
A1	AGRICULTURAL One-Family Dwellings Parks Playgrounds Community Centers Golf Courses Truck Gardening Extensive Agricultural Uses			20% lot depth 25 Ft. max.	25 Ft. Maximum 10% Lot Width 3 Ft. minimum	25% lot depth 25 Ft. max.	5 Acres	2½ Acres	300 Ft.	Two Spaces Per Dwelling Unit
A2	AGRICULTURAL A1 Uses	3	45 Ft.				2 Acres	1 Acre	150 Ft.	
RA	SUBURBAN Limited Agricultural Uses One-Family Dwellings				10 Ft.–plus 1 Ft.–3 Stories–less than 70 Ft. width 10% lot width 3 Ft. min.		17,500 Sq. Ft. (1)	17,500 Sq. Ft. (1)	70 Ft. (1)	Two Covered Spaces Per Dwelling Unit

One family residential

ZONE	USE	STORIES	FEET	FRONT	SIDE	REAR	PER LOT	PER DWELLING UNIT	MIN LOT WIDTH	PARKING
RE40	RESIDENTIAL ESTATE	3	45 Ft.	20% lot depth 25 Ft. Max.	10 Ft. min. plus 1 Ft.–3 stories	25% lot depth 25 Ft. Max.	40,000 Sq. Ft. (1)	40,000 Sq. Ft. (1)	80 Ft. (1)	Two Covered Spaces Per Dwelling Unit
RE20	One-Family Dwellings Parks						20,000 Sq. Ft. (1)	20,000 Sq. Ft. (1)	80 Ft. (1)	
RE15	Playgrounds Community Centers Truck Gardening				10 Ft. max. 10% Lot Width 5 Ft. min.–plus 1 Ft. 3 stories		15,000 Sq. Ft. (1)	15,000 Sq. Ft. (1)	80 Ft. (1)	
RE11					5 Ft., less than 50 Ft. width 3 Ft. Min.		11,000 Sq. Ft. (1)	11,000 Sq. Ft. (1)	70 Ft. (1)	
RE9							9,000 Sq. Ft. (1)	9,000 Sq. Ft. (1)	65 Ft. (1)	
RS	SUBURBAN One-Family Dwellings Parks Playgrounds Truck Gardening			20% lot depth 25 Ft. Max.	5 Ft., less than 50 Ft. 10% Lot Width 3 Ft. Minimum	20 Ft. Min.	7,500 Sq. Ft.	7,500 Sq. Ft.	60 Ft.	
R1	ONE-FAMILY DWELLING RS Uses	3	45 Ft.	20% lot depth 20 Ft. Max.	Plus 1 Ft. 3 Stories	15 Ft. Min.	5,000 Sq. Ft.	5,000 Sq. Ft	50 Ft.	
RZ 2.5	RESIDENTIAL ZERO SIDE YARD				None(3) or 3 Ft. plus 1 Ft.–3 stories	None(3) or 15 Ft.	2,500 Sq. Ft.	2,500 Sq. Ft.	30 Ft. with driveway, 25 Ft. w/o driveway	Two covered spaces per dwelling unit
RZ 3	Dwelling across not more than five lots (2)			10 Ft. Min.			3,000 Sq. Ft.	3,000 Sq. Ft.	20 Ft.–flag curved or cul-de-sac	
RZ 4	Parks Playgrounds						4,000 Sq. Ft.	4,000 Sq. Ft.		
RZ 5							5,000 Sq. Ft.	5,000 Sq. Ft.		
RW1	ONE-FAMILY RESIDENTIAL WATERWAYS ZONE	2	30 Ft.	10 Ft. min.	10% width 3 Ft. Minimum	15 Ft. Min.	2,300 Sq. Ft.	2,300 Sq. Ft.	28 Ft.	

(1) 'H' Hillside or Mountainous Area designation may alter these requirements in the RA-H or RE-H Zones, subdivisions may be approved with smaller lots, providing larger lots are also included. Each lot may be used for only one single-family dwelling. See minimum width and area requirements below.

ZONE COMBINATION	MINIMUM TO WHICH NET AREA MAY BE REDUCED	MINIMUM TO WHICH LOT WIDTH MAY BE REDUCED
RA-H	14,000 Sq. Ft.	63 Ft.
RE9-H	7,200 Sq. Ft.	60 Ft.
RE11-H	8,800 Sq. Ft.	63 Ft.
RE15-H	12,000 Sq. Ft.	72 Ft.
RE20-H	16,000 Sq. Ft.	72 Ft.
RE40-H	32,000 Sq. Ft.	No Reduction

(2) See Section 12.08 B 1 of the Zone Code.
(3) See Section 12.08 C4 of the Zone Code.
† As in force in February 1988.

GENERALIZED SUMMARY OF ZONING REGULATIONS: CITY OF LOS ANGELES

ZONE	USE	MAXIMUM HEIGHT		REQUIRED YARDS			MINIMUM AREA		MINIMUM LOT WIDTH	PARKING REQUIRED
		STORIES	FEET	FRONT	SIDE	REAR	PER LOT	PER DWELLING UNIT		

Multiple residential

ZONE	USE	STORIES	FEET	FRONT	SIDE	REAR	PER LOT	PER DWELLING UNIT	MIN. LOT WIDTH	PARKING REQUIRED
RW2	TWO-FAMILY RESIDENTIAL WATERWAYS ZONE	3	45 Ft.	10 Ft. Min	10% Lot Width 3 Ft. Minimum plus 1 Ft. each story over 2nd (4)	15 Ft. min.	2,300 Sq. Ft.	1,150 Sq. Ft.	28 Ft.	Two covered Spaces per Dwelling Unit
R2	TWO-FAMILY DWELLING; R1 Uses; Two-Family Dwellings	3	45 Ft.	20% lot depth 20 Ft. Max.	5 Ft., less than 50 Ft. 10% Lot width 3 Ft. Min. plus 1 Ft. 3 stories	15 Ft. min	5,000 Sq. Ft.	2,500 Sq. Ft.	50 Ft.	Two Spaces One Covered
RD 1.5	RESTRICTED DENSITY MULTIPLE DWELLING ZONE; Two-Family; Apartment Houses; Multiple Dwellings	Height District No. 1 3 Stories 45 Ft.		15 Ft. Min.	5 Ft., less than 50 Ft. 10% lot width 3 Ft. min. plus 1 Ft. each story over 2, 16 Ft. Max.	15 Ft. Min.	5,000 Sq. Ft.	1,500 Sq. Ft.	50 Ft.	One space each dwelling unit of less than three rooms, one and one-half spaces each dwelling unit of three rooms, two spaces each dwelling of more than three rooms, one space each guest room (first thirty).
RD2								2,000 Sq. Ft.		
RD3		Height District Nos. 2, 3 or 4 6 Stories 75 Ft.			5 Ft. or 10% lot width 10 Ft. Max.		6,000 Sq Ft.	3,000 Sq. Ft.	60 Ft.	
RD4							8,000 Sq. Ft.	4,000 Sq. Ft.		
RD5		Height District No. 1 3 stories 45 Ft.		20 Ft. Min.	10 Ft. Min.	25 Ft. Min.	10,000 Sq. Ft.	5,000 Sq. Ft.	70 Ft.	
RD6							12,000 Sq. Ft.	6,000 Sq. Ft.		
R3	MULTIPLE DWELLING; R2 Uses; Apartment Houses; Multiple Dwellings; Child Care (20 Max.)	Height District Nos. 2, 3 or 4 6 Stories 75 Ft.			5 Ft., less than 50 Ft. 10% lot width, 3 Ft. min. plus 1 Ft. each story above 2nd, 16 Ft. Max.	15 Ft. Min.	5,000 Sq. Ft.	800 to 1,200 Sq. Ft.	50 Ft.	One space each dwelling unit of less than three rooms, one and one-half spaces each dwelling unit of three rooms, Two spaces each dwelling of more than three rooms
R4	MULTIPLE DWELLING; R3 Uses; Churches; Schools; Child care	Unlimited (6)		15 Ft., key lots 10 Ft. min.		15 Ft. plus 1 Ft. each story above 3rd, 20 Ft. Max.		400 to 800 Sq. Ft.	50 Ft.	one space each guest room (first thirty)
R5	MULTIPLE DWELLING; R4 Uses; Clubs; Lodges; Hospitals; Sanitariums							200 to 400 Sq. Ft.		

(4) For two or more lots the interior side yards may be eliminated, but 4 Ft. is required on each side of the grouped lots. See Section 12.09.5C of Zone Code.

(5) Sec. 12.17.5 B.9.(a) Dwellings considered as accessory to industrial use only (watchman or caretaker including family).

(6) HEIGHT DISTRICT

No. 1	Floor Area of Main Building may not Exceed Three Times the Building Area of the Lot
No. 1L	Same as No. 1 and Maximum Height — 6 Stories or 75 Ft.
No. 1-VL	Same as No. 1 and Maximum Height — 3 Stories or 45 Ft.
No. 1-XL	Same as No. 1 and Maximum Height — 2 Stories or 30 Ft.
No. 2	Floor Area of Main Building may not Exceed Six Times the Buildable Area of the Lot
No. 3	Floor Area of Main Building may not Exceed 10 Times the Buildable Area of the Lot
No. 4	Floor Area of Main Building may not Exceed 13 Times the Buildable Area of the Lot

GENERALIZED SUMMARY OF ZONING REGULATIONS: CITY OF LOS ANGELES

ZONE	USE	MAXIMUM HEIGHT		REQUIRED YARDS			MINIMUM AREA PER LOT/UNIT	MINIMUM LOT WIDTH	LOADING SPACE	PARKING REQUIRED
		STORIES	FEET	FRONT	SIDE	REAR				

Commercial

ZONE	USE	STORIES	FEET	FRONT	SIDE	REAR	MINIMUM AREA PER LOT/UNIT	MINIMUM LOT WIDTH	LOADING SPACE	PARKING REQUIRED
CR	LIMITED COMMERCIAL Banks, Clubs, Hotels, Churches, Schools, Business and Professional Child care, Parking areas, R4 uses	6	75 Ft.		10 Ft. 10% lot width, 5 Ft. min. for corner lots; same as R4 for residential uses or adjoining an 'A' or 'R' Zone	15 Ft. plus 1 Ft. each story above 3rd	Same as R4 for Residential purposes Otherwise None	40 Ft. Comm. use; 50 Ft. residential use	Hotels, Institutions, and with every building where lot abuts an alley Minimum Loading Space 400 Sq. Ft.	One space per 500 Sq. Ft. of floor area within all buildings on any lot.
C1	LIMITED COMMERCIAL Local retail stores Offices or Businesses, Hotels, Hospitals and/or Clinics, Parking Areas CR uses except churches, schools and museums R3 Uses	Unlimited (6)		10 Ft. min.	Same as R3 for corner lots, or residential uses or adjoining an 'A' 'R' Zone	15 Ft. plus 1 Ft. each story above 3rd, 20 Ft. max. Residential Use or abutting an 'A' or 'R' Zone.	Same as R3 for Residential purposes, except 5,000 Sq. Ft. per unit in C1-H Zones Otherwise None		Additional Space Required for Buildings containing more than 50,000 Sq. Ft. of floor area. None required for apartment buildings 30 Units or Less.	One space per 200 Sq. Ft. of total floor area of medical service facilities.
C1.5	LIMITED COMMERCIAL C1 Uses Department Stores, Theatres, Broadcasting Studios, Parking Buildings, Parks and Playgrounds R4 uses.					Yards provided at lowest residential story. Otherwise None	Same as R4 for Residential purposes Otherwise None			
C2	COMMERCIAL C1.5 Uses Retail Businesses with Limited Manufacturing, Auto Services Station and Garage, Retail Contractors Businesses, Churches, Schools R4 uses.	Unlimited (6)			None for Commercial buildings Residential uses— same as in R4 Zone Yards provided at lowest residential story.	Same as R4 for Residential purposes Otherwise None	40 Ft. Comm. Use; 50 Ft. residential use	Hospitals, Hotels, Institutions, and with every building where lot abuts an alley Minimum Loading Space 400 Sq. Ft. Additional Space Required for Buildings containing more than 50,000 Sq. Ft. of floor area. None required for buildings 30 units or less.	One space per 500 Sq. Ft. of floor area within all buildings on any lot. One space per 200 Sq. Ft. of total floor area or medical service facilities.
C4	COMMERCIAL C2 Uses— (With Exceptions, such as Auto Service Stations, Amusement Enterprises, Hospitals Second-Hand Businesses) R4 Uses									
C5	COMMERCIAL C2 Uses—Limited Floor Areas for Light Manufacturing of the CM-Zone Type, R4 Uses									
CM	COMMERCIAL MANUFACTURING Wholesale Business, Storage Buildings, clinics, Limited manufacturing, C2 Uses— Except Hospitals, Schools, Churches, R3 Uses				None for Industrial or Commercial buildings Residential Uses—same as in R4 Zone		Same as R3 for Residential purposes Otherwise None			

GENERALIZED SUMMARY OF ZONING REGULATIONS: CITY OF LOS ANGELES

ZONE	USE	MAXIMUM HEIGHT		REQUIRED YARDS			MINIMUM AREA PER LOT/UNIT	MINIMUM LOT WIDTH	LOADING SPACE	PARKING REQUIRED
		STORIES	FEET	FRONT	SIDE	REAR				

Industrial

ZONE	USE	STORIES	FEET	FRONT	SIDE	REAR	MINIMUM AREA PER LOT/UNIT	MINIMUM LOT WIDTH	LOADING SPACE	PARKING REQUIRED
MR1	RESTRICTED INDUSTRIAL Uses First permitted in CM Zone Limited Commercial and Manufacturing Uses, Clinics, Limited Machine Shops, Animal Hospitals and Kennels	Unlimited (6)		5 Ft. for lots 100 Ft. in depth or less, 15 Ft. for lots over 100 Ft. in depth	None for industrial or commercial buildings Residential Use— Same as in R4 Zone (5)	None for industrial or commercial buildings Residential Uses— Same as in R4 Zone Yards provided at lowest residential story (5)	Same as R4 for watchman or caretaker dwellings (5)		Institutions, and with every building where lot abuts an alley Minimum Loading Space 400 Sq. Ft. Additional space required for buildings containing more than 50,000 Sq. Ft. of Floor Area None Required for apartment buildings 30 Units or Less	One space for each 500 Sq. Ft. of floor Area in all buildings on any lot. Must be located within 750 Ft. of building.
MR2	RESTRICTED LIGHT INDUSTRIAL MR1 Uses Additional Industrial Uses, Mortuaries, Agriculture									
M1	LIMITED INDUSTRIAL CM Uses Limited Industrial and Manufacturing Uses No 'R' Zone Uses, No Hospitals Schools or Churches any enclosed C2 Uses									
M2	LIGHT INDUSTRIAL M1 and MR2 Uses—Additional Industrial Uses, Storage Yards of All Kinds, Animal Keeping— No 'R' Zone Uses			None	Residential Uses— Same as in R5 Zone (5)		Same as R5 (5)			
M3	HEAVY INDUSTRIAL M2 Uses Any Industrial Uses— Nuisance Type— 500 Ft. From any Other Zone— No 'R' Zone Uses				None	None	None			

Parking

ZONE	USE	STORIES	FEET	FRONT	SIDE	REAR	MINIMUM AREA PER LOT/UNIT	MINIMUM LOT WIDTH	LOADING SPACE	PARKING REQUIRED
P	AUTOMOBILE PARKING—SURFACE AND UNDERGROUND Land in a 'P' Zone may also be classified in 'A' or 'R' Zone Parking Permitted in lieu of Agricultural or Residential Uses			10 Ft. frong where any combination of an 'A' or 'R' Zone with 'P' Zone			None Unless also in an 'A' or 'R' Zone			
P8	PARKING BUILDING Automobile Parking within without A Building 'P' Zone Uses	MAXIMUM PS ZONE HEIGHTS No. 1 — 2 Stories and Roof No. 2 — 6 Stories No. 3 — 10 Stories No. 4 — 13 Stories		0 Ft., 5 Ft. or 10 Ft. depending on zoning frontage and zoning across street	5 Ft. plus 1 Ft. each story above 2nd if abutting or acrooss street and frontage in 'A' or 'R' Zone	5 Ft. plus 1 Ft. each story above 2nd if abutting an 'A' or 'R' Zone	None	None		

Special

T — TENTATIVE CLASSIFICATION
Used in Combination with Zone Change Only—Delays issuance of Building Permits until Subdivision or Parcel Map Recorded or other conditions met as required by City Council.

Q — QUALIFIED CLASSIFICATION
Further restrictions on Property; used in Combination with Zone Changes Only (Except with RA, RE, RS or R1 Zones) Restricts Use of Property and Assures Development Compatible with the Surrounding Property

D — DEVELOPMENT LIMITATION CLASSIFICATION
Restricts absolute building heights, floor area ratio, percent of lot coverage and building setbacks

SL — SUBMERGED LAND ZONE
Commercial Shipping
Navigation
Fishing
Recreation

F — FUNDED IMPROVEMENT CLASSIFICATION
An Alternative means of Effecting Zone Changes and Securing Improvements (When No Subdivision or Dedications are involved)

Supplemental use districts

Established in Conjunction with Zone(s)

G — Surface Mining
O — Oil Drilling
RPD — Residential Planned Development
K — Equine Keeping
CA — Commercial and Aircraft

rezoning of the area, amending the condition that offends. An extreme example of such a condition is the requirement to provide signs on buildings around Times Square, New York City. A 1 million square foot mixed use development, comprising offices, shops and cinemas, planned for that area is required to be adorned by 16,000 sq ft of signs, and some of them must be illuminated, to maintain the character of the area. Moreover, the signs have to be reviewed by the Department of City Planning, presumably to ensure sufficient gaudiness. According to one developer[8], the cost per building of such signs will be between $1m and $3m.

Another example of a condition that looks a bit intrusive to British eyes is applied in the Pinelands area of New Jersey, where the need is to protect the current agricultural and forest uses from encroachment. In forest and farmland areas residential dwelling units may be permitted provided that:

- the dwelling unit will be the applicant's principal place of residence

- he has not built a dwelling unit for at least five years

- the applicant can demonstrate a cultural, social or economic link to the essential character of the Pinelands

To fulfil this last requirement, the property must have been owned by the applicant or his family in 1979, and he must be either a member of a two generation extended family residing in the Pinelands for at least 20 years, or employed in a Pinelands resource related activity. Such conditions are rather tougher than can be applied in British National Parks, where tough development control is justified.

Zoning can be used to ensure that almost nothing can happen outside very clearly determined objectives of the municipality concerned. Consider the following entry for Carmel in a California guidebook[9]:

'Carmel is a unique community in California. It began as a seaside colony for professors from Stanford and Berkeley and for writers, artists, musicians, and others seeking peace, quiet and natural beauty. The mile square village is chiefly known for its setting and what it does not have. Restrictive zoning passed in the 1920s preserves the residential character of the village of 5,000 and strictly controls all commercial development. There are no neon signs, no tall buildings, and no paved sidewalks or streetlights in the residential areas. Houses have no numbers; mail is picked up from the post office, which serves as the nerve center for the village. So zealous is the village about preserving its character that a few years ago it passed an ordinance forbidding outdoor plastic plants!'

This only serves to underline how far the police power can be stretched, especially in California. Driving through Carmel reveals it to be a quite special place, almost precious with its small wooden signs where in many other places illuminated hoardings and billboards would be the norm. There is also sign control in Breckenridge, Colorado, an old silver-mining town now winter resort, that ensured that Wendys' Hamburgers could erect only a carved wooden sign. But, in the week that the planning officer was away on vacation the necessary permit was obtained to repaint the building itself a gaudy lemon yellow – the company colours, but quite out of character with the historic district. So much for tight zoning controls!

Special permits, variances and conditional uses

The extracts of the Jersey City residential zone ordinance quoted above include the concept of a *conditional use* – that is, a use that is permitted in a zone, but only after the planning board has had the opportunity to appraise an individual application. The planning board meeting will be a public hearing at which neighbours to the potential new use may come and make their views known. Sometimes the ordinance will specify conditions that are to be met; sometimes the board will apply conditions of its own where the unique circumstances of the site demand them or where there is need to pay regard to public opinions voiced. There is a range of mechanisms such as this, and terms such as conditional use, special use permit and special exception are used in various ways in different states and localities, and according to whether it is the planning board (similar to a British planning committee), or the zoning board (a local appeals body for which there is no exact equivalent) that is responsible for taking the decision.

These exceptions and permits are generally applicable only in circumstances defined in the ordinance, for example where a particular use is envisaged that is likely to cause a nuisance. By contrast, all aspects of the ordinance may be the subject of an application for a *variance*. Such applications should be successful only in limited circumstances, where the physical configuration of the plot would make a strict application of the ordinance bear unfairly on one individual. Some state enabling legislation also permits the concept of a use variance, again to allow an individual to appeal to the zoning board on the grounds that the ordinance treats him too harshly. With all these different mechanisms it is sometimes quite difficult to know which is the proper channel, and indeed there may even be a choice according to where the applicant considers that he has a better chance of success.

Site plan review and subdivision control

A whole series of specialised developments and uses of the zoning power are described later in this Chapter. But first the potential developer will probably have to submit most significant developments to two other local review processes.

(a) Site plan review

Zoning indicates for each part of a local government area the types of use and building that are to be permitted as of right, with no need for a public hearing unless the ordinance demands it (for example, in the case of conditional uses). Site plan review is a means frequently used to ensure that the various standards set out in the zoning ordinance are followed in major developments that comply with the zoning ordinance. The proportion of developments reviewed depends on the local government concerned. For example, in West Windsor, a central New Jersey municipality, all development other than single family detached dwellings and associated accessory uses comes under scrutiny in order to:

'a. Preserve existing natural resources and give proper consideration to the physical constraints of the land.

b. Provide for safe and efficient vehicular and pedestrian circulation.

c. Provide for screening, landscaping, signing and lighting.

d. Ensure efficient, safe and aesthetic land development.

e.   Provide for compliance with appropriate design standards to ensure adequate light and air, proper building arrangements, and minimum adverse effect on surrounding property.

f.   Develop proper safeguards to minimize the impact on the environment including but not limited to soil erosion and sedimentation and air and water pollution.

g.   Ensure the provision of adequate water supply, drainage and storm water management, sanitary facilities, and other utilities and services.

h.   Provide for recreation, open space and public use areas.

i.   Encourage cost-performance methods and designs to enable the construction of low and moderate impact on the public health, safety and general welfare of the township or for the future residents of the development.'

In West Windsor, site plans are reviewed in a two stage process, preliminary and final review; an informal discussion and review sketch stage is also encouraged. An appointed body, the Site Plan Review Advisory Board, advises and assists the planning and zoning boards in carrying out their site plan review function. Other officials are invited to contribute, namely,

'a.   The township engineer.

b.   The township planning consultant.

c.   The township board of health.

d.   The township fire inspection officer.

e.   The township environmental commission and its consultant.

f.   The township shade tree committee.

g.   The township chief of police.

h.   Mercer County Planning Board and where applicable, the State Department of Transportation.

i.   The township sewer operating committee.

j.   Such other boards or professionals as the planning board may deem necessary (eg Delaware and Raritan Canal Commission, school board, etc.)'

The main purpose of the review process is to encourage, cajole and even bully developers to submit and implement plans that conform as far as possible with a whole range of performance standards, such as technical standards relating to odorous matter and noise on lot lines. Public scrutiny extends to car parking standards, tree planting, street lighting, signs, street furniture and even the size of swimming pools to be provided. The regulations specify in great detail the sort of information that the applicant must provide. The British development control system is criticised from time to time for the supplementary information that local authorities sometimes demand; but such demands seem small compared with the cross examination of experts by board members in the West Windsor process.

The policy on site plan review in Jersey City, in the same state and hence under the same state enabling legislation, is to review far fewer projects. There, the trigger is 10 dwellings, or 10,000 square feet lot size (moderately set in a densely developed city), or 50 per cent additions. Looking further afield, in Billings Montana the site plan review is part of the process of obtaining a building permit, and is thus much more akin to building regulations approval of construction standards, although the details required for that and the subdivision review process do overlap significantly. Wherever you look, the details of administration are different; it is difficult to make generalisations.

(b) Subdivision control

Subdivision is the process of creating legally defined parcels of ground, usually lots or tracts, and usually for the purpose of transferring the ownership of the subdivided parcels to others. It is a process that has always been subject to careful control in the United States. Originally the aim was to ease the conveyancing of legal title to land from one owner to another and to make sure that an up-to-date record of land ownership was maintained. This process was known as 'platting' and subdivision ordinances refer to a preliminary plat, when the outline proposal to divide the land is approved, and to a final plat when the process is formally complete and the actual transfer of ownership can proceed. The main purposes of the control now are to ensure that the lots created are sensibly sized in relation to the development that the zoning ordinance will permit, and will be adequately served by the streets on the site. Sometimes new housing developments are referred to as subdivisions because it is here that the process is most clearly at work, turning virgin land in one ownership into a large number of parcels on which homes will be built, and served by the necessary new streets. Subdivision control also takes account of the extension of other infrastructure – water and sewerage, access to services such as the fire brigade, and the provision of parks, schools and streetlamps. From an original voluntary way of easing conveyancing, subdivision control has developed into a mandatory requirement, one which can be conditioned to require the setting aside of land for streets and parks, and more recently one which can require dedication of land to the public.

Aesthetic controls

Two other control systems may also be relevant, especially in larger, older cities.

(a) Landmark controls

There is a rapidly increasing awareness in the United States of the importance of attempting to conserve some elements of the built heritage, whether through preserving historic buildings, or by ensuring that new development in historic districts is sympathetic in scale and design with the character of such districts. In New York City it was the loss of the old Pennsylvania Railroad terminal to redevelopment that led to the creation in 1965 of a Landmarks Preservation Commission, responsible for identifying and designating landmark buildings and historic districts, and regulating the alteration of designated properties to ensure the preservation of their architectural, historical, cultural and aesthetic qualities. Before an owner may change a protected feature of any individually designated landmark or property feature of any historic district, approval must be obtained from

Figure 4.4 upper St Bartholomew's Church is on Park Avenue, New York City and protected by landmarking, but a battle rages over a proposal to develop an office tower on the ancillary structure to the right. *lower* Historic housing in Pittsburgh, renovated with the aid of grants and protected by being in a historic district.

the Landmarks Preservation Commission. By 1986 the Commission had designated 730 individual landmarks and 48 historic districts.

The controls that have evolved seem analogous to the British listed building consents and controls in designated conservation areas; demolitions may not take place without the consent of a city commission, and controls can extend to the interior of selected buildings (in this last case the effect may only be to delay demolition for a couple of years while efforts are made to find a new use for an old building). Many cities have established landmark commissions to designate individual landmarks and historic districts. The extent of control varies from city to city and from state to state. The position is complicated by the existence of federally designated landmarks and districts. In Pittsburgh, for example, there is the incongruous

Figure 4.5 The Seagram Building, on Park Avenue, New York City is considered a modern masterpiece, by architects Mies van der Rohe and Philip Johnson; recent arguments concerned whether it was too young to be designated a landmark.

position that locally designated historic districts are subject to more control than federally designated districts, simply because of the political and financial cost of extending the local controls and accompanying grant availability to all the federal districts.

Landmark controls are important; combined with special tax reliefs for restoration they are preserving the heritage districts in many cities and encouraging re-use of buildings that only a few years ago would have been torn down. The premier example of this is Grand Central station, New York City, an enormous beaux arts building housing a cathedral of a passenger concourse. Despite the landmarks control, to save it took a US Supreme Court decision with tremendous popular support from those who remembered the fate of the old Pennsylvania Terminal. But more modest survivors that would previously have been at risk are to be found in the historic housing of Pittsburgh, and the warehouse districts of Cleveland and Denver, to mention just three.

(b) Design review

Some cities have separate design review processes over and above the normal building codes. For example, no project in downtown Portland Oregon may proceed without review by either the Design Commission, the Landmarks Commission (for historic districts and structures) or the Bureau of Planning (for projects which the Planning Director and Design Commission judge will not significantly affect the character, use and development of the surrounding properties). The requirements for an application are pretty daunting (including for example a landscape plan showing all the planting areas, street furniture, street trees, outdoor art and other outdoor features of the project, including a list of materials and colours). Every case involves a public hearing, which must take place between 15 and 60 days of the application, and decisions may be appealed to the City Council. An illustrated book[10], issued free, explains the four goals of downtown design:

'1.   Enhance the existing character of Portland's downtown

2.   Promote the development of diversity and areas of special character within Portland's downtown

3.   Provide for a pleasant, rich and diverse pedestrian experience

4.   Provide for the humanization of downtown through promotion of the arts and excellence in design.'

It goes on to illustrate some 20 general guidelines and additional special district guidelines using pictures of the city. The content of the book is supposed to give certainty to the review process by indicating the importance of certain design elements. All this is rather at odds with the current British guidance to planning authorities not to involve themselves with the design details of developments, such as the shade of bricks to be used. But I found Portland, in its modest way, to have the most coherent sense of place of all the medium sized cities I visited. Design can only be a matter of judgement; Portland contains little that is outstanding, but it fits together as a remarkable whole and the net result of that has been to attract steady development despite the apparent bureaucracy.

Master plans

At the detailed level the planning administrator's tool kit might comprise zoning and subdivision regulations, building codes, plus perhaps landmarking and design control. These would fit into a framework of master or comprehensive plans, and infrastructure or capital improvement programmes. In practice, planning and phasing infrastructure, and coordinating the actions of various departments at the state and local level are often some way removed from detailed development control processes. Also, arrangements differ greatly between areas, depending on the relationships between different agencies and local government units. As this paper concentrates on development control, I have avoided references to these broader plans except where they impinge on development control itself, for example, where a deliberate programme of phased infrastructure provision has been devised in order to control growth.

However, it is important that, in some states more than others, zoning regulations must demonstrably conform with a comprehensive plan. Local governments are empowered to create zoning regulations generally as a result of state enabling legislation. Such enabling legislation is frequently based on a model Act published by the US Department of Commerce in 1922. That contains the phrase:

'Such regulations must be made in accordance with a comprehensive plan . . .'

Figure 4.6 Portland Oregon; shaped partly by Design Commission.

Other efforts have been made to ensure that there is a properly considered rational basis for the zoning and subdivision regulations of local governments. For a long time Federal funds were available to support the preparation of master plans. Many state land use laws require that master plans are not only prepared but reviewed regularly, and a local government not carrying out this requirement will find its zoning decisions more susceptible to legal challenge in the state courts. After all, how can the zoning ordinance be rationally based if the broad policy goals of the community are not reasonably up-to-date and based on recent data?

One example of prominent local comprehensive planning is in California, where each county or municipality must prepare a general plan. That plan must contain policies on land use, traffic circulation, open space, conservation of natural resources, housing welfare, noise, pollution and public safety (including earthquake protection). All these policies within the plan must be internally consistent. Every public works programme must also be consistent with the plan or there will be a real risk of successful legal challenge. Zoning ordinances must also be consistent or they too will be invalidated. Ultimately, therefore, provided there is sufficient citizen interest to enforce the master plan by taking local governments to court for non-compliance, all development should be in accord with its content. In practice in other states the courts have been reluctant to go so far, or there is not the same degree of public willingness to institute court challenges. In many states the courts have held that the drawing up of a zoning map (such as in the frontispiece to this chapter) is sufficient to constitute a comprehensive plan.

Comprehensive plans tend, to my untrained eyes, to resemble British development plans. They contain general maps to indicate the long term goals for different land uses planned over the area concerned for the next twenty or so years. They provide information about expected changes in population and employment, and policies designed to accommodate or stimulate those changes. Roads and open space, job preservation, action to co-ordinate public service provision and to preserve neighbourhoods are all issues relating to the long range physical development of the community and might be found in a master plan. But the absence of a plan does not necessarily mean that a city has none of those objectives. The biggest city of all, New York, has no master plan, but its zoning ordinances are sufficiently backed with information and evidence to avoid the appearance of being capricious.

Zoning devices, constructive and otherwise

Over its 70 year life, straightforward zoning has not proved to be sufficiently flexible to achieve all the objectives that planners have wanted of it. Various refinements have been developed and added to the menu of mechanisms available. The paragraphs below describe some of the refinements which are important as an indication of the limitations that planners and politicians have sought to overcome. By way of read across, these adaptations provide clues as to how it may be necessary to shape simplified planning zone or other zoning mechanisms if they were ever to become a widely adopted development control tool in England.

(i) Floating zones

Floating zones are perhaps a political cop-out. As we have seen, zoning generally requires the division of a local government area into districts in each of which regulations determine what buildings may be erected and what uses permitted. A *floating zone* involves the creation of those regulations for a district but without designating any part of the map as the area where that zone will apply. It represents a recognition that a district needs a particular use, such as a regional shopping centre, but a political failure to identify an area where such a use might be acceptable. A developer wishing to build in accordance with the floating zone must first propose the amendment of the zoning map to accommodate what he proposes, and if his application is successful, the map will be amended and the zone will no longer float. The burden is on the developer rather than the local government to promote development that might be opposed by local electors, while the local government can still continue to promote itself as open to growth proposals.

From the planners' point of view the advantage of this way of zoning is that it is less important to establish in a thorough way all the technical elements that will apply in the zone. Such elements can be dealt with by way of condition when the individual developer proposes locating the zone on the map. Also, it makes it much easier to keep down the number of less desirable uses and focus development. Let us suppose that a developing area needs a shopping centre, but that there is no obvious place to locate it. With traditional zoning, a series of potential sites might be identified, because it was not clear which landowner might react to his site being zoned for retailing and actually proceed to provide that use. Then, if several landowners decided to develop at the same time, the locality might suddenly gain rather more of that kind of development than it intended. The area might even become some sort of specialist retail centre, a development far removed from the planners' original vision. The same effect can emerge, even with floating zones, if two developers come along at more or less the same time, and have to be treated equally. But, keeping uses off the map until the developer himself makes a proposal has its advantages. Land use planners in Britain will recognise this process as reversing zoning into the sort of reactive discretionary control system that operates under the 1971 Town and Country Planning Act. Then the challenge is to persuade the developer to come forward with the right proposals in the right place!

(ii) Spot zoning

Floating zones can generally only apply to quite large developments where there are policies in the master plan that give guidance as to how the device will be applied. The reason is the risk that bringing special provisions to bear on individual small sites will constitute *spot zoning*. This practice is frowned upon because it is the opposite of zoning in accordance with a comprehensive plan. Once the practice has been conceded for one site and special provisions made, the chances are that others will apply for variations in the zoning regulations applying to their sites, demanding equal treatment. It is thus vulnerable to legal challenge as unconstitutional.

With zoning the theory is that it should be quite difficult to change the pattern of development provided for in the plan and zoning ordinances. Variances for individual sites should be available only when there is hardship to the applicant arising uniquely from the application of the ordinances to his site. (In practice this strict intention is observed rather more in the breach.) The proper way to change what may happen on a particular site, rather than letting floating zones settle on a small area, is to amend the ordinance itself. This will require proper notice, a planning board hearing, and possibly action by the elected members. It might even be necessary to amend the master plan.

(iii) Planned unit developments

If with floating zones the purpose is to set out likely or necessary uses in the ordinance, without designating land on the zoning map, planned unit developments can be regarded as the opposite. They are generally areas designated on the map, capable of taking a range of different uses or densities, and thus for which development types are not fully detailed. They are more likely to be appropriate on the edge of a developing area than in an area where most sites have already been developed. In such areas there is really no need for artificial lines to be drawn by planners to separate the uses that are envisaged; a developer may well come along with an alternative plan that is equally acceptable. In these circumstances the answer is to designate the area for planned unit development (known as a planned residential development if only residential uses are to be located on the site).

Planned unit or residential developments have several advantages. First, the planners need only set down broad guidelines for the mixtures of uses or densities that might be permitted. The developer's own team can prepare a plan in accordance with the guidelines, but with the flexibility to put together components in such a way as to maximise the potential of the site. On approval, that plan is effectively bound into the ordinance. This gives the developer the certainty that a large project will go forward without needing a succession of later approvals. Dealing with all the details in response to an application does take rather longer than would consideration of a whole series of minor elements against a rigid zoning ordinance. But the development concerned may well benefit from larger scale site design. In addition, subdivision and zoning controls may be combined, with a resultant time saving. A whole series of affordable housing case studies published by the US Department of Housing and Urban Development demonstrate that anything up to a year in processing time can be saved if the planned unit or residential development option is open.

It is possible for a planned unit development provision in the zoning ordinance to be a floating zone too. In other words the local government is setting normal standards in its zoning ordinance for normal types and sizes of development, but allows the freedom to turn to some other approval if a large scale planned development is proposed. This recognises the unnecessary constraints on the design of large development tracts that traditional zoning can bring. Where a floating zone of this kind comes to rest, it replaces the zoning that otherwise applied over that area of land. This practice is combined with an innovatory points analysis system to establish appropriate development densities in rapidly growing Fort Collins Colorado, where dense development is only accepted where it embraces good urban design concepts (see Chapter 5 below).

(iv) Cluster zoning

Where local governments determine that low density development is all that can be accommodated in their area, perhaps because of inadequate infrastructure and services, then residential zoning densities can be set at 2 or perhaps 5 acres to a house. This can create lots that are larger than the market demands, and which are difficult to maintain. At the same time it can fail to meet the objectives of a community wishing to retain some of its rural character. It can also lead to high infrastructure costs, as roads, pipes and cables have to cover the whole site, and if there are difficult physical features such as wetlands or steep slopes, it may be difficult to arrive at a sensible estate design. One widely adopted answer is *cluster zoning*. The same number of units is placed on the site, but the garden sizes are much reduced and the balance of the site is dedicated as open space. Such space can incorporate the wetlands, areas needed for drainage, or the mature trees that are to remain as features of the development. The developer would be required to satisfy the local government concerned about the arrangements for the management of the open space; these arrangements are not unlike those applying to the common areas of leasehold blocks of flats in England.

(v) Mixed use zoning and special districts

In the face of the rigidities of the zoning system, latest development trends show that it is possible to create mixed use developments which are more likely to be self sustaining. Larger office and research developments are increasingly likely to incorporate shops, restaurants and coffee shops, open to all but of greatest interest to the employees on site. The environment is likely to be better landscaped, with water, trees, lawns and outdoor sitting areas. Moreover, there may be executive clubs, swimming pools, tennis courts and other recreational facilities, and a hotel to serve business visitors and provide the conference room a business may need only occasionally. Costs of security, utilities, insurance and taxes may be shared between the various businesses on the park. And the overall aim, apart from the economics of this shared environment, is to avoid the need for employees to leave the site during the day, thus reducing pollution and congestion.

In developed areas too there seems to be a realisation that the trend towards separation of uses, as non-conforming uses gradually became fewer, was leading to sterile single purpose districts. Downtown areas in particular are now seen as healthier places if an element of residential use can be incorporated with the more traditional shop, office, hotel and cultural uses. Zoning can be used to promote this by the creation of special districts in which combinations of uses may be permitted.

The preservation of unique combinations of uses has led the City of San Francisco to create 16 neighborhood commercial special use districts, and a newspaper size fold out matrix summarises exactly what is permitted in each one (see the four page spread in Figure 4.7). There were originally 11 generic districts in the city, comprising residential, commercial and industrial zones at different densities. These were complemented by a series of

No.	Zoning Category	References	NC-1 Sec. 710#	NC-2 Sec. 711	NC-3 Sec. 712	NC-S Sec. 713	Broadway Sec. 714	Castro Sec. 715
			Controls					
GENERAL BUILDING STANDARDS								
.10	Height and Bulk	§§ 102.11, 105, 106, 250–252, 260, 270, 271	Varies See Zoning Map	Generally, 40-X See Zoning Map	Generally, 40-X See Zoning Map	Generally, 40-X See Zoning Map	P up to 40 ft. C 41 to 65 ft. # § 253.1	40-X to 65-B See Zoning Map
.11	Lot Size [Per Development]	§§ 790.56, 121.1	P up to 4999 sq.ft., C 5000 sq.ft. & above § 121.1	P up to 9999 sq.ft., C 10,000 sq.ft. & above § 121.1	P up to 9999 sq.ft., C 10,000 sq.ft. & above § 121.1	Not Applicable	P up to 4999 sq.ft., C 5000 sq.ft. & above § 121.1	P up to 4999 sq.ft., C 5000 sq.ft. & above § 121.1
.12	Rear Yard	§§ 130, 134, 136	Required at grade level and above § 134(a)(e)	Required at the second story and above and at all residential levels § 134(a)(e)	Required at residential levels only § 134(a)(e)	Not Required	Required at residential levels only § 134 (a)(e)	Required at the second story and above and at all residential levels § 134(a)(e)
.13	Street Frontage		Required § 145.1	Required § 145.1	Required § 145.1	Required § 145.1	Required § 145.1	Required § 145.1
.14	Awning	§ 790.20	P § 136.1(a)	P § 136.1(a)	P § 136.1(a)	P § 136.1(a)	P § 136.1(a)	P § 136.1(a)
.15	Canopy	§ 790.26	P § 136.1(b)	P § 136.1(b)	P § 136.1(b)	P § 136.1(b)	P § 136.1(b)	P § 136.1(b)
.16	Marquee	§ 790.58	P § 136.1(c)	P § 136.1(c)	P § 136.1(c)	P § 136.1(c)	P § 136.1(c)	P § 136.1(c)
.17	Street Trees		Required § 143	Required § 143	Required § 143	Required § 143	Required § 143	Required § 143
COMMERCIAL AND INSTITUTIONAL STANDARDS AND USES								
.20	Floor Area Ratio	§§ 102.8, 102.10, 123	0.75 to 1 § 124(a)(b)	1.75 to 1 § 124(a)(b)	3.6 to 1 § 124(a)(b)	1.0 to 1 § 124(a)(b)	2.0 to 1 § 124(a)(b)	2.5 to 1 § 124(a)(b)
.21	Use Size [Non-Residential]	§ 790.130	P up to 2499 sq.ft. C 2500 sq.ft. & above § 121.2	P up to 3499 sq.ft. C 3500 sq.ft. & above § 121.2	P up to 4999 sq.ft. C 5000 sq.ft. & above § 121.2	P up to 4999 sq.ft. C 5000 sq.ft. & above § 121.2	P up to 2999 sq.ft. C 3000 sq.ft. & above § 121.2	P up to 2499 sq.ft. C 2500 sq.ft. & above § 121.2
.22	Off-Street Parking, Commercial and Institutional	§§ 150, 153–157, 159–160, 204.5	Generally, none required if occupied floor area is less than 5000 sq.ft. §§ 151, 161(g)	Generally, none required if occupied floor area is less than 5000 sq.ft. §§ 151, 161(g)	Generally, none required if occupied floor area is less than 5000 sq.ft. §§ 151, 161(g)	Generally, none required if occupied floor area is less than 5000 sq.ft. §§ 151, 161(g)	Generally, none required if occupied floor area is less than 5000 sq.ft. §§ 151, 161(g)	Generally, none required if occupied floor area is less than 5000 sq.ft. §§ 151, 161(g)
.23	Off-Street Freight Loading	§§ 150, 153–155, 204.5	Generally, none required if gross floor area is less than 10,000 sq.ft. §§ 152, 161(b)	Generally, none required if gross floor area is less than 10,000 sq.ft. §§ 152, 161(b)	Generally, none required if gross floor area is less than 10,000 sq.ft. §§ 152, 161(b)	Generally, none required if gross floor area is less than 10,000 sq.ft. §§ 152, 161(b)	Generally, none required if gross floor area is less than 10,000 sq.ft. §§ 152, 161(b)	Generally, none required if gross floor area is less than 10,000 sq.ft. §§ 152, 161(b)
.24	Outdoor Activity Area	§ 790.70	P in front; C elsewhere § 145.2(a)	P in front; C elsewhere § 145.2(a)	P in front; C elsewhere § 145.2(a)	P/C § 145.2(a)	P in front; C elsewhere § 145.2(a)	P in front; C elsewhere § 145.2(a)
.25	Drive-up Facility	§ 790.30				C		
.26	Walk-Up Facility	§ 790.140	P if recessed 3 ft.; C otherwise § 145.2(b)	P if recessed 3 ft.; C otherwise § 145.2(b)	P if recessed 3 ft.; C otherwise § 145.2(b)	P if recessed 3 ft.; C otherwise § 145.2(b)	P if recessed 3 ft.; C otherwise § 145.2(b)	P if recessed 3 ft.; C otherwise § 145.2(b)
.27	Hours of Operation	§ 790.48	P: 6 a.m.–11 p.m. C: 11 p.m.–2 a.m.	P: 6 a.m.–2 a.m. C: 2 a.m.–6 a.m.	No Limit	P: 6 a.m.–2 a.m. C: 2 a.m.–6 a.m.	P: 6 a.m.–2 a.m. C: 2 a.m.–6 a.m.	P: 6 a.m.–2 a.m. C: 2 a.m.–6 a.m.
.30	General Advertising Sign	§§ 262, 602–604, 608.1–.10, 609		P § 607.1(e)1	P# § 607.1(e)2	P § 607.1(e)1	P § 607.1(e)2	
.31	Business Sign	§§ 262, 602–604, 608.1–.10, 609	P § 607.1(f)1	P § 607.1(f)2	P# § 607.1(f)3	P § 607.1(f)2	P § 607.1(f)3	P# § 607.1(f)2
.32	Other Signs	§§ 262, 602–604, 608.1–.10, 609	P § 607.1(c)(d)(g)	P § 607.1(c)(d)(g)	P § 607.1(c)(d)(g)	P § 607.1(c)(d)(g)	P § 607.1(c)(d)(g)	P# § 607.1(c)(d)(g)

			NC-1 1st	NC-1 2nd	NC-1 3rd+	NC-2 1st	NC-2 2nd	NC-2 3rd+	NC-3 1st	NC-3 2nd	NC-3 3rd+	NC-S 1st	NC-S 2nd	NC-S 3rd+	Broadway 1st	Broadway 2nd	Broadway 3rd+	Castro 1st	Castro 2nd	Castro 3rd+
		§ 790.118	**Controls by Story**																	
.38	Residential Conversion	§ 790.84	P			P	C		P	C		P			P	C		P	C	
.39	Residential Demolition	§ 790.86	C	C	C	C	C	C	C	C	C	C	C	C	C	C	C	C	C	C
Retail Sales and Services																				
.40	Other Retail Sales and Services [Not Listed Below]	§ 790.102	P			P	P		P	P	P	P	P		P	P		P	P	
.41	Bar	§ 790.22	P#			P			P	P		P	P		P	P				
.42	Full-Service Restaurant	§ 790.92	P#			P#			P	P		P	P		P	P				
.43	Small Fast Food Restaurant	§ 790.90	C#			P#			P#	P#		P	P		C	C				
.44	Large Fast Food Restaurant	§ 790.91				C#			C#	C#		C	C							
.45	Take-Out Food	§ 790.122	C#			C			C	C		C	C		C	C				
.46	Movie Theater	§ 790.64				P			P	P		P			P	P		P		
.47	Adult Entertainment	§ 790.36							C	C					C	C		C		
.48	Other Entertainment	§ 790.38	C			P			P	P		P	P		P	P		C		
.49	Financial Service	§ 790.110				P			P	P		P	P		C			C		
.50	Limited Financial Service	§ 790.112	P			P			P	P		P	P		C			C		
.51	Medical Service	§ 790.114	P			P	P		P	P	P	P	P		P	P		P	P	C
.52	Personal Service	§ 790.116	P			P	P		P	P	P	P	P		P	P		P	P	C
.53	Business or Professional Service	§ 790.108	P			P	P		P	P	P	P	P		P	P		P	P	C
.54	Massage Establishment	§ 790.60 § 2700 Police Code				C			C	C		C	C		P	C		P	C	
.55	Tourist Hotel	§ 790.46				C	C	C	C	C	C				C	C	C	C	C	C
.56	Automobile Parking	§§ 790.8, 156, 160	C			C	C	C	C	C	C	P	P		C	C	C	C	C	C
.57	Automotive Gas Station	§ 790.14				C			C			C								
.58	Automotive Service Station	§ 790.17				C			C			P								
.59	Automotive Repair	§ 790.15				C			C	C										
.60	Automotive Wash	§ 790.18				C			C			C								
.61	Automobile Sale or Rental	§ 790.12				C			C											
.62	Animal Hospital	§ 790.6				C			C	C		C	C		C			C		
.63	Ambulance Service	§ 790.2							C											
.64	Mortuary	§ 790.62							C	C	C	C	C							
.65	Trade Shop	§ 790.124	P			P#	C#		P	C	C	P	P		P#	C#		P	C	
.66	Storage	§ 790.117							C	C	C	C	C							
Institutions and Non-Retail Sales and Services																				
.70	Administrative Service	§ 790.106							C	C	C	C	C							
.80	Hospital or Medical Center	§ 790.44							C	C	C									
.81	Other Institutions	§ 790.50	P	C		P	C	C	P	P	P	P	P		P	C	C	P	C	C
.82	Public Use	§ 790.80	C	C	C	C	C	C	C	C	C	C	C	C	C	C	C	C	C	C
RESIDENTIAL STANDARDS AND USES																				
.90	Residential Use	§ 790.88	P	P	P	P	P	P	P	P	P	P	P	P	P	P	P	P	P	P
.91	Residential Density, Dwelling Units	§§ 207, 207.1, 790.88(a)	Generally, 1 unit per 800 sq.ft. lot area § 207.4			Generally, 1 unit per 800 sq.ft. lot area § 207.4			Generally, 1 unit per 600 sq.ft. lot area § 207.4			Generally, 1 unit per 800 sq.ft. lot area § 207.4			Generally, 1 unit per 400 sq.ft. lot area § 207.4			Generally, 1 unit per 600 sq.ft. lot area § 207.4		
.92	Residential Density, Group Housing	§§ 207.1, 790.88(b)	Generally, 1 bedroom per 275 sq.ft. lot area § 208			Generally, 1 bedroom per 275 sq.ft. lot area § 208			Generally, 1 bedroom per 210 sq.ft. lot area § 208			Generally, 1 bedroom per 275 sq.ft. lot area § 208			Generally, 1 bedroom per 140 sq.ft. lot area § 208			Generally, 1 bedroom per 210 sq.ft. lot area § 208		
.93	Usable Open Space [Per Residential Unit]	§§ 135, 136	Generally, either 100 sq.ft. if private, or 133 sq.ft. if common § 135(d)			Generally, either 100 sq.ft. if private, or 133 sq.ft. if common § 135(d)			Generally, either 80 sq.ft. if private, or 100 sq.ft. if common § 135(d)			Generally, either 100 sq.ft. if private, or 133 sq.ft. if common § 135(d)			Generally, either 60 sq.ft. if private, or 80 sq.ft. if common § 135(d)			Generally, either 80 sq.ft. if private, or 100 sq.ft. if common § 135(d)		
.94	Off-Street Parking, Residential	§§ 150, 153–157, 159–160, 204.5	Generally, 1 space per unit §§ 151, 161(g)			Generally, 1 space per unit §§ 151, 161(g)			Generally, 1 space per unit §§ 151, 161(g)			Generally, 1 space per unit §§ 151, 161(g)			Generally, 1 space per unit §§ 151, 161(g)			Generally, 1 space per unit §§ 151, 161(a)(g)		
.95	Community Residential Parking	§ 790.10	C	C	C	C	C	C	C	C	C	C	C	C	C	C	C	C	C	C

LEGEND

P – Permitted as a principal use.

C – Permitted as a conditional use, subject to the provisions set forth in Sections 178, 179, and 316 through 316.8 of this Code.

– A blank space on the table or the symbol 'NP' indicate that the use or feature is not permitted. Unless a use or feature is permitted or required as set forth in the Zoning Control Tables or in those sections referenced in Section 799 of this Code, such use or feature is prohibited, unless determined by the Zoning Administrator to be a permitted use.

\# – See specific provisions listed by Section and Zoning Category number at the end of the table.

1st – 1st story and below

2nd – 2nd story

3rd + – 3rd story and above

PROPOSED CONTROLS FOR NEIGHBORHOOD COMMERCIAL DISTRICTS: CITY OF SAN FRANCISCO (continued)

Inner Clement Sec. 716	Outer Clement Sec. 717	Upper Fillmore Sec. 718	Haight Sec. 719	Hayes-Gough Sec. 720	Upper Market Sec. 721	North Beach Sec. 722	Polk Sec. 723
Controls							
GENERAL BUILDING STANDARDS							
40-X	40-X	40-X	40-X	50-X to 65-A See Zoning Map	40-X to 80-8 See Zoning Map	P up to 40 ft. C 41 to 65 ft. # § 253.1	65-A to 130-E See Zoning Map
P up to 4999 sq.ft., C 5000 sq.ft. & above § 121.1	P up to 4999 sq.ft., C 5000 sq.ft. & above § 121.1	P up to 4999 sq.ft., C 5000 sq.ft. & above § 121.1	P up to 4999 sq.ft., C 5000 sq.ft. & above § 121.1	P up to 9999 sq.ft., C 10,000 sq.ft. & above § 121.1	P up to 9999 sq.ft., C 10,000 sq.ft. & above § 121.1	P up to 4999 sq.ft., C 5000 sq.ft. & above § 121.1	P up to 9999 sq.ft., C 10,000 sq.ft. & above § 121.1
Required at the second story and above and at all residential levels § 134(a)(e)	Required at grade level and above § 134(a)(e)	Required at the second story and above and at all residential levels § 134(a)(e)	Required at grade level and above § 134(a)(e)	Required at residential levels only § 134(a)(e)	Required at residential levels only § 134(a)(e)	Required at the second story and above and at all residential levels § 134(a)(e)	Required at residential levels only § 134(a)(e)
Required § 145.1	Required § 145.1	Required § 145.1	Required § 145.1	Required § 145.1	Required § 145.1	Required § 145.1	Required § 145.1
P § 136.1(a)	P § 136.1(a)	P § 136.1(a)	P § 136.1(a)	P § 136.1(a)	P § 136.1(a)	P § 136.1(a)	P § 136.1(a)
P § 136.1(b)	P § 136.1(b)	P § 136.1(b)	P § 136.1(b)	P § 136.1(b)	P § 136.1(b)	P § 136.1(b)	P § 136.1(b)
P § 136.1(c)	P § 136.1(c)	P § 136.1(c)	P § 136.1(c)	P § 136.1(c)	P § 136.1(c)	P § 136.1(c)	P § 136.1(c)
Required § 143	Required § 143	Required § 143	Required § 143	Required § 143	Required § 143	Required § 143	Required § 143
COMMERCIAL AND INSTITUTIONAL STANDARDS AND USES							
1.75 to 1 § 124(a)(b)	1.0 to 1 § 124(a)(b)	1.75 to 1 § 124(a)(b)	1.5 to 1 § 124(a)(b)	2.5 to 1 § 124(a)(b)	2.5 to 1 § 124(a)(b)	1.75 to 1 § 124(a)(b)	2.0 to 1 § 124(a)(b)
P up to 2499 sq.ft., C 2500 sq.ft. & above § 121.2	P up to 2499 sq.ft., C 2500 sq.ft. & above § 121.2	P up to 2499 sq.ft., C 2500 sq.ft. & above § 121.2	P up to 2499 sq.ft., C 2500 sq.ft. & above § 121.2	P up to 2999 sq.ft., C 3000 sq.ft. & above § 121.2	P up to 2999 sq.ft., C 3000 sq.ft. & above § 121.2	P up to 2499 sq.ft., C 2500 sq.ft. & above § 121.2	P up to 2999 sq.ft., C 3000 sq.ft. & above § 121.2
Generally, none required if occupied floor area is less than 5000 sq.ft. §§ 151, 161(g)	Generally, none required if occupied floor area is less than 5000 sq.ft. §§ 151, 161(g)	Generally, none required if occupied floor area is less than 5000 sq.ft. §§ 151, 161(g)	Generally, none required if occupied floor area is less than 5000 sq.ft. §§ 151, 161(g)	Generally, none required if occupied floor area is less than 5000 sq.ft. §§ 151, 161(g)	Generally, none required if occupied floor area is less than 5000 sq.ft. §§ 151, 161(g)	Generally, none required if occupied floor area is less than 5000 sq.ft. §§ 151, 161(g)	Generally, none required if occupied floor area is less than 5000 sq.ft. §§ 151, 161(g)
Generally, none required if gross floor area is less than 10,000 sq.ft. §§ 152, 161(b)	Generally, none required if gross floor area is less than 10,000 sq.ft. §§ 152, 161(b)	Generally, none required if gross floor area is less than 10,000 sq.ft. §§ 152, 161(b)	Generally, none required if gross floor area is less than 10,000 sq.ft. §§ 152, 161(b)	Generally, none required if gross floor area is less than 10,000 sq.ft. §§ 152, 161(b)	Generally, none required if gross floor area is less than 10,000 sq.ft. §§ 152, 161(b)	Generally, none required if gross floor area is less than 10,000 sq.ft. §§ 152, 161(b)	Generally, none required if gross floor area is less than 10,000 sq.ft. §§ 152, 161(b)
P in front; C elsewhere § 145.2(a)	P in front; C elsewhere § 145.2(a)	P in front; C elsewhere § 145.2(a)	P in front; C elsewhere § 145.2(a)	P in front; C elsewhere § 145.2(a)	P in front; C elsewhere § 145.2(a)	P in front; C elsewhere § 145.2(a)	P in front; C elsewhere § 145.2(a)
P if recessed 3 ft.; C otherwise § 145.2(b)	P if recessed 3 ft.; C otherwise § 145.2(b)	P if recessed 3 ft.; C otherwise § 145.2(b)	P if recessed 3 ft.; C otherwise § 145.2(b)	P if recessed 3 ft.; C otherwise § 145.2(b)	P if recessed 3 ft.; C otherwise § 145.2(b)	P if recessed 3 ft.; C otherwise § 145.2(b)	P if recessed 3 ft.; C otherwise § 145.2(b)
P: 6 a.m.–2 a.m. C: 2 a.m.–6 a.m.	P: 6 a.m.–11 p.m. C: 11 p.m.–2 a.m.	P: 6 a.m.–2 a.m. C: 2 a.m.–6 a.m.	P: 6 a.m.–2 a.m. C: 2 a.m.–6 a.m.	P: 6 a.m.–2 a.m. C: 2 a.m.–6 a.m.	P: 6 a.m.–2 a.m. C: 2 a.m.–6 a.m.	P: 6 a.m.–2 a.m. C: 2 a.m.–6 a.m.	P: 6 a.m.–2 a.m. C: 2 a.m.–6 a.m.
P § 607.1(f)2	P § 607.1(f)2	P § 607.1(f)2	P § 607.1(f)2	P § 607.1(f)2	P # § 607.1(f)2	P § 607.1(f)2	P § 607.1(f)2
P § 607.1(c)(d)(g)	P § 607.1(c)(d)(g)	P § 607.1(c)(d)(g)	P § 607.1(c)(d)(g)	P § 607.1(c)(d)(g)	P # § 607.1(c)(d)(g)	P § 607.1(c)(d)(g)	P § 607.1(c)(d)(g)

Inner Clement			Outer Clement			Upper Fillmore			Haight			Hayes-Gough			Upper Market			North Beach			Polk		
Controls by story																							
1st	2nd	3rd +	1st	2nd	3rd +	1st	2nd	3rd +	1st	2nd	3rd +	1st	2nd	3rd +	1st	2nd	3rd +	1st	2nd	3rd +	1st	2nd	3rd +
P			P			P	C		P			P	C		P	C		P			P	C	
C	C	C	C	C	C	C	C	C	C	C	C	C	C	C	C	C	C	C	C	C	C	C	C
Retail Sales and Services																							
P	C		P			P	P		P	C		P	P		P	P		P	P		P	P	
												P			C			C			C		
												P			C			C			C		
												P			C			C			C		
												C											
												C			C			C			C		
P			P			P			P			P			P			P			P		
C			C			C			C			C			C			C			C		
			C			C			P			P			C			C/NP #			C		
C			C			C			P			P			P			C			P		
P	C		P			P	P			C		C	P	C	P	P	C	P	P		P	P	
P	C		P			P	P		P	C		P	P	C	P	P	C	P	P		P	P	
P	C		P			P	P		P	C		C	P	C	P	P	C	C	P		P	P	
C						C			C			C			C	C		C			C		
C	C					C	C	C	C	C		C	C	C	C	C	C	C	C	C	C	C	C
C	C	C	C	C		C	C	C	C	C	C	C	C	C	C	C	C	C	C	C	C	C	C
									C						C			C			C		
C			C			C			C			C			C			C			C		
P	C		P			P			P			P	C		P	C		P #	C #		P	C	
Institutions and Non-Retail Sales and Services																							
P	C	C	P	C	C	P	C	C	P	C	C	P	C	C	P	C	C	P	C	C	P	C	C
C	C	C	C	C	C	C	C	C	C	C	C	C	C	C	C	C	C	C	C	C	C	C	C
RESIDENTIAL STANDARDS AND USES																							
P	P	P	P	P	P	P	P	P	P	P	P	P	P	P	P	P	P	P	P	P	P	P	P
Generally, 1 unit per 600 sq.ft. lot area § 207.4			Generally, 1 unit per 600 sq.ft. lot area § 207.4			Generally, 1 unit per 600 sq.ft. lot area § 207.4			Generally, 1 unit per 600 sq.ft. lot area § 207.4			Generally, 1 unit per 400 sq.ft. lot area § 207.4			Generally, 1 unit per 400 sq.ft. lot area § 207.4			Generally, 1 unit per 400 sq.ft. lot area § 207.4			Generally, 1 unit per 400 sq.ft. lot area § 207.4		
Generally, 1 bedroom per 210 sq.ft. lot area § 208			Generally, 1 bedroom per 210 sq.ft. lot area § 208			Generally, 1 bedroom per 210 sq.ft. lot area § 208			Generally, 1 bedroom per 210 sq.ft. lot area § 208			Generally, 1 bedroom per 140 sq.ft. lot area § 208			Generally, 1 bedroom per 140 sq.ft. lot area § 208			Generally, 1 bedroom per 140 sq.ft. lot area § 208			Generally, 1 bedroom per 140 sq.ft. lot area § 208		
Generally, either 80 sq.ft. if private, or 100 sq.ft. if common § 135(d)			Generally, either 80 sq.ft. if private, or 100 sq.ft. if common § 135(d)			Generally, either 80 sq.ft. if private, or 100 sq.ft. if common § 135(d)			Generally, either 80 sq.ft. if private, or 100 sq.ft. if common § 135(d)			Generally, either 60 sq.ft. if private, or 80 sq.ft. if common § 135(d)			Generally, either 60 sq.ft. if private, or 80 sq.ft. if common § 135(d)			Generally, either 60 sq.ft. if private, or 80 sq.ft. if common § 135(d)			Generally, either 60 sq.ft. if private, or 80 sq.ft. if common § 135(d)		
Generally, 1 space per unit §§ 151, 161(a)(g)			Generally, 1 space per unit §§ 151, 161(a)(g)			Generally, 1 space per unit §§ 151, 161(a)(g)			Generally, 1 space per unit §§ 151, 161(a)(g)			Generally, 1 space per unit §§ 151, 161(a)(g)			Generally, 1 space per unit §§ 151, 161(a)(g)			Generally, 1 space per unit §§ 151, 161(a)(g)			Generally, 1 space per unit §§ 151, 161(a)(g)		
C	C	C	C	C	C	C	C	C	C	C	C	C	C	C	C	C	C	C	C	C	C	C	C

LEGEND

P – Permitted as a principal use.

C – Permitted as a conditional use, subject to the provisions set forth in Sections 178, 179, and 316 through 316.8 of this Code.

– A blank space on the table or the symbol 'NP' indicate that the use or feature is not permitted. Unless a use or feature is permitted or required as set forth in the Zoning Control Tables or in those sections referenced in Section 799 of this Code, such use or feature is prohibited, unless determined by the Zoning Administrator to be a permitted use.

– See specific provisions listed by Section and Zoning Category number at the end of the table.

1st – 1st story and below

2nd – 2nd story

3rd + – 3rd story and above

PROPOSED CONTROLS FOR NEIGHBORHOOD COMMERCIAL DISTRICTS: CITY OF SAN FRANCISCO (continued)

GENERAL BUILDING STANDARDS

Sacramento Sec. 724	Union Sec. 725	Valencia Sec. 726	24th-Mission Sec. 727	24th-Noe Valley Sec. 728	West Portal Sec. 729	References	Zoning Category	No.
40-X	40-X	40-X to 50-X See Zoning Map	40-X to 105-E See Zoning Map	40-X	26-X	§§ 102.11, 105, 106, 250–252, 260, 270, 271	Height and Bulk	.10
P up to 4999 sq.ft., C 5000 sq.ft. & above § 121.1	P up to 4999 sq.ft., C 5000 sq.ft. & above § 121.1	P up to 9999 sq.ft., C 10,000 sq.ft. & above § 121.1	P up to 4999 sq.ft., C 5000 sq.ft. & above § 121.1	P up to 4999 sq.ft., C 5000 sq.ft. & above § 121.1	P up to 4999 sq.ft., C 5000 sq.ft. & above § 121.1	§§ 790.56, 121.1	Lot Size [Per Development]	.11
Required at grade level and above § 134(a)(e)	Required at the second story and above and at all residential levels § 134(a)(e)	Required at the second story and above and at all residential levels § 134(a)(e)	Required at the second story and above and at all residential levels § 134(a)(e)	Required at grade level and above § 134(a)(e)	Required at grade level and above § 134(a)(e)	§§ 130, 134, 136	Rear Yard	.12
Required § 145.1	Required § 145.1	Required § 145.1	Required § 145.1	Required § 145.1	Required § 145.1		Street Frontage	.13
P § 136.1(a)	P § 136.1(a)	P § 136.1(a)	P § 136.1(a)	P § 136.1(a)	P § 136.1(a)	§ 790.20	Awning	.14
P § 136.1(b)	P § 136.1(b)	P § 136.1(b)	P § 136.1(b)	P § 136.1(b)	P § 136.1(b)	§ 790.26	Canopy	.15
P § 136.1(c)	P § 136.1(c)	P § 136.1(c)	P § 136.1(c)	P § 136.1(c)	P § 136.1(c)	§ 790.58	Marquee	.16
Required § 143	Required § 143	Required § 143	Required § 143	Required § 143	Required § 143		Street Trees	.17

COMMERCIAL AND INSTITUTIONAL STANDARDS AND USES

Sacramento Sec. 724	Union Sec. 725	Valencia Sec. 726	24th-Mission Sec. 727	24th-Noe Valley Sec. 728	West Portal Sec. 729	References	Zoning Category	No.
1.5 to 1 § 124(a)(b)	2.5 to 1 § 124(a)(b)	1.75 to 1 § 124(a)(b)	1.75 to 1 § 124(a)(b)	1.5 to 1 § 124(a)(b)	1.5 to 1 § 124(a)(b)	§§ 102.8, 102.10, 123	Floor Area Ratio	.20
P up to 2499 sq.ft., C 2500 sq.ft. & above § 121.2	P up to 2499 sq.ft., C 2500 sq.ft. & above § 121.2	P up to 2999 sq.ft., C 3000 sq.ft. & above § 121.2	P up to 2499 sq.ft., C 2500 sq.ft. & above § 121.2	P up to 2499 sq.ft., C 2500 sq.ft. & above § 121.2	P up to 2499 sq.ft., C 2500 to 3999 sq.ft., NP 4000 sq.ft. & above § 121.2	§ 790.130	Use Size [Non-Residential]	.21
Generally, none required if occupied floor area is less than 5000 sq.ft. §§ 151, 161(g)	Generally, none required if occupied floor area is less than 5000 sq.ft. §§ 151, 161(g)	Generally, none required if occupied floor area is less than 5000 sq.ft. §§ 151, 161(g)	Generally, none required if occupied floor area is less than 5000 sq.ft. §§ 151, 161(g)	Generally, none required if occupied floor area is less than 5000 sq.ft. §§ 151, 161(g)	Generally, none required if occupied floor area is less than 5000 sq.ft. §§ 151, 161(g)	§§ 150, 153–157, 159–160, 204.5	Off-Street Parking, Commercial and Institutional	.22
Generally, none required if gross floor area is less than 10,000 sq.ft. §§ 152, 161(b)	Generally, none required if gross floor area is less than 10,000 sq.ft. §§ 152, 161(b)	Generally, none required if gross floor area is less than 10,000 sq.ft. §§ 152, 161(b)	Generally, none required if gross floor area is less than 10,000 sq.ft. §§ 152, 161(b)	Generally, none required if gross floor area is less than 10,000 sq.ft. §§ 152, 161(b)	Generally, none required if gross floor area is less than 10,000 sq.ft. §§ 152, 161(b)	§§ 150, 153–155, 204.5	Off-Street Freight Loading	.23
P in front; C elsewhere § 145.2(a)	P in front; C elsewhere § 145.2(a)	P in front; C elsewhere § 145.2(a)	P in front; C elsewhere § 145.2(a)	P in front; C elsewhere § 145.2(a)	P in front; C elsewhere § 145.2(a)	§ 790.70	Outdoor Activity Area	.24
						§ 790.30	Drive-Up Facility	.25
P if recessed 3 ft.; C otherwise § 145.2(b)	P if recessed 3 ft.; C otherwise § 145.2(b)	P if recessed 3 ft.; C otherwise § 145.2(b)	P if recessed 3 ft.; C otherwise § 145.2(b)	P if recessed 3 ft.; C otherwise § 145.2(b)	P if recessed 3 ft.; C otherwise § 145.2(b)	§ 790.140	Walk-Up Facility	.26
P: 6 a.m.–12 a.m. C: 12 a.m.–2 a.m.	P: 6 a.m.–2 a.m. C: 2 a.m.–6 a.m.	P: 6 a.m.–2 a.m. C: 2 a.m.–6 a.m.	P: 6 a.m.–2 a.m. C: 2 a.m.–6 a.m.	P: 6 a.m.–2 a.m. C: 2 a.m.–6 a.m.	P: 6 a.m.–2 a.m.	§ 790.48	Hours of Operation	.27
						§§ 262, 602–604, 608.1–.10, 609	General Advertising Sign	.30
P § 607.1(f)2	P § 607.1(f)2	P § 607.1(f)2	P § 607.1(f)2	P § 607.1(f)2	P § 607.1(f)2	§§ 262, 602–604, 608.1–.10, 609	Business Sign	.31
P § 607.1(c)(d)(g)	P § 607.1(c)(d)(g)	P § 607.1(c)(d)(g)	P § 607.1(c)(d)(g)	P § 607.1(c)(d)(g)	P § 607.1(c)(d)(g)	§§ 262, 602–604, 608.1–.10, 609	Other Signs	.32

Controls by Story

Sacramento			Union			Valencia			24th-Mission			24th-Noe Valley			West Portal			References	Zoning Category	No.
1st	2nd	3rd+	1st	2nd	3rd+	1st	2nd	3rd+	1st	2nd	3rd+	1st	2nd	3rd+	1st	2nd	3rd+	§ 790.118		
P			P	C	C	P			P			P			P			§ 790.84	Residential Conversion	.38
C	C	C	C	C	C	C	C	C	C	C	C	C	C	C	C	C	C	§ 790.86	Residential Demolition	.39
																			Retail Sales and Services	
P	C		P	P		P	C		P			P	C		P	P		§ 790.102	Other Retail Sales and Services [Not Listed Below]	.40
C			C									C			C			§ 790.22	Bar	.41
C						P			C						C			§ 790.92	Full-Service Restaurant	.42
C						P			C						C			§ 790.90	Small Fast Food Restaurant	.43
						C												§ 790.91	Large Fast Food Restaurant	.44
C						C			C						C			§ 790.122	Take-Out Food	.45
P			P			P			P			P						§ 790.64	Movie Theater	.46
																		§ 790.36	Adult Entertainment	.47
C			C			C			C			C						§ 790.38	Other Entertainment	.48
C			C			P			P			C						§ 790.110	Financial Service	.49
C			P			P			P			C			C			§ 790.112	Limited Financial Service	.50
	P		P	P	C	P	C		P	C		P	C		C	P		§ 790.114	Medical Service	.51
P	P		P	P		P	C		P	C		P	C		P	P		§ 790.116	Personal Service	.52
C	P		P	P	C	P	C		P	C		P	C		C	P		§ 790.108	Business or Professional Service	.53
						C			C			C						§ 790.60 / § 2700 Police Code	Massage Establishment	.54
C	C		C	C	C	C	C		C	C		C	C					§ 790.46	Tourist Hotel	.55
C	C	C	C	C	C	C	C	C	C	C	C	C	C	C	C	C		§§ 790.8, 156, 160	Automobile Parking	.56
																		§ 790.14	Automotive Gas Station	.57
						C									C			§ 790.17	Automotive Service Station	.58
						C			C									§ 790.15	Automotive Repair	.59
																		§ 790.18	Automotive Wash	.60
																		§ 790.12	Automobile Sale or Rental	.61
C			C			C			C			C			C			§ 790.6	Animal Hospital	.62
																		§ 790.2	Ambulance Service	.63
																		§ 790.62	Mortuary	.64
P	C		P	C		P	C		P			P	C		P			§ 790.124	Trade Shop	.65
																		§ 790.117	Storage	.66
																			Institutions and Non-Retail Sales and Services	
																		§ 790.106	Administrative Service	.70
																		§ 790.44	Hospital or Medical Center	.80
P	C	C	P	C	C	P	C	C	P	C	C	P	C	C	C	C		§ 790.50	Other Institutions	.81
C	C	C	C	C	C	C	C	C	C	C	C	C	C	C	C	C		§ 790.80	Public Use	.82
																			RESIDENTIAL STANDARDS AND USES	
P	P	P	P	P	P	P	P	P	P	P	P	P	P	P	P	P	P	§ 790.88	Residential Use	.90
Generally, 1 unit per 800 sq.ft. lot area § 207.4			Generally, 1 unit per 600 sq.ft. lot area § 207.4			Generally, 1 unit per 600 sq.ft. lot area § 207.4			Generally, 1 unit per 600 sq.ft. lot area § 207.4			Generally, 1 unit per 600 sq.ft. lot area § 207.4			Generally, 1 unit per 800 sq.ft. lot area § 207.4			§§ 207, 207.1, 790.88(a)	Residential Density, Dwelling Units	.91
Generally, 1 bedroom per 275 sq.ft. lot area § 208			Generally, 1 bedroom per 210 sq.ft. lot area § 208			Generally, 1 bedroom per 210 sq.ft. lot area § 208			Generally, 1 bedroom per 210 sq.ft. lot area § 208			Generally, 1 bedroom per 210 sq.ft. lot area § 208			Generally, 1 bedroom per 275 sq.ft. lot area § 208			§§ 207.1, 790.88(b)	Residential Density, Group Housing	.92
Generally, either 100 sq.ft. if private, or 133 sq.ft if common § 135(d)			Generally, either 80 sq.ft. if private, or 100 sq.ft if common § 135(d)			Generally, either 80 sq.ft. if private, or 100 sq.ft if common § 135(d)			Generally, either 80 sq.ft. if private, or 100 sq.ft if common § 135(d)			Generally, either 80 sq.ft. if private, or 100 sq.ft if common § 135(d)			Generally, either 100 sq.ft. if private, or 133 sq.ft if common § 135(d)			§§ 135, 136	Usable Open Space [Per Residential Unit]	.93
Generally, 1 space per unit §§ 151, 161(a)(g)			Generally, 1 space per unit §§ 151, 161(a)(g)			Generally, 1 space per unit §§ 151, 161(a)(g)			Generally, 1 space per unit §§ 151, 161(a)(g)			Generally, 1 space per unit §§ 151, 161(a)(g)			Generally, 1 space per unit §§ 151, 161(a)(g)			§§ 150, 153–157, 159–160, 204.5	Off-Street Parking, Residential	.94
C	C	C	C	C	C	C	C	C	C	C	C	C	C	C	C	C		§ 790.10	Community Residential Parking	.95

LEGEND

P – Permitted as a principal use.

C – Permitted as a conditional use, subject to the provisions set forth in Sections 178, 179, and 316 through 316.8 of this Code.

– A blank space on the table or the symbol 'NP' indicate that the use or feature is not permitted. Unless a use or feature is permitted or required as set forth in the Zoning Control Tables or in those sections referenced in Section 799 of this Code, such use or feature is prohibited, unless determined by the Zoning Administrator to be a permitted use.

\# – See specific provisions listed by Section and Zoning Category number at the end of the table.

1st – 1st story and below

2nd – 2nd story

3rd+ – 3rd story and above

Proposed Neighborhood Commercial Zoning Map and Text Amendments

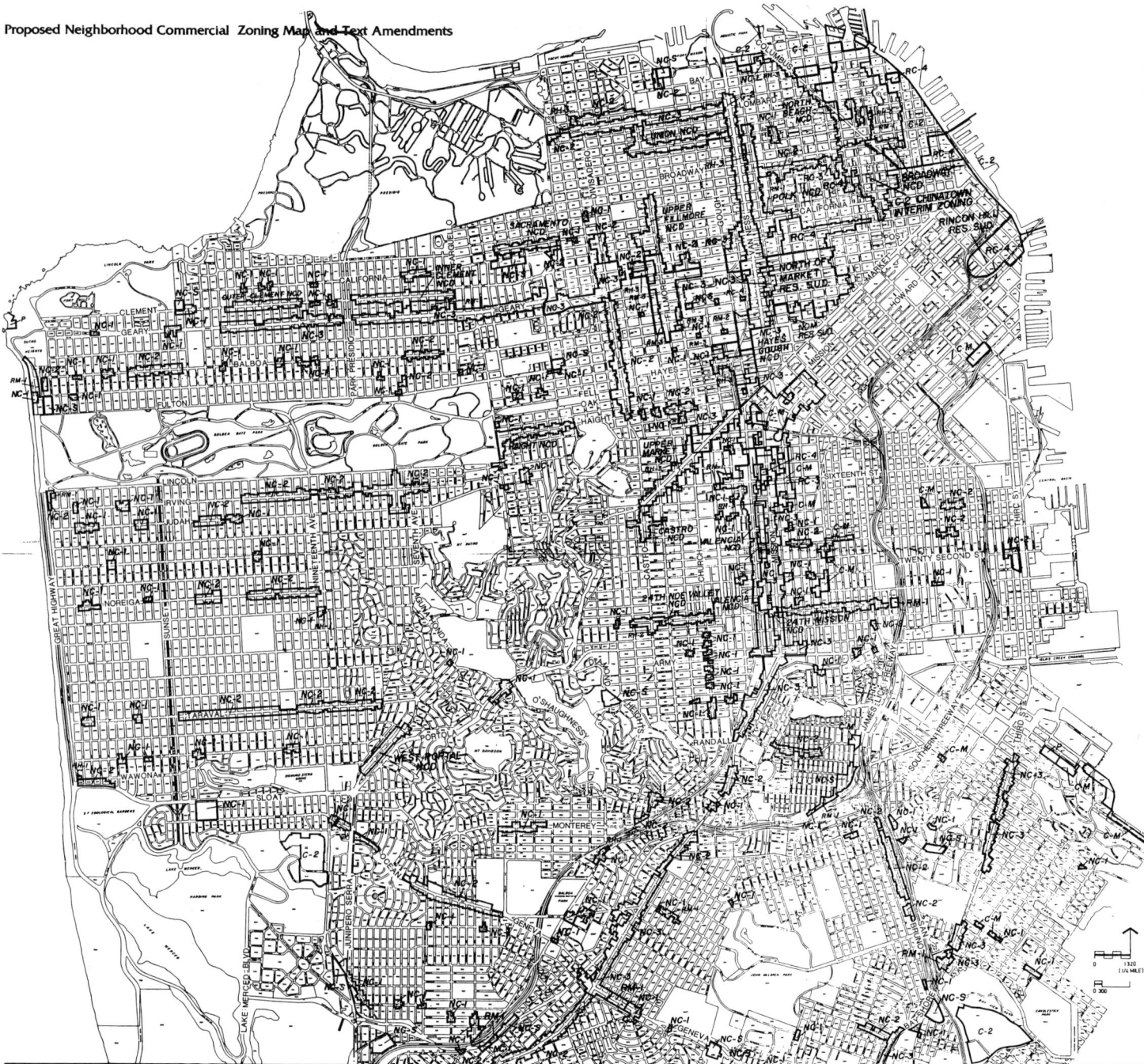

SPECIFIC PROVISIONS

Section		Zoning Controls
§ 710.12 § 710.20 710.24 710.27 710.41 710.43–45 § 701.49	§ 780.1	**LAKESHORE PLAZA SPECIAL USE DISTRICT**
	Boundaries:	Applicable only for the Lakeshore Plaza NC-1 District as mapped on Sectional Map 13 SU
710.51–53 710.58 710.65 710.81–82 710.90–93 710.95		*Controls:* Special controls on commercial floor area, various features and uses, and residential standards
§ 710.41 § 710.42		*Boundaries:* All NC-1 Districts
		Controls: P if located more than one-quarter mile from any NC district with more restrictive controls; otherwise, same as more restrictive control
710.43 710.44 710.45		*Boundaries:* All NC-1 Districts
		Controls: C if located more than one-quarter mile from any NC district with more restrictive controls; otherwise, same as more restrictive control
710.42 710.43 710.44	§ 781.1	**TARAVAL STREET RESTAURANT AND FAST FOOD SUB-DISTRICT**
		Boundaries: Applicable only for the two Taraval Street NC-1 districts between 40th and 41st Avenues and 45th and 47th Avenues as mapped on Sectional Map 5 SU
		Controls: Full-Service Restaurants and Small Fast Food Restaurants are C; Large Fast Food Restaurants are NP
711.42 711.43 711.44	§ 781.1	**TARAVAL STREET RESTAURANT AND FAST FOOD SUB-DISTRICT**
		Boundaries: Applicable only for the Taraval Street NC-2 district between 12th and 36th Avenues as mapped on Sectional Maps 5 SU and 6 SU
		Controls: Full-Service Restaurants and Small Fast Food Restaurants are C; Large Fast Food Restaurants are NP
§ 711.43 711.44	§ 781.3	**OCEAN AVENUE FAST FOOD SUB-DISTRICT**
		Boundaries: Applicable only for the Ocean Avenue NC-2 District from Manor Drive to Phelan Avenue as mapped on Sectional Map 12 SU
		Controls: Small Fast Food Restaurants and Large Fast Food Restaurants are NP

Section		Zoning Controls
§ 711.42 711.43 711.44	§ 781.2	**IRVING STREET RESTAURANT AND FAST FOOD SUB-DISTRICT**
		Boundaries: Applicable only for the portion of the Irving Street NC-2 district between 19th and 27th Avenues as mapped on Sectional Map 5 SU
		Controls: Small Fast Food Restaurants are C; Full-Service Restaurants and Large Fast Food Restaurants are NP
§ 711.65	§ 236	**GARMENT SHOP SPECIAL USE DISTRICT**
		Boundaries: Applicable only for the portion of the Pacific Avenue NC-2 District east of Hyde Street as mapped on Sectional Map 1 SU[a]
		Controls: Garment Shops are P at the 1st and 2nd stories
§ 712.30 712.31 712.32	§ 608.8	**MARKET STREET SPECIAL SIGN DISTRICT**
		Boundaries: Applicable only for the portion of the Market Street NC-3 District from Franklin to Octavia Streets as mapped on Sectional Map SSD
		Controls: Special restrictions and limitations for signs
§ 712.30 712.31 712.32	§ 608.10	**UPPER MARKET STREET SPECIAL SIGN DISTRICT**
		Boundaries: Applicable only for the portion of the Market Street NC-3 District from Octavia to Church Streets as mapped on Sectional Map SSD
		Controls: Special restrictions and limitations for signs
§ 712.43 712.44	§ 781.5	**MISSION STREET FAST FOOD SUB-DISTRICT**
		Boundaries: Applicable only for the portion of the Mission Street NC-3 District between 14th and Randall as mapped on Section Map 7 SU
		Controls: Small Fast Food Restaurants are C; Large Fast Food Restaurants are NP
§ 712.44	§ 781.4	**GEARY BOULEVARD FAST FOOD SUB-DISTRICT**
		Boundaries: Applicable only for the portion of the Geary Boulevard NC-3 District between 14th and 28th Avenues as mapped on Sectional Maps 3 SU and 4 SU
		Controls: Large Fast Food Restaurants are NP

Section		Zoning Controls
§ 714.10	§ 253.1	**65-A-1 HEIGHT AND BULK DISTRICT**
		Boundaries: Applicable for all of the Broadway NCD from Columbus Avenue to Osgood Place as mapped on Sectional Map 1H
		Controls: Building Height and Bulk Limits are P up to 40 feet; C between 40 feet and 65 feet
§ 714.65	§ 236	**GARMENT SHOP SPECIAL USE DISTRICT**
		Boundaries: Applicable only for the portion of the Broadway NCD as mapped on Sectional Map 1 SU[a]
		Controls: Garment Shops are P at the 1st and 2nd stories
§ 715.31 715.32	§ 608.10	**UPPER MARKET STREET SPECIAL SIGN DISTRICT**
		Boundaries: Applicable only for the portions of the Castro Street NCD as mapped on Sectional Map SSD
		Controls: Special restrictions and limitations for signs
§ 721.31 721.32	§ 608.10	**UPPER MARKET STREET SPECIAL SIGN DISTRICT**
		Boundaries: Applicable only for the portions of the Upper Market Street NCD as mapped on Sectional Map SSD
		Controls: Special restrictions and limitations for signs
§ 722.10	§ 253.1	**65-A-1 HEIGHT AND BULK DISTRICT**
		Boundaries: Applicable for portions of the North Beach NCD as mapped on Sectional Map 1H
		Controls: Building Height and Bulk Limits are P up to 40 feet; C between 41 feet and 65 feet
§ 722.49	§ 780.3	**NORTH BEACH FINANCIAL SERVICE SUB-DISTRICT**
		Boundaries: Applicable only for portions of the North Beach NCD south of Union Street as mapped on Sectional Map 1 SU[a]
		Controls: Financial Services are NP at all stories
§ 722.65	§ 236	**GARMENT SHOP SPECIAL USE DISTRICT**
		Boundaries: Applicable only for the portion of the North Beach NCD as mapped on Sectional Map No. 1 SU[a]
		Controls: Garment Shops are P at the 1st and 2nd stories

'overlays', special additional requirements that applied only in certain designated areas, such as the garment district, or near the waterfront where there was a need to sustain marine based industries. But gradually a series of special districts has been created for various unique areas of the city – an area of steep hills, Chinatown, areas known as 'residential enclave districts', affordable housing districts, and so on. The conditions that apply in these areas designed for mixed uses can be quite stringent[11]. For example, they include conditions on business opening hours. Some uses are not permitted in the ordinance, but are present and tolerated nevertheless; the City attempted and failed to devise a watertight means of keeping out new fast food outlets while retaining neighbourhood delis that traditionally have served a similar role. However, by excluding the use from the zone altogether, but not acting against non-conforming uses, the character of the neighbourhood can be preserved. That is often the aim of such special mixed use districts in Boston, New York City, Chicago and elsewhere. The subject is interesting enough to warrant a whole book[12].

Floating zones, planned unit developments, cluster development, and special mixed use districts are all reactions to the rigidity of original city-wide zoning ordinances. They reflect the reality that separation of uses and rigid construction and subdivision requirements do not necessarily deliver the most efficient use of land. The market is sometimes capable of delivering a better structure of uses for the community than if the zoning was immutable. On the other hand zoning can be used to protect certain areas against the undesirable effects of market pressures. No doubt, if zoning had been in operation in Britain, a special district would have been created to cover the area of Savile Row where tailors occupy low rental workshops. These benefited from effective rent control for many years because planning permission was needed, and was difficult to obtain, to change their use to much more profitable offices. When the rules about planning permission for a change of use were altered nationally, it was not possible to single out the area for special treatment. The effective rent control was removed in some cases and, so the Federation of Master Tailors suggested, that change was suffient to put the future of their local industry in jeopardy. An American response would have been to create a special district; in that way the public would have received a benefit from continuing to enjoy the presence of that use, without paying the real cost. In the Savile Row case, that cost of maintaining the rents without the planning control, would have amounted to a $40 a square foot subsidy. But neither zoning nor British development control are often looked at in such purely economic terms.

(vi) Zoning bonuses

A variant on the same theme is the use of zoning to obtain public benefits at no direct cost. Where a bonus scheme applies, either in a special district or city-wide, the developer is entitled to a bonus in the shape of extra floor space or a denser development, but only if he agrees to provide some community benefits. Examples of such benefits might be a public plaza, an improved rapid transit system access point, a through-block walkway or arcade, financial support for a theatre, or flowers in Fifth Avenue. It is open to the developer to choose not to take the bonus, and abide by the as-of-right zoning in force. But the incentive is there inviting him to trade.

The ethical worry about zoning bonus schemes is whether the original zoning has been set at the right level in the first place. Initially, it might seem just another element of flexibility to allow a building to exceed the bulk standards set to protect light and air at the street level, if the extra bulk was to be offset by more public open space in the shape of a plaza. In that case at least there would be a clear link between the two items traded. The difficulty comes when the introduction of a bonus scheme is combined with a widespread downzoning, so that buildings of the size previously permitted as of right become permitted under the revised ordinance only if the developer contributes some public amenity. In that way the incentive zoning device can be brought into disrepute. Nevertheless, it can be a very effective way of encouraging development, especially if time-limited. In the west Midtown area of New York City, a 6 year time limited bonus has been very effective not only in encouraging development, but encouraging it in an area identified by the City as being best placed to take growth. I consider this issue in more detail in Chapter 10.

(vii) Transfer of development rights

Bonus schemes represent one way in which development rights are traded for public amenities. Another method of trading development rights for public benefits is represented by transfer of development rights schemes. Following the inevitable legal challenge, such schemes have been blessed by the courts. They are used to secure designated landmarks, or an important natural environment, or perhaps farmland in the outer suburbs. Here again the purpose is to introduce flexibility to the basic zoning background. One example of its use is to take the air rights above historic landmarks, the basic volume of building that a developer would ordinarily be entitled to build, and transfer it to a nearby site, thus securing the landmark concerned from redevelopment pressure. The community can be seen to be conceding a greater density of development on one site in return for a lower than envisaged density on another. The need for such a scheme arises only because constitutional constraints rule out zoning individual plots in such a way that no redevelopment is permitted. The result is often to dwarf the landmark among the taller buildings permitted as the result of

Figure 4.8 New York City; one of the most complex urban structures, the design of which now represents the effects of a complex mesh of zoning ordinances, zoning bonus systems and transfer of development rights mechanisms, to name a few.

the transferred air rights. In Britain, where there are no such constitutional constraints, the planning system would simply not routinely grant development rights in such circumstances where they would need to be bought back by concessions elsewhere.

Other transfer of development rights schemes are used to reduce the densities of development on open countryside beyond what is thought can be achieved by using zoning alone. Here, the principle is to convert some of the development rights held by the farmer landowner into credits that can be sold to developers and applied elsewhere. So, in the Pinelands area of New Jersey, landowners are prevented from building by a zoning ordinance effectively banning all development, and are provided with development credits by way of compensation. These can be purchased by developers of land around the edges of the sensitive area, and applied to increase the density of development in those areas above what would ordinarily be allowed. Chapter 8 contains more details. Again, the introduction of such schemes raises ethical questions about what the original zoning ordinance should contain – whether a picture of how the planners and community want the area to become in the future, or some lower degree of freedom designed to stimulate developers to haggle over the possibility of doing more. My view is that zoning bonus schemes are an indictment of zoning itself; zoning cannot go as far, or apply specifically to specific buildings, as the majority of local people would like, without risking constitutional difficulties.

(viii) Exclusionary zoning   Another example of local governments setting zoning freedoms at a lower than reasonable level is where they practise what is known as *exclusionary zoning* – not a particularly praiseworthy invention. Exclusionary zoning means creating large minimum lot sizes, or minimum house sizes, while making no provision in the ordinance for mobile homes or apartment blocks, in order to ensure that only a certain class of person is able to afford to live in the community. The motivation of those suburban communities using such devices, and many do, is to exclude on the grounds of income, and hence class and race. As Chapter 11 explains, in New Jersey at least, the courts and subsequently the state government have acted to try to secure more balance and more equal opportunity of access to suburban areas. But an important contributory factor to America's affordable housing crisis must surely be the difficulty of making land available for denser housing. And dense in America is rather less dense than in Britain or Europe.

An early example of ordinances designed to keep undesirable people out is to be found in an 1865 ordinance for Cape May. The ordinance, which now seems rather quaint, states:

> 'Our local government is rigid and definite in its ideas of right and wrong, and is to a great extent responsible for the city's high moral tone. The cultured and refined people who patronize our hotels diffuse about the place a high bulwark, which patrons of disreputable habits cannot penetrate'[14]

The city, at the very southern tip of New Jersey, had few equals as a resort in the late Victorian era. However, it became less accessible in the motor age until the construction of the Garden State Parkway in the 1960s, a motorway extending all the way down the coast from New York City. As a result its many picturesque Victorian houses survived long enough for a preservation movement to become established to save them. Although not so exclusive as in 1865, Cape May City is still a cut above most other New Jersey resorts.

(ix) Inclusionary zoning

A few communities have deliberately gone in the opposite direction than exclusionary zoning, by providing in their ordinances that a certain proportion of new housing built should be set aside for low and moderate income households. A typical requirement would be for 10 per cent of units to be set aside for households with incomes of less than 50 per cent of the median for the area, and for 10 per cent to be set aside for those with incomes of less than 80 per cent of the median. Occupancy of the low and moderate income units is regulated by restrictive covenant, which has the effect of keeping the market prices of the units artificially low. Often, the only way to fund such units is to offer the developer a density bonus, whereby he can build more units per acre in return for an undertaking to provide the affordable housing. Alternatively, instead of actually providing the housing in return for the density bonus, he might be asked to contribute to a fund to be used for low and moderate income housing on the understanding that those who do not contribute do not benefit from the density bonus.

A recent step further in this process has been what is known as 'linkage', which operates most notably in Boston and San Francisco. Linkage effectively requires developers of major projects such as offices requiring some discretionary approval by the city government to either provide low income housing, or contribute in lieu. The contribution is intended to reflect that major developments create demands for low income workers for whom there is no affordable housing in the city. The contribution is therefore necessary to *maintain* the social and economic balance.

It is a matter for debate whether inclusionary zoning or linkage can hope to contribute to the solution of the affordable housing crisis. Some say that linkage in particular is no more than a local tax on development in areas of high growth potential, where local governments are limited in their revenue raising powers and need to be inventive.

(x) Performance standard zoning

In British development control, whether a particular light industrial use falls within the general business class or the general industrial class of the Use Classes Order depends on whether that use is capable of being carried out in a residential area without detriment arising from noise, vibration, smell, fumes, smoke, soot, ash, dust or grit. The classification of the use depends on the way in which the business is carried out. A change in the way the business is operated may give rise to the need for planning consent. This is performance zoning at its most basic. Its disadvantage is the basis of judgement needed to determine whether detriment to amenity has indeed been caused.

Some American zoning ordinances adopt a similar performance related approach to categorise the uses that may be permitted in different zones. Instead of attempting to draw up and categorise a comprehensive list of all the potential uses in an area, the ordinance simply classifies according to whether the use can meet criteria relating to noise, vibration, smoke, odours, heat, glare and traffic generation. Those criteria are often quite complex and make use of standards prepared by state or Federal agencies, or standards associations. The zoning ordinance might, for example, contain a table showing for different octave bands the amount of noise permissible at different times of day, and according to whether the lot abutted on a residential or industrial district.

Another way of looking at performance zoning is to regard it as simply the imposition of a long list of standard conditions on any development that is to go ahead in the area to which it applies – often the whole community. Fewer artificial constraints on industry should arise in such a system, by comparison with one which simply determined that manufacture of metal goods would always be too noisy to tolerate in a general business zone. The difficulty comes in monitoring the uses established and negotiating appropriate action should the standards be breached. Faced with the need to obtain sophisticated measuring equipment, many local governments find it more straightforward to take the crude and easy way out, even though that may make it more difficult for certain types of development. But perhaps that is the sort of development that would be better placed in another community . . . ?

Environmental Impact Statements

While strictly speaking, the requirement to produce environmental impact statements is not a development control mechanism but a procedural requirement, it is an important element in the development control process. This is because it costs a great deal and takes a long time to produce an environmental impact statement, which may in turn lead to the imposition of planning conditions. In New York City, any project requiring a variance of the zoning is susceptible to environmental review, taking perhaps 6 to 12 months, or even 2½ years in some extreme cases. It is not simply the element of the development triggering the need for a variance that is considered in the review. All adverse aspects of the development on traffic, air pollution, sewerage and so on have to be identified, and measures to mitigate those adverse effects have to be undertaken to the maximum feasible extent in the judgement of those administering the review. By contrast a marginally smaller, or perhaps even larger, building permitted under the as-of-right zoning ordinance is not subject to the review process. It is not surprising that in recent years so many more developments have been tailored to fit the zoning ordinances without the need for a variance or rezoning.

The types of development requiring such statements vary from state to state. Most states have modelled their review processes on those necessary for the examination of the projects of Federal agencies under the National Environmental Policy Act. Whatever the dividing line, one important effect is to discourage development that would barely trigger the mechanism, if there is an alternative way of proceeding. In other words, developers are likely to make greater efforts to comply with the ordinances, or else will propose much more substantial breaches in order to fund the preparation of the impact statement, the mitigations that may be required and the interest costs that will mount up while the review process proceeds.

In California, the enactment and amendment of local general plans and zoning ordinances, the granting of zoning variances, and the approval of tentative subdivision maps are all actions which, if they may have 'a significant effect on the environment', must be preceded by an environmental impact review. However, the state agency concerned has exempted certain small residential or commercial construction. Some idea of the procedure can be gleaned from the flow chart in Figure 4.9, drawn from the California legislation[14].

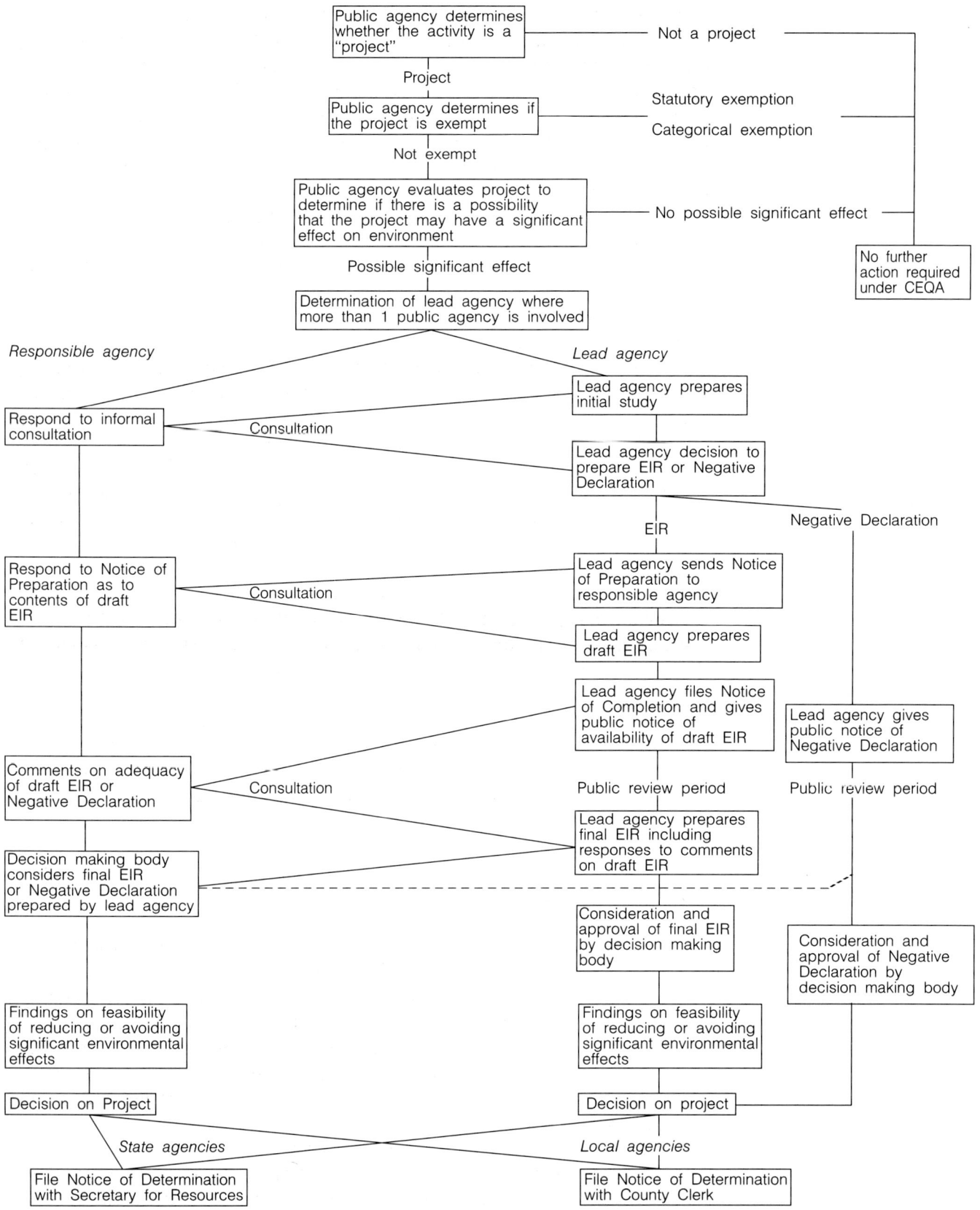

Public agency determines whether the activity is a "project"

Not a project

Project

Public agency determines if the project is exempt

Statutory exemption

Categorical exemption

Not exempt

Public agency evaluates project to determine if there is a possibility that the project may have a significant effect on environment

No possible significant effect

Possible significant effect

No further action required under CEQA

Determination of lead agency where more than 1 public agency is involved

Responsible agency

Lead agency

Lead agency prepares initial study

Respond to informal consultation

Consultation

Lead agency decision to prepare EIR or Negative Declaration

EIR

Negative Declaration

Respond to Notice of Preparation as to contents of draft EIR

Consultation

Lead agency sends Notice of Preparation to responsible agency

Lead agency prepares draft EIR

Lead agency files Notice of Completion and gives public notice of availability of draft EIR

Lead agency gives public notice of Negative Declaration

Comments on adequacy of draft EIR or Negative Declaration

Consultation

Public review period

Public review period

Decision making body considers final EIR or Negative Declaration prepared by lead agency

Lead agency prepares final EIR including responses to comments on draft EIR

Consideration and approval of final EIR by decision making body

Consideration and approval of Negative Declaration by decision making body

Findings on feasibility of reducing or avoiding significant environmental effects

Findings on feasibility of reducing or avoiding significant environmental effects

Decision on Project

Decision on project

State agencies

Local agencies

File Notice of Determination with Secretary for Resources

File Notice of Determination with County Clerk

Figure 4.9 California's Environmental Quality Process Flow Chart

76

If there is doubt about the need for a full environmental impact review, or a likelihood that there will clearly be no impact, the first step is to carry out an 'initial study'. This is a 45 day process carried out by the local government responsible for the zoning action that has triggered the review. The purpose is to determine whether the project will have a significant effect; in other words will it substantially degrade the environment (ie land, air, water, minerals, flora, fauna, ambient noise, and objects of historic or aesthetic significance), reduce essential wildlife habitats, harm endangered species, or eliminate important historic sites? Will there be cumulative effects when taken together with other developments and, after consideration of all the natural environmental protection issues, will there be a substantial adverse effect on humans?

If the project passes all these tests, the local government may issue a negative declaration, and give notice and time for review before proceeding to approve the zoning change. But faced with a dividing line case, against the background of the power of public challenge through referenda or in the courts, many local governments will invariably err on the side of requiring a full environmental impact review. More development projects are held up, and the consequent shortage of housing supply has led to a sharp escalation of house prices, one that cannot be relieved by quick provision to relieve the demand for affordable housing.

If a full review is required, the first step is to prepare a draft statement for review and public scrutiny. Preparation of the statement is the formal responsibility of the local government body, but they will draw heavily on the input of the developer and consultants. In practice, the developer might as well be regarded as mainly responsible. In New York City this stage of the process can take anything between 12 and 24 months, depending on the size of the project and the amount of information available about the impacts of the development. Moreover the developer will be charged a fee ($43,000 for a more than 500,000 square feet development[15].

Draft California statements must include:

- a thorough project description;

- a description of the present environmental setting of the project;

- an analysis of all significant effects on the environment, set against a baseline of pre-project conditions, including
  - all possible significant, direct and indirect, short and long term effects
  - effects caused cumulatively with other projects
  - effects that cannot be avoided if the project is implemented in any form
  - measures that might mitigate the adverse effects
  - alternatives to the project, including a specific no project alternative
  - effects of encouragement of future development in the area; and

- a statement explaining why particular identified effects were dismissed as not significant.

Once the draft has been published, there is a review period during which the public and other public sector agencies have the opportunity to make representations. This period, which might be as long as 90 days, may include public hearings as a way of focusing debate, or allowing better presentation of the issues. At the end of the period for comment, the local government or other agency must prepare the final environmental impact review document. This comprises the original draft, together with any changes now proposed, and a full analysis of the comments received from interested parties together with the reasons for not reflecting them in the final document.

In the case of a private sector development the approving agency can now proceed with its zoning or subdivision action. The environmental impact review will influence the decisions because there will be an expectation that mitigation measures identified in the final report will be incorporated in the development. Where such measures would be economically or socially infeasible, the local government is required to identify sufficient social and economic benefits to outweigh the unavoidable environmental risk. If insufficient regard is paid to reflecting the mitigation measures, the expectation is that some public interest group will challenge the decision in the courts.

Statistics from the City of Los Angeles Planning Department[16] show that about 6/7,000 new construction projects led to 1,384 exemptions from the need for environmental impact review, 870 initial assessments and 22 full impact reports. In San Francisco, 194 cases were received for initial review in 1985/86, and of these, 47 were determined not to require an evaluation and 95 had a negative declaration filed. Only 7 (3%) required a full environmental impact report.

The importance of other controls

Figure 4.1 illustrated the range of controls other than local land use planning controls that can nevertheless be important as controls over development. In this context, the actions of a few states are gaining in significance. New Jersey is drawing up a State Development and Redevelopment Plan. In this rapidly developing state, there is a clear need for growth management. One method of achieving that is to introduce new state controls; those that exist already have some bite, and the role of these individual controls is likely to become more significant. The paragraphs below describe a few of these control systems in more detail. The state planning process itself is explained in Chapter 8.

Under the proposed state planning arrangements in New Jersey, the state will influence the content of zoning ordinances to a much greater degree. Other state systems such as that in Oregon have had the same effect. At the time of writing New Jersey's state planning process is in the 'cross acceptance' stage. A 3-volume Preliminary State Development and Redevelopment Plan was released in January 1989, together with some very detailed maps breaking the state down into 7 tiers in which different degrees of development are to be expected. Each of the 567 municipalities in the state must consider the plan. Differences between the state's proposals and the local government reaction are then to disappear in a sort of mutual coming together called 'cross acceptance' and involving the counties. It is neither a top-down nor a bottom-up approach. But in the end, if the plans are not consistent, or if the state plan is not reflected in local decision taking, local government actions will be at risk in the courts. In both Oregon and Florida, state planning has been accompanied by the founding of citizens' advocacy groups designed to keep public sector decisions on track. No doubt New Jersey too will find it has a pressure group prepared to take legal action to secure sound planning. So, zoning itself is becoming shaped by state considerations, and the local independence is being eroded, but in New Jersey's case by persuasion.

(i) Coastal permits

Among New Jersey's existing state development control mechanisms, that which most closely duplicates the municipalities' land use planning functions was established under the state's 1973 Coastal Area Facility Review Act. That Act was itself encouraged by Federal support, under the Federal Coastal Zone Management Act of 1972, at the time when the shoreline nationally was first perceived to be under threat and environmental concerns were running high. The state Act provides that a Department of Environmental Protection permit (a CAFRA permit) must be obtained before any significant development proceeds in a strip of varying width (up to 20 miles in parts) running along most of New Jersey's shore. The main aim was to protect the coastal strip, including the tidal marshes which permeate some way inland, from inappropriate large scale development. But a wide range of other developments is caught, including any residential development of more than 25 units, and the reviews often lead to imposition of conditions on car park sizes, provision of pavements and landscaping that have to be reconciled with the zoning requirements of the municipality concerned. The New Jersey Builders Association[17] say that the review process is cumbersome and inefficient, and contains a great deal of uncertainty as to the standards used in reviewing applications. Although 90 per cent of applications for permits are granted, it is not surprising that developers have seen fit to construct a large number of 24 unit blocks of flats along the coast. They can avoid as much as a year's delay, as well as the uncertainty of the outcome of the review process.

(ii) Contaminated land restoration

Another part of New Jersey's Department of Environmental Protection is responsible for the operation of the Environmental Cleanup Responsibility Act (ECRA) permit process. This is said to be the toughest such law in the United States. It requires industrial establishments with contaminated land, and there is quite a lot of it in urban New Jersey, to clean their facilities before closing an operation or disposing of land. The burden of clean up costs is therefore effectively transferred to the owner of the site, who can dispose of a site only once he has obtained from the state either an approved negative declaration or an approved clean up plan. Failure to comply can cost $25,000 a day. Just as with CAFRA, there are criticisms of inconsistent policies. But the reason this scheme is important to development control decisions is that it means more delay in obtaining approval to redevelop urban land, and thus creates more pressure for development of green field sites further out in the suburbs.

(iii) Wetlands

Wetlands are another example of a particular type of land where state permits are required, this time covering almost any works on the land. Federal regulations govern the filling of wetlands; New Jersey's state legislation regulates dredging and excavation, the cutting of trees and other preliminaries or consequentials of building projects. More far reaching controls over buffer zones surrounding wetlands came into force in mid-1989, and other controls seem likely on development near streams. A substantial area will be covered by the controls. The state contains 323,000 acres of wetlands, representing about one twelfth of its surface area, but there hardly seems to be a development site without some portion affected. Wetlands are important for flood control, for water cleansing and for wildlife habitats. The controls are significant in that they represent another functionally compartmentalised control. Despite the local expertise applied, for example, by those carrying out site plan reviews, the direction is clearly towards more state control of development. According to one conference brochure, 'the new wetlands program . . . will create exciting opportunities for environmental planning aimed at the conservation of stream corridors, greenways and open spaces throughout the state'. According to one developer's attorney[18], 'The regulatory climate is leading toward making development in New Jersey so problematic, and so uncertain, it may kill the goose that laid the golden egg.'

(iv) Sewer permits

Another important control over new development is the sewer ban. Here, all the developer needs is a permit to connect his development to the system, but the difficulties arise when the local treatment plants are operating at more than capacity. The State Department of Environmental Protection can then impose a sewer extension ban, in which case no new sewer extension permits can be issued, although developments that already have permits can still be connected as they are completed. Before that stage is reached, however, the town or sewerage authority should already have been required to prepare a plan for expanding its facilities. Some areas are reluctant to do so, using capacity of facilities as a method of development control, directing development to the already adequately serviced urban areas. Meanwhile development on lots of more than one acre can continue, relying on septic systems rather than requiring a sewer hook up. The result is to encourage more dispersed development, and a more rapid conversion of agricultural land to suburban uses.

Federal control systems

Federal controls affecting land development are a comparatively recent phenomenon, mainly having their roots in a rapidly increasing environmental awareness at the end of the sixties. Rather than being direct control systems, they often work indirectly, by requiring or using grants to encourage the states themselves to establish a permitting regime. An example of this is the *Coastal Zone Management Act* of 1972, which we saw above has an impact on development control for example in New Jersey, by requiring a state permit, separate from zoning, for developments of certain kinds. The Act was intended to encourage individual states to implement state run coastal zone management systems. Grants encourage the states to adopt programmes that met the detailed criteria set down by the Federal government. The idea is that the states designate areas of land and water along the coast, including those needing special management because of erosion, or sensitive wildlife concerns. They then draw up plans to manage the coastal resource, and mechanisms aimed at delivering the objectives of those plans. The mechanisms may be direct control of development by the state, as in New Jersey, or the establishment of criteria for local implementation, or state intervention in development plans and other planning mechanisms, as in Oregon. There is an audit process intended to ensure that the states receiving grants treat the programme seriously.

An important aspect of the coastal zone programme is that the management objectives can extend to Federally owned land which would otherwise fall within a zone. This is important in a state like Oregon, where so much land is Federally owned. The effect of the requirement for 'consistency', as it is called, is rather like the development control regime applying to Crown land in England. The Federal government is not actually prohibited from certain activities or construction. But it must go through a long series of bureaucratic processes before it develops in a way inconsistent with the development control regime in the zone.

A similar cross fertilisation has occurred with the *National Environmental Policy Act*. Stimulated by the review processes applying to development projects in which the Federal government has an interest, many states have established requirements for environmental impact reviews of major projects, whether private or public sector development. The important aspects of the review process are the breadth of development caught, the scope for environmental activists to challenge projects, and the fact that the outcome is not actually binding. The breadth of control extends the need for review to any development going ahead with Federal resources, including redevelopment that will receive relatively small historic buildings grants, major highways, electricity generation infrastructure, sewers, reservoirs and so on. While I was in Oregon, a case was being prepared to challenge the way in which tax reliefs influence forest management in ways not consistent with the state plan; the contention was that tax relief represents a use of Federal resources.

The Act does not create a permitting regime. It simply ensures that government agencies must:

> 'include in every recommendation or report on proposals for legislation and other major Federal actions significantly affecting the quality of the human environment, a detailed statement by the responsible official on:
>
> • the environmental impact of the proposed action,
>
> • any adverse environmental impacts which cannot be avoided should the proposal be implemented,
>
> • alternatives to the proposed action,
>
> • the relationship between local short term uses of man's environment, and the maintenance and enhancement of long-term productivity, and
>
> • any irreversible and irretrievable commitments of resources which would be involved in the proposed action should it be implemented.'

Many groups have seen the procedures required by the Act as a way of challenging Federal government projects, for delay is often as effective a tool to stop development as a permit refusal. In *Local Government Law*[19], David Callies illustrates this phenomenon by referring to a figure of 1052 law cases filed against Federal agencies in the first 10 years of the Act.

The *Clean Air Act* can involve the Federal government in development review. This is because there is a reserve power for the Federal agency itself to establish an implementation plan, designed to secure clean air standards, if the state and local government agencies fail to do so. In practice major stationary sources of pollution are controlled. In Summer 1988 an order was issued banning all such new developments in Los Angeles until pollution levels had been stabilised. But in practice only the biggest polluting developments were likely to be affected, and these were unlikely to have been acceptable to the local governments in the area. Usually, the impact of the Clean Air Act is more indirect, featuring for example in cost benefit analyses of major highway developments by comparison with public transit alternatives, or in supporting applications for other Federal government grants.

In some areas of rapid development where local government was fragmented, Federal investment in roads and sewers was formerly one of the strongest determinants of the shape of development. The office controlling sewerage investment north west of Philadelphia was an example of a powerful Federal agency acting in this way. The source of its power was the *Clean Water Act* designed to control and reduce discharges of pollutants, including sewage effluent, to inland waters. The discharge permit system was used in such a way as to direct as much of the pollutants as possible into treatment plants funded by Federal government grants.

Over time responsibility for the permitting aspects under the Act has been transferred to the states. The waste water management plans were strong influences over the shape of development, and given the pressure to control growth in some areas, they can be used to prevent development. The existence of a strict discharge control regime means that local government areas choosing not to invest in sewage treatment facilities can effectively delay development, or make it more costly by forcing the developer either to install his own infrastructure, or to develop houses at the greater spacing needed if septic tanks are to be used.

Conclusions

This chapter has attempted to provide a basic explanation of the main development control systems operating in different parts of the United States. Generally, the Federal role is either non-existent or detached so that it influences decisions indirectly – for example by requiring or encouraging environmental impact statements. Most of the control mechanisms are at the local level, although the trend is towards more state regulatory systems and some state co-ordination of local government actions.

Zoning, subdivision and their variations are the main mechanisms adopted by local governments. Zoning can be as straightforward or sophisticated as the local community demands – provided that it does not go so far as to transgress the boundaries of the police power. Subdivision control and site plan review can represent additional detailed examinations of development proposals. They may be complemented by landmark controls or review by a design commission; and they may fit into a master or comprehensive plan. Over time some interesting variants of zoning have been developed by way of innovations to achieve certain social objectives or to bend the development market.

British practitioners can learn from these adaptations about the limitations of zoning as a development control method. In particular, floating zones and mixed use districts underline the realisation in the United States that separating uses into exclusive zones does not create the appropriate solution of social and environmental problems. Zoning bonuses represent a way of achieving compensation for the community where it chooses to concede more development rights than it would otherwise achieve, but it is all too easy to make zoning bonuses an automatic feature – which is a case of planning permissions for sale. Transfer of development rights schemes become necessary because the Constitution does not allow zoning to treat individual plots in such a way as to take all value from them. Saving historic buildings or open countryside can only be achieved by selling extra development rights on nearby sites, or sites not so nearby on less environmentally sensitive land.

These systems are beginning to be overlaid by new state initiatives, and complemented by specialised environmental control permit systems. On top of the fragmentation that the multiplicity of local government brings, with different variations of control in each town, fragmentation of permit systems between different environmental elements is also happening. The time will surely come when the US Supreme Court are faced with a takings case where no single development control mechanism can be said to be unreasonable, but where a combination of all the mechanisms that apply sums to a complete removal of economic value. If a regulatory taking is found in those circumstances, who pays? Chapter 5 describes some of the ways in which the controls are being combined, and details some specific initiatives.

NOTES TO CHAPTER 4

1. Directory of State Programs for Regulating Construction, published by the State of New Jersey, January 1985.

2. An example of the end result of such a review is the report of Florida's Environmental Efficiency Study Commission: 'Managing Florida's Environmental Assets' published February 1, 1988. Despite a range of permits as wide as the New Jersey example, the report concluded that the structure of reviews was basically sound. It is clearly very difficult to remove or combine review procedures and create a streamlined system that developers and others involved in the development review process might find easier to understand.

3. Tom Black, Staff Vice President, Research and Education, in an interview with the author, January 1988.

4. Professor Frank Popper in 'Understanding American Land Use Regulation Since 1970', Journal of the American Planning Association Volume 54, Number 3, Summer 1988.

5. Information extracted, with the assistance of the State's Office of Business Advocacy, from the New Jersey Directory of State Programs for Regulating Construction, published 1985.

6. All quotes from volume II (Strategies, Policies and Standards) of the Draft Preliminary State Development and Redevelopment Plan for New Jersey (January 1988)

7. Both these examples from New Jersey were reported in the Princeton Packet in late 1987 and early 1988.

8. According to an architect, Alan Lapidus, quoted in 'A Major Mall in a Broadway Building', New York Times, Real Estate Section February 21, 1988.

9. California: a Guidebook, by Randolph Delahanty, published by Harcourt, Brace, Jovanovich (1984)

10. Downtown Design Guidelines, Portland Oregon, January 1983, published by the City of Portland Planning Bureau.

11. See 'Neighborhood Commercial Zoning', published by the Department of City Planning, City and County of San Francisco, February 1985.

12. Richard Babcock and Wendy Larsen are currently working on a book about the use of special districts as part of the zoning process.

13. Quotation reproduced from 'The Great Weekend Escape Book' by Michael Spring, published by E P Dutton (1985)

14. California Administrative Code tit.14 R.83 Chapter 3, Appendix A.

15. According to Lauren Otis, New York City Planning Department in an interview with the author.

16. In a quarterly program effectiveness report submitted to the City Administrative Officer by the Director of Planning, December 7, 1987.

17. Quoted in Coastal Disturbances by Erlinda Villamor in New Jersey Reporter, November 1987.

18. Robert Greenbaum, quoted in the Princeton Packet, April 26, 1988.

19. Local Government Law, published by Callaghan & Co, 1986. The figure is quoted in Chapter 16, Land Development Regulation, by David Callies.

5 The Extent of Control

Measuring the extent of control

Having described some of the mechanisms of development control, the next step is to consider how they are applied. Not all the various mechanisms apply everywhere. Indeed, if they did the expectation might be that nothing would be developed anywhere. But, because it is almost entirely in the hands of each local government unit to decide how to exercise its powers, there are effectively perhaps 10,000 development control systems in place across the country, depending on the combination of control mechanisms adopted locally. In some places there is neither zoning nor subdivision control. But in such places there is probably little pressure for development either, and only rudimentary building control codes exist. Such areas are to be found for example in the centre of the country, and in up-state New York, or in the Carolinas. At the other end of the scale are the most densely populated cities and the most environmentally aware parts of California. In these areas development control mechanisms are complex and sophisticated. By contrast with the cities, in suburban municipalities the ordinances need not be so complicated, because there will be fewer uses of land to cope with, but enforcement may well be much more stringent. In these areas the boundaries of development control may be no stricter on paper than in the city, but the local character will ensure that the regime is effectively tougher as a result of more rigid enforcement.

In England, the extent of development control is largely set by central Government through primary legislation, through the General Development Order, which exempts a large amount of minor development from control, and through the Use Classes Order, which determines the changes of use of property that are not significant enough in planning terms to require local authority consent. Every other development or change of use of land will require a specific application for planning permission. The exemptions from this requirement are set in a uniform way across the whole country, except in conservation areas, National Parks, and areas of outstanding natural beauty, where a stricter but still standard set of controls applies. It is therefore easy to measure the extent of control, by considering the national rules. If a particular house extension is subject to control in the London Borough of Richmond it will also be subject to control in neighbouring boroughs, and in other cities too. It is easy to identify changes in the boundary of control over time, by considering the changes in the relevant national rules. It is also easy to identify the limited variations that local authorities are from time to time able to secure through special local (Article 4) directions under the General Development Order.

What is not so easy is to compare the extent of American development control with that in Britain. There is no standard against which to measure American local governments. The individual ordinances are hand crafted by the land use counsels employed by the individual municipalities, sometimes guided by professional handbooks containing specialised foolproof definitions. The ordinances are often loose leaf documents capable of frequent amendment without reprinting the entire ordinance, and prepared and circulated by private contractors. The mind boggles at the prospect of 10,000 Encyclopedias of Planning Law! Most applicants' lawyers simply buy the up-to-date issue of the relevant ordinances when they are brought into a case. A rigorous analysis of development control standards within a even limited area would be a daunting task.

Such an analysis would also require consideration of the characteristics of the land itself, which tend to vary with so many small local government units of vastly different sizes. For example, establishing a 250 foot set-back from rural state highways would bite more harshly in an area where many such highways meet than in an area where local roads predominate. Minimum lot sizes in rural Pennsylvania represent a much less dense standard than in the suburbs of Philadelphia, but might in themselves be the maximum feasible density because of rural sewage standards.

Measuring the extent of discretionary control

One way of contrasting the bite of American controls with that in Britain is to compare the number of discretionary planning decisions per head of population. In Britain the rate of planning applications per head of population can be calculated from the statistics collected from local authorities by the Department of the Environment. A map showing these data is reproduced in Figure 5.1. The variations it shows across the country may be due to many factors, and I am not aware of any rigorous analysis of the underlying data. But looking at the map it is possible to speculate that the extent of the pressure of growth (greatest in the home counties and the south west) and the effect of tighter controls (in areas of outstanding natural beauty and National Parks) are together responsible for much of the difference in the shading. Whatever the reasons for the variation, the overall figure is about 8.5 planning applications per thousand residents per year.

Although there are no comprehensive data available for the United States on an equivalent basis, a sample of local governments kindly provided me with data for the purposes of this paper. Figure 5.2 shows, for a series of big cities and a small sample of other local government units, information which gives a feel for the degree of control in the United States compared with Britain. I say 'feel' because I would be the first to acknowledge the scientific shortcomings of my data; it was very difficult to put the information from the different cities on to a consistent basis. Different cities use different terms for the same processes; they also have different points at which particular bodies – such as the planning board and city council – wield power. Nevertheless, I use the data here because I believe that it is the best available; it would require a detailed research study of administrative processes to start to do a truly comparative study. That is why I draw no comparative conclusions, but rely on the aggregate data as a reasonable indicator for my purposes.

The data demonstrate the variable application of planning controls between different locations. It is necessary to bear in mind that the number of applications is a relatively crude measure. It cannot account for the difference in the size of development contained in permit applications in different parts of the country. Nor can it be adjusted to account for all the variations in different development control systems; in particular, there may be some double counting where a project requires both an amendment to the zoning map, and a subsequent subdivision approval. And finally, the figures are not adjusted to account for different growth rates.

Planning applications received:
per 100,000 population
England – by district, 1987/88

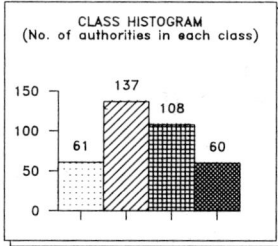

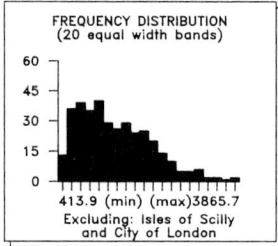

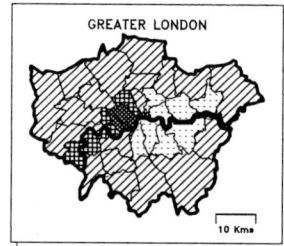

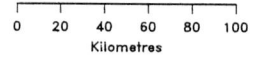

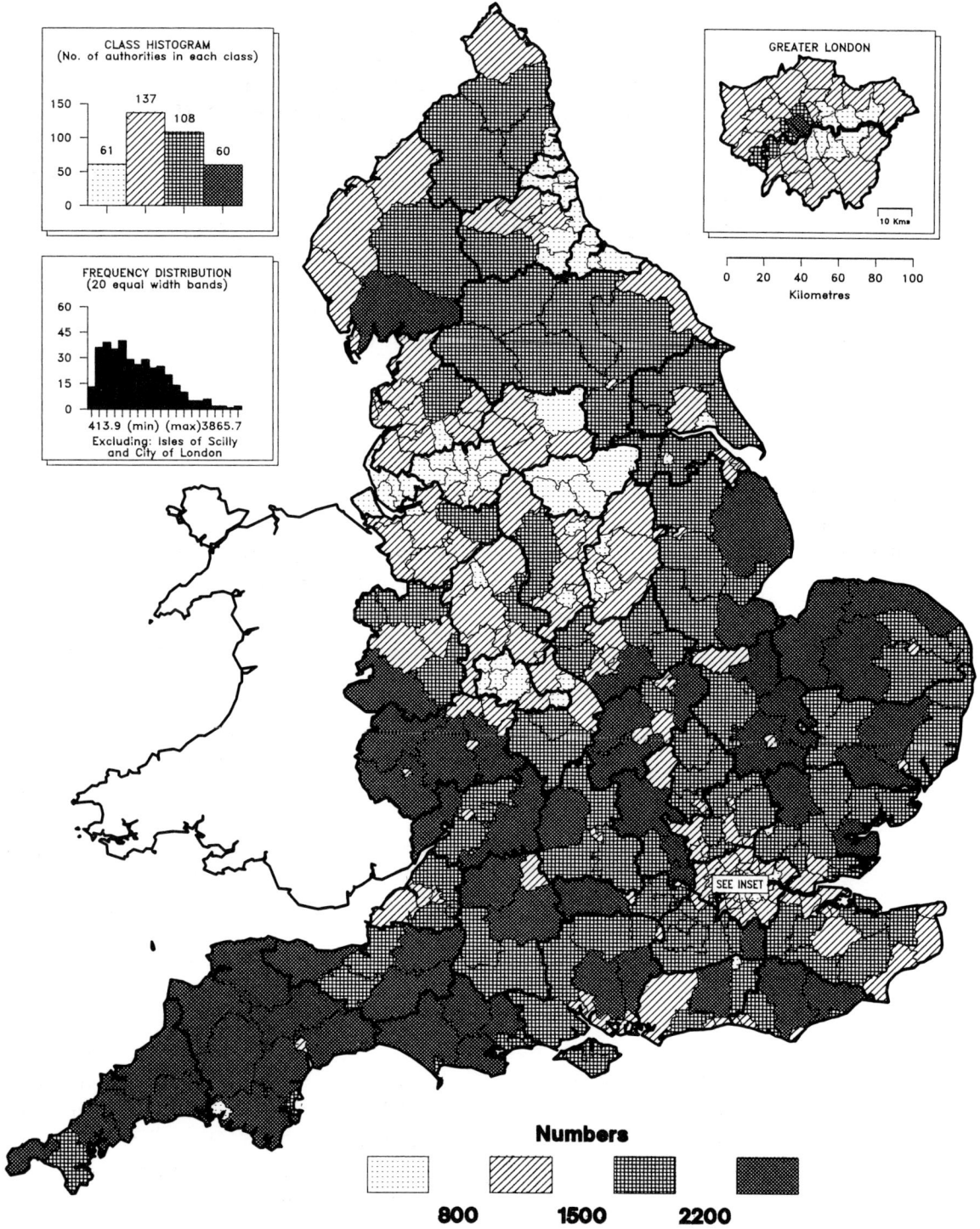

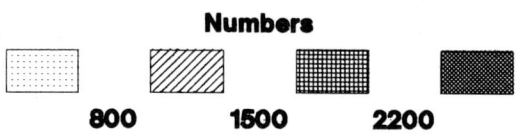

CLASS HISTOGRAM
(No. of authorities in each class)

150
100
50
0

61 137 108 60

FREQUENCY DISTRIBUTION
(20 equal width bands)

60
45
30
15
0

413.9 (min) (max)3865.7
Excluding: Isles of Scilly
and City of London

GREATER LONDON

10 Kms

0 20 40 60 80 100
Kilometres

SEE INSET

Numbers

800 1500 2200

LGS1 – DMTU0293/3/89/LGS2CV8
Department of the Environment
© Crown copyright 1989

Source: LGS/DOE
Boundaries as at 1981
Colour original

Figure 5.1 Development control applications received per 100,000 population in England by district, 1987/88 (Dept of the Environment)

Using data published in Zoning News[1], Figure 5.3 shows a more limited analysis of zoning appeals board caseload per head of population, in other words not taking into account the work of the planning commission itself, which will vary according to local legislative requirements and administrative practice.

Figure 5.2 shows a figure of about one discretionary planning application or decision per thousand population. Figure 5.3 shows a similar, slightly higher rate, perhaps because the units of local government are not so large on average than those surveyed in Figure 5.2 (I assume that smaller governments are more accessible, and more likely to enforce control, and thus more likely to generate variance requests). In England, the number of planning applications per year is about 425,000. Assuming a population of the order of 50 million provides a figure of 8.5 applications per thousand population. In other words in Britain the developer (often the householder himself) is about 8 times more likely to require a discretionary approval from the local government, and probably more since there is likely to be an element of double counting in the American data.

Comparing the bite of zoning mechanisms and planning permission

Yet, these figures should not be taken to suggest that development in Britain is much more tightly controlled. It is necessary to take account of the different approaches of the two development control starting points: in Britain development rights rest with the state, except in certain narrowly defined cases. In America, zoning provides substantial development rights to the individual owner of land. But zoning ordinances define in great detail exactly what use can be made of a piece of land, for example prescribing that houses should be 'single family', the amount of floor space that can be placed on the plot, and the width of the gardens or 'yards' between the house and its curtilage. Controls can even extend to the colour of the paintwork, or the materials out of which fences may be built.

My point is simply that in the more densely developed parts of America the zoning code can affect construction just as much as in Britain, but it does it by imposing standard conditions over the design. The developer shapes his proposed development to fit in with the code, rather than trying to seek a variance on the grounds of hardship, or because of the unique characteristics of the site.

By contrast, in Britain it is open to the developer to submit whatever design he chooses once he is in the position of needing a discretionary permission, which is usually the case. In Britain the General Development Order sets out what developments can proceed without any need for a planning application (that does not mean that such developments are free of all permit requirements; there will probably still be a need for building regulations approval, but that is much more of a predictable review process of certain technical standards which development must meet; provided the appropriate notices are sent at the right time, giving the building inspectors appropriate notice, there is no need for this approval process to interfere with the construction timetable). In considering whether to grant permission for development not covered by the General Development Order, the planning authority is expected to start with a presumption in favour of the development, and only refuse permission or impose conditions if there is a clear public reason for so doing. A number of documents will inform that process.

Figure 5.2 Development control data for a sample of local government units: Overall planning activity

local government	1	2	3	4	5	6
Atlanta Ga	431	8,441	423	19.6	0.98	0.05
Charlotte NC	460	6,940	354	15.1	0.77	0.05
Chicago Il	3,010	10,645	475	3.5	0.16	0.04
Cincinnati Oh*	369	1,741	80	4.7	0.22	0.05
Columbus Oh	593	625	362	1.1	0.61	0.58
Dallas Tex	1,003	13,430	716	13.4	0.71	0.05
Fort Worth Tex	440		290		0.66	
Indianapolis Ind	785	39,728	1,135	50.6	1.45	0.03
Los Angeles Ca	3,071	45,000	3,538	14.7	1.15	0.08
Louisville Ky	693		388		0.56	
Milwaukee Wis	600		754		1.26	
Nashville Ten	526	3,278	1,526	6.2	2.90	0.47
New Orleans La	563	5,058	310	9.0	0.55	0.06
Norfolk Va	275	13,000	386	47.3	1.40	0.03
Omaha Neb	397	7,172	718	18.1	1.81	0.10
Phoenix Az	947	15,896	1,823	16.8	1.93	0.11
Pittsburgh Pa	385	3,253	704	8.4	1.83	0.22
Portland Or	407	1,344	681	3.3	1.67	0.51
Rochester NY	242	2,500	409	10.3	1.69	0.16
San Francisco Ca	700	7,400	612	10.6	0.87	0.08
Seattle Wa	491	6,000	883	12.2	1.80	0.15
Tampa Fl	276	4,759	550	17.2	1.99	0.12
Tulsa Ok	377	3,070	575	8.1	1.53	0.19
TOTAL	17,041	220,000 (est)	17,692	12.9	1.04	0.08
Billings Ma	78	1,844	295	23.6	3.78	0.16
Bozeman Ma	31		74		2.39	
Brooklyn Park Mn	53	1,344	115	25.4	2.17	0.09
Clearwater Fl	99	7,667	431	77.4	4.35	0.06
Covina Ca	42	835	69	19.9	1.64	0.08
Culpeper Va	23	305	58	13.3	2.52	0.19
El Paso Co. Co	350		225		0.64	
Lane Co. Or	372	1,059	398	2.8	1.07	0.38
Mequon Wis	17	419	71	24.6	4.18	0.17
Middletown Oh	46	350	47	7.6	1.02	0.13
Missoula City/Co. Ma	112	918	133	8.2	1.19	0.14
Multnomah Co. Or	75		89		1.19	
Pueblo Co. +	100	5,465	111	54.7	1.11	0.02
Redwood City Ca + +	59	239	94	4.1	1.59	0.39
Santa Clara Co. Ca	110		122		1.11	
Skokie Il	60	434	100	7.2	1.67	0.23
Sweetwater Co. Wy	8	87	35	10.9	4.38	0.40
Tippecanoe Co. Ind	127	701	157	5.5	1.24	0.22
Weld Co. Co	142	2,131	88	15.0	0.62	0.04
TOTAL	1,904	26,000 (est)	2,712	13.7	1.42	0.10

column 1: population (thousands)

column 2: total number of building permits issued per year (based on latest year for which figures available)

column 3: total number of planning applications includes developer stimulated requests for rezoning variance and conditional use applications, major subdivisions and other discretionary development control permits

column 4: building permits per thousand population, a measure of the extent of activity by developers but also dependent on the building code itself

column 5: planning applications per thousand population

column 6: column 5 expressed as a percentage of column 4, an indicator of the relative degree of planning control (a higher figure suggests more detailed control)

*figures exclude variances. +building permit figures inflated by hailstone damage. + +building permit figures for new construction only

Figure 5.3 Development control data for a sample of local government units: Zoning appeals only

local government	1	2	3
Huntsville Al	143	218	1.52
Mobile Al	200	84	0.42
Mesa Az	152	191	1.26
Scottsdale Az	88	165	1.88
Little Rock Ark	159	77	0.48
Bridgeport Conn	143	240	1.68
Stamford Conn	102	150	1.47
Aurora Col	159	24	0.15
Wilmington Del	70	147	2.10
Coral Gables Fl	43	162	3.77
Gainesville Fl	81	129	1.59
Athens Ga	5	30	6.00
Evanston Il	74	45	0.61
Skokie Il	60	45	0.75
Crown Point Ind	16	20	1.25
Fort Wayne Ind	172	183	1.06
Ames Iowa	46	47	1.02
Iowa City Iowa	51	33	0.65
Kansas City Kansas	161	13	0.08
Portland Maine	62	78	1.26
Annapolis Md	32	27	0.84
Barnstable Mass	33.5	140	4.18
Dearborn Mich	91	126	1.38
Southfield Mich	76	144	1.89
Bloomington Mn	82	42	0.51
Lincoln Neb	172	80	0.47
Paterson NJ	138	120	0.87
Farmington NM	31	24	0.77
Huntington NY	201	439	2.18
Raleigh NC	150	234	1.56
Winston Salem NC	132	180	1.36
Cleveland Heights Oh	57	85	1.49
Allentown Pa	104	200	1.92
Mount Lebanon Pa	34	20	0.59
Newport RI	29	120	4.14
Charleston SC	70	400	5.71
Oak Ridge Tenn	28	92	3.29
Arlington Tex	160	165	1.03
Irving Tex	110	31	0.28
Salt Lake City Utah	163	344	2.11
Alexandria Va	103	200	1.94
Virginia Beach Va	262	544	2.08
Burlington Vt	38	67	1.76
Wheeling WV	43	59	1.37
Green Bay Wis	88	134	1.52
Madison Wis	171	161	0.94
TOTAL	4,586	6,259	1.36

column 1: population (thousands)
column 2: total number of cases (variances, appeals and special exceptions)
column 3: number of variances, appeals and special exceptions per thousand population

One document which the relevant legislation[2] specifies should be taken into account is the development plan for the area, rather like its American master plan counterpart. But this is most unlikely to impinge on other than major developments, or developments that clearly stand out from policies that apply over the local government area. In addition to the development plan, some local authorities have design guidelines – locally adopted documents which, provided they were the subject of public consultation, can be material considerations in the planning approval process. But in general, these considerations are not sufficiently specific to amount to rules shaping the actual developments; and, as considerations only, they do not bind the local authority, which has the discretion to go against its own guidelines if it so resolves with good reason.

Development plans are more likely to influence decisions about where major housing or industrial growth might be directed (for example, in Oxfordshire the County structure plan encourages growth in four country towns – Witney, Banbury, Bicester, and Didcot – as a way of ensuring that the City of Oxford does not have to bear the entire burden of meeting the demand for housing in the county, much of it related to Oxford generated employment). Local development plans prepared by districts are more likely to have sets of policies directed towards an individual place (for example, identifying the sites where particular development types might be granted permission). Design guidelines are more likely to contain policies encouraging the use of local building materials. None of these policies are binding on local authorities, but they must be taken into account to the extent that they are material.

By contrast, as we have seen in Chapter 4, zoning is precise, rather like the General Development Order writ large. It determines what can be built (or rather what the local administrator is bound to give permission for, since the zoning ordinance itself, unlike its British counterpart, does not do away with the need for an application for a permit, but simply states what sort of rules proposed developments must meet if the permit is to be issued). Moreover, it does so for substantial development proposals rather than for just the building extensions and few changes of use within the scope of the British general permissions. It represents the control mechanism to help facilitate the goals of the master plan, and thus needs to identify the land which is suitable for housing, whether dense or scattered, and that for industry. Each zone has its own pattern of standards set out in the ordinance, and the discretion to vary the zoning standards is not supposed to be wide – see Chapter 6 on the role of zoning boards of adjustment. So, although zoning permits much more development, it automatically applies much more rigid constraints on quite large developments than a British discretionary permit would have attached to it in the way of planning conditions.

Moreover, there is a sense in which the zoning controls in America can be more restrictive – some would say more effective – than those in Britain. The zoning code continues to apply to all developments and use of the land in each particular zone. If the zone restricts floor area, setbacks from roads and boundaries and so on, those restrictions continue to apply. It does not create the difficulty that arises in the denser parts of Britain, where local planning authorities are often unsure what maximum development to allow on a site. In such circumstances the authority always has in mind that whatever development they permit on the site, the General Development Order rights will allow to be expanded by as much as a quarter. Their quandary is whether to permit something less than the maximum that they believe that the site could take in urban design terms, thus leaving some leeway for individual flexibility in the way that additions may be added, or to permit the maximum and take away the extension rights by applying a suitable condition to the consent. The risk in the latter course is of having the condition removed by the Secretary of State on an appeal by the developer. It is a difficult judgement for the authority to make because they are not entirely in control.

In such circumstances, the American solution looks much more attractive – namely, a basic zoning code *continuing to apply* through the life of the buildings, backed up by the planned unit development option where a local government and developer agree to waive the normal rules in a special agreement for the site concerned. That is the clear position in places such as Fort Collins, Colorado, described later in this chapter, where rapid growth but a need to stop sprawl has led to planning solutions which deliver well designed developments. The special features of these developments – child care facilities, landscaping, swimming pools run by residents associations – can all be assured, since in theory it would be open to the City to take enforcement action if any feature of the agreed development did not continue to be provided. To take a simpler example, we saw in the previous chapter how Jersey City requires street lighting to be provided to a given standard in foot candles. Once provided, that would have to be maintained, or there would be a code violation which could lead to enforcement action. (Whether it would in fact be enforced would depend to a large degree on the mobilisation of local community groups prepared to bring pressure on the City, as well as on the resources of the City itself, which might not regard enforcement as its most pressing priority.)

There is another aspect to the difference of incidence between zoning and British development control. I have suggested that despite the much smaller extent of discretionary intervention in the United States, there is nevertheless scope for the community to impose considerable constraints on the shape and design of development. The worst effects of this can be seen in suburban America, although perhaps I should qualify my remarks by acknowledging that it is all a matter of judgement. It is in the suburbs of the fifties and sixties that one can see 'cookie cutter' lots on a grand scale, with so many houses sharing the basic constraints of common setbacks, side yard widths, building height and so on. Variation for individual buildings to break up the uniformity in the zone, except perhaps in the choice of 'siding' (cladding) materials, is limited by the difficulties that would arise if a land in the zone did not receive equal treatment under the Constitution.

So, perhaps it is better to give the architect or urban designer freedom to propose, while leaving the local planning authority freedom to dispose. There may be less certainty in having a wider local discretion, and it may be that the local authority could be accused of imposing its own conservative design tastes on developers and on its inhabitants; but in considering the extent of control, it seems preferable to me to have those design tastes imposed on an individual basis, rather than through a zoning ordinance automatically shaping the starting point for every development proposal.

Examples of tight controls It is interesting to look at the type of zoning and other controls which developers believe most obstructs their objective of converting land to a higher use and taking a reasonable profit for so doing. The US Government's Housing and Urban Development Department sponsors research, and from

91

time to time publishes guidance to help smooth the development process, in particular in circumstances where that process could be said to be hindering the delivery of low-cost housing. That guidance points up some of the controls which cause most difficulty and are perhaps unnecessarily burdensome. For the purposes of this report, I have separated consideration of burdensome regulations from procedural inefficiencies which supposedly also increase housing costs. I deal with the latter in Chapter 7.

In a Department of Housing and Urban Development report[3] designed to improve the availability of affordable housing, a range of regulatory steps is suggested to reduce the costs imposed by (unnecessary) provisions in ordinances. The corollary of each proposed step is a suggestion that the extent of control is too great. The steps suggested are:

Upzoning: ensuring that land in different zoning categories reflects the proportionate market demand for the housing types permitted, for example by including sufficient provision for multi-family housing. The criticism here is that zoning is requiring too high a minimum lot size. The reason may be local unease at the vision of a whole local government area developing at higher densities, a consequence of the difficulty in clawing back development rights once granted, except at high cost. It may also be a desire to exclude poorer people.

Flexible zoning: allow automatic increases in density for those developments that incorporate open space, landscaping or other amenities. Again, the ordinances may be cautious to start with, because of the worry that developers will build the houses and do no more, leaving denser housing but not a better environment. I discuss such zoning 'bonuses' in more detail in Chapter 10.

Reducing minimum area for PUDs: as planned unit developments usually incorporate a higher density, it clearly helps developers to keep land cost elements down if more sites potentially qualify. But I would question why there has to be a minimum area at all. The danger to avoid is spot zoning (see Chapter 4) but I regard this inflexibility as a major indictment of zoning.

Zero lot line zoning: a method of waiving the normal restriction preventing detached houses being built to the side edge of lots. The criticism here is of the standard requirement in a zoning ordinance for a set distance between the house and its curtilage.

Reducing setbacks: the same criticism as immediately above, but this time relating to the front of the house and its distance from the street. If the zoning did not specify a prescribed setback, then the increased flexibility might allow more effective use of land. Some urban design professionals would rather see maximum setbacks than minimum as is the normal practice.

Allowing substandard lots to be developed: this criticism is a localised version of the problem of over-zoning. If there were some flexibility, then land could be used more efficiently, rather than leaving odd corners underdeveloped simply because they were not of an adequate area to satisfy the zoning requirement.

Lot splitting: subdivision controls can prevent development, simply by requiring lots to remain of a certain size. It is an odd feature of

American law, to British eyes, that local government approval can control the sale of a portion of garden to a neighbour. But without it, the lot size requirements of the zoning ordinance could be easily evaded over time, and there is an equivalent worry in England over inset development (whether between houses or in back gardens) in relatively spacious areas of towns now under severe development pressure in south east England.

Accessory dwellings: in Britain planning permission is required for any subdivision into two separate dwellings. In America ordinances often restrict the sharing of accommodation by two families, as well as the division of a house into flats. The problem again is equal treatment or equal protection; in drawing up the zoning ordinance the worst case scenario is often borne in mind, in other words the prospect of every house being subdivided and requiring twice as much parking and road provision. If the ordinance permits it for one house in the zone, it must permit it for all. If it permits it for none, it is very difficult to obtain a variance, although personal hardship in the shape of the needs of an elderly relative may help. British discretion allows a local authority to say enough is enough for this street; the fact that a neighbour was granted permission last week is material, but does not create a binding precedent.

Site improvement standards: the same principles of inflexibility arising from the requirement to abide by specified standards results in the areas covered by subdivision control and building codes. The report points out as particularly costly, street, sidewalk and utility requirements. Street widths and radii should not be regarded as sacrosanct; curbs and sidewalks may not be invariably needed; off-street parking requirements could be tailored more to the likely needs of the new home dwellers. In all these cases, it is the imposition of a standard that introduces inflexibility through higher cost.

Lot frontage: a similar problem results when the subdivision code requires each house to have a minimum lot frontage of say 100 feet, when 50 feet would suffice. The zoning could assure the same density of development, but less road length would be needed.

Structure types: some communities prohibit row houses (terraced housing), duplexes (semi detached), quads or low rise multi-family housing. Thus again, the standard regulations constrain the types of development that are likely to be proposed.

Floor area: some communities insist on minimum floor areas for particular types of dwellings, which has the same effect as minimum lot size in making housing more expensive.

Combining restrictions on floor area, height, lot frontage, setback distances, and lot size, it is easy to see how the imposition of zoning can bring inflexibility and constraints on good design; certainty is a significant attraction of zoning, but it turns out to be quite expensive.

Limits to taut control

One of the reasons why American development control seems to impinge on fewer developments than in England is the constitutional background to the system itself. It would be very difficult for an American local government to operate a development control system requiring the incidence of discretionary permitting that operates in England. An important reason for this is found in the constitutional constraints on the 'taking' of property rights without just compensation, and requiring 'equal protection'.

(i) Takings

Perhaps the most important constraint on the extent of control is the constitutional requirement not to take land for public purposes without just compensation. Whether specific local government actions amount to takings gives rise to a large number of references to the courts. Zoning creates a much clearer picture of the value of land than is the case where there are no development rights until the local authority decides an individual application for consent. Americans place property rights very high on any list of important freedoms. So, there is great resistance to any action by a local government that appears to result in a reduction of the value of land.

The reason that there are so many court cases is that there are plenty of circumstances where a local government can take actions greatly reducing the value of land, or even requiring public dedication of land, but still not constituting a taking. This is because zoning comes within the police power, and as we saw in the previous chapter the burden is on the person complaining to show why the local government was not justified to act as it did to promote the public health, safety or welfare of its citizens. Many actions that might constitute takings are never challenged, because the cost of mounting a challenge would be substantially more than the value of the property right at stake (each party pays its own legal costs in the United States when it comes to planning and many other legal proceedings; there is no award of costs against the losing party). Examples of such actions specified by Richard Babcock, in his *Zoning Game*[4] are requirements to remove billboards, and architectural design requirements.

Most legal challenges are decided by the courts of the individual states–a process which provides the individual states with planning systems with different characteristics, according to the structure of case law set up by each different judiciary. That in turn may depend on how judges are appointed or elected, and on how close are the relationships between the judiciary and the legislature. The US Supreme Court has ruled in only a handful of cases since the Euclid case in 1926, but in 1987 chose to review three. The media coverage they attracted brought the subject of takings on to many conference agendas. The prospect of local government zoning actions becoming more difficult to defend in the courts caused some consternation among planning boards and their officials.

The history of takings cases in the courts began in 1887. In that year the Supreme Court held that restricting the use of a building in Kansas City by preventing its use as a brewery did not constitute a taking in the face of a claim that the building had no other practical use. A string of cases followed relating to the damming of rivers. Clearly land that was flooded as a result of dam construction was taken for a public purpose, but what about the interests of water mill operators downstream who found that the flow of water available to them was much reduced? A more modern parallel can be found in looking at the land around airports. How much restriction on use might the need to accommodate overflights create before a taking resulted?

The US Supreme Court's landmark case on taking, widely quoted in the various zoning law textbooks, was Pennsylvania Coal Company v. Mahon[5].

In this 1922 case a coal mining company had sold the surface rights of land but retained the right to mine. The question addressed by the Court was whether a restriction that mining could not take place if it would result in subsidence amounted to a taking. The mining company successfully argued that if they had to operate in such a way as to avoid subsidence the operation would be hopelessly uneconomic. Justice Oliver Wendell Holmes stated that:

'The general rule is that while property may be regulated to a certain extent, if the regulation goes too far it will be recognized as a taking.'

The question whether a particular regulatory action constituted a taking was therefore to be determined on a case by case basis. It would be a question of degree, and it has proved far from easy to recognize in many cases since. Perhaps the real significance of this decision was that the distinction between regulation and physical taking had been removed. In future, cases would be balanced to see whether there had been a taking – by weighing the public health, safety and welfare goals served, against the degree of property value diminution.

In the period from 1922, cases have been considered on their merits at the level of the state courts and the incursions of the US Supreme Court have been relatively few. The trend has been for the state courts to support more and more regulation in the public interest. One hundred years after the Kansas City brewery case, participants in the American land use planning process were therefore keen to see what the US Supreme Court would make of three relevant cases before it in 1987.

In a commentary[6] and in public presentations on the cases, the prominent land use planning lawyer Charles Siemon concluded that they did little to relieve the tensions between developers and local governments stemming from the lack of definitive legal precedents. He observed that the first case[7] was similar to the 1922 Pennsylvania case, except that legislation on subsidence had developed rather further since then. The question was whether a taking was involved in the requirement to leave pillars of coal underground. This differed from the earlier case, which had been concerned with regulation of one private concern to protect the private interests of other private individuals. In the 1987 case there was no distinction in the regulation concerned between the protection of private and public interests. The Court carried out an economic analysis, looking at the entire unit of ownership, and concluded that 4% of coal had to remain underground. These 4% pillars could be seen as the equivalent of the traditional set-back prohibiting building closer than a prescribed distance from the street. The requirement to leave pillars was not a taking.

Siemon observed that this decision was of particular interest to those engaged in the preparation of a state plan for New Jersey. It confirmed the need to look at whole units of property (for example quite large development tracts, or whole farms) in order to assess whether any taking was involved. It also underlined that the courts would be more likely to uphold restrictions if there were a clearly defined public program objective related to public health, safety or nuisance. He suggested that another factor that would influence individual decisions would be the condition or nature of the land. The value of the land is often created by the installation of public services. There was no inherent right, he thought, to use unserviced land for intensive development. In assessing whether there had been a taking it was necessary to establish the reasonable expectations for the land. These might well be *influenced* by the forward plans of the utility companies and authorities, although there might be a reverse duty on them to service land that was likely to be developed. (There is a parallel here with the question of whether new retirement homes can be permitted in the coastal resorts of England, where there is already a shortage of medical facilities; in the British case the right answer is not to refuse the development but to reorder medical priorities to reflect the demographic change.)

The second case, involving the First English Evangelical Lutheran Church[8], touched on the taking issue in looking at whether compensation was necessary as a result of a temporary taking. In this case rain had resulted in floods which had washed away the Church's summer camp. The County therefore temporarily designated the area, along a creek, as a flood protection area in which no development was to take place. Whether this represented a taking was not considered in the Supreme Court: the only question was whether compensation was payable if there had been a taking, given that the Church had sought damages instead of pursuing the remedies specifically available under California State Law, namely declaratory relief from the deprivation of use or *mandamus* to force a decision. The Court concluded that compensation could be an appropriate remedy for a total regulatory taking, and was payable so long as the taking was effective. They sent the case back to the California Court to decide whether the flood plain restriction represented a taking or a justifiable step as part of the State's authority to enact safety regulations. If there had been a taking, the state court would also have to establish how much compensation might be paid. In this the reasonable use of the land concerned would need to be addressed.

One of the dissenting Justices commented that this decision would generate a great deal of litigation. Local government officials do seem to be more concerned about the risk of compensation accruing while any temporary moratorium on development is in place. There was a comment in one of the planning journals that local governments might find it harder to obtain insurance cover against their liability in a case of unreasonable delay. But overall the feeling seems to be that local governments will simply need to ensure that they have very clear justification for their actions. There is similar pressure on British local authorities who do not give sound, adequate and clear-cut reasons for refusing planning permission; the consequence might otherwise be an award against the authority of the costs incurred by the applicant in taking the case to the Secretary of State on appeal. However, the British Government has so far not been prepared to extend awards beyond simply the costs associated with the appeal.

The difficulty that many American local governments have is knowing how far they can go without becoming liable to pay compensation. This is especially true of municipalities standing in the way of growth. A common reaction to infrastructure and quality of life complaints is simply to downzone by doubling required lot sizes. Provided that there is adequate justification for such an action to protect the health, safety and public welfare of the community, such a step can probably be successfully achieved without challenge. But there is no absolute limit. One area might be able to achieve control by limiting development to one unit per 39 acres. Another area might find it difficult to defend 1 acre zoning. In the absence of hard and fast rules caution is the watchword.

The third Supreme Court case referred to by Charles Seimon in his presentation and article was the Nollan case[9]. In this, a regulation imposed by a planning condition went too far; a condition attached to a building permit was not properly related to the objective of the regulatory system concerned. The Nollans applied for permission to demolish a small beach house on the California coast, and replace it with a structure almost three times as large. The California Coastal Commission, pursuing an acknowledged objective of protecting public views of the beach, granted the necessary permit, but attached a condition requiring the Nollans to cede an easement to allow a public right of way along the beach – in other words between the house and the high water mark. The court decided that this condition was not linked to the effect of the new construction: in Britain it would have failed the test which requires conditions attached to planning consents to be relevant to the development to be permitted. The following quotation from the Supreme Court ruling is a good illustration of the impact of the US Constitution on planning administration, determining the extent of control by opening the way to legal challenges of other regulations or decisions that go too far:

> 'Thus, if the Commission attached to the permit some condition that would have protected the public's ability to see the beach notwithstanding the construction of the new house – for example, a height limitation, a width restriction, or a ban on fences – so long as the Commission could have exercised its police power (as we have assumed it could) to forbid construction of the house altogether, imposition of the condition would also be constitutional. Moreover (and here we come close to the facts of the present case), the condition would be constitutional even if it consisted of the requirement that the Nollans provide a viewing spot on their property for passers by with whose sighting of the ocean their new house would interfere. Although such a requirement, constituting a permanent grant of continuous access to the property, would have to be considered a taking if it were not attached to a development permit, the Commission's assumed power to forbid construction of the house in order to protect the public's view of the beach must surely include the power to condition construction upon some concession by the owner, even a concession of property rights, that serves the same end. If a prohibition designed to accomplish that purpose would be a legitimate exercise of the police power rather than a taking, it would be strange to conclude that providing the owner an alternative to that prohibition which accomplishes the same purpose is not.'

I have considered this case in relation to exactions of public benefits in Chapter 9 below.

(ii) Equal protection

In considering the limitations which the Constitution imposes on the extent of control, Chapter 3 above touched on the need for land use regulations to abide by the rules of due process and equal protection. Due process simply means that all citizens should expect to be treated fairly in accordance with the laws governing the situation, and this need not concern consideration of the scope of control. However, equal protection is significant, in that it means that people in equal positions should be treated equally, in other words that a zoning ordinance that applies certain provisions to all landowners in a given zone should not be capable of different implementation as between individuals in a similar position. The same rules have to apply throughout the zone, and generally a unique hardship is needed to warrant a variance. It is the shadow of equal protection threats that means that zones cannot be too tightly drawn – a zoning map that made different provision for individual plots of land would be suspect. This is the same phenomenon which discourages what is known as spot zoning (see previous chapter), and which keeps up the minimum size of planned unit development sites. This constitutional constraint, although clearly understandable as a protection against discrimination on grounds of race, age, sex, health, religion, and so on, can be seen as a source of inflexibility in zoning.

The result is that the zoning system follows quite large areas of land. The numbers of zones in a particular city are generally relatively small, as can be seen from the map of Jersey City at the start of Chapter 4. Each contains standard requirements for height limitation, setbacks and so on. The result is more certainty for the developer, but more wasteful use of land. Within a given zone, there may well be sites where greater heights or reduced setback requirements might be acceptable; with good design a denser layout might make more sense on such sites. The inability of zoning to be more site specific, or at least to be more locally differentiable, is in my view a major disadvantage.

Fort Collins, Colorado

It was exactly this problem that led Fort Collins to design its innovative development control system. The zones are still in place, but there is an alternative application procedure which is tantamount to considering every proposed development on a planned unit development basis. The importance of the system is that a market has been created in which positive desires of the community are valued in a kind of currency, which can be used to buy density. Looked at from the side of the local community, the densest developments come with mitigating features such as extra landscaping, or a community swimming pool. The system can also be used to influence where development takes place, again by providing extra density in return for development on particular streets or in less attractive parts of the city.

Fort Collins has a recent history of extremely rapid expansion, both in terms of population, and in terms of land annexed (annexation takes place as city services are extended into the unincorporated areas outside the city). The population has increased from 15,000 in 1950, through 25,000 in 1960, 43,000 in 1970 to 65,000 in 1980[10]. The growth continues. Until 1979 the city coped with the growth by conventional zoning, backed up by a planned unit development ordinance and a requirement for payments of impact fees by developers to cover the cost of new infrastructure. In the late 1970s there was increasing citizen concern, part of what now seems to be known as the first wave of 'growth management'. Just down the road in Boulder the electorate had used the initiative process to put a cap on development, limiting the number of building permits to be issued each year. But in Fort Collins, the citizens voted against such an initiative, preferring to support the Fort Collins City Council in controlling the quality rather than the quantity of growth. A report prepared by consultants[11] summarised the Council's aims as:

1. Controlling fringe growth and encouraging it to follow sound planning principles.

2. Encouraging concentrated land use patterns and infill development.

3. Encouraging the juxtaposition of uses (ie mixed use development).

4. Encouraging higher densities and discouraging lower densities.

5.   Encouraging alternative transportation modes (mass transit, bike and pedestrian routes), and siting new development or access to new development in harmony with the road hierarchy.

This sort of set of policies is not so unusual in the United States (it would fit well in Britain); what is unusual is the way it is achieved.

One key overlay was the agreement with the surrounding Larimer County, establishing an urban growth boundary around the city. The county agreed to require development in that area to urban densities, and to apply city development standards for streets, water, sewer, storm damage and street lighting (so that at a given time the city boundary would be extended). Had such an agreement not been reached with the County, it would have been impossible for the City to achieve its aims of denser development in the city; strengthening controls in the city would simply have encouraged development outside the city where the standards were lower and compliance cheaper. Another key feature was the joint work by the City and the Colorado Homebuilders' Association to identify whether new developments were paying a fair share of the costs imposed on the local community. This was subsequently incorporated into an impact fee scheme, with the fees subject to annual review.

The Land Development Guidance System is available as an alternative to zoning, but to all practical purposes it has supplanted zoning for most developments of more than a few houses. All developments have to meet certain absolute criteria. The applicant must give affirmative answers to 43 questions on subjects such as neighbourhood compatibility, comprehensive plan compatibility, public facilities and safety, resource protection, environmental standards, and site design. It all looks very daunting, from the first requirement that the developer and neighbourhood meet together at an informal meeting chaired by the planning staff, where the objective is for the developer and local community to 'resolve any differences as to the social compatibility of the project'.

In addition there are variable criteria through which a development proposal can accumulate points – two points for an excellent implementation of the criterion, one for an adequate job of implementing the criterion, and none for no effort or failure. The criteria have multipliers assigned to them, ranging from 1x to 5x, depending on their relative importance. For commercial/retail centres of up to 15 acres, the total number of points accumulated must reach 50 per cent of the potential maximum; figure 5.4 sets out the criteria and maximum scores, indicating the City's relative priorities. From this figure it is easy to see that the City is anxious to discourage development of further retail uses along the existing long commercial strip (South College Avenue) but would rather see it in North Fort Collins, and preferably at some distance from existing shops (the idea

Figure 5.4   Maximum point scores for commercial/retail development in Fort Collins.

Contiguous to an existing transit route	4 points
Located at key street intersection	6 points
Located within 'North' Fort Collins	4 points
Located more than 0.75 or 1.5 miles from an existing or approved shopping centre	2 or 4 points
Located outside the South College Avenue corridor	8 points
Primary vehicle access from a non-arterial street	6 points
Supermarket/grocery store included	6 points
Special attention to energy conservation, and renewable resources such as existing buildings	8 points
At least ⅛th of the boundary contiguous to existing urban development	10 points

is for shopping centres to be local and to include grocery stores so that traffic levels, and the consequent pollution, can be kept down). The points system is also designed to discourage access from through routes, and to encourage developments that fill sites in areas already partly developed.

Figure 5.5 sets out the maximum points available for housing development. In residential projects, the more points the greater the density that can be permitted, so for example, a project earning 50 percentage points can be built to 5 units per acre. Projects which do not achieve the appropriate number of points for the density proposed can only be made acceptable by the developer earning bonus points from up to eleven different criteria. These mechanisms ensure that maximum densities are permitted on the best located and best planned sites. They also enable trading of bonuses for features judged to be of benefit to the community.

Figure 5.5 Maximum point credits for residential development in Fort Collins, Colorado

Base criteria

Within 2,000 feet of existing or approved neighbourhood shopping centre	20 points
Within 650 feet of existing transit stop	10 points
Within 4,000 feet of regional shopping centre	10 points
Within 3,500 feet of existing or reserved neighbourhood or community park or facility	20 points
Within 1,000 feet of a school	10 points
Within 3,000 feet of a major employment centre	20 points
Within 1,000 feet of a child care centre	5 points
In North Fort Collins or the Central Business District (where residential development is to be encouraged)	20 points
Contiguous with other development	30 points

Bonus options

Energy conservation in excess of building code requirements	5 points for each 5% reduction
Large site bonus	1 point for each 50 acres
On-site recreational space Off-site open space	according to the ratio of recreational to total development acreage
Transit expenditure in excess of building code requirements	2 points per $100 per unit
Neighbourhood facilities in excess of code requirements	1 point per $100 per unit
Low income housing Handicapped housing	points according to the percentage of qualifying units

There are also bonuses for sympathetic treatment of historic buildings, for enclosed parking on certain projects, and for the installation of automatic fire extinguishing systems.

If the currency created is weighted correctly by the City Council, it should not be necessary for them to intervene by using other cruder land use controls. It will be for the market to respond within the framework and certainty of the established system, and deliver the development the city wants, with the denser developments coming with appropriate higher standards and mitigations for the existing community. I was impressed because in this city, unlike most others I visited, there seemed to be much more concentration on efficient uses of the land. It was noteworthy that residential development was taking place right next door to neighbourhood shopping, and that small apartment blocks were being created only in landscaped sites with common recreational space, perhaps a swimming pool and a child care day centre. The City appears to have achieved a kind of certainty for developers through a clear system which awards development value to those prepared to supply the community's identified needs. At the same time the system is encouraging mixed development because that reduces the use of cars, and thus achieves energy and pollution savings. The system is also capable of rapid adaptation; when the relatively depressed North Fort Collins has come up to the level of the rest of the city, it will be an easy matter to amend the points in the ordinance to reflect changed priorities; there will be no need to go through a much more time consuming rezoning review, possibly involving amendments to the master plan.

Figure 5.6 Fort Collins, Colorado; community facilities such as this swimming pool and child care centre can be used to 'pay' for apartment blocks such as those in the background

Figure 5.7 Fort Collins, Colorado; new neighbourhood shopping centres (centre) as close to housing as this (right of picture) are rare in the United States.

The fact that, despite the base zoning, the Land Development Guidance System enables applications for any type of development on any land in the city makes it rather like the British system. There is no starting point of a uniform assumption that particular areas are for family housing, and particular corners are for shopping strips. It is for the developer to propose the type of development he estimates will bring him the best return. However, by contrast with the British system, there is certainty in that the developer can work out precisely what is permitted and can make trade-offs, for example between the number of housing units and the amount of land he dedicates for open space. He is free to pursue a wide range of options within a range of certainty, unlike the British system, where a sensitive site might take several time-consuming applications before the 'right' level of development is settled by the local planning authority.

The evaluation and conclusions in the report on the Fort Collins system for the Urban Land Institute suggest that the system works well. In particular, some of the key principles in the City plan have been attained; concentrated growth patterns and infill development are being achieved, with less fringe development; access performance points and the spread of neighbourhood shopping centres are encouraging a safe and free flowing local road network. The report also comments favourably on the administration of the system, with its key element an informal meeting with the developer to review concepts and identify the likely degree of compliance with the points scheme.

Breckenridge

A Colorado town more familiar to British visitors, because of its excellent skiing facilities, is Breckenridge. It is an old silver mining town which now finds its wealth through winter and summer visitors. Here tight development control is essential to maintaining the character of the community, and thus to its economy. This town also has a points-based development control system, which operates along similar lines to that in Fort Collins. There are absolute standards, to which new developments must adhere, and relative policies with relative weights reflected through multipliers. Positive or negative scores depend on the extent to which the town's policy objectives will be satisfied by the proposed development.

The Town's Development Code sets out 39 development policies, many of which are divided into absolute and relative. For example, all developments must comply with the Town's parking code; but plus and minus point scores can be accumulated depending on the design standards employed, on landscaping standards, on whether the space is to be available to the general public, and on whether the space is shared with other businesses or has shared accesses. Positive points gained may then be used to offset other aspects of the development which do not meet Town objectives. In this way a shared entrance to a car park might be used to offset a failure to provide public transit facilities or the installation of non-conforming wood burning fireplaces (these attract negative points, while installing stoves to state standards would be neutral, and installing no fireplaces at all and imposing a covenant on successive owners not to do so would gain positive points). Air pollution and traffic congestion are serious threats in the Colorado skiing areas in winter. Similar trade-offs might be smaller building setbacks in return for solar heating, and a density bonus in return for a shuttle-bus.

The Town's Director of Development, John Humphreys, suggests[12] that flexibility, the comprehensive scope of the scheme and the capacity for negotiation, are the major benefits of moving away from zoning. In addition most requests for rezoning or for variances have evaporated since the scheme was introduced. In discussing the scheme with Mr Humphreys, I also deduced that putting relative values on their policy priorities was a sensible discipline on both the planning staff and the elected and appointed boards; it was much more difficult for minor prejudices to stand in the way of an otherwise satisfactory development.

The weaknesses of the system have proved to be in staff and commission shortcomings, the length of review time, and in the inability of the code to reconcile master planned developments with the system. Commission shortcomings revealed themselves in an initial unwillingness to let certain minor aspects of a development pass, even when not provided for in the code. Staff difficulties were due to subjectivity in scoring certain aspects of the developments in the appraisal process (clear guidance has had to be drawn up). Discussion in the planning commission of the relative scores for different relative policies has proved time consuming, while major developments comprising different components have caused difficulties in that it is not clear to which elements of a major project the plus points gained by conformity with the master plan attach.

Whether it would be possible to take such a system and build it on to British development control is an interesting question. Essentially, a precise local plan would be needed, setting out the plus and minus points that proposed developments would attract and their relative importance, as well as the absolute requirements not open to negotiation. In one sense the local government would be advertising the conditions on which it would grant planning permissions for different types and densities of development. Whether this would work in our relatively densely populated island, where communities do not usually grow at the rate of Fort Collins or Breckenridge, is hard to judge. Whether the certainty would be illusory given that the development plan can only guide development control decisions, not mandate them, is another question. There can be no advance guarantee that planning permission would be granted if a developer could show that he had conformed with a set proportion of the local planning authority's objectives.

I find the idea attractive; and I take back my disdain which I expressed once when a Planning Inspector on a training course I was addressing suggested something on similar lines to make planning appeal decisions more rigorous. Perhaps he too had been to Fort Collins! I think it might increase the communication and understanding between local planning authorities and applicants if there were a well designed pro-forma available, setting out a list of policies, with relative priorities attached. In completing the boxes, it would then become apparent to a developer that, for example, however much landscaping or additional car parking he might provide, other more important policy disadvantages would weigh more heavily against him. More certainty for the developer would be accompanied by a more structured and objective review by local officials and local councillors.

Houston, Texas

If Fort Collins and Breckenridge have devised ways to overcome some of the rigidities of zoning, and have got into a 'post-zoning era', then it is important to say something about the development control system in place in Houston. This city is renowned for being the only city of any size in the United States without zoning. But that does not make it a city without development control; it is just that the combination of measures that apply do not include zoning *per se*. As Dick Babcock put it in 1966[13]:

> 'Land-use control in Houston has for generations depended upon the private restrictive covenant placed in the deeds and plats by the developer. Almost every acre of land in the city is subjected to private restrictions over use, size, or cost of house, yard requirements, height of building, and all the other baggage customarily found in our zoning ordinances'

In addition, in the absence of zoning, the city has obtained the power to enforce those private deed restrictions. Any resident who wishes to enforce a restrictive covenant is encouraged to bring the matter to the city through a civic club, a local community association, together with a copy of the appropriate deed restrictions. The city then considers whether and how best to take action. So, there is zoning enforcement without zoning.

Most of Houston has been privately planned. The amount of space and the adequacy of water supplies have permitted the city to expand by way of large developments. These have needed to incorporate a certain degree of private planning to protect against devaluation of the property in order to sell the housing units in a competitive market. This expansion is directed by the provision of water and sewerage services by the city government, provision that is in turn shaped by the comprehensive plan. Major roads and transport infrastructure provided or directed by the city also shape development trends. The effects of this can be seen from the air by any user of Houston's 'hub' airport. The suburbs of the city are vast areas of well laid out, spacious subdivisions, and the newest ones are clearly built only after the roads, water and sewerage facilities are installed in large areas of land. Near the main roads and the airport there are clusters of shopping centres and office buildings, generated by the infrastructure that supports them.

What observers seem to like least about Houston is the juxtaposition of uses in older parts of the city, and the visual rash of billboards and incompatible architecture. Yet others admire the city *because* of the way in which the uses are determined by the land market. Indeed, in a paper by the Director of City Planning[14] it is suggested that the mixed land use pattern in certain parts of the city is not all bad.

> 'In a lower income area, the availability of car-repair services, eating establishments, bars and such service outlets, makes for an 'attractive' neighbourhood in the sense of convenience for a group that has a low mobility. The ability to establish a business in one's garage or in one's home contributes to easy entry of individuals into the economic system. Many a small business has been started in a home or garage.'

In addition to encouraging private sector planning and directing development by infrastructure provision, the City has also used its police powers to achieve some of what zoning ordinances provide elsewhere. For example there are strict off-street parking requirements, and even a fence ordinance requiring the fencing of junk yards.

So, although Houston is a city without zoning, it is not a city without planning. Some of the benefits of not having zoning show up in the more mixed uses that can occur – and in this Houston has features in common with Fort Collins, where bringing shops and houses closer together was a priority, and where some house-like buildings on housing estates are in fact the neighbourhood offices. In practice, by not getting into zoning, or in overcoming the disadvantage of inflexibility that can flow from zoning, both cities are showing that in choosing a development control package no one ingredient is essential.

Conclusions

Comparing the extent of control between the US and Britain is difficult because although zoning permits so much more, it also applies standard conditions on development that are difficult to vary. By contrast, British development control is sufficiently flexible to react more sensitively to development proposals. In crude numerical terms there are at least eight times more developments per head of population requiring consent in Britain. This means that a far greater proportion of developments are individually designed, rather than shaped to meet the restrictions of the code. The restrictions imposed by the code can be substantial and unnecessary, and yet difficult to remove. The list of examples of initiatives that could be considered as ways of reducing housing costs is long. It identifies the cost of zoning – or rather the price of certainty which zoning provides by comparison with a British development control system.

We have seen in this chapter how different combinations of development control measures have been chosen in different places. One large city has even managed without zoning, although some say that it shows through poor living quality in some areas; others say it shows in the wealthy economy of Houston. The needs in different places vary according to such factors as the amount of space, the need to conserve character, the need to reduce pollution and so on. In the United States there are probably 10,000 different development control regimes, and there does not seem to be any easy way of categorising them. Perhaps there is scope for more detailed study of the systems in, say, a hundred places with the aim of categorising measures according to objective criteria – in other words identifying the existence of particular controls whether in the zoning, subdivision or some other permit mechanism. That would help to demonstrate which communities had more controls than were needed; it would make it easier for HUD to tackle the sorts of burdens which make housing development more costly than it needs to be.

The absence of any basic categorisation means that teaching the next generation of planners is done by reference to innovative case studies and to practice in certain larger cities, especially New York City where zoning started. It makes it difficult to comment on the absolute effect of land use planning controls on the shape of America today. Yet I believe that effect to be every bit as significant as in Britain, where the universal demands of planning control are apparently much more stringent. Perhaps the nearest to universal categorisation comes through the Constitutional constraints I have described. Although those apply differently in different states, according to the influence of the state constitutions, the effect is to apply a pattern of administration, such as that requiring equal treatment of all landowners within a particular zone.

Despite the rigidities of zoning, and the potentially undesirable effects it can have on urban design, it does have some advantages compared with the British system. Apart from certainty for the developer (which I have only touched on in this chapter, and which may be illusory in many places), I would identify the continuing applicability of the code even after a development is complete. In this way it is possible to allow the most intensive development of land in the code, secure in the knowledge that all future alterations and adaptations will also have to abide by those rules. There is no need to consider such actions as taking away General Development Order rights.

But in this chapter too we have seen that zoning has its disadvantages, and innovatory alternative combinations of control mechanisms have been put together to overcome these. The Fort Collins process seems particularly attractive in bringing certainty for developers and a more rigorous approach to decision taking by a city council. It could be applied as an administrative overlay to British discretionary development control decisions.

These innovatory systems bring American development control closer to British practice – or rather to what British practice would become if there were less influence by central Government through its operation of the planning appeals system, and more freedom for local government to negotiate deals with developers for the provision of public infrastructure. I return to this last theme in Chapter 9. Meanwhile, the next chapters develop further the questions of efficient administration and co-ordination of development control procedures. And Chapters 10 and 11 explain further how development control systems, such as those in Fort Collins, can be used to create artificial currencies which can then be traded by communities and developers in a local development market.

Postscript: approval rates and relative incidence of permits

Although I have not drawn on the material in Figure 5.8, it is of interest to conclude this chapter and its comparisons between English and American incidence of control with more numerical data. These, presented following the footnotes, show the approval rates for different types of permit issued by American local governments (the English approval rate for planning applications is about 85% on average, but rather less for major developments), and the relative incidence (and perhaps importance) of the different methods of control in the United States. This table underlines the tremendous variation between different cities in the methods of controlling development.

NOTES TO CHAPTER 5

1. Zoning News, published by the American Planning Association, June 1985 and May 1986.

2. The Town and Country Planning Act 1971, Section 29.

3. Affordable Housing: How Local Regulatory Improvements Can Help, by Stevenson Weitz, published by US Department of Housing and Urban Development Office of Policy Development and Research, September 1982.

4. The Zoning Game; Municipal Practices and Policies by Richard F Babcock, published by the University of Wisconsin Press (1966).

5. Pennsylvania Coal Co v. Mahon, 260 US 393 (1922)

6. Exactions and Takings After Nollan, by Charles Siemon and Wendy Larsen, in Land Use Law and Zoning Digest, September 1987.

7. Keystone Bituminous Coal Association v. DeBenedictus, 480 US 107 (1987)

8. First English Evangelical Lutheran Church v Los Angeles County, 482 US 107 (1987)

9. Nollan v. California Coastal Commission [ ] US 107 (1987)

10. I am grateful to Joe Frank of the Fort Collins Department of Planning and Development for explaining how the innovative planning system has been developed, and for showing me some of the results on the ground. I have also drawn on a report (Fort Collins Colorado, Land Development Guidance System) prepared for the Urban Land Institute by John Rahenkamp Consultants Inc (October 1986).

12. John Humphreys, in an article in Planning, published by the American Planning Association, October 1985, page 23.

13. The Zoning Game, by Richard F Babcock, published by the University of Wisconsin Press (1966)

14. Houston: a City without Zoning by Roscoe H Jones, Director of City Planning, September 15, 1976 (sent to me by Patricia Knudsen, the current Assistant Director).

Figure 5.8 Development control data for a sample of local government units: Analysis of relative incidence of different types of permits (and proportions allowed)

Local government	Rezoning requests prompted by developers	Zoning and use variances	Conditional use permit applications, special use permits, PUDs	Major subdivisions	Other
Atlanta Ga	23 (75%)	273 (84%)	38 (40 + %)	59 (90%)	10 (100%)[1]
Charlotte NC	154 (25%)[2]	62 (66%)		138 (90%)	
Chicago Il	152 (90%)	125 (95%)	143[3] (70%)	5 (90–95%)	
Cincinnati Oh	15 (95%)		52 (90–95%)	13 (95%)	
Columbus Oh	120 (94%)	77 (80%)	165 (74%)		
Dallas Tex	47	151	111	381[4]	26[5]
Fort Worth Tex	145 (66–75%)	130 (95%)	15 (75%)	[6]	
Indianapolis Ind	258 (50–60%)	683 (60–70%)	60 (70–80%)	134 (50%)	
Los Angeles Ca	1706	144	144		[7]
Louisville Ky	113	186	39	50	
Milwaukee Wis	114 (93.9%)	420 (89.3%)	220 (90.9%)	0	48[8] (100%)
Nashville Ten	213 (30%)	263	510 (ca70%)	540 (50%)	
New Orleans La	21 (57%)	256 (91%)	30 (90%)	3 (100%)	
Norfolk Va	20 (65%)	96 (60%)	92 (79%)	178 (90%)	
Omaha Neb	81 (73%)		103 (79%)	43 (77%)	56 (86%)
Phoenix Az	205 (65%)	1278 (70%)	31 (78%)	309 (na)	
Pittsburgh Pa	6 (50%)	582 (85%)	9 (60%)	2 (100%)	16[9]
Portland Or	54 (80%)	258 (65%)	177 (80%)	19 (96%)	173[10] (90%)
Rochester NY	22 (93%)	245 (40%)	49 (85%)	47 (98%)	66[11] (100%)
San Francisco Ca		152 (99%)			
Seattle Wa		103 (50%)	77 (21%)		
Tampa Fl	114 (80%)	250 (85%)	78 (78%)	34 (100%)	74 (86%)
Tulsa Ok	74 (85%)	25 (68%)	366 (85%)	27 (95%)	183[12] (85%)
Billings Ma	10 (50%)	41 (83%)	34 (90%)	176 (na)	
Bozeman Ma	4 (50%)	33 (66%)	34 (97%)	3 (100%)	
Brooklyn Park Mn	14 (100%)	14 (29%)	41 (88%)	17 (35%)	29[13] (100%)
Clark Co Wa	24	28	45	47	
Clearwater Fl	19 (75%)	203 (77%)	107 (85%)	18 (98%)	
Covina Ca	3 (100%)	12 (75%)	51 (98%)	2 (100%)	
Culpeper Va	6 (100%)	22 (64%)	16 (94%)	7 (86%)	
El Paso Co Co	13 (100%)	23 (83%)	106 (76%)	37 (100%)	46[14] (76%)
Lane Co Or	8	39	304	2	45[15]
McHenry Co Il	32 (94%)	9 (89%)	6 (66%)	10 (100%)	
Mequon Wis	24 (80%)	20 (30%)	12 (90%)	5 (90%)	10[16] (80%)
Middletown Oh	3 (100%)	29 (90%)	9 (100%)	6 (100%)	
Missoula City/Co Ma	53 (90%)	63 (95%)	6 (90%)	11 (95%)	
Multnomah Co Or	4 (100%)	16 (95%)	26 (10%)	6 (33%)	37[17] (15%)
Pueblo Co	14 (80%)	47 (95%)	23 (95%)	20 (na)	7[18] (95%)
Redwood City Ca	3 (100%)	24 (87.5%)	55 (95%)	12 (100%)	
Santa Clara Co Ca	5 (60%)	82 (70%)	34 (na)	1 (0%)	
Skokie Il	3 (100%)	64 (91%)	20 (90%)	2 (100%)	11[19] (82%)
Sweetwater Co Wy	10 (90%)	8 (37.5%)	13 (85%)	1	3 (100%)
Tippecanoe Co Ind	38 (76%)	60[20] (83%)	35[21] (90%)	34 (100%)	
Weld Co Co	8 (75%)	23 (91%)	55 (91%)	2 (100%)	

For notes to table see page 108.

NOTES TO TABLE 5.8

1. special river corridor permits and administrative permits for elderly family care homes.

2. Low because many requests require site plan changes.

3. Special use and PUDs only; Chicago's ordinances do not permit conditional use permits or uses.

4. All subdivision applications in Dallas require a public hearing.

5. Hearings to determine proper zoning.

6. Subdivisions do not require hearings in Fort Worth.

7. The work indicators I received from Los Angeles' City Planning Department show that about 45,000 permits are issued each year for this city of just over 3 million inhabitants. Of these 38,000 are issued over the public counter (for interior alterations and house extensions). About 6,000/7,000 are for new construction and require a full plan check. The planning activities broke down, in 1986/87, into Zone Hearings (469), Plan Approvals (1,706), Commission Agendas (1,105), Board of Adjustment Appeals Agendas (213), Tentative Tract and Private Street Maps (334), Parcel Maps (115 completed, 122 exemptions, 129 violations), Certificates of Compliance (72), Exemptions from Environmental Impact Reports (1,384), Initial Environment Assessments (870), Full Environmental Impact Reports (22), Public Works Approvals (229), Zone Variances (144), Conditional Uses (144), Area/yard/height Variances (214), Slight Modifications (188), Other Modifications (97), Coastal Permits (37), Coastal Administrative Actions (572), Code Amendments (103), and Other Zoning Administration Cases (992).

8. Certified survey maps

9. Project development plans for the Central Business District

10. Greenway permits, adjustments, minor partitions, revocable permits.

11. Site plan reviews

12. Subdivisions of 4 lots or less

13. Waiver of platting

14. Sketch plans, subdivision exemptions, variation of lot lines, variation of rights of way.

15. Partitions

16. Commercial site plan approvals.

17. Site plan review: the low approval rate may reflect that most applications are amended as they are processed and are thus not properly regarded as approved in the form proposed by the developer.

18. Vacations.

19. Amendments to zoning ordinance initiated by Village.

20. No use variances are permitted by Indiana state law.

21. Special exceptions and planned unit developments.

6 The Exercise of Control

Introduction

This chapter explains *who* is responsible for public control of private development in the United States. As with other aspects of American land use planning, a wide variety of arrangements has evolved locally in response to local requirements and often in such a way as to diffuse power and make it difficult to identify responsibilities in the development control process.

The main contrast with the arrangements in Britain is the key role played by lay citizens appointed to serve the local government body. This is true in the biggest cities and in the smallest municipalities. This feature may flow from the smaller numbers of elected councillors in both cities and suburban municipalities than in Britain. As a result there are insufficient representatives to support the elaborate structures of local councillor committees that characterise British local government. But it is more likely rooted in the progressive era of American urban politics at the turn of this century, a time when it became important to keep planning free of politics and away from the corrupting influences of the political machines. It was at this time that planning was emerging as a professional drive to make urban development conform to pre-stated priorities and guidelines, both physical and economic. Those reformers responsible for bringing planning into the urban political pattern were determined that the planning should be in the general public interest, rather than in the private interest of some influential minority. State legislation governing zoning reflects that earlier determination.

State legislation generally prescribes all the arrangements for preparing a comprehensive master plan and a compatible zoning ordinance and map, for deciding applications to amend that ordinance or to develop at variance to it, and for other procedures such as enforcement of control, approval of special permits and so on. Those arrangements are often based on the separation of legislature, executive and judicial branches of government, although the distinctions are sometimes unclear at the local government level. Adopting ordinances is a legislative function which is usually the formal responsibility of the elected city or municipal council or the mayor or perhaps both. This governing body may also have a role in hearing appeals from the bodies it creates, or there may be appeals to other bodies such as a board of public utility commissioners.

The key body in the planning process is the planning commission or board. Assisted by the full time planning staff and consultants, it generally prepares draft plans and ordinances, grants permits for subdivision of land, for conditional uses, and certain variances from the ordinances. Another board, the zoning board of appeals, considers applications for other types of variance, requests for interpretation of the ordinances, and appeals against the actions of officials. There may well be further boards that impinge on the planning process (for example development agencies, authorities and corporations, landmark agencies, environmental review boards of various kinds and site plan review boards). The arrangements are different in each state and locality. The complexities only serve to underline the diffusion of power and lack of uniformity in American local government. The planning system as a whole is nowhere near as distant from political influence as the fathers of the profession might originally have hoped.

The planning commission   The main participant in any land use planning issue affecting a city or municipality is the planning board or commission. Supported by the full time planning department staff, its overall role is to co-ordinate the development in the city. To play this role, it is generally responsible for:

> i   preparing a master plan, which may or may not require approval by the elected members of the local government body;

> ii   devising a mechanism for implementation, namely draft zoning and other ordinances for adoption by the elected body;

> iii   reviewing development proposals that come before it, to check conformity with the ordinances, a function generally carried out by administrative staff in the zoning or building control office;

> iv   managing citizen participation, by arranging public hearings in connection with tasks i to iii above; and possibly,

> v   reviewing the annual capital budget of the city, to ensure that expenditure proposals are consistent with the long term aims expressed in the master plan.

The larger planning bodies that cities and counties can support, unlike the suburban municipalities, seem be able to take on the wider role that v implies. Here the planning commission will concern itself with such matters as roads, sewers, water supply, the appropriate mix of development types, ownership and financing, inclusion of low income housing, urban design aspects of developments they would like to see, and how the overall strategies of the various departments of local government mesh together. Regional planning boards have been established in some metropolitan areas to coordinate these more strategic issues, and Chapter 8 explains more of this regional perspective.

In areas of smaller local government units, federal and state government action has dramatically increased the extent of planning. For example, until funds were withdrawn as part of President Reagan's budget cuts, section 701 Housing Act grants provided Federal support for local planning. At the state level Florida has progressive requirements on each city and county in that state to prepare a plan, and, more recently, to show in that plan how development will be constrained so as not to outpace infrastructure provision. Even so, the local planning effort in many small municipalities is very limited, either by the size of the administration, and hence what it can afford to devote from local taxes, or indeed by a lack of any need for planning in that part of the country.

Planning commission members are generally appointed by the mayor. There are usually either 7 or 9 members, perhaps with additional alternate members in order to assure a quorum if members are absent. Members are generally unpaid and appointed for their judgement in land use planning issues. This means that members are often experienced in real estate, architecture, engineering or government service. The usual lack of remuneration for preparing for and attending meetings, which may be held weekly in some places, means that retired people are frequently represented. But it can also lead to a rapid turnover of members appointed without knowing the nature of the demands the task will put on them. In some places the planning board may include among its members the mayor or city manager, one other elected governing body member, and an appointed official of the local government body concerned. These overlaps with other boards or departments are intended to ensure some liaison between the various aspects of planning and other functions, but they are generally limited by law so as to secure the independent nature of the planning board[1]. This represents a great contrast with the appointment of a planning committee in England, where generally a rather larger committee is formed of the elected councillors of the local authority, with the result of a sometimes all too parochial approach to planning as members looking after the interests of their ward constituents. Only occasionally are appointments made of non-elected members, and even this practice has been frowned upon in recent years[2].

Planning boards may appoint their own attorneys and other specialist staff, none of whom need to be the same people as those serving the other committees dealing with planning matters. A township committee may have one attorney, the planning board another, and the zoning board yet another. Moreover, a change of appointees on a board may lead to a wholesale change of staff[3]. It causes great difficulty and uncertainty for applicants when the board changes together with its attorney, engineer and planning consultant. The only mitigating factor is that board appointments are generally timed to overlap so that some continuity is assured.

Some statutes provide for the planning board to be supplemented by a citizens' advisory committee to assist and collaborate with the board, but not to vote. One of the best examples of such an arrangement is to be found in the New York City structure, where community boards have a role in the development review process, making recommendations to the City Planning Commission. Each community board – there are 62 for this city of over 7 million inhabitants – covers a population approaching that of some London boroughs. However, in the absence of any real power to take even minor decisions and the constraining influence that might bring, it is perhaps not surprising that the appointments to some of the boards are thought to be uninspired and their actions subject to question. One City Planning Department publication[4] asserts:

> 'While the local planning boards have advisory powers only, they frequently exert an important influence on the planning process.'

However, difficulties with the activities of the community boards led the Mayor, in 1987, to propose guidelines to constrain the process. As Sylvia Deutsch, Chair of the City Planning Commission, put it in a statement to the Bar Association of New York[5]:

> 'In one recent project, Commission learned that the developer had made a commitment to the community board to provide funds to those neighbourhood groups which would be recommended . . . by the community board. This commitment appeared to have been made either at the request of, or with the concurrence of the community board.'

How can you rely on community advice when there is a risk that it could be tainted? On the other hand, is this not the market economy where more efficient decisions would flow from individual negotiation of amenities between developers and the local people affected most by plans to build outside the zoning envelope? In Chapter 11 I describe more of the work of the Bar Association review.

The United States is a country of great contrasts, and planning administration is not excluded from these. It seems strange to an outsider that a body representing over 100,000 people has power only to make recommendations, akin to an English parish council, while just down the road in New Jersey, municipalities with only a few thousand people are more or less free to decide applications to build 1,000 unit residential developments. One can only observe that this contrast has arisen because the local government structure itself is largely the function of local decision rather than being determined by any pattern handed down by the federal government. However, such local decisions on powers and their location are largely a matter of history, given the difficulty now of taking any steps to change the location of decision responsibilities. Small suburban municipalities are unlikely to submit to any change that could erode their powers to protect the property values of their residents. Eventually, in New York City, residents would have the chance to vote on a new Charter, but its contents would be largely constrained by the input of those already involved in the process. There is pressure for neighbourhood advisory committees to be elected. However, elected community boards and a degree of local power over minor development decisions in New York are most unlikely to feature in proposed reforms, however attractive such a modest administrative delegation might seem.

Figure 6.1 Local government can be small

Where planning boards fit in

Big cities have different arrangements from suburban jurisdictions for the linkages between the various planning bodies. The most common structure, found for example in New York and Philadelphia, is to have the planning commission or board, advised by the city planning department, make recommendations to the elected city council for final decision. By contrast, in Chicago, the planning department works to a commissioner appointed by the mayor, and proposed decisions are not made public until the mayor

112

himself has endorsed them. (Chicago is also renowned for the role of the ward elected aldermen, whose approval for a project is essential if it is to get through the final stage in the process–City Council approval. For that reason, most developers will work closely with the local alderman from the start of the process–an involvement that could seem rather risky in terms of the potential for allegations of corruption.) The planning department is one of the mayor's operational departments, and therefore has less independence in this model. In theory, by cutting out a layer of control the Chicago model ought to be faster, though there is no data to prove either that or the contrary. In particular, Chicago's arrangements do not seem either fast or slow by comparison with other large cities (see the tables in Chapter 7).

The delivery of rapid development in a stagnant city was one factor leading Boston to set up a third type of structure. In this, all the development and planning functions were centralised in a 'superagency', the Boston Redevelopment Authority (BRA). Development control responsibilities were removed from the city commissioners and effectively placed in the new functional agency, whose board and director are appointed by the mayor. A planning commission and zoning board of adjustment, also appointed by the mayor, have the formal final say in approving zoning changes and variances, but the scale of professional support available to the BRA ensures that the commission and board are unlikely to gainsay the Authority's advice. The BRA was immediately successful in attracting government grants and stimulating development in the city, although whether it is efficient now that the downtown area is under such great development pressure is less clear. A major downtown development might now take between 6 and 10 years to obtain all the necessary approvals[6].

The BRA's Development Review Procedures explain why this might be the case. The aim is to evaluate the 'quality and appropriateness of a proposal based on objectives stated in plans, guidelines, and regulations'. The review is conducted by the 'Authority and staff from its design, development, transportation, environment, zoning, and engineering departments with assistance on a project by project basis from citizen advisory groups, professional associations, and other constituencies'. The procedures are as follows:

Step 1: For a privately initiated project, the developer first briefly describes the project in a letter of interest. The BRA then meets the developer to discuss the development concept, government regulations and procedures, and to outline the information needed in the formal submission. (The list is very long and complex, but not all information is required for all projects).

Step 2: The next step is a schematic review, intended to secure agreement on the basic development concept. Schematic materials submitted by the developer are reviewed by BRA staff who may recommend revisions. There is an environmental review to determine 'microclimate and other impacts', and the project may need to be changed to mitigate adverse impacts. Once the schematic design has been accepted by BRA staff, the next stage of review is initiated.

Step 3: The developer next submits design development materials, which are reviewed by BRA staff, who may request modifications. A final environmental review is conducted, and when the BRA staff are content the proposal goes to the BRA Board.

Step 4: The Board holds public hearings and, in the light of these, recommends appropriate zoning actions to the Zoning Commission and Zoning Board of Appeal.

Step 5: The BRA staff review the final working drawings and then issue a building permit.

Given all this, and the additional burden represented by the 'linkage' scheme (see Chapter 9), it may seem surprising that development goes ahead at all in downtown Boston. In fact, the effect is partly to divert development to other parts of the city and to the suburbs, but as fewer buildings are being constructed there is a shortage of accommodation in the downtown area. This in turn allows the rents to rise, and the resultant increased potential profit is sufficient to sustain the interest of developers. Boston is clearly an unusual city, and not only because of the combination of development review and city construction in the same department.

The building and zoning inspection department

Frequently, the planning department and commission are not directly concerned with monitoring conformity with the zoning ordinances. This task falls to the specialist staff of a separate technical department. Their tasks include:

i inspection of plans before construction to assess compliance with various building regulations and zoning ordinances and issue of permits accordingly;

ii inspection of buildings during construction to ensure conformity with plans; and,

iii certification of buildings before occupancy.

The first line of protection of the integrity of the zoning ordinance is thus the possibility of the refusal of an occupancy permit. Illegal occupation can be an expensive response to such a refusal. However the effectiveness of this approach where the zoning ordinance is very complex relies on the training of the technical staff. The second line of defence is often more effective, that is the interest in monitoring development taken by local community groups, for example New York City's community boards. Perhaps it is not inappropriate that a regulatory system designed to protect the health, safety and welfare of citizens should ultimately rely on those citizens themselves to monitor compliance. From the fairly frequent newspaper reports, it seems that the suburbs are the places where enforcement of quite petty ordinances (for example governing where washing may be hung, or dustbins kept) is regarded as important.

Zoning Boards of Appeals

The third local government body sharing responsibility (with the planning commission and governing body) for the development control system is the zoning board of appeals. This body is sometimes called the zoning board of adjustment, and the term is frequently shortened to simply ZBA. Like the planning boards, these are usually appointed bodies, typically with 7 voting members and 2 alternates. The alternates may participate in the hearings, but may only vote when a voting member is absent. Generally, no holder of an elected office may be appointed to a ZBA, and quite often no member of the planning board may be appointed either, although some states do permit an overlap, for the purpose of liaison.

The main role of the ZBA is a quasi-judicial one. The board hears applications for variances from zoning ordinances, appeals against the actions of municipal officials, requests for interpretation of the ordinances, and sometimes applications for special exceptions, when the ordinance provides for that method of obtaining consent. No zoning ordinance can anticipate every likely contingency, even if every possible step has been taken to ensure that it is the soundest possible document. For that reason it is necessary to provide a mechanism to vary the application of the ordinance in cases where the result would otherwise be unnecessary hardship. However, the mechanism, known as a variance, can only be applied where there will be no substantial detraction from the public interest in seeing the ordinance sustained – as the Standard Zoning Enabling Act so succinctly put it, '. . . so that the spirit of the ordinance shall be observed and substantial justice done'[7].

The hardship in question must relate to the physical character of the property, and must be shown to be unnecessary and undue. Its amelioration is limited to bringing the zoning status of the land up to that of the other land in the area, and it should not result in any adverse effect on neighbouring property. This means that variances should not be granted if the hardship alleged applies equally to other properties in the neighbourhood; the proper remedy then is to petition for an amendment of the zoning ordinance or map itself. In addition the hardship which might justify a variance is limited to that caused by the zoning ordinance; the personal circumstances of the applicant should be discounted.

This means that, in theory, applications for variances should be refused in cases where in the equivalent situation in Britain, the local planning authority would have no hesitation in granting consent. One case mentioned in the APA 'handbook'[8] concerns the construction of new houses on a road that has been widened. Some had been built before the widening, with front yards set back the amount determined by the zoning ordinance. After the road widening, vacant lots on the road could not be developed with new houses sharing the same building line as the earlier ones, because the setback requirement could not be met. Nor could a variance be granted to achieve that effect, because more than one property was involved – the circumstances would not be unique. The proper way forward would be by amendment of the zoning ordinance itself, a function of the planning board and the elected members of the municipality.

Other functions of the ZBA are to consider requests for interpretation of the zoning map or ordinance – equivalent to a British 'Section 53' determination – and applications for so-called 'special exceptions'. These are not variances requiring a relaxation of the rules in response to hardship, but are an administrative responsibility delegated by the zoning ordinance in larger cities in order to avoid the need for special use permits which would otherwise unduly burden the governing body.

Of course, the extent to which the ZBA will restrict itself to its proper role will vary from case to case, and may even lead to conflict with the planning board. It is possible for the two bodies to seem to be in competition to implement different planning regimes in a locality – with the planning board making firm rules and the ZBA granting variances that undermine their intent. This is particularly so in states, such as New Jersey, where the ZBA is empowered to grant use variances, and variances permitting the expansion of non-conforming uses. In Jersey City, an inner city area where substantial new developments are under way or planned, one reason quoted by officials for adopting redevelopment plans (which effectively suspend the normal zoning ordinance) was to ensure that the planning board retained total control of development standards. In other areas, one of the considerations of land use attorneys is to decide whether to take their client's case to the planning or the zoning board, a decision that may turn on the individuals appointed to those boards.

On the other hand, there is a clear advantage in terms of more efficient operation of the development control process if the planning board, and possibly the elected council itself can be spared the consideration of mainly minor matters.

Decisions by more than a simple majority

One interesting feature of the American process is the inclusion of weighted voting, and the need for more than a simple majority in certain circumstances. For example, use variances in New Jersey can be granted only by affirmative vote of 5 out of 7 members. (It is in this sort of case that the function of alternates or reserves is so important: if members cannot get to every board meeting, or are disqualified from voting by reason of a personal interest in the application under consideration, there should still be a sufficient voting attendance to allow decisions to be taken).

Taken in combination, weighted voting and weighted majorities can lead to difficulties. The New York City Board of Estimate is the centre of the City's current form of government which must approve noncompetitive contracts, franchises, the budget and land use decisions. A two thirds (8 out of 11) majority is needed to approve projects without competitive bidding. A recent plan[9] to renovate a historic landmark school building in exchange for a transfer of its air rights to a neighbouring plot, allowing an extra 12 stories than the zoning would normally allow, ran into trouble when the mayor disqualified himself from voting because of a conflict of interest. The plan had been developed over 5 years and had gained approval with the local community board, with the City Planning Commission and with the Landmarks Preservation Commission. Without the mayor's votes, it would only take an adverse reaction from one of the others with two votes, the City Comptroller, and the City Council President, or from two of the 5 borough presidents on the Board, to prevent the project proceeding as negotiated. Perhaps there is a need for alternates on this Board too? In any case, at the time of writing it seemed unlikely that the Board would survive for long in its present form. The City Charter Revision Commission, in reviewing the government of the city, received legal advice that it would be impossible to reconstitute the Board so as to conform with the constitutional and legislative requirements for relating representation to the number of voters. The US Supreme Court would consider the issues before a new Charter emerged.

Development agencies, authorities or corporations

Cities involved in urban renewal in the fifties and sixties often created redevelopment agencies. These were established by state legislation and located in the cities to receive federal grants. As implementing agencies, their initial task was to get public projects built that needed grant aid to proceed. The key power available to them was that of 'eminent domain', or compulsory purchase as it is known in Britain. This enabled the acquisition of sites in officially designated blighted areas in fragmented ownership, and the disposal of the entities created to developers in the public or private sectors.

The creation of independent agencies was not an essential prerequisite to receiving federal funds; cities could designate themselves or their own planning commissions as the appropriate agency. However, in some cities the political interests of the central business district – an alignment of corporations, banks, provincial newspapers and construction unions – began to urge the strengthening of city-wide interests as the only way of securing economic regeneration. All powers in Boston, for example, became effectively centred in the mayor and his appointees. From the early 1960s the Boston Redevelopment Authority began to succeed both in attracting federal funds and assembling land which, after appropriate planning input, became available for profitable development[10].

As urban renewal has given way to community development, as specific grants have given way to block grants, and as the whole climate has changed to one in which wholesale clearance is not politically acceptable, so the role of redevelopment agencies has changed to become more involved with individual development projects. And as federal grants have reduced in both amounts and variety, these agencies have come to depend more on obtaining a slice of funds from parent cities or states in order to make their input to such projects.

More recent development authorities or corporations have reflected this change in emphasis. They are special purpose bodies designed to carry out development in partnership with the private sector. A key role is the attraction of economic development, although for this function whether the agency is now located in the public or private sectors seems largely irrelevant. For example, Elizabeth is a city and port located in the older industrial part of New Jersey, and has housing and industry that would benefit from inward investment. Its development company is a private non-profit corporation, but it clearly operates closely with the City Council, making direct loans at low interest rates, as well as being a certified lender of Federal Government Small Business Administration monies and assisting the securing of Urban Development Action Grants and aid from the state Economic Development Authority. In effect it is a part private, part public sector one stop shop for potential investors.

Many more cities are shaping development by becoming directly involved with individual projects. For example, Fairfield California is an equity partner in a large regional shopping mall, Cincinnati has a stake in a Westin hotel, and New York City is a partner in an office building with Morgan Stanley and Company[11]. The incentive for such involvement stems partly from voter led initiatives to prevent property tax increases. Local governments have had to become more entrepreneurial. The difficulty about such initiatives, especially given the apparent susceptibility of local government to corruption, is the propriety of government acquiring land, then by action such as zoning, increasing its income potential. One way of reducing such doubts is to set up development agencies as separate entities and treat them exactly as if they were private sector developers. New York City has such an entity in the shape of its Public Development Corporation (formed in 1966), which by 1987 had more than 100 projects under way with a total value of close to $13 billion. What is never clear is how much at arms length such agencies are; if they were really treated just as any developer, it is hard to see why there should be a need for them. In practice they probably gain from a good knowledge of how to minimise the bureaucratic hurdles on the way to approval of projects, as well as not being bound by quite the same constraints on taking risks. However, there is a political advantage in encouraging the more difficult, but probably more sensible decisions, in removing the agency from the direct purview of the city concerned. The reverse of this benefit arises whenever political imperatives drive them to different decisions than their private sector counterparts would reach.

One advantage originally available to New York State's Public Development Corporation equivalent, the Urban Development Corporation (formed in 1968), was that it could override local zoning in its mission to build moderate income housing. In that way it could overcome exclusionary zoning requirements and build more densely than the suburban communities would have liked. But, this exemption did not last. Following the promotion of 9 projects in Westchester County, an expensive suburban area north of New York City, the state passed legislation stripping the zoning freedoms, except in city areas. It is interesting that the cities did not join the suburbs in this action; it may reflect a tacit admission that successful housing projects are more likely to come to fruition if city bureaucracy can be bypassed. The Urban Development Corporation also has its own bond raising powers and building codes, the power to condemn land and dispose of it, to initiate public works projects, to grant tax abatements, and ultimately to manage its own estate without interference with any surpluses generated. It became very much the builder of major, last resort housing projects, benefiting at one time from 50 per cent of the Federal government budget for public housing.

In 1975, the Urban Development Corporation defaulted on its bonds, in the light of President Nixon's moratorium on Federal housing programs. Ultimately it was reborn, bringing its unique powers into play on commercial and industrial, rather than housing, development. Its current flagship project is the World Financial Center at Battery Park City, Manhattan. This enormous project is taking shape on landfill from the foundations of the World Trade Center. The project is so successful that substantial surpluses are being generated and devoted to low and moderate income housing elsewhere in the city. Here the UDC is acting in the same way as its British namesakes, by taking the risks on a project in an area that the private sector would not take on. It was able to do this because of the freedoms granted it by the state and city, in particular to act as an urban redevelopment agency.

Having consolidated in safer fields, the UDC once again is reported as changing course[12]. The aim seems to be to transform the corporation into a broader purpose economic development agency, concentrating on the creation of jobs through encouraging the expansion of private industry throughout the state.

The line between the UDC and other development entities can be measured in the extent of powers available directly to it, rather than it needing to go to the city or state for special aid programmes. If, instead of granting powers to an agency, a series of aids are simply made available to a non-profit agency, the result is a body like the Community Preservation Corporation, which also operates in New York City. This is not a local government body, but the creation of a large number of banks, prepared to pool their risks and lend for rehabilitation of housing for moderate income households in areas previously 'redlined'. Its strength is the ability to negotiate advantages like future relief from property tax, cash grants-in-aid, mortgage guarantees, low interest loans, rent support and so on, in return for which the city is able to see development of a type it wishes in a neighbourhood in need of development. The degree of complexity in the funding arrangements can be very great, often stemming, it seems, from the political need to avoid giving straight rental support (because such expenditure would have to compete with other priority spending items, whereas tax foregone does not need to be justified in the same way), even though such support would be economically most efficient in leveraging moderate income housing[13].

The term generally used to describe initiatives such as that of the Community Preservation Corporation, is public-private partnership. Private sector and community leaders, motivated by the links between self interest and community interest, become involved in economic redevelopment in a whole range of ways. Frequently cooperation between these groups and local government leads to the creation of formal development entities, involved in planning, stimulating and carrying out development projects. The projects concerned range from convention centres at one extreme, through community housing projects of various sizes, to the most local projects such as finding a new use for a historic building. Such groups thrive, though many fall by the wayside, in a society where local government seems far more often to delegate reviews and projects to outside groups, and where there seem many interested and qualified people prepared to give their time.

All this is some way from the action of the city as a planning agency or development control authority. But it serves to show how in the American experience, development control merges into any number of functions of the city, and how a myriad range of public and private agencies is often created to deal with the problems of the day. It also reinforces the message that the American planning profession takes a very wide view of its own constituency and the tools available.

Metropolitan planning agencies

There are other planning agencies with rather less influence on development control. During the 1960s, the Federal government began to earmark funds for regional planning agencies. To be eligible for certain specific grants metropolitan areas needed to have one of these agencies in place, and the agency's plans would influence the local application of Federal aid for development purposes. The review power was vested in regional planning commissions directed by councils of local elected officials. In 1983, the power of oversight of the rapidly reducing number of Federal programs was placed with the states. The role of the regional bodies now seems mainly to be as a research resource able to put out reports on a region wide basis on subjects such as population analysis, industrial trends, land use, transportation, water supply, pollution, open space and recreation[14]. Their impact on development control is therefore remote, as my more detailed explanation of their role, in Chapter 8, reveals.

Landmark agencies

Historic preservation commissions, such as New York City's Landmarks Preservation Commission, tend to work independently of the planning process. They designate landmarks, subject only to appeal direct to the Board of Estimate, the City's highest elected body, which rarely overturns designations. Special approval is then needed before development applications may be made to the City Planning Department. The New York regime is regarded as particularly stringent, surprisingly so in this city where the tradition has been to tear down the old and replace it without sentiment, and was under review at the time of writing. But a general national awareness of the value of preserving historic buildings is leading to the establishment of such bodies more widely.

Contrasts with the British process

Planning and zoning boards seem to deal with far fewer cases, but in much more detail than in Britain. In developing areas where there is concern from the neighbourhood about the effects of growth, these boards have to be very careful to exercise their power in a way that reflects that concern. In West Windsor, for example, the number of interested people attending the fortnightly planning board meeting quite often reaches over one hundred. Some development hearings take several hearings to reach an decision, and several sets of hearings may be needed for each stage of the process – for example, for preliminary site plan review, subdivision and zoning approvals. Some would say that this interest in planning can only be healthy. But there is a risk that it could bring the whole system into disrepute.

Attorney Henry Hill of Princeton has appeared before such heated meetings in various municipalities. It is his view that this public participation could become dangerous;

> 'What we are seeing in some towns is a deterioration from orderly legal procedures to a form of anarchistic populism where the will of the majority prevails over the rights of the minority. I feel much more comfortable before a court than before a planning board in a room full of people who have already decided the merits of an application based on the number of units'[15].

He must have had in mind the particularly controversial process in New Jersey for securing a degree of racial and income integration through forcing local governments to zone to ensure the provision of low and moderate income housing in every developing area, a process that has involved the courts a great deal, as we shall see in Chapter 11.

He continued,

> 'The process seems to be breaking down because of the great anti-growth outcry. There is huge and popular anti-development pressure. There is more and more pressure on local government to become anti-growth. Those who get elected are those who express the most antipathy for the developer. The mob is being listened to more and the constitutional tenets less. We're beginning to reach a state of anarchy.'

The situation described may sound familiar to planning inspectors at the more controversial public inquiries in Britain, where the local planning authority has refused permission for a major development and the applicant has exercised his right to appeal to the Secretary of State. The difference in America is that many more proposed developments are subjected to detailed public examination and cross examination, by a board of perhaps 7 relatively less qualified people. Questions by the board are followed by questions from the professionals, and finally by questions from the floor. Everyone who can demonstrate a legitimate interest has a right to be heard. As a result a single planning application might take a whole evening to determine; a major subdivision may require a series of sessions during which various experts will be led by the presiding counsel through the various aspects of the project, partly to get the essential facts onto the record in case there is a later challenge in the courts.

English local authorities' peremptory decision taking may flow from their much greater caseload or it could be that the staff resources enable the review of the proposal by officials to become much more developed; whatever the reason, many more cases are decided on the basis of information on paper and the analysis of the professional planning team. Though the developer may be present at the hearing, the chance that he is able to participate is much less than in the United States where he has the right, indeed the duty to appear, usually represented by his lawyer or planning consultant, or perhaps both. Such representation is important because, should there be a need for a legal challenge, the evidence given and the documents taken in evidence form part of the record; there is no review from scratch such as the English planning inspector would undertake.

Despite the time consuming nature of the American process, the constitutional requirement for a public hearing and 'due process' does seem rather more healthy. I am sure that people would have more respect for a process where they could have their say about proposed development, and where the Parish Council planning chairman could appear to give evidence of the views of the local people. But I am equally sure that with the current incidence of control, British local government cannot afford that luxury.

Conclusions

The single greatest contrast between the American and British organisations of people to take development control decisions is in the scale of *appointed* memberships. Because appointed members of planning and zoning boards are more likely to be formally qualified than their British counterparts, they tend to rely less in the smaller jurisdictions on the advice of planning professionals. Indeed, many authorities rely on contract professionals, and conscious of the expenditure, do not always require them to attend meetings. By contrast, there is always likely to be a legal presence because of the risk of local proceedings being part of a later court action. Cities can support larger planning staffs and projects there are more likely to have complicated impacts on existing structures and communities. The position of professional planning staff seems stronger therefore, although the position is complicated by the political appointments at the top of the organisation (again by contrast with British practice). Generally these features and the division of responsibilities between various boards and agencies make for a more diffuse relationship between the adoption of development control policies and the implementation of those policies.

The wide range of size of planning authorities, for example between suburban municipalities, rural and suburban counties, and major cities, makes it difficult to judge on the effectiveness of particular structures. So much depends on the size of the local government unit. The judgement of many of those involved in the process is that the optimum model is to be found in the county government of Maryland, where there are few municipalities. (The size of these counties is probably somewhere between British counties and districts). Another model that is praised is where a major city and county surrounding it have merged, as in the case of Jacksonville, Florida. Units of this sort of size are likely to extend over different types of land characteristic and use, and can direct growth pressures by special mechanisms within their jurisdiction. They can also afford to employ a full time professional planning team whose recommendations gain enough respect to enable the appointed committees to scrutinise recommendations from a policy viewpoint rather than make policy on the hoof.

Another difference between the British and American organisation is the separation of major actions (rezoning, possibly to facilitate a large development) from minor issues (where a garage cannot be built without a variance due to the shape of the plot). If the problems of defining overlap could be satisfactorily resolved, a two tier development control committee structure in Britain, with responsibilities split between major new developments and smaller matters, might have something to be said for it. But, in practice there are better options, such as delegating minor decisions to the planning director. Because there is usually no public hearing with cross examination of witnesses at a British planning committee meeting and the number of items taken on an agenda is so much higher, the extra time for considering applications created by splitting the planning committee's work would not be all that great, though it might allow more time to consider more major applications.

The possibility of internal appeals is an interesting one, where the governing body reviews the decision reached by the planning board. But there does not seem to be much use made of this power. It is regarded rather cynically by attorneys. Moreover, the British parallel does not lend itself to quite the same mechanism. In the British case the councillors would be reconsidering the decisions of a sub-group of their members, rather than those of a body of outsiders appointed by the mayor.

In the field of urban renewal, just as in Britain, there is a wide range of structures reflecting different legislative thrusts at different times. And just as in Britain, it is crucial for these agencies and city planners to work closely together, and to take an overall and objective view of the resources available. (Some American systems are set up to maximise the input of funds from sources such as the state and federal government, without necessarily considering the most economic combination of measures for the public sector input as a whole). In both countries there is plenty of opportunity for accusations that planners have taken decisions purely to benefit city agencies. The key to minimising these accusations is openness of procedures. American arrangements seem to permit a wider involvement of different enterprise agencies in the planning process – and planners seem to take a wider view of the scope of their responsibilities than their English counterparts. There seems to be a current lack of confidence in planning in England, while American environmental problems in particular give planners a wider agenda and a wider acceptance.

Finally, there is the crucial role of lawyers in the process – whether coordinating the presentation of a development, or ensuring that boards keep within the requirements of the constitution. Regular advice from all quarters is not to embark on a development proposal requiring even a small variance, without engaging a lawyer. This must partly stem from the nature of American bureaucracy and the ease of performing an illegal act without realising it. Be warned for example, that is not permitted to take any photographs from the New Jersey Turnpike, even from the rest areas, or to carry out building work for payment in Princeton without a $75 licence. It is equally easy, given the complexity of zoning ordinances, which vary from place to place, and the difficulty of knowing from case law when constitutional rights might have been breached, to find oneself on the wrong side of the municipality. Given that everything said or done before the planning board might compromise the chances of success in court later, it is not surprising that the lawyers are in charge. It is a pity that planning cannot be more user friendly, but equally we in Britain have a lot to learn – perhaps from cities such as Fort Collins – about how to conduct the local planning process in public. It might force planning committees to delegate more, but I believe that greater public participation in development control decisions would engender a greater respect for the decision process.

NOTES TO CHAPTER 6

1. See for example the Municipal Land Use Law of New Jersey C40:55D-23.

2. Widdicombe Committee Report

3. It did in Neptune Township, New Jersey, early in 1988.

4. Plans, Programs and Policies 1980–1985, published by the New York City Department of City Planning (1985)

5. Her testimony to the committee's meeting on January 12, 1988 was made available to the public attending the meeting.

6. According to Gregory Perkins, BRA, in a meeting with the author

7. Standard State Zoning Enabling Act, published by the US Department of Commerce (1922).

8. The Zoning Board Manual, by Frederick Bair, published by the American Planning Association

9. Koch's Abstention Throws School and Tower Plan into Doubt, in the New York Times, 28th January 1988.

10. See chapter 4 of The Contested City by John Mollenkopf, published by the Princeton University Press (1983).

11. Cities Turn into Entrepreneurs in the New York Times, Saturday April 4, 1987

12. After a record of achievement, a shift in course, by Robert Ponte, in New York Affairs, Vol 8 No 2, 1984.

13. According to Jack Freeman of the Community Preservation Corporation.

14. A summary description of the rise and fall of metropolitan planning is to be found in Chapter 12 of Political Change in the Metropolis, by John J Harrigan published by Little, Brown and Company (1985).

15. Quoted from 'Lawyer Henry Hill lets his foes know they have been in a fight' a profile of one of the more prominent land use lawyers in New Jersey in the Princeton Packet of Tuesday April 12, 1988.

7 The Efficiency, Effectiveness and Enforcement of Control

Introduction

The previous chapters of this report describe some of the tools used to control development, mainly at the local government level, the extent to which those controls impact on and shape development, and some of the structures of administration which have evolved. In this basic review of development control mechanisms it remains to consider how fast or slow the process is, how costly it is for those affected, how effective it is, and the extent that its effectiveness is driven by enforcement action.

The British context

In Britain over the past decade, the efficiency of the planning process has become an increasingly important issue. As part of a drive to make local government more accountable and more business-like, data relating to the speed of decision are collected and published quarterly by the Department of the Environment[1]. The Audit Inspectorate, responsible for most of the auditing of local government, published a report to demonstrate ways of improving the efficiency of the development control process without unduly increasing costs[2]. The National Development Control Forum published guidelines, launched by a Government Minister, to help stimulate an interest in efficiency on the part of elected council members[3]. The Government carried out efficiency scrutinies of the planning appeals process for which it is responsible[4]. And in other aspects of policy, such as the preparation of development plans, a crucial factor has been the need to make the process faster and more responsive to changes in the development climate. 'Streamlining' the system has meant reducing overlapping tiers of control and increasing the extent of additions to dwellings that can be carried out without the need for planning permission.

Equivalent action in the United States

'Streamlining Land Use Regulation' was the title of a guidebook for American local government prepared jointly by the American Planning Association and Urban Land Institute for the United States Department of Housing and Urban Development[5]. It contains a great deal of useful guidance on how to improve the efficiency of the permit processes, including tips on how to deregulate, of which more later. But nowhere does it contain any *facts* about the current speed of the process, even in the authorities included in the case studies. Very rarely is any information given that local governments might use as an objective measure of their own performance.

At the state level too there seems little interest in the speed of the local process. Generally, it is the state that would legislate, if legislation were necessary to tighten up the timetables for decision. California, for example, has legislated to impose time limits on local government consideration of development permits[6] in the case where an environmental impact report is required. New Jersey imposes limits in its Municipal Land Use Law[7], requiring for example, major subdivisions to be approved or otherwise within 45 days of the application being complete, or such longer period as may be agreed with the applicant. But in practice such time limits are illusory. For a start, it is open to the local government to ask for extra information, as a way of extending the time available for considering what its response to the application ought to be. Second, and more important, no applicant wishes to upset a local government that may be on the verge of approving the application; local government requests for extension are therefore invariably accepted. An applicant who refused such a request would promptly receive a 'without prejudice' refusal, and challenging that in the courts would take far longer than simply acceding to the original request. No state can pass a law stringent enough to force early decisions without prejudging the proper consideration of the most complicated proposals. Delay may be cited in many court challenges, but delay alone never seems at the root of any challenge.

Against this background, one view is that a local government unit needing development to improve its financial position will be very keen to speed the process as much as possible. On the other hand, local governments in areas under pressure from developers will not be so quick, but developers will be more patient given the likely scale of profits that attracted them there in the first place. In this way the planning stages of a project in Newark, New Jersey, ought to be very much shorter than those of projects in Princeton, where residents believe that quite enough development has already taken place. I was not able to collect sufficient data to test this hypothesis.

Information that gives clues about the performance of the planning system seems to appear rarely. I did find information about Vermont's Environmental Boards which review all major development proposals (see Chapter 8 below). In a recent review[8] of the effectiveness of these boards between 1970 and 1983, the time taken to issue those permits issued between 1 January and 31 March 1983 was measured. The results show that 26% of permits were issued within 30 days, 43% within 60 days, 70% within 90 days and 83% within 120 days. But it should be borne in mind that this is a measure of the *additional* time needed for the state input in a special land use decision process catching only the most significant developments for review. Much more time would have to be first spent dealing with the local government concerned.

Similar information on handling times does also appear, albeit rarely, in some local government publications. A request for any relevant reports to around 120 local government units, some selected because they had been associated with some initiative designed to improve efficient administration, drew only a handful of documents with data about time taken. The most impressive information came from the Seattle Department of Construction and Land Use. They had set themselves clear management targets for deciding proportions of their workload–30% in less than 2 months, 50% in less than three and so on. Performance against these targets was measured both overall, and in relation to different types of permit. A second report– called a permit process update–indicated current average turnaround times for different types of permit, achievements in the previous month, as well as the availability of officials for appointments to discuss development. Another type of document set out all the various actions needed by projects of different types, plotted on time lines. In this way the developer could see where progress had been made on his application and judge how much longer a permit would take. A cynic would comment on the management consultancy cost behind all this material; but given the structure of the permitting system, set out in Figure 7.1, perhaps it is important for that City to manage its affairs well.

Los Angeles City also produced a great deal of management information, including measures such as man hours per case, but the average time taken for each type of permit did not feature. Atlanta provided a comprehensive report, with clues about the time cases take, and Tulsa gave some turn round time information in one report. But, in general, time taken featured less as a performance indicator than numbers of cases, proportions approved, degree of concurrence between officials and elected members, caseload in hand and so on.

The results of a pilot survey

In order to try to establish more information about decision taking times, I approached just over 100 local government units with a request for data on handling times. Of those approached, about half were the 50 largest cities and about half were smaller counties and cities who had previously expressed an interest in more efficient development control procedures. I asked each local government to complete a pro forma setting out decision times for different types of permitting processes. I was very pleased to receive information from a high proportion of those I approached; the response rate was greater than I had expected. The responses are summarised in Figure 7.2. It is important to bear in mind that, despite my attempts to ensure uniformity of input data, there is no doubt that different local governments have calculated their estimates in different ways. Some of the reported times were in round months, which led me to suspect that these were the type of estimated times that officials might give the public in response to enquiries about processing times rather than precise measurements; others were clearly times calculated by taking the number of case weeks and dividing by the number of cases, as I had requested (I preferred not to suggest the use of medians, probably a better comparative measure than arithmetic means, but the one less likely to be used by local governments).

Figure 7.2 sets out the results of the survey; the main features are:

> **Rezoning requests:** to complete action on a rezoning request generally takes between 10 and 17 weeks in most big cities, with a few such as Los Angeles, Seattle and San Francisco taking over twice as long. In the smaller local governments the time spread is narrower, at between 10 and 14 weeks.

> **Variances:** by contrast with rezoning, the big cities are rather quicker, with most decisions averaging between 4 and 6 weeks. The smaller units reported average handling times mainly in the 4 to 9 week range. From the odd notes of explanation, it would appear that the main reason for this difference is the need for a public hearing, which seems to add about 4 or 5 weeks. Perhaps there is a greater propensity to require public hearings in the smaller local government units?

> **Conditional and special use permits (including planned unit developments):** in this category there seems to be no significant difference between the speed of large and small local governments. There is also a rather wide band covered by the average times – between 5 and 14 weeks. The reason for this may be the bringing together in this category of relatively straightforward permitting (for example, where a city decides to approve particular changes of use on the basis of an

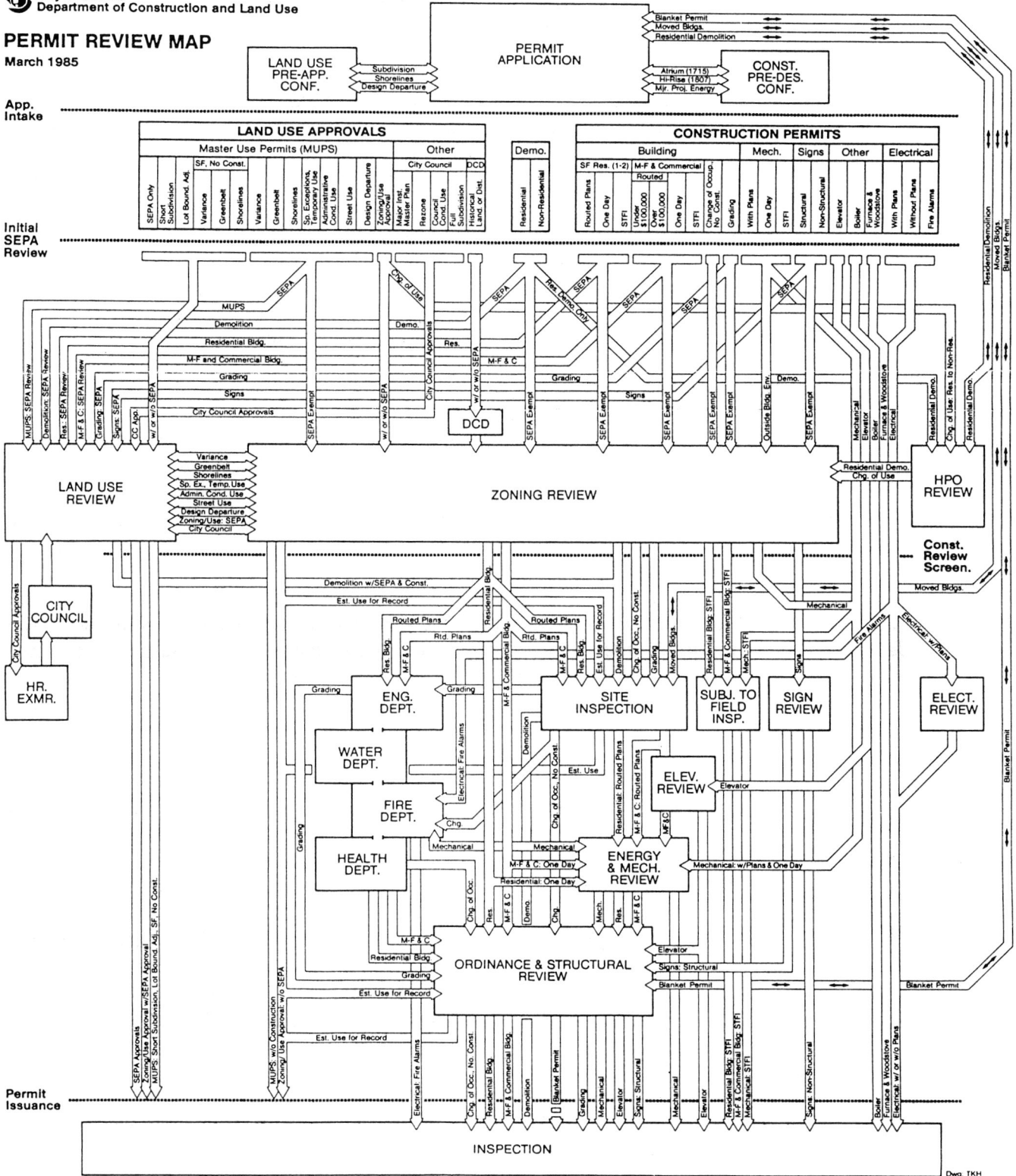

Figure 7.1 A diagrammatic representation of the permitting procedures operating in the City of Seattle

individual application) and planned unit developments. The latter are akin to large subdivision permits and can be expected to take much longer.

Major subdivisions: here too there was a very wide variation, depending on the point at which the substantial review of major projects occurs. The point is that some local governments can regard the subdivision approval as a relative formality, given the work that has already been done on a rezoning or a PUD application.

The data would need more thorough checking for consistency before any conclusions were drawn about the relationship between permitting times and the need for development. However, generally the California governments seem the slowest, and that is where there is some of the greatest resistance to growth, the most complex regulation, and the most frequent recourse to law.

Reasons for accelerating the regulatory process

Local governments need to be concerned about the time that the development control process takes for a whole series of reasons. At its most basic, delayed decisions mean that development is not coming on stream as fast as could otherwise be the case. Such delays are therefore likely to create a shortage of accommodation of the type delayed, and will also damage the local development industry. Shortages often mean price increases, which are the last thing many communities want in their search for affordable housing on the one hand, and to remain attractive for investment on the other. Some of the savings, and hence unit cost reductions, that were made in some demonstration affordable housing projects are described later in this Chapter. Delayed project competition also means delayed local tax revenue increases.

It may be that the time taken in reviewing projects in one area as compared with another itself influences developers' location choices. Jersey City sits just across the Hudson River from some of the most expensive offices in the world, and yet it is only recently that the attractions of developing there have led to a boom in construction. One major factor in Jersey City's favour is that development reviews there take about half the time of those of similar sized projects across the water that require environmental impact reviews because they cannot be accommodated within the as-of-right zoning ordinance. Mayor Koch of New York City has had to conclude some major agreements granting tax concessions to certain firms considering moving from his city. It may be that rents are higher than they need to be because environmental impact reviews take a long time, not so much when the formal review is under way, but in the informal stages when the planning department and developer must accumulate and analyse all the necessary information. Without giving away tax concessions, certain cities might be able to increase their rate of inner city regeneration simply by offering and publicising a speedy approval process. It remains to be seen whether President Bush and his Secretary for Housing and Urban Development, Mr Jack Kemp, will grant exemptions from planning regulations in their enterprise zone legislation – as the British zones do.

There may be a further incentive to measure delays, flowing out of one of the 1987 trio of US Supreme Court cases. In considering whether compensation should be payable to someone deprived of the use of their land by virtue of a temporary zoning moratorium, Chief Justice Rehnquist conceded that 'normal delays . . . and the like' would not constitute periods for which

Figure 7.2 Development control data for a sample of local government units: speed of permitting measured by time from application to decision for different types of permit

local government	average time to process rezoning requests	average time to process zoning and use variances	average time to process conditional and special use applications	average time to process major subdivision proposals
Atlanta Ga	11 weeks	6 weeks	11 weeks	2–3 weeks[1]
Charlotte NC	13–52 weeks	4/5 weeks		9–18 weeks
Chicago Il	9–13 weeks	9 weeks	9–13 weeks	19–23 weeks
Cincinnati Oh	24 weeks		5–12 weeks[2]	6–8 weeks
Columbus Oh	21 weeks	14 weeks	8 weeks	
Dallas Tex	17 weeks	4–6 weeks	21 weeks	4 weeks
Fort Worth Tex	9 weeks	4 weeks	13 weeks	
Indianapolis Ind	17 weeks	9–13 weeks	13–17 weeks	4–9 weeks
Los Angeles Ca	39 weeks	11 weeks	11 weeks	26 weeks
Louisville Ky	16–24 weeks	4 weeks	6–8 weeks	8 weeks min.
Milwaukee Wis	11 weeks	7 weeks	10 weeks	
Nashville Ten	10 weeks		4–6 weeks	7 weeks
New Orleans La	14 weeks	4 weeks	13 weeks	4 weeks
Norfolk Va	17 weeks	9 weeks	13 weeks	1.5 weeks
Omaha Neb	13 weeks min.	2/3 weeks	4/5 weeks	17 weeks
Phoenix Az	15 weeks	3 weeks	15 weeks	
Pittsburgh Pa	20 weeks	5 weeks	18 weeks	3–7 weeks[3]
Portland Or	10 weeks	6 weeks	10 weeks	10 weeks
Rochester NY	12 weeks	6 weeks	8 weeks	12 weeks
San Francisco Ca	26 weeks plus[4]	13 weeks	13 weeks	
Seattle Wa	30–39 weeks	9–13 weeks	13 weeks	
Tampa Fl	10 weeks	6 weeks	10 weeks	26 weeks
Tulsa Ok	12 weeks	5 weeks	5 weeks[5]	24 weeks[6]
Bozeman Ma	6 weeks	3 weeks	6 weeks	6 weeks
Brooklyn Park Mn	10 weeks	7 weeks	7 weeks	12 weeks
Clearwater Fl	14 weeks	25 weeks	5.5 weeks	11 weeks
Covina Ca	15 weeks	9 weeks	3–7 weeks	23 weeks
Culpeper Va	10 weeks	4 weeks	7–8 weeks	20 weeks
El Paso Co Co	13 weels plus	9 weeks	3–9 weeks plus	9 weeks plus
Lane Co Or	34 weeks	7 weeks	8 weeks	17 weeks
McHenry Co Il	11.3 weeks	11.6 weeks	12 weeks	22–26 weeks
Mequon Wis	9 weeks	4 weeks	6–13 weeks[7]	13 weeks
Middletown Oh	12 weeks	3 weeks	9 weeks	12 weeks
Missoula Ma	12 weeks	12 weeks	1 week	4 weeks
Multnomah Co Or	13–17 weeks	4–13 weeks[8]	13–17 weeks	13–17 weeks
Pueblo Co	13 weeks	4 weeks	4 weeks	13 weeks
Redwood City Ca	13 weeks	4 weeks	4–17 weeks[9]	4–9 weeks
Santa Clara Co Ca	14 weeks	10 weeks	13 weeks	13 weeks
Skokie Il	10–12 weeks	6–8 weeks	12–16 weeks	10–12 weeks
Sweetwater Co Wy	8 weeks	8 weeks	8 weeks	26 weeks
Tippecanoe Co Ind	10.3 weeks	5 weeks	6.1 weeks	
Weld Co Co	12 weeks	5 weeks	11 weeks	8 weeks

1 Special administrative permits for subdivisions require no public hearings.
2 Conditional use applications take 12 weeks, while special use permits and PUD applications take 30–35 days
3 Depending on whether a hearing is needed
4 A further 12 months needed for cases requiring an environmental impact report.
5 12 weeks for PUD permits
6 Of this only 4–6 weeks are staff time; much of the remainder depends on the developer and his engineer.
7 Conditional use permits take 1.5 months and Planned Unit Developments 3 months.
8 Depending on whether a hearing is necessary.
9 One month for use permits and 3–4 months for planned developments.

compensation would be due. But this statement raises questions whether, for example, 'normal' should relate to the time normally taken by the particular local government to progress the action in question, or whether normality might be measured by the performance of the average authority acting in a reasonable way. Whatever approach is adopted, in the future there seems likely to be more examination of the time local governments take to carry out their various development control functions. Certainly there is evidence that courts are being asked to examine whether or not delays were reasonable; in one California case the court examined evidence about the time taken by a decision before concluding that there was no showing that the interim delay was anything more than the normal period of time for government decision making.

For purposes of sound management, for reasons of attracting industry or keeping down affordable house prices, or to avoid problems of regulatory takings, it seems that local government will need to do more to measure and monitor its processing efficiency. It may be that the American Planning Association should be thinking about gathering some hard and comparable facts in this rather unsexy area.

That is not to say that no-one is pressing to improve the efficiency of the administrative process. For example, at the 1988 American Planning Association convention in San Antonio, Texas a firm of planning consultants presented the contents of a report they had prepared at the request of the Oregon Department of Land Conservation and Development[9]. The document and the conference session were very well presented, using a questionnaire to identify the areas of administration that individual local government officials might need to review (remember that the 10,000 development control systems make it necessary to start from a point of generality), and going on to identify the sorts of consideration that might be given to various stages of the permitting process. Other papers have been published by the International City Management Association[10] and the National League of Cities[11].

The most comprehensive document came about through a Housing and Urban Development Department sponsored research project conducted by American Planning Association staff. The results were published as *Streamlining Land Use Regulation*[12]. The authors identified the reasons for streamlining as:

- to contain rising administrative costs, especially in the light of new constraints on local government expenditure; not all application fees meet the costs of processing applications;

- to control one of the factors that increase the price of new housing; in other words a more efficient and predictable process means lower overheads for the developer;

- to save time for public officials (allowing more time for constructive comprehensive planning!);

- to encourage the kind of development the community wants (by giving it a competitive edge over neighbouring slower local governments);

- to establish better relationships between applicants and reviewers (because delay will no longer be an antagonism);

- to structure citizen participation (by making it more timely);

- to make the regulatory system more accountable (reducing the scope for back room deals); and,

- to assure fairness and due process (in a simpler system it is easier to see what should happen).

Many of these reasons would apply to British local governments too, except that much of the regulatory structure is laid down in Britain by central Government. It is therefore interesting to review some of the potential administrative improvements identified in this and other documents.

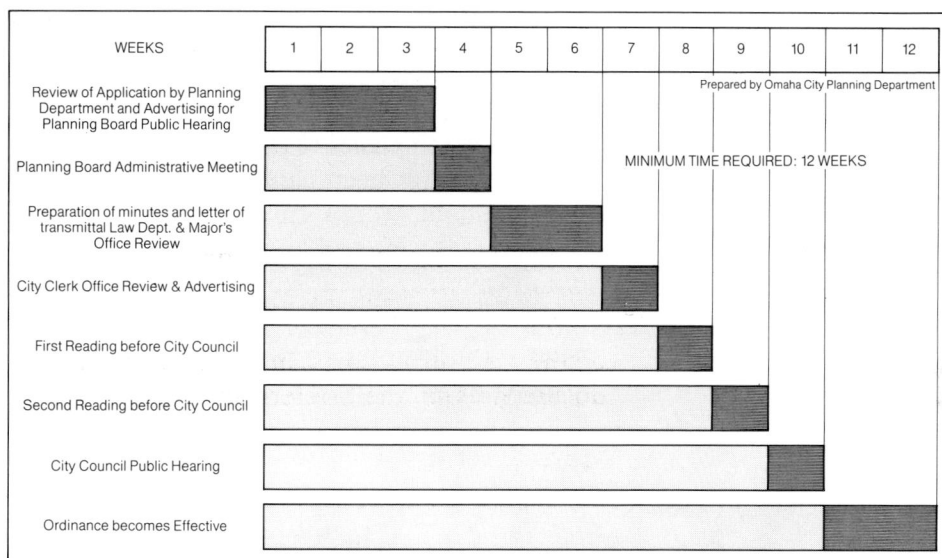

Figure 7.3 Minimum timetable for rezoning applications; Omaha City Planning Department

Streamlining techniques

The HUD sponsored research identified a range of techniques that different local governments had used in order to streamline their development control processes. I have reproduced the headings here and explained what each might involve. Many have equivalents in the British development control process, but I suppose that only serves to demonstrate the universality of management improvement techniques.

(i) Use of handouts, manuals, registers, and other written materials

(ii) Improvement of application forms

These help the efficiency of the process by explaining to the potential applicant or developer in simple terms the procedures involved in obtaining the necessary permits, with checklists of the information that will be required at each stage, the timescale within which a decision will be taken, the fee schedules, the relevant legal documents and ordinances, and the terms used. This kind of information is especially important in the United States because the large number of local governments, each with their own permitting procedures and ordinances, gives rise to even more confusion. In Britain, at least the need for planning permission and the application fees are uniform, but there are still local variations in procedure, and the need to explain the coverage of local plans and other locally adopted policies. One fascinating recommendation in *Streamlining Land Use Regu-*

lation promotes the use of design manuals, as something for which developers and consultants frequently lobby. The idea is that an up-to-date manual would offer design principles and examples that embody the standards used by the officials reviewing the projects. Aesthetic control through the consideration of planning applications is not encouraged by the British government[13], except in special areas such as conservation areas; but there are other aspects of land use design which local councillors will take into account in reaching their decisions, and it seems fair to explain the principles to the developer at the outset and thus avoid nugatory preparatory work. Such documents can also help to contain maverick decisions, by providing a source of guidance to decision takers and constraining unpredictable actions by councillors.

(iii) Holding informal pre-application meetings

Some British local authorities have been reported as being cool towards the idea of discussing proposed developments (even to the extent of charging for advice) before a concrete proposal is submitted. That attitude is similar to one in some places in America where the staff are not keen on discussions before a fee has been paid to help cover the consultation. This is especially understandable for a small community because it costs money to bring their planning consultant in for such a meeting. At the other extreme, some American local governments have made pre-application meetings compulsory. In general the American attitude to pre-application meetings seems more positive than the British, but that may simply reflect the more positive attitude towards development generally.

The Uniform Land Use Review Procedures in New York City require pre-certification of plans as a way of promoting an orderly review process. During the period before a formal application, the intention is that plans can be examined to ensure completeness. A 1986 report[14] suggested that this technical phase had evolved into a negotiating process that delayed construction and increased costs. The phase was also controversial because the community boards, which have a statutory right to comment on applications, dislike the shaping of the application by the City before they are shown the plans. Nevertheless, the Department of City Planning insisted that the pre-certification phase allowed the controversial aspects of projects to be reviewed and modified, thus shortening subsequent formal reviews, and enhancing development.

(iv) Reorganisation or revision of ordinances

Where local governments are devising their own legal ordinances and procedural requirements, for example, to define the relationships between zoning and subdivision control, there is a great responsibility to ensure that the resulting documents are clear, correct and drawn up in a way to deliver a reasonably efficient outcome. In Britain, the local responsibilities in these matters are fewer. But as district councils obtain more local responsibility for planning, there will be an increasing responsibility for clear presentation of local policies.

(v) Central computer applications

(vi) Use of computer in some phase of processing

I need not embellish this. British local government has access to different types of systems, from the relatively home grown product at Stafford, to the sophistication of such systems as Wakefield's planning and building regulations control.

(vii) Reorganisation of central regulating departments	Again, reorganisations of departments to ensure proper accountability and motivation are as frequent in Britain as in the States.
(viii) Use of permit expeditors or ombudsmen	Some cities that are particularly interested in attracting new commercial and industrial development, or in ensuring that adequate housing provision is made for low and moderate income households, have appointed 'permit expeditors'. Their task is to take personal responsibility for ensuring that particular projects move through the administrative process with the minimum of delay; the aim is that they should be seen as individually accountable by the developer. As with the simplification of ordinances, there may be a greater need for such an official in American local governments which do rather more administrative permitting than British local authorities. This is the sort of trouble shooting role that an economic development officer might undertake for relatively few projects, rather than a way of making the process as a whole more efficient.
(ix) Preparation of master environmental impact reports	Many states now require some environmental impact assessment of major development projects, and these can be quite time consuming, as some of the data in Chapter 5 showed. One way of overcoming these delays, employed by Sacramento County in California, is to create a series of overlay zones for each of which an individual series of planned unit development standards are drafted. In other words the County act in advance of the developer to create zones in which rather more specific requirements or performance standards are laid down. These standards are designed in such a way as to minimise any subsequent requirement for an environmental impact review. In addition, once the overlay zone has been created (with the necessary public consultation), it is possible to delegate decisions to officials and to avoid public hearings. The English equivalent would be to delegate authority to the planning officer to decide all applications in accordance with a detailed local plan for the areas of the district most likely to be developed.
(x) Elimination of duplicate hearings	In practice, very few planning applications in England are the subject of a public hearing. Most local authority decisions are taken on the basis of paper applications and reports by officials. Even at the planning appeals stage, four out of every five appeals can be decided on the basis of written representations and a site visit. The British reader may therefore be forgiven for raising an eyebrow at the following paragraph, quoted from *Streamlining Land Use Regulation*:

> 'The typical sequence of land review as envisioned under most state laws was supposed to entail one, or at most two, public hearings per project. But where an applicant must obtain a change in zoning before submitting a subdivision approval, this can add another two public hearings, and perhaps upwards of four in states such as California, which require corresponding plan amendments. In these cases it is not unusual for even relatively uncontroversial projects to go through three to seven hearings. The separate review procedures of zoning changes, subdivision approvals etc were designed as closed systems, complete in themselves with all the elements of due process. When they are added together, however, the composite process becomes redundant.'

(xi) Use of joint staff project review committees	Such committees might bring together not only the planners, but also the fire officer, the water and highways engineers, and those responsible for the building code. This reflects the more fragmented rules which tend to have evolved in most American local governments, and the need for co-ordination if developers are not to be totally frustrated.
(xii) Use of a hearings official	Hearings officials or examiners are professional planners or lawyers appointed to conduct quasi-judicial hearings on minor rezonings, variances, subdivisions, special use permits and appeals against administrative decisions. They write up findings based on the record of the hearing and make either a final decision, or a recommendation to a legislative body[15]. They are the Planning Inspectors of America, and their use to take local decisions is interesting for two reasons. First, it demonstrates the feasibility of settling land use conflicts at a local level; in other words, a local alternative to the planning appeal for less significant developments. Second, it has proved in America to be a way of removing the more irrelevant and overtly political considerations from land use decision making. (I shall not easily forget the questions put by the West Windsor Planning Board, at one of a number of meetings when a particularly large development of some 2000 houses was under consideration. The applicant's consultants were questioned on whether the drainage pools would be stocked with fish, on whether flower boxes would be installed on the senior citizens' dwellings, and on whether the sign at the entrance (proposed to be 10 feet by 3 feet at ground level) could be permitted in the light of the local ordinances).
	I have detailed later in this chapter the advantages and disadvantages claimed for the American hearings officer.
(xiii) Simultaneous processing or review of permits	These are obvious reforms; the management consultant should always look for things that can be done in parallel instead of in series, and for things that do not need to be done at all.
(xiv) Elimination or consolidation of review steps	
(xv) 'Fast track' processing of minor applications	The key decision with this type of initiative is to identify the right cases for fast tracking. Often the best dividing line is between those requiring a public hearing and those not; in British terms, between those delegated to the planning officer and those that need to go to the planning committee. There is always the counter-question; why slow track big developments?
(xvi) Institution of more project review deadlines	I commented on the effect of these earlier in this chapter.
(xvii) Delegation of decision making authority to lower levels in administration	This is also a sound technique, provided that the political masters are prepared to trust the officials they employ, and do not take back the power at the first sign of controversy.

(xviii) Strengthening or revising of appeals process	The reason for this is apparently to increase fair play, by knowing when unfair play can be appealed against.
(xix) Holding more frequent commission meetings to improve regulatory process	English planning authorities are frequently urged to do this.
(xx) Improvement of citizen input procedures	The measures suggested under this heading are improving public hearing procedures, and encouraging the developer to hold informal meetings with neighbourhood groups. Despite there being one tenth as many discretionary decisions as in Britain, some being duplicate decisions on the same proposal but for different permits, there seem to be quite as many hours, if not more, spent in public meetings of American planning boards and similar bodies. The legal obligations of procedural due process require a fair public hearing with a right to be heard. Some courts have supplemented this by requiring a written record of the proceedings, written decisions based upon written findings of fact, and the right of rebuttal and cross examination. In practice this can make planning board meetings very tedious indeed. Witnesses are sworn in, plans and documents are numbered and certified by the clerk to the meeting, and evidence is recorded on tape in case the written record is questioned later. Opening statements by the attorney representing the developer are followed by supporting evidence from the planning and engineering experts. They can then be questioned by the members of the board, then the staff of the local government, and finally by the members of public present. This last stage can be particularly time consuming; hence the recommendation to find ways of improving this process, and perhaps cutting it short by arranging a forum for the developer and local community to settle some of their differences before the application comes before the local government. In Britain, at the local authority stage as distinct from the planning appeal stage, the public have very little say, and indeed there is frequently expressed dissatisfaction about the extent to which the public can influence the development control process. The American experience points very clearly to the way in which even the best directed public input can slow the process by a considerable amount.
(xxi) Revamping of record keeping procedures	This is the final component of administrative improvements through better information dissemination, improved application forms, and use of computers.
(xxii) Abolition of planning commission or zoning board *(xxiii) Dual planning commissions*	Many local governments believe that they have instituted innovative arrangements for decision taking. In practice there is a wide range of arrangements that could be made, depending also on the structure of permit requirements set up by the local government concerned. One significant aim is frequently to separate the comprehensive planning role from the tasks of deciding small development proposals, otherwise the latter swamp the former at the expense of longer term planning. In the local political climate, with different groups of elected or appointed officials vying with each other to influence development in their area, tension and dissatisfaction are likely. Changes in committee structure may be possible under particular states' legislation, but in practice there does not seem to be any general theme of change that might interest the British reader.

Abolishing the planning commission or zoning board can bring more single mindedness to decision taking, given the involvement of fewer individuals, and thus more predictability for the applicant. On the other hand, splitting a planning commission into a dual commission, with one set of members handling casework and the other set long term planning, can ensure that the permitting process is not held up for other agenda items. I sense that there is no right answer, or perhaps as many right answers as there are local governments.

(xxiv) Staff training programs

(xxv) Public education programs

(xxvi) Training for commissioners

In Britain, just as in America, it is probably the first of these that is best provided for. The American Planning Association is very keen to recruit commissioners as members, and organises, for example, a specially designed programme for them at its annual conference. It is easy to neglect training and education programmes, and there is similar scope in Britain for more work by local authorities to convey to the public the legitimate role of the development control process, which seems almost narrower than is potentially the case in America. It is understandable that local government should be unwilling to explain the limitations of their powers, and yet it might make it easier for the public to understand why decisions are taken in a particular way.

Figure 7.4 Drive-in permitting in Jacksonville, Florida; in practice nothing complicated can be transacted, but in a country of drive-ins and take-aways, there had to be an example of a drive-in planning permission somewhere!

(xxvii) Use of consultants to study procedural reforms

(xxviii) Formation of a task force or committee to implement reforms

In other words it is not enough to read all the foregoing points; action has to follow.

Hearings officials or examiners

I suggested above that the growing tendency to appoint hearings examiners was interesting to the British reader for two reasons–because it pointed to the possibilities of local government being able to handle its own minor planning appeals caseload, and because it had proved a way of reducing the irrelevant and political inputs to planning decisions taken by elected councillors or political appointees. Hearings examiners are professional planners or lawyers appointed to conduct quasi-judicial hearings on minor rezonings, variances, subdivisions, special use permits and appeals against administrative decisions. Following the hearings they write up findings based on the record of the hearing and make either a final decision, or a recommendation to a legislative body. They are used especially in Maryland, California, Oregon and Washington states, generally replacing a hearing of the planning or zoning board that would otherwise have been needed, and sometimes acting instead of the local government itself in deciding appeals.

Streamlining Land Use Regulation identifies a number of benefits of the appointment of hearings examiners:

(i) the process becomes more relaxed and informal for individual applicants, who previously would have appeared before a board of 7 or 9 appointed commissioners. This also means that small applicants do not need to be represented.

(ii) queuing time is cut for both large and small developments, because small applications that no longer need to go to the planning commission do not hold up those for larger developments which still do.

(iii) the procedural requirements are complied with more efficiently by an appointed expert than by a lay board.

(iv) the planning commission or board has more time to devote to policy formulation and planning, work which in the long term should reduce still further the case load of variances and rezoning requests.

(v) the quality of staff input to the decision making body improves, and this reduces the likelihood of successful local challenge.

(vi) staff time and cost savings can be achieved. This is because simple cases can be despatched within about 12 to 15 minutes.

(vii) often, the hearing examiner can be employed on an hourly basis, so allowing adjustment of availability to match a varying caseload. Alternatively, a staff member might be appointed (akin to the delegation of decisions to planning officers in Britain), but that course does give rise to constitutional propriety problems.

The major disadvantages occur if the hearing examiner's decisions are so clearly out of line with the local government that decisions become subject to further routine appeals, and if too much power is seen to have been placed in the hands of one individual. The authors of the book mentioned above stress that the hearing examiner's role must be limited to applying policy, and not making it.

In some jurisdictions hearings examiners are carrying out the same role as the local government planning officer in Britain might do under delegated powers, albeit without the constitutional right of the individuals and others affected to be heard. Perhaps it is the absence of that right which enables a typical British planning committee to take so many decisions at a sitting. Clearly delegation can bring some of the benefits outlined above, provided that the terms of the delegation and the policy background are clear. In this context, delegation may become easier as the local plan coverage at district council level expands, bringing relevant policies to bear on more decisions. The American experience is that planning decisions are more likely to be limited to legitimate considerations when taken by an individual than by a group of 7 or 9 people; what can that tell those who sit on British planning committees of tens of members?

But the promise of the hearings examiner for the British system might be at the point where considerably more time per case is spent – at the appeal stage. Perhaps there is scope for reducing the large number of appeals on relatively small development proposals by legislating to provide alternative systems, either:

- a hearings officer appointed by a local authority to review their decisions that were challenged, and to decide or recommend on the basis of the facts elicited at a 'small claims court' type hearing; or,

- the statutory appeal decided by the Secretary of State.

Both queuing time and administrative fees could encourage the small development into the local process. Alternatively, all appeals might go into the local 'pot' unless called in by the Secretary of State. The hearings examiner might be scheduled to appear at the local authority on a regular timetable dovetailed with that of the planning committee for maximum efficiency. The American experience with hearings examiners suggests that the idea of despatching planning appeals through informal hearings on a sessional basis, floated in an efficiency scrutiny for the Department of the Environment[16], might be worth reconsidering.

Efficiency in New York City

In the paragraph above outlining various initiatives for increased efficiency, the use of permit expeditors was mentioned as being useful for applications of a particular economic type. In New York City in 1986, Mayor Koch set up an Office of Housing Coordination, intended to speed socially desirable housing projects through the City's complicated regulatory system. The Office is a special kind of permit expeditor. Its aims include:

- coordinating approvals for projects in the City's own housing program;

- coordinating approvals for a 3,000 unit program that developers are implementing on a non-profit basis for the City, itself a novel idea;

- streamlining the construction process by implementing a whole catalogue of measures recommended by two of the Mayor's committees.

The Office has only 6 staff for a city covering 7 million residents and quite a few homeless people. In an interview with the New York Times[17], the Director of the Office said that their best results had been obtained by bringing development problems to the attention of high ranking staff in the regulatory agencies concerned, or by bringing together representatives from several agencies that have conflicting requirements. In implementing reforms, the role of the Office is to ensure that the appropriate decision makers consider the various regulations and act on the legislative issues involved. In this area no big successes have been achieved, but many small processing improvements have been implemented.

The Deputy Director of the Office, Frances Pandolfi, explained to me[18] that only major projects and those involving historic landmarks suffered great difficulties with the land use review process in the city. Most normal projects were held up by the excessive bureaucracy in the Department of Buildings and other agencies that monitor the construction of buildings. One of the reports that led to the creation of the Office of Housing Coordination was the Report of the Mayor's Blue Ribbon Panel on Building Plan Examination and Review[19].

That report identified a whole raft of problems in the plan approval process. While it is a digression from the main subject of this report, the reader may find some of the practices of interest. The burden of regulation at home may not seem so great after all, after reading these examples:

(i) Except in Manhattan, application forms for different purposes (300 different forms are available, although only some 120 are active) are available at different, unlabelled windows in different offices, and often come without sufficient instructions about completion and processing.

(ii) Once a plans examiner is assigned to a project, he remains with it, and development can be held up by his summer holidays.

(iii) After a permit to start construction is issued, permits are also required for the separate stages of construction (excavation, foundation, building construction), for connection to water and sewer systems, for the sidewalk installation, for placing materials or equipment on the street, for opening the street for the installation of services, for installing fuel burning equipment, and for the installation of fire safety systems. Then comes the Certificate of Occupancy process, requiring notarized application forms, inspection by a construction inspector who then alerts other inspectors who must look at plumbing, elevators, fire protection devices and the sidewalks. Any objections lead to modifications that have to be approved by the functional inspector concerned.

(iv) Applicants have to submit any materials or equipment, proposed for use but not on the Buildings Department file, to independent laboratories for testing at their own expense.

(v) Installing a sidewalk that is formed of anything other than poured concrete is particularly demanding, involving permits from both the city

Art Commission and the Department of Transportation demonstrating approval of both materials and design, and a maintenance declaration to bind the owner to maintain the sidewalk in perpetuity.

(vi) Before a start on each construction phase the developer must obtain a certificate of adequate insurance from the Bureau of Highways and submit it to the Buildings Department. To get the certificate each time requires the posting of a street obstruction bond, proof of compliance with the State laws on workers compensation and disability benefits, and the filing of a general liability insurance policy.

No doubt some of the practices here will have been simplified as a result of the efforts of the Bureau of Housing Coordination. No doubt too, New York City is the place to see regulation at its most complicated. It is the most complicated and fascinating of cities.

But it is not only in New York that complaints of delays and inefficiency in the building inspection operation are to be heard. Such delays can sometimes be seen to flow from the small scale and diffuse nature of much of the local government operation. Small municipalities are often not large enough to warrant employment of building inspectors qualified to approve the larger development projects. They rely on state agencies to carry out what amounts to a building regulations approval process together with the necessary inspections. But, state agencies are notorious for delay, and municipalities anxious not to discourage development come under pressure to employ better qualified staff at greater cost in order to satisfy the local development community. Delays not only cost the developer, they also seem to arise during construction, leading to environmental unsightliness. In New Jersey, the State will allow a municipality to review its own 'class 1' projects, only if all the staff involved in the building inspection department are trained to a prescribed high standard[20]. Municipalities must thus pay a substantial financial price to remove the State from the review process, a price that the builder will have to pay through increased inspection fees for a more rapid service.

The costs of control

Delays lead to costs to developers and to the community. It has proved difficult to track down generalised data about delays themselves, or to discover any research attempting to quantify the costs of delay to developers or to the national economy. There seems to be no equivalent to the work of Paul Cheshire and Charles Leven of the University of Reading Department of Economics[21]. They suggested that the costs of delay imposed by the British process of development control amounted to about £300m in 1980 prices. In the United States, the question of whether society can afford the costs of delay does not appear to have been approached in any similar analytic way. Yet, it is a matter for concern that soft costs (construction financing, marketing, overheads and profit) have risen to 30 per cent, expressed as a proportion of total development costs, an increase of 50 per cent over 15 years. Some of this must be attributable to the increasing costs of delay in the process.

Many policy makers and housing advocates are concerned about a shortage of affordable housing (see Chapter 11 below). If delay leads to fewer completions, at a time of demand that will lead to higher price rises than would otherwise occur. So delay adds to the costs of development and rations output to the disadvantage of the less well off.

Material obtained from the National Association of Home Builders[22] does demonstrate concern about the administrative and processing costs of different aspects of affordable housing development. In a series of case studies financed jointly with the Federal Government agency concerned, the cost savings accruing from such initiatives were identified. Not all contained cost savings attributable to the development control procedures. But, the following examples give the unit cost savings that it was estimated could be achieved by various specified improvements in procedure:

Local government	cost saving per unit	Measure identified
Valdost Ga	$300	Elimination of the need for a separate city government review
Phoenix Az	$2000	Giving special fast tracking to affordable housing development proposals, and allowing flexibility in the trading of zoning rights
Oklahoma City Ok	$180	Planned Unit Development ordinance could save 30 days in the processing
Blaine Mn	$280	Fast tracking
Lincoln Neb	$1116	Telescoping approval processes
Knox Co Tn	$443	Saving of 75 days if planned residential development ordinances were in place, thus avoiding the need for a discretionary review

A study quoted in the publication *Streamlining Land Use Regulation* found that a 5 month increase in processing time between 1967 and 1976 cost the home buyer in Houston a minimum of $560 to $840 per lot in the projects surveyed.

Effectiveness of controls

I turn now to the effectiveness of controls. It is simply not possible to generalise about the effectiveness of land use and development controls in the United States. There are so many different systems of control, each designed to serve a specific purpose in the community that adopted it. To the extent that there are still major efforts continuing to improve control systems at the state level (see the next chapter) and given the development of new control methods such as exactions and linkage fees (see Chapter 9) and transfer of development rights schemes, it could be said that the land use controls already in place are not sufficiently effective in achieving all that people want everywhere. But, I think it would be difficult to start to build consensus about the objects of control in the first place. Then, if those objects are not being achieved fully, it would be necessary to distinguish whether it is the system itself (ie the way the rules are drawn up; Chapters 4 and 5) that hinders achievement, or the operation of the system (the way the rules are administered; Chapters 6 and 7). To look at the British control system, for example, as planning permission is necessary for just about all development, local authorities would seem to have a system capable of delivering whatever pattern of development they wished. But first they must somehow ensure that the county structure plan or local development plan reflect their objectives; then they must stick to their objectives in exercising their discretion in deciding applications; and finally the Secretary of State may still frustrate their objectives by taking different decisions on development proposals put to him on appeal or on cases he decides to 'call-in'.

Certainly to an Englishman some of the development patterns and land uses in the United States seem alien. For example, the rate at which central New Jersey is being converted from farmland into landscaped spacious suburban development is astounding. I was far from convinced that the development control system was doing enough to keep development provided with the necessary schools, roads, and sewers. In fact, the pace of the development was actually encouraged by another aspect of the planning system intended to help deliver social infrastructure in the shape of affordable housing, subsidised by the new suburban tracts (see Chapter 11). People in the state were convinced that there was a need to control growth, and to direct development pressure to the needier cities such as Newark and Camden. Yet that same population, when broken down into constituent townships and municipalities, saw the need to encourage development locally as a way of increasing overall property tax revenues and thus reducing household bills; the general opinion was that it was the development in the *neighbouring* jurisdiction that needed to be stopped. Reconciliation of these approaches may prove possible through the state plan that is being developed (see Chapter 8). Similar problems have been tackled by the state planning process in Florida where there is a 'concurrency doctrine' which prevents local governments from issuing development permits unless all the infrastructure for urban growth is in place. In practice the pressure for development will force the developer to meet the infrastructure costs, and planning for growth will become that much more effective.

Perhaps the biggest hindrance to the achievement of objectives flows out of the constitutional constraints. These make it necessary, for example, to devise very complicated transfer of development rights systems, cluster zoning, and exactions, as the only affordable ways of preventing development so as to conserve open space. A secondary hindrance is the difficulty of timing development. If a whole community is zoned for a different range of uses making up an overall balance, there is no way to be sure that any sort of balance will be maintained; for all the land designated for offices may be developed at once, without the industry, housing or shops that were proposed to make up the balance. Having zoned the four corners of a road intersection for petrol stations, because the community needs one and there is no indication which land might be developed for that purpose, it is not possible easily to call a halt after the first on the grounds that the community is adequately served. If the market will support them, it is far more likely that all four corners will be developed for the same purpose.

Underlying the zoning system, therefore, is the American pro-development sentiment – the feeling that land is there to be exploited, and that bureaucrats should not have the power of frustration. On the other hand, the list of police power requirements that can be applied to that development which the zoning permits is long indeed. Those requirements are accepted in the sense that they do not take away development rights, they simply delay the profit; and delay is acceptable since it does not interfere with the principle of freedom to develop and make a profit.

So, it is not for me to start to judge how effective are American development control systems. I am not qualified to do so, and I should certainly be trespassing if I attempted to measure achievements against the objectives of the British planning system, tailored as it is to the needs of a nation with very much less space at its disposal. Ultimately it is for the American people, through the various steps available to them, to decide the balance between development rights and development control that suits them best. And it is open to me, as I have done in this report, to say where I think the American control systems have attractive and unattractive features to offer those responsible for devising control systems to achieve the land use planning objectives of Britain.

Enforcement

Before completing this chapter, and this part of the report – on the control systems, how they work, who operates them, and how efficiently – it is worth mentioning enforcement. For it is on enforcement that achievement of the objectives of a development control system depends. To my mind, one of the key problems in American development control is that enforcement is so often separated from the planning and zoning process. Usually, enforcement is the responsibility of the building inspectors. They sometimes do not appreciate the relative importance of particular aspects of zoning; in more complicated one-off permit situations, such as planned unit developments, they may not have the time or inclination to get to know just what the ordinance requires. For that reason, many local governments have appointed specialist zoning enforcement officers as part of wider enforcement agencies such as Sacramento's Division of Nuisance Abatement.

Although detailed zoning requirements can be attached to new developments and enforced by threatening not to grant a certificate of completion, enforcement on existing buildings is much more patchy. It can depend very much on the locality. Communities undergoing change are much more likely to contain citizens prepared to lobby their local representatives to take action. This was certainly the case in suburban West Windsor where a group led by a long time resident, Rae Rayder, succeeded in persuading the Township to take on an additional member of staff simply to carry out enforcement work. In some places the enforcement officers carry out thorough surveys area by area, identifying problems and taking action. But more widely, enforcement is very variable; this situation is tolerated by the average community, which is likely to be cynical about the effectiveness of its local government. The attitude of expecting inaction goes along with the ever present suspicion of municipal corruption. And there is a reluctance to pay more taxes in order to get the regulations implemented, without clear political pressure to the contrary.

In the American way, it is often only the richer local government units that can afford to enforce the controls they devise. Jersey City's ordinances, from which I drew examples in Chapter 4, seem to require some admirable standards of street lighting, car parking standards, landscaping and so on. But the City cannot afford a planning department big enough for its needs. Its efforts are largely concerned with getting right the waterfront development, capitalising on its spectacular views of New York across the Hudson River. If that is got right, then in time the City will become rich enough to devote resources to enforcement.

According to an article in *Planning*[23], the latest trend, given that more and more people are demanding a proper enforcement service, is to set up a system of fines sufficient to cover the cost of enforcement administration. Some communities are also taking powers to put right what is wrong and then send violators a bill for the work. Hillsborough County, Florida hires contractors to clear overgrown properties and then bills the owner (the county highways staff impound illegal signs that they come across).

With the fast growing complexity of zoning and other environmental regulations, not always matched by staff resources, it is not surprising that enforcement is frequently regarded as the weakest aspect of American development control. Often, communities take little action unless pressed by local residents' groups. The role of New York's Community Boards was quoted in this context in the previous chapter. It is similar to the local 'civic clubs' in Houston which petition the City to enforce the private covenants that govern ancillary activities on that city's suburban tracts.

143

Court Backs New York's Right To Order Building's Top Razed

By THOMAS J. LUECK

New York State's highest court ruled yesterday that New York City can force the developer of a 31-story apartment building, erected on a site zoned for no more than 19 stories, to tear down the top 12 floors.

In ruling on the highly unusual case, the New York State Court of Appeals found that the apartment building at 96th Street just off Park Avenue, begun by Parkview Associates of Manhattan in 1985, vastly exceeds its allowable height because city employees and the development company made a series of mistakes that got out of hand.

But the floors will not be torn down right away. City officials said yesterday that they would hold off further action on the building until the Board of Standards and Appeals rules on an application by the developer for a zoning variance. If it is approved, the variance would retroactively change the zoning on the building site so that a 31-story building would be allowed.

The developer was granted a building permit based on an erroneous map published by the city. In effect, the court found, the permit for a 31-story building — instead of a 19-story one — was granted because a dotted line on the zoning map was in the wrong place.

The court said it found no evidence of illegal action by Parkview Associates when it applied for and received the building permit. But in ruling in favor of the city, and upholding lower court decisions, it said that the developer should have realized earlier that the building permit was based on erroneous zoning information, and called it to the city's attention.

"Reasonable diligence by a good-faith inquirer would have disclosed the true facts and the bureaucratic error," the court said its eight-page opinion.

Possible $10 Million Loss

"With due respect to the court, we disagree," said Jeffrey L. Braun, a New York lawyer representing the developer. "My client is in a terrible predicament primarily because of the mistakes of the city."

He added that Parkview Associates would suffer at least $10 million in losses if it were forced to tear down the top 12 floors of the building. The exterior of the building, at 108 East 96th Street, is nearly complete, but extensive work needs to be done to complete the interior of the contested top 12 flors.

Mr. Braun said it would cost the developer $1,025,000 to demolish the 12 floors, and an additional $874,000 to put a new roof over the 19th floor. He added

that large additional losses had already been sustained because the developer had hoped to begin selling condominiums in the building last spring, but has been carrying the taxes, maintenance and other costs of a vacant building.

Mr. Braun said he expected the Board of Standards and Appeals to rule on the variance request sometime in the next six months.

Approval of the variance "would be absolutely unprecedented," said Charles M. Smith Jr., Commissioner of Buildings for New York City, who issued a "stop-work" order in June 1986. At the time, steel girders, plumbing ductwork and some electrical equipment was already rising the full 31 stories on the 96th Street site. Mr. Smith added that the city had never approved a variance that allowed construction of a building so much higher than is allowed by normal zoning.

Others said they doubted that the board would approve the variance application because it rejected a 1986 appeal by the developer of Mr. Smith's order, effectively bringing work to a halt on the project.

"The importance of this ruling lies in its reaffirmation of the fact that the city can't be barred from enforcing the law even though it has made a mistake," said Robert S. Davis, an attorney representing Civitas, an organization of residents of Manhattan's East Side that has opposed the 96th Street building since its inception. Citivas pointed out the error in the approval of the building permit to the City Department of Buildings in 1986.

Parkview Associates has notified the city that it has prepared a suit seeking monetary damages that would compensate it for its losses if it is required to tear down 12 stories of its building.

Special Zoning District

Lawyers on both sides of the case said yesterday that the development company also has the option of appealing the Court of Appeals ruling to the United States Supreme Court. Mr. Braun said Parkview Associates was "considering all options," but for the time being was concentrating on its application for a zoning variance from the city.

The apartment building is within a special zoning district that was created in 1973 and runs 150 feet east of Park Avenue. Buildings within the district are limited to 210 feet in height, or 19 stories, whichever is less.

In its opinion, the court said yesterday that changes in the boundaries of the special zoning district enacted by the city in 1983 had allowed construction of taller buildings nearby, but not on the site owned by Parkview Associates. The developer acquired the property in 1982.

A zoning map published by the city, and used by the developers and the Department of Buildings when the building permit was issued, erroneously included Parkview Associate's site in the area — delineated on the map by a dotted line — where bigger buildings were allowed.

The 31-story apartment building at 108 East 96th Street was ruled to have exceeded its allowable height (dotted line.)

Figure 7.5 Not so tall stories in the New York Times: the courts back the City's right to demand partial demolition, but can the City carry through their threats into practice?

Such groups take an interest in monitoring development, and bring political pressure to bear where breaches of control are sufficient to cause local alarm. Perhaps it is not inappropriate that a regulatory system designed to protect the health, safety and welfare of citizens should ultimately rely on those citizens themselves to monitor compliance. Indeed, perhaps this is the most pragmatic approach to enforcement of any ordinance. If local people are not concerned about a breach of regulation, perhaps that regulation was not entirely justified in the first place.

That approach fails to deliver enforcement of ordinances designed to secure wider social objectives. For example, local people would be unlikely to complain if a New Jersey housing development did not contain its fair share of low and moderate income housing. They would prefer to remain select, and let the social provision be made elsewhere. Indeed, it might be difficult for them to have access to information on household income to check compliance with the covenants imposed to restrict housing to low income people. An enforcement by the people approach might also compromise the need to enforce to serve as an example to others to follow the rules. New York City Planning Commission recently refused retroactive approval for additions to a Manhattan skyscraper that was built 11 feet too high, 814 feet instead of 803 feet, as a result of a need to thicken each floor slab by 2 inches. They could not accept the developer's suggested ameliorations, of floor space dedicated to artists' groups or improvements to a nearby historic building. The clear aim of the Planning Commission here was to set an example, and the developer was faced with a need to persuade the courts that the land-use issue was not significant enough to warrant the action taken by the Commission. A solution announced by the developer and the City in April 1988[24] would cost the developer $2m; he would provide rehearsal space in the development, next to the City Center of Music and Drama, and donate this to the City for letting to non-profit dance groups. However, this solution gave rise to some criticism, because the mitigation offered did not relate to the land use planning difficulty to be overcome, namely a building too tall.

The New York State courts were also involved in a dispute over another tower block during our time in the States. This one was built 12 stories too tall, allegedly because a City official drew the boundary line of an area of special control in the wrong place on the zoning map. The State's highest court affirmed that the City was entitled to require the removal of the top 12 stories. Whether that would in fact transpire remained to be seen when we left. The developer was applying to the City's Board of Standards and Appeals (the ZBA) for a retroactive variance, and also considering further legal action, in the direction of the Supreme Court, and separately to seek monetary damages from the City to compensate for the costs the administrative error caused.

An example of a much more trivial nature is described in the *Planning* article referred to above. It started when someone complained about their neighbour's basketball hoop. After enforcement action was taken, confirmed in the light of an appeal to the planning commission, the hoop and the backboard were removed, but the pole was painted orange and a flag hung from it (flagpoles are generally permitted in the United States in the light of national pride and the number of occasions when it is appropriate to demonstrate it by flying the Stars and Stripes; out of town shopping centres and car dealers generally fly the largest flags to draw attention to themselves by a device of a size that in any other shape would not be permitted). After national publicity, the local government concerned relaxed its ordinance to permit basketball hoops.

One of the difficulties about enforcement in the United States is that offences against criminal offences have traditionally been regarded as criminal misdemeanors. When they come to court they appear trivial by comparison with the other workload of the court and offenders are treated leniently. Perhaps the fine is small by comparison with the violation, which is still not put right. For that reason, some local governments are making zoning violations into civil offences. The *Planning* article describes the revised procedure in Fairfax County, Virginia, a procedure which is very close to that in operation in Britain. Notices are sent out to violators, explaining the problem and setting a period of grace in which action should be taken. If the violation is not corrected, a fine is imposed; at this point the violator can challenge the charge by appealing to the court, and the court will also become involved if fines are not paid or the violation not corrected. Fairfax County, just as British local authorities, have found that there are some persistent offenders prepared to drag out the process and go to court and take a chance rather than comply immediately.

New York City is also taking action to put on to computer the names of developers, builders and architects accused of repeated violations, so that future decisions can be taken in the light of the past record of the applicant for a discretionary permit. San Francisco, where subdivisions of large houses are a great problem (leading to overcrowding, lack of parking space etc), the City inspects every time multi family houses change hands to ensure that illegal conversion works have not been carried out. Another supporting actor in the enforcement process can be the bank or lending institution. Such bodies are reluctant to lend money for the construction or use of a building that will not accord with the zoning ordinance. This is because of the risk that the local government concerned may take action that will prevent occupation. Illegal occupation in turn may not be consistent with insurance covering the occupants; the owner might find himself liable if some claim against him was forthcoming. Of course, there will always be those prepared to take risks, but San Francisco City Council relies on the banks to determine whether a particular commercial use of a building is properly regarded as falling within the definition of a 'back office' in an area where those are the only uses permitted.

Information about the enforcement of development control is difficult to obtain[25]. The annual reports by various large cities do not seem to mention this aspect of the planning system. The reason for the lack of data may be that responsibility for enforcement is dispersed. It is for the building inspectors to check compliance of new development projects as they are built. Later breaches of control are enforceable under the police power and administrative arrangements for enforcement of breaches of local ordinances do not seem to feature in much of the material describing the planning systems in place.

Yet, the rapid development of new controls without adequate resources for enforcement was a weakness in Florida's processes identified by that state's Environmental Efficiency Study Commission[26]:

> 'Conditions placed on permits, compliance schedules and mitigation are meaningless without effective monitoring and enforcement . . . .With so little agency enforcement permit violations occur frequently . . . .The expense of [ongoing surveillance] can be reduced by educating

citizens to report violations and developing systems that ensure that such reports are investigated'.

Comments such as these can be applied to every development control system, and recognition of the private role in supporting government is an interesting theme. Enforcement, rather like auditing of accounts, may not be the most exciting and constructive activity. But a degree of enforcement must be necessary if the community is to be satisfied that action is being taken to achieve its objectives, which the development control system is designed to deliver.

Conclusions

So, how efficient and effective is American development control in a narrow administrative sense? Basically, we have seen that there is sufficient awareness of the costs of delay to persuade bodies such as the Federal Government, the American Planning Association, the Urban Land Institute and various consultants to disseminate literature with useful guidance about good practice. Yet, the local governments themselves, even the larger ones with sound annual reporting procedures, are remarkably reticent about how long it actually takes to get all the necessary permits. Perhaps the American Planning Association should consider gathering material for some league tables, with the aim of improving the speed of the system and encouraging a positive appreciation of the efficiency with which planners discharge their administrative functions. There are classes of cities and suburbs where the local community is not interested in very much new development, and in these areas the need for an efficient development control process is not to the foremost. On the other hand, there are plenty of communities competing to attract development. It is surprising that some of these have not made more of their permit turnaround times.

In comparison with the British process, the figures seem to show that some minor matters such as variances can be decided in as little as 4 weeks. Not many English planning permissions can be issued that quickly. But even allowing for the fact that the incidence of permitting is at about one tenth of the English level (meaning that American development proposals are likely to be for more significant developments), the time consumed in public hearings seems to make American development that does not conform with the zoning ordinance more time consuming than its English equivalent.

In my view, there is scope for economists to try to do more to estimate the total cost of planning and construction delays to the United States economy. It may be possible to demonstrate that cities with rapid review processes do better in attracting development (as it appears some New Jersey and Connecticut cities have done at the expense of New York City). Indeed planning officials might even be able to make a case for increased resources based on the payback from earlier and greater local property tax receipts.

It is possible to compare the measures recommended to increase efficient administration in America with similar measures in England. Some of the measures that the various reports have recommended reveal the short-comings or costs of an American way of administration, constrained by the Constitution, particularly in the requirement to hold public hearings. But others have their parallels in the advice that the English local authority associations have given to their members aimed at speeding up the development control process. I believe that the American experience with hearings examiners does illustrate the benefits of an individual taking decisions against policies properly set out by the local planning committee (perhaps the district development plan under the British Government's latest policy proposals). The political board might then be entitled to select applications to call-in from the planning officer. Such decisions might then be capable of appeal in defined circumstances, and again there could be a twin track system. A hearings examiner could be appointed to act rather as a small claims court, dealing with all appeals for an area on a sessional basis, except those specifically called in by the Secretary of State. This procedure offers the potential for localising some of the planning appeals in England which currently the Secretary of State or his appointed inspectors must decide.

As for the effectiveness of American development control, I am tempted to say that 'you get what you pay for', because so often the barrier to the controls that the majority of the local community seek is the financial cost of a regulatory taking. Much of that cost derives from the constraint of the Constitution. Some local governments have devised cheaper ways of achieving their objectives by creating a zoning currency, in the shape of a bonus system, or transfer of development rights. In general, the regulatory systems seem to result in new development that accords with the rules set, because of the close enforcement by building inspectors. But it is impossible to generalise on whether the rules themselves are effective in delivering land uses that meet the community's objectives.

Effectiveness goes hand in hand with enforcement. With regulations much more locally determined, to protect the health, safety and welfare of local citizens, it is appropriate that enforcement efforts too should depend largely on local discretion and local action. The shortcoming of that approach is the failure to attain wider than local objectives, unless there are individuals prepared to group together to take their local government to court. Increasing environmental awareness in the United States is also reflected in action to conserve local environments, and that means more enforcement action. Slowly the American approach to enforcement is being improved by making the process pay for itself, by improving the effectiveness of the legal action taken and by making the local enforcement effort part of a wider process of nuisance abatement, rather like environmental health. But rarely is it suggested that planners themselves should enforce their own decisions as is the case in England; that would encourage better ordinances, as officers saw the effects of their rules carried through to the purpose of those rules, to secure the health, safety and public welfare of the community.

NOTES TO CHAPTER 7

1. See, for example, Development Control Statistics: England 1986/87–1987/88, published by the Department of the Environment 1989.

2. Local Planning:– The Development Control Function; a report of the Department of the Environment Audit Inspectorate (1983).

3. Guidelines for the Handling of Planning Applications, published by the National Development Control Forum (February 1988).

4. Two reports entitled 'Speeding Planning Appeals' were published by Her Majesty's Stationery Office in 1986 and 1987. One dealt with the appeals decided on the basis of written representations and a site visit by a person appointed to decide the appeal on behalf of the Secretary of State. The other reviewed the handling of the 20% or so of appeals where a public inquiry was necessary– those involving the more significant development taking rather longer times to decide.

5. Streamlining Land Use Regulation, a Guidebook for Local Governments by John Vranicar, Welford Sanders and David Mosena (1980), reprinted by the American Planning Association in 1982.

6. California State Government Code 65950 and 65952.

7. Chapter 291, Laws of New Jersey 1975 (as amended).

8. Managing Rural Growth; The Vermont Development Process, published by the Environmental Board, State of Vermont (1983).

9. Permit Aerobics: Getting Your Process In Shape, prepared by Cogan Sharpe Cogan, consultants in planning, community and government relations, July 1987.

10. Streamlining Local Regulations: A Handbook for Reducing Housing and Development Costs, by Stuart Hershey and Carolyn Garmise, published by the International City Management Association, May 1983.

11. Streamlining Your Local Development Process by Douglas Porter (of the Urban Land Institute), published by the National League of Cities, 1981.

12. See Note 5.

13. See for example Department of the Environment Circular 31/85.

14. The Report of the Mayor's Blue Ribbon Panel on Building Plan Examination and Review, published in July 1986 by the City of New York.

15. For more details see Zoning News, May 1987, published by the American Planning Association.

16. Speeding Planning Appeals (Annex D); see note above.

17. The New York Times, Real Estate section, November 14, 1987

18. In an interview on 24 May 1988.

19. Published by the City of New York, July 1986.

20. Editorial in the Princeton Packet, February 16, 1988.

21. On the Costs and Consequences of the British Land Use Planning System, published by the University of Reading (1985).

22. From Joseph R Molinaro AICP, Senior Land Use Planner, National Association of Home Builders, 15th and M Streets, NW, Washington DC 20005.

23. Throwing the Book at Zoning Violators, by Todd W Bressi, in Planning, December 1988

24. Pact Reached on Skyscraper Built Too Tall, in the New York Times, Wednesday April 20th, 1988, page B1.

25. I understand that there is now an American Planning Association Planning Advisory Service report, written by Eric Damian Kelly.

26. Managing Florida's Environmental Assets, the final report of the Environmental Study Commission, published February 1, 1988.

8 Co-ordination of Control Systems

Introduction

In Britain anyone who wishes to build on land or change its use goes to local government for a permit. Local government staff give advice on whether a permit is needed for minor development, or on how the planning committee are likely to react to an application. Ultimately a decision is taken, perhaps by the planning director under delegated powers, or by a planning committee of the elected local council, or where really significant development is involved, by the full council. Most people on the receiving end of this process perceive it as an essentially local one.

The applicant in the United States perceives the process in the same, local light. The permit may be one that is available from the local officials on a reasonably automatic certification. Or the planning board of local political appointees may become involved. It may be necessary to decide whether the proposed development requires a variance or a zone amendment, in which case different locally appointed boards may become involved. The city or municipality's own elected members may need to deal with an appeal or a zone change. But again, the decision is seen to be one that is the entire responsibility of the local government concerned.

The British applicant does not usually appreciate the amount of central government influence over the processing of his application for planning permission. Whether the application is needed at all is determined by central government regulations, in the shape of the Use Classes Order and the General Development Order. The scope for local variation of these orders to vary the boundaries of development control is limited. Similarly the national planning legislation requires the local government to have regard to the development plan for the area in deciding permit applications. Although this plan will have been prepared by a local government unit, either the county or the borough or district council, it will have been formally approved by the Secretary of State for the Environment (or if it is a local rather than a structure plan, it will be certified as consistent with a central government approved document). With the proposed changes to the development planning process in England, the Secretary of State will still be able to call in elements of plans for review.

Finally, there is the appeals process. Any applicant aggrieved by a local government refusal to grant a permission, or by the conditions attached to a permission, may appeal to the Secretary of State. In practice, only about 5 per cent of applications result in appeals. However, the existence of the right of appeal, and the range of central government circulars explaining how the Secretary of State is likely to decide a case in a particular policy area have an important influence on local decisions. If the local government appears to go against clear policy guidance from the Secretary of State, then the well informed applicant can be expected to appeal. The appeal results in a complete reconsideration of the application from scratch. Few local governments welcome the intrusion of central government reconsidering local decisions, unless their original aim was to avoid the political stigma of approving major development proposals in the face of hostile public opinion.

Central government influence over the British planning process is significant, therefore, because of the central role in rule making, the government review of structure plans, and the availability of the appeals process backed by circulars promulgating government policies. By contrast, in the United States the Federal influence over planning decisions is largely limited to specific environmental review regimes where government spending is likely to have environmental impacts, and to specific grant regimes designed to encourage particular standards (for example, only if the roads serving a development are constructed to a particular standard will the costs of construction be eligible for a grant).

The state's normal roles are the setting of ground rules to govern the process (for example, covering the size, constitution and appointment procedures for of planning boards), further environmental controls (for example, requiring the clean up of industrial sites) and the addition of another layer of decision influencing specific grants.

There is generally no ordained structure of local government determining which tiers of local and state government are responsible for planning and development control functions. Each state has its own arrangements. Just as in Britain, the powers of local authorities are constrained by statute; in most states local government has only the powers that the state legislatures see fit to grant. But local determination of local land decisions seems to be the rule almost everywhere. Perhaps state politicians are astute enough to appreciate that planning issues do not generally generate good political capital. More likely it is the pervasive localism, that expectation that decisions will be taken at the lowest possible level in the hierarchy of government, that leaves most planning issues for reasonably unfettered local decision.

In addition much depends on the nature of the local government. In Pennsylvania, where counties comprise a number of cities and townships of different sizes, some cities may look after themselves while other smaller units have ceded land use responsibilities to the county to administer. In other areas the county role might be purely advisory, but its decisions on roads and public transport issues would constrain local plans and decisions. Within metropolitan areas fragmented planning systems reflect the fragmented local government structure, with small suburban units clustered around the center city. Within larger cities and indeed in some small ones too there is also likely to be a functional fragmentation, in the separation of planning and redevelopment agencies, or in the creation of special purpose authorities, perhaps to improve certain areas or to administer certain estates or stadiums. In several cities, planners indicated to me the difficulty of carrying out their task where they could have little influence over transit or car parking policies that were the responsibility of separately appointed authorities. These policies could be crucial in the planning of adequate parking, or traffic arrangements for major downtown developments.

Such intra-government problems are for local resolution; ultimately the mayor or city council must be persuaded of the need for reform – reform that is a matter for that local government unit alone. The structure of each local government's organisation is rarely regulated by outside bodies. This chapter is not about such intra-governmental problems. It is about attempts to overcome the problems that arise when decision taking is an entirely local responsibility within a fragmented framework over a wider area. These are the problems that result from a pattern of local decision taking over a period of time where only the interests of the local people have been taken into account, and not the broader interests of the people in the wider area, or the need for proper planning of that area.

Generally the problems of fragmented decision taking need to acquire major political significance before new administrative structures can be implemented. This is simple political reality; state legislators need to be persuaded of the problems, and that the solutions will bring a sound political return. But in a few areas in the United States circumstances have demanded that planning decisions should be taken in a wider context. This issue is of particular interest in Britain, with the publication of a Government White Paper in January 1989 proposing what some have described as a more fragmented, more local development plan process.

Examples of broader structures

In the history of urban politics in the United States, the earliest examples of co-operative planning efforts emerged from the political reform movement. In a few instances city and surrounding county administrations merged in a way that should have led to broader, more enlightened planning decisions. The needs of the city centres and the inner suburbs could be tackled with the resources in the outer suburbs, and planning for the wider metropolitan area should become more comprehensive. The extent to which these ideals have been achieved is hard to judge. The more recent merger of Jacksonville Florida with Duval County, in 1967, provides some clues.

A second type of regional co-operation in planning matters are the councils of governments (CoG). These are voluntary associations of cities, counties, and special purpose agencies concerned with matters such as water and transit. Their purpose is to co-ordinate policies and thus to achieve more efficient service delivery and infrastructure provision over metropolitan areas. They may have responsibility for sharing out state or federal grants. They may also be able, through their scale, to carry out a crucial research role in examining regional trends in population and economic activity. But, councils of governments have rarely been able to carry much weight in the decision making process. That is because they lack the powers to ensure implementation of their plans. They are purely advisory bodies, appointed by and accountable to the individual local governments in the areas concerned, and have no tax or rule making powers.

A body rather stronger than a CoG was created by the Minnesota State legislature in the so-called Twin Cities metropolitan area of Minneapolis/ St. Paul. Local and national commentators consider the metropolitan council a successful innovative approach to planning over a very large area. Its scope is wide enough to cover even the outer suburbs. It fits somewhere between a state and local government unit, with sufficient direct responsibilities to enforce the policies it settles. But, it probably cannot be replicated elsewhere; Minnesota is an unusual state where there is only one urban area, and urban affairs can still dominate the legislature (rather than the interests of suburbs). Furthermore, the relatively minor urban problems of the inner city areas of Minneapolis and St Paul do not frighten the suburbs from co-operation.

Other states are acting to introduce special arrangements to protect areas of environmental significance. New Jersey, for example, has significantly modified the planning powers of municipalities in the Hackensack Meadowlands (a large swamp and wetland area no more than 5 miles from New York City, surrounded by urban areas and largely used for solid waste disposal). A similar regional planning body has been established for the Pinelands (one million acres of natural resource in the shape of pygmy pines, cranberry bogs and pure water aquifer). The state has also established a special permitting regime for the coastal zone, so that major developments are scrutinised by the state Department of Environmental Protection as well as the municipality concerned. This was encouraged by Federal legislation in the shape of the Coastal Zone Management Act 1972, which makes available grants for cities and counties in coastal areas in return for regulatory regimes designed to achieve certain coastal management standards. Many states have agencies and special planning arrangements to protect their coasts. New Jersey is in the process of filling in the gaps, by a comprehensive development and redevelopment plan covering all the state that is not covered by the earlier arrangements.

Other states have instituted state-wide mechanisms intended to influence and constrain decision taking by local governments. The original motivation and mechanisms in each state have been different, but no state could act without persuading public opinion of the need to protect the environment. For example, in Oregon the main thrust was the need to protect substantial areas of prime farmland from development pressure, but the measure passed because of an extraordinary environmental pride that its citizens shared in the 1970s. Hawaii too saw the need to protect its extraordinarily rich agricultural land. In Vermont the traditional agricultural industry is fast disappearing, but the construction of Interstate highways had brought the state much closer in travelling time to both Boston and New York City. There was a perception that a failure to direct the growth would ultimately damage the assets of fine mountain scenery and clean water responsible for the state's healthy diversified economic base. Florida too is suffering from enormous growth, but here the current state planning initiative is intended mainly as a discipline to protect areas of environmental importance and ensure that infrastructure provision in the shape of water supply and pollution control keeps pace with growth. The overall need is to protect environments while catering for thousands of new residents each week. John DeGrove's very readable book, *Land, Growth and Politics*[1] details the background and development of these systems.

In most of these areas and systems the emphasis is on directing growth. This reflects one of the underlying traits of the American character – that economic growth, and the development that goes with it, is good and to be encouraged. Even in areas under intense pressure from developers the mechanisms adopted are known as 'growth management' tools. In the states that have adopted planning control mechanisms, the challenge is to encourage economic growth without destroying the environment.

How is this of interest to the British reader?

The aim of this chapter is to explain some of the different mechanisms for control outlined above, and the intergovernmental relationships that result. In any planning system there is always tension between local demands for local control and the need for some more strategic overlay in order to achieve more effective overall use of the land and other resources. It is in exploring this tension that there is the most potential for the British reader to learn from the various American experiences. How can we devise the best structures to achieve the ideal balance between local control and accountability on the one hand, and the needs of the region as a whole on the other? New Jersey is one of the latest states to immerse itself in this question, and the approach there might seem to have most relevance to Britain. It has the densest population in the United States. After some years in the economic doldrums it has made a significant turn around, suffering pressures in some parts rather like those in south east England outside London. And New Jersey has a strong sense of home rule – local expectation that local people through local government should determine their own local destinies.

In preparing its state-wide plan and administrative structure to co-ordinate planning policies and decisions New Jersey must learn from the experiences of those that have gone before. This chapter therefore looks at structures in place in city counties such as Jacksonville, in the Meadowlands and Pinelands National Reserve of New Jersey, in the Twin Cities area, on the coast in North Carolina, and in the state-wide systems of Oregon, Florida and Vermont. My aim is to point up the common themes and differences, some of the problems that have emerged and the potential solutions. The common themes ought to give clues as to the ideal structure of agencies and policy responsibilities; the differences ought to illustrate a range of administrative mechanisms to deliver effective control, some of which might have read across as incremental improvements in British planning mechanisms, especially in the context of the White Paper mentioned above.

Jacksonville, Florida

In the last century it was a relatively frequent occurrence for the largest cities to expand and merge with the county in which they sat. In the case of New York City that merger was with four counties (hence the existence in the City of separate borough presidents of Brooklyn, Queens etc). Such mergers have been much less frequent in this century, partly because of suspicion by those in the county outside the city that their taxes would rise, and that undesirable aspects of city life might spread to fill the new boundaries. Jacksonville was one of three major consolidations that took place in the sixties (the others were Nashville and Indianapolis). In his book, *The Politics of Metropolitan Reform*[2], John Harrigan suggests three background factors prominent in encouraging consolidation in these cases: a breakdown or crisis in public service provision, special political conditions, and a population outside the city not already organised into municipalities. In the 1960s, Jacksonville was threatened by a loss of accreditation in its school system, and a breakdown of its sewage system, which was polluting the St Johns River. According to Harrigan, the city was also riddled with corruption, eight city officials having been indicted on charges including grand larceny. There were only a few suburban governments, and they were unaffected by the merger of city and county. Another political aspect was that racial polarisation was tending to increase the black influence over the city government. In other words the move might have been prompted by those wishing to prevent black control of city government, by diluting the urban black population with suburban whites.

Twenty years after the city and county merged, it is not clear that any more sensible planning arrangements have emerged. Jacksonville is not noticeably different from other cities, with suburban development expanding in the suburbs (in this case still within the city boundary), with suburban office and shopping centers, and with a downtown area of limited health surrounded by empty land, car parking lots and housing mainly occupied by poor blacks. The city is making the most of its attractive waterfront,

Figure 8.1 Jacksonville Landing, a James Rouse development, sits looking over the St Johns River, turning its back on a struggling downtown studded with offices.

where Jacksonville Landing – a shopping and leisure centre – has been developed by the James Rouse Company. But the difficulty of doing more to force the pace of development in the more depressed urban areas is an economic one. If Jacksonville makes it too difficult for developers, the new office developments will locate elsewhere in faster developing places in central and southern Florida, such as Orlando, Tampa and Miami. Growth is important as the means of bringing in extra revenue needed to tackle the urban problems, but it has to be carefully husbanded, and that means not putting too many obstacles in the way of developers. I found it hard to see that combining city and county had made very much difference to the planning arrangements. I grant that the suburban development value helps the city as a whole, and not just the suburban areas in which it locates, but the example of Jacksonville suggests that wider measures are necessary in the region before the city can direct development to where it is needed.

The Meadowlands, New Jersey

New Jersey is the location of two special purpose planning arrangements in which the state has created regional commissions designed to secure proper planning of land with particular characteristics in areas of fragmented local government. The first is in the Hackensack Meadowlands. These comprise some 19,000 acres of salt and freshwater marshes, tidal pools and marginal land to the west of the string of communities on the hills edging the Hudson River's Jersey shore. They are crossed by railroad tracks on embankments, and by the New Jersey Turnpike and other roads on enormous viaducts. The only relief is provided by huge garbage mountains. The state's Hackensack Meadowlands Reclamation and Development Act 1968 defined an area in which responsibility for land use administration would be transferred to a development commission appointed by the state.

155

The aim was to co-ordinate comprehensive development of an area that was previously regarded as only the forgotten corners of several small municipalities, and to secure an ultimate end (achieved in 1988) to the disposal of solid waste in the area. A master plan for the area is accompanied by standards for regulation such as zoning, and there is a shared responsibility for permitting, with the local governments free to permit development in accordance with the master plan and zoning standards. The model here is widely regarded as a successful exercise of state power to bring order to development, although there remain conflicts between those who are concerned to conserve wildlife in these wetlands so close to New York City, and those who see this area as ideal for light industrial development that has brought the state recent economic success, and for regional sports stadia. The regional arrangements are generally thought to provide a better balance in those conflicts than the earlier fragmentation.

The Pinelands National Reserve, New Jersey

New Jersey followed the same model when it came to consider how best to plan for the future of the Pinelands area. This area is of particular interest to those concerned with development control in Britain because of the parallel with our national parks. In the United States the national parks are wilderness areas in the main, and development there is controlled directly through ownership by the Federal government. Similarly, state parks are recreational areas operated by the individual states; again, complete control over development is achieved by ownership. The Pinelands area is rather different. The Federal legislation enabling the establishment of special controls in the Pinelands declared the Pinelands to be the nation's first national reserve – a slogan that appears today on Pinelands Commission notepaper. These reserves were intended to protect American landscapes of outstanding ecological, scenic, cultural, historic and recreational importance that were too populated, complex and costly to protect through national park designation. Controlling use and development without widespread acquisition of property is exactly the challenge facing British national parks.

The history of the battle to establish the Pinelands as a national reserve is described in an entertaining way in Babcock and Siemon's *The Zoning Game Revisited*[3]. It is characterised by the struggles of individual landowners to retain their development rights (and hence their ability to obtain maximum capital value for their assets at the time of their choosing) and by the objections of the individual municipalities in the area covered by the reserve (who would lose the power to determine the shape of their own areas). Ranged against them were those concerned to see preservation of the natural resources of the area. I cannot better David Callies' description[4] of these resources:

> '. . . the pine-oak forests, wild and scenic rivers and cedar swamps of the Pinelands area comprise vast undeveloped tracts of land which provide habitat for a wide diversity of rare, threatened and endangered plant and animal species and contain many other significant and unique ecological, historical, recreational, and other resources. In addition, this area overlies the estimated 17 trillion gallon Cohansey Aquifer, one of the largest virtually untapped sources of pure water in the world.'

The area now protected covers more than 20% of New Jersey – more than 1500 square miles, or 4 Dartmoor National Parks. There are 52 municipalities – equivalent to English district planning authorities – covered

Figure 8.2 Pinelands landscape; very much an acquired taste

by the area of the reserve, as well as 7 counties, concerned with more strategic planning but lacking direct development control powers.

The Pinelands Commission was established by executive order of the state governor in February 1979, who at the same time instituted a moratorium on development while a plan for the Pinelands was being prepared[5]. The Pinelands Protection Act 1979 authorised the Commission to devise a comprehensive management plan for its area, and after a very public battle, described in Babcock and Siemon's book, in 1981 a plan was approved by the State Governor and the Federal Secretary of the Interior. All counties and municipalities within the Pinelands area were then required to revise their master plans and zoning ordinances to conform with the comprehensive management plan. By 1988, when I met the Commission's Executive Director, the process of certifying compliance was almost complete. Some local governments had been extremely reluctant to accept the imposition of the Commission as a superior planning agency. However, the benefits of greater local freedom that come with certification finally encouraged all into the fold.

Obtaining the necessary permit for development means an initial application to the Pinelands Development Commission. No application to a local government can be regarded as complete, and thus capable of being processed unless accompanied by the certificate that the preliminary application to the Commission has been lodged. The local government then process the application in the normal way, but at each stage notify the Commission in case it wishes to make an input, perhaps to determine conditions that might be imposed. Once the local government has taken a final decision, the Commission has 15 days to intervene, by 'calling up' the application. In practice only about 3% of the 1800 or so applications for development in the area each year are called up. Of these about half are ultimately approved after a hearing; but a significant proportion of applications are withdrawn after an informal indication to the applicant of the likely outcome, given the planning background, and this saves the time that hearings absorb. Some of the more complex cases go to the State Office of Administrative Law, where a judge makes a recommendation based

157

on an objective hearing record for review prepared by the Commission. The system is not unlike that which applies to certain English planning applications that must be notified to the Secretary of State before approval, in case he wants to call them in, and where the Secretary of State calls in the application and appoints an inspector to hold a public inquiry and make a recommendation.

The general view of most commentators outside the area is that the Pinelands Commission is an unmitigated success. There are landowners and local governments in the area who would disagree. The local people would regard the system as failing to deliver what they want, while a wider population in the state would see the process as meeting their concerns and objectives.

What is particularly interesting is that the state has succeeded in securing what is almost a national park designation, but without the need for public ownership of the land. Almost total control in the Pinelands is achieved in the main by planning mechanisms rather than by ownership, and thus resembles the control over English National Parks. It has proved a particularly successful control; inappropriate development has been staunched and nearly every legal challenge to its decisions has been rejected in the courts.

A good illustration of how much control over development has been achieved in an area that was about to take off is shown by a 1988 case[6] in the Superior Court of New Jersey, in which the Pinelands Commission's second comprehensive plan was challenged as having resulted in a 'taking'. The owner of a 216.5 acre farm in Shamong Township, whose farm had been in his family since 1902, alleged that before the Pinelands Commission was established, he would have been entitled to subdivide his land into 200 building lots. After the first comprehensive management plan, the zoning was reduced to one dwelling per 10 acres, and he started to draw up plans for subdivision into 17 'farmettes'. After the second plan, the permissible density was again reduced, to one house per 40 acres, with clustering, and this decision was upheld by the court. So only 5 units could now be built on the farm; these would have to be clustered on one acre lots, and the remainder of the parcel would, as a consequence of permitting this development, have to be made the subject of deed restriction permanently restricting it to agricultural use. In this way the Commission have succeeded in clawing back development rights previously given away.

Another safeguard against such legal challenges of alleged regulatory takings has been established in a transfer of development rights scheme in the Pinelands, said to be the first in the United States to operate on a regional scale. This provides a way for owners in the most environmentally sensitive regions, and subject to stringent development control, to share in the economic benefits of increased land values in other Pinelands areas more suitable for home building. Land in the Pinelands is designated under the development plan as Preservation, Forest, Agricultural Production, Rural Development, Regional Growth, Military and Federal, or Villages and Towns. The plan limits development by different amounts according to the designation. Concentrated residential development is allowed in the Villages and Towns and in the Growth Areas. In the Preservation and Agricultural Production areas development is much more limited. Landowners in these areas are allocated development credits, which may be used in the Regional Growth Areas to allow more homes to be built on a property than would otherwise be possible–in other words as a density bonus. Each credit can allow 4 extra homes to be built. The idea is that the farmer will sell these for use in the development areas in preference to building on his own land on the very limited basis permitted. It is a case of carrots and sticks – in the shape of density bonuses and regulation.

The Pinelands Commission has worked well as a regional agency because it has had political backing from the state, it has been single minded as a single purpose authority, and has employed a number of devices to restrict development and to encourage it in the more appropriate areas. It has worked because it had strong regulatory powers from the start, and the ability to override local governments. The scale of existing public land ownership gave a good springboard for extending control into adjacent privately owned areas sharing the same environmental sensitivity. Through deed restrictions and through land acquisition the Pinelands Commission is securing the future use of the most sensitive land in the way best secure from legal challenge – through acquisition. Indeed, in an interview with the author, the Executive Director, Terrance Moore, suggested that expanding acquisition programmes would be needed as the designated growth areas filled up and development credits become impossible to apply. The task of the Commission was therefore a temporary one of holding back development until the land could be permanently preserved. But the main lesson, so far as this chapter is concerned, is that because cooperation among the many local governments was impossible, the state stepped in to secure its wider objectives for an area of more than local importance.

Metropolitan government in the Twin Cities area

Another example of a single purpose body that is judged to have succeeded against the tide is the Metropolitan Council of the Twin Cities Area in Minnesota. Like the Pinelands Commission, it has no operational responsibilities. But it has adequate powers to be seen as a major shaper of development in the Minneapolis/St Paul metropolitan area.

(i) Metropolitan regional planning across boundaries

To appreciate its success, it is necessary to step back and look at the recent history of regional metropolitan planning. Attempts to institute wide scale regional planning over metropolitan areas in the United States seem generally to have met with little success. Certainly, a large number of metropolitan planning commissions have been established, especially in the light of Federal legislation in the 1960s. The Housing and Urban Development Act 1965 authorised the payment of Federal grants towards research and planning by regional planning agencies. The Demonstration Cities and Metropolitan Development Act 1966 made some 30 Federal grant programs conditional on review by a metropolitan agency. In other words, if cities did not co-operate with their suburbs, key funds they needed, for example grants towards transport infrastructure, would simply be foregone. Two years later, the Intergovernmental Co-operation Act required the grants to be consistent with and to further the objectives of state, regional and local comprehensive planning. Regional planning commissions comprising representatives of the elected officials in the region began to wield power in determining how Federal funds were spent. However, this regional planning era was short lived; the requirement for oversight ceased in 1983, when President Reagan handed over responsibility to the states, and Federal funds were reduced.

It is the comparative lack of influence that these regional agencies seem to wield over local development control decisions that leads me to think that they have not been effective in influencing local planning. Certainly, major infrastructure provision in sewers, roads, or public transport has influenced the location of major developments. With the aid of Federal funds, the agencies were able to draw up large scale plans for the installation of infrastructure, for the establishment of park systems and open space and so on. They also engaged in planning research of a breadth that individual cities and municipalities are unable to justify. But, the extent to which that research, or the plans the agencies prepare, can be useful depends crucially on the political clout of those concerned. The power over the distribution of Federal money was important, but Federal money alone does not shape the metropolis. Most decisions lay with local politicians and local money. Frustration with formal regional planning agencies has led to the establishment of voluntary groups, advocating good planning, and seeking to influence both locally elected and state officials.

The most frequent model for the regional agency is the so-called Council of Governments. Counties, municipalities and functional agencies such as port and transit authorities get together to form a voluntary coordinating body to deal with specific problems, often including regional planning problems. But power can only be exercised at the lowest common denominator of its component elements; the domination of independent suburban communities can prevent the resolution of the very problems that the central city faces because of the flow of the middle class population to those suburbs.

(ii)   The Minneapolis/St Paul example

Standing out against this poor profile of the council of governments model is the example of the Twin Cities Metropolitan Council, which covers some 2 million population in the area of Minneapolis/St Paul in Minnesota. It is more than a council of governments in that it is not an advisory body made up of representatives of local governments, but a policy setting body of people appointed by legislature for districts that do not coincide with individual local government boundaries. It does not become constrained by the need of local government appointees to do their best for their areas, and it does not depend on local government for its income.

The Metropolitan Council was created in 1967 by a state legislature which had just been reorganised so that the urban areas were properly represented. It was created in response to a sewerage and water supply problem resulting from the fragmentation of the local governments in the area. Over 130 incorporated municipalities had together failed to plan properly for the increase in development in the region, and they were not opposed to the creation of the Council. It was created in a part of the United States which many regard as most civilised. Scandinavian social values predominate, and the region is remote enough to have escaped the type of population movements that have created substantial urban problems elsewhere. John Harrigan's *Political Change in the Metropolis*[7] contains an analysis of the political factors that led to the establishment of the Council.

(iii)   Functions of the Metropolitan Council

The primary function of the Council is to adopt policies and set standards for regional development. Their *Metropolitan Development Guide* is a statutory comprehensive statement of policies and objectives for the region's development, prepared after thorough public review. Its chapters cover:

Health; the Council acts jointly with another regional board in preparing the Federally required health systems plan.

Airports; the Council's comprehensive regional airports development plan requires actions by the Council, the Metropolitan Airports Commission (the budget of which is open to review, and its capital expenditure on large projects is subject to veto by the Council) and by local governments (their development plans are subject to review by the Council).

Housing; as Metropolitan Housing and Redevelopment Agency, and as a designated agency for other purposes including the review of Federal grant aid, the Council is able to wield power in the provision and location, for example, of affordable housing in the region.

Recreational open space; the parks and open space elements of the guide provide for a comprehensive system of regional parks and park reserves, trail corridors and special use areas. The Metropolitan Parks and Open Space Commission is appointed by the Council. Implementation of the plan elements on this subject is through that Commission and 10 implementing agencies.

Transportation; there is no doubt in the United States about the fundamental linkage between transport systems and development. A new road can act as a spur to major development all along it; new public transport facilities can contribute to the reshaping of downtown areas. It is not surprising that the Council's plan is for more efficient use of the existing public and private transport infrastructure, upgrading the bus service, reducing reliance on cars, encouraging car pooling, exploring light rail transit as a higher capacity and less labour intensive mode, and evaluating the costs and benefits of peak hour only bus services.

Solid waste management; in this section of the Guide, recycling and resource recovery are identified as the preferred practices in a strategy designed to prevent air and water pollution in collecting and processing solid waste and thus protect the health and safety of the people. The Council sets policies, and reviews processing practices and proposed disposal locations. The critical problem is persuading the counties to adhere to the regional guidelines.

Sewage disposal; the Council also appoints the metropolitan commission responsible for all sewage interceptors and treatment facilities in the region. In this way it can assure high standards of water quality, and also control the location of new development by controlling the location of sewers.

Surface water management; this part of the Guide deals with the problems which melting snow and storm water runoff can cause by carrying pollutants into water resource areas and by erosion and flooding.

Water use and availability; here the aim is to improve coordination of the units of government responsible for managing water resources.

Law and justice; a strategy for regional coordination of law enforcement.

On top of these comes the most important chapter of the Guide, the Metropolitan Development and Investment Framework. This establishes an overall policy for ensuring that all new development has the appropriate major regional facilities, like sewers and highways (for which priorities are determined in the Framework), and sets a general direction for development within the metropolitan area. The general aim is to designate urban growth areas in which most new development will take place, thus making the best use of existing infrastructure and relying on efficient extension to keep the costs of provision down. Outside these areas, the policy is that urban services will not be provided. The decisions about the location of new development have been controversial with some communities which would have liked the property tax revenue that new development brings. But in the end, it seems that rurally designated areas have chosen to toe the line rather than pay for their own major infrastructure.

All government units in the region are bound by law to prepare long range plans that are consistent with the Council's framework of sewers, highways, public transport, airports and parks. The Council review these plans and negotiate or require modifications necessary to bring them into line with the regional framework. This power of review extends even into the capital expenditure plans of school districts. In a typically American way, the Council wields a great deal of authority on the basis of relatively little by way of formal powers. For example, in bringing the local governments into line, it might use powers such as reviewing major development proposals, or allocating state and Federal grants. Bob Hoffman, an attorney who has been very closely involved with the Council[8], suggested that it had lost some of its power as a result of the substantial restriction of Federal grant aid by the Reagan Presidency. It is not so easy now for the Council to ensure provision of low income housing in a particular county by refusing otherwise to endorse an application for some unrelated Federal grant aid. But the Council still has other grants in its gift, such as for regional parks.

One other feature of the Minneapolis/St Paul region which helps to encourage more orderly development, or rather to discourage the precipitate rush for property tax ratables, is the regional tax-base sharing programme. Every dollar of new tax revenues from commercial and industrial development is shared 60:40 between the local government concerned and a regional fund from which payments are made on the basis of fiscal capacity and population. (This could be viewed as rather like the 1990 English innovation, the uniform non-domestic rate.) In this way, the benefits of rapid growth in Bloomington, the third largest city in the region, may be shared among neighbouring areas which need to finance the services demanded by their population who commute to Bloomington. In fact, Bloomington's Interstate 494 strip, leading away from the Twin Cities' airport, is said to employ more than either Minneapolis' or St Paul's downtown areas. To that will be added a 9 million square feet 'megamall' otherwise known as the fashion plaza for America[9]. The Metropolitan Council reviewed the proposals for the megamall and were criticised for delay; the cities with regional shopping centres and Minneapolis and St Paul, worried about their downtown shopping, were opposed. Eventually, the Council determined that the new mall would capture only 30 per cent of the likely growth in the area, and the project could go ahead in a modified form. The response of downtown Minneapolis has been to upgrade the Nicollet Mall, an axis where public transit has priority and where all the shops are linked by covered skyways. In addition the City is creating more multi storey parking garages, and money is flowing into the downtown area in order to compete with the rival attraction out of town, which will also require public money for highway provision. The metropolitan council could only delay the project and impose conditions; ultimately Bloomington got what it wanted.

(iv) The structure of the Metropolitan Council

The Metropolitan Council is an appointed body, with its chairman and all its members being appointed by the state governor, with all members apart from the chairman being appointed to represent groups of local governments after consultation with the legislators for the district concerned. In turn, the Council makes a whole series of its own appointments; the most important of these are the members of the sewer, public transport and regional parks agencies. Having an appointed rather than an elected Council was intended to lead to a body less constrained and more independent. But it does tend to reduce public awareness of the body.

Several people I interviewed in the region commented that the power and influence of the Metropolitan Council depended crucially on the relative strength and vitality of the appointed chairman and members, and over the years the powers have been amended by the legislature according to the political climate in the various commissions in the region. At present the view in some quarters is that the Council is busily looking for new fields to take the lead in, when there are more traditional regional planning policy tasks that demand more priority. I suspect that the Council is probably more important at times of sustained growth. Local governments are traditionally suspicious of the Council, as they would be of any agency with powers to direct local priorities. It is the limited powers that bring the Council some respect. Local governments need to work to influence the decisions; they cannot afford to opt out.

(v) Effectiveness of the Council

An interesting slim volume published by the Council, entitled *Making One Community out of Many*[10], describes the Council's work and history, and provides an analysis of the recent attention to redefinition of the Council's role. Professor Naftalin, the author, suggests that the Council has been very successful in resolving most of the problems it was set up to deal with, but was by 1986 at a crossroads. The reasons for this were conflicts between the roles of the Council as a policy setting and as an operating agency, and the reluctance of the state legislature to devolve more of its powers to the Council, even though that might be necessary to tackle what is perceived as an ever widening regional agenda.

All those I spoke to in a short visit to the region were genuinely proud of the concept of the Metropolitan Council, although they also had specific reservations about some aspects of the work. As Professor Naftalin comments, it is not easy to measure effectiveness of a programme such as this. For who can tell what would have happened in its absence? Certainly, the planners of Minneapolis can see the benefits of the programme, because the constrained suburbs ensure better land values and hence more private development and less decay in the city. It also makes more effective the traditional process of urban redevelopment, involving declaration of blight, compulsory purchase as a way of site assembly, followed by disposal to a developer. Regional planning is contributing to keeping the costs of urban regeneration relatively low. The threat of withdrawal of Federal grants, which are administered through the Metropolitan Council, is also generating substantial investment in new multi storey car parks around the fringes of Minneapolis' downtown area. Combined with 10 cent park-and-ride buses, these are intended to keep air pollution levels down to appropriate levels so as not to endanger grants for other projects, such as the improvement of public transport and possibly the construction of a light rail system (essentially two-car tramway systems) in the region. (Grants depend on the achievement of pollution targets)

Perhaps the best way of measuring effectiveness would be to identify similar regions elsewhere without such a programme, and compare the outcomes. But, there are all sorts of reasons why Minneapolis/St Paul stands out from other metropolitan areas in the United States, including the low proportion of minorities, the relatively small incidence of urban problems, the traditional Democratic party politics of the state, as well as the high proportion of the state's population and wealth in the Twin Cities. Other regions may not have the right political climate for a straight copy. Interest by other regions in the Council's work and success was originally great, but slower growth in the 1980s has reduced the need for such mechanisms. Only recently has the second wave of regional and state wide planning started to take off, with Vermont adjusting its system, Florida struggling with growth rates that show no sign of abating, and New Jersey suddenly particularly attractive to suburban developers. The fact that each of these states has seen the need for stronger regional planning suggests that something along the lines of the Metropolitan Council is needed where growth pressures are great. The Council seems to offer a good model, with its limited powers sufficient to stimulate considerable local government interest in its work, and with its influence over regional agencies sufficient to shape priorities and impinge on investment decisions, while not unduly hampering the work of the state legislature.

Indeed I wonder whether the Council might form a good model for England, after the development plan reforms announced by the Government in early 1989[11]. The individual local governments in the Twin Cities area must draw up their plans in 'conformance' (awful word) with the Metropolitan Development Guide. The guide itself is drawn up in consultation with local interests and is rather like the proposed English county strategies. Another similarity is that local governments in English counties and the Twin Cities region can keep more of the local tax revenue from new housing than from commercial and office development (although in England the accountability is rather spoilt by the redistributive elements of the Rate Support Grant, which tend to even up local government financial resources and in Minneapolis the City believes that the redistributive element is quite inadequate to compensate for the offices and shopping malls 'lost' to the suburbs)[12]. In terms of powers the counties can determine the road network and have public transport and solid waste disposal responsibilities. Perhaps the one element of the Minneapolis/St Paul example that would justify stronger county involvement is the provision of new sewer and water supply infrastructure. In England, the tradition is that such infrastructure must be provided by the water and sewerage undertakers on demand. In Britain, it is clearly for the planning system to shape developing areas, rather than some method of sewer permitting.

Coastal planning control in North Carolina[13]

One of the factors in getting the Twin Cities' Metropolitan Council into place was the dominance of the metropolitan area in the state of Minnesota, and the proper representation of the electorate of the urban areas in the state legislature of 1965. In other states there is not the same dominance and it has been more difficult for electors to bring about state wide systems. We now come to consider some of the other state planning systems that have begun to emerge in more recent years; I start with the example of North Carolina's coastal zone controls created following the Federal government's lead in passing the Coastal Zone Management Act in 1972.

(i)   What development is caught by the control?

In 1975, North Carolina introduced a development control process in 20 counties in its coastal zone, as part of a comprehensive coastal management programme, designed to balance the needs for economic growth and resource preservation along the coast and over 2 million acres of estuary. All development is potentially the subject of control (except agriculture and forestry, and minor maintenance and improvements unlikely to cause any environmental damage).

In 13 designated 'areas of environmental concern' (coastal wetlands, estuaries, aquifers, prime agricultural and forest land, historic sites and sites of natural or scenic importance, and areas where major development could be expected to have an impact on the area), all development needs a permit.

(ii)   The procedures for control

Each coastal zone county, or municipality if it has the resources, maintains a land use plan consistent with the original legislation and with Coastal Resources Commission guidelines – effectively a framework of state policies. This plan must be based on data of population trends, an analysis of current land uses, zoning ordinances and other regulations, current land use problems and projections of economic demands and future land use needs. The implications of these demands on the ability of local governments to provide cost-effective water, sewer, fire and police protection, transportation, schools, parks, solid waste disposal, and public access to the ocean must be analysed and constraints identified. In other words, communities are forced to consider the implications of the growth they expect.

Permits are then required for all developments, and in considering whether to grant a permit, local governments must pay due regard to the policies set by the Coastal Resources Commission. The procedures differ according to the scale of the development proposal.

Major developments are those requiring an input from more than one state agency, or extending over at least 20 acres, or involving drilling or excavation, or comprising more than 60,000 sq ft. In areas of environmental concern, these need a permit from the Coastal Resources Commission, a 15 member body appointed by the state governor mainly from lists of nominees from local government. Minor development applications in these areas are considered by the local governments which must abide by the rules of the Commission, or risk losing their authority to the Commission itself. The Commission also hears appeals against permit decisions of local governments. Failure to act on a major permit within 90 days, or on a minor permit within 30 days is deemed to constitute a consent. Enforcement is carried out by a monthly aerial survey, and is also encouraged by fines and requirements to restore land to its original condition.

(iii)   The criteria employed in exercising control

Eight grounds for the refusal of a permit are listed in the legislation. In particular, permits in areas of environmental concern can be granted only for developments consistent with both the land use plan and the Coastal Commission guidelines.

(iv) What are the results? The major achievement has been to force the improvement of the local planning process, while retaining a state role in the consideration of the most damaging development proposals in the sensitive areas. The planning process has been sold successfully to the local constituencies, so that local governments who previously saw no need for a planning function now find it essential. There has been constructive co-operation between the state and local governments through two rounds of plan making and the state considers the planning/permitting links to have worked well. The process has been helped along by substantial infusions of state and federal money into local government planning efforts.

Most permits, about 95 per cent, are being approved, but often subject to conditions. Development control is therefore just what it says, and not the device for stopping economic development that some had feared. Development has been largely steered away from the most sensitive areas, although there are reportedly proposals to undermine the control regime. The system emerged after some damaging winter storms showed the short-sightedness of developments on the beach front. I heard it said that North Carolina needed another damaging storm to remind itself of the need for control, and perhaps the hurricane of fall 1989 will have had that effect.

There have been some efforts on the efficiency front to consolidate the different permitting regimes in the environmental field so that a Coastal Area Management Act permit is all that is required. Ultimately, that has not proved possible, partly because of the unwillingness of federal government agencies to relinquish control such as the Corps of Engineers control over wetlands. Because the permitting process itself has not proved popular with applicants, some consideration is now being given to positive incentives to good planning (for example, removing the availability of flood insurance for barrier island development).

Oregon: a comprehensive state wide approach

Oregon's state-wide land use planning process is widely regarded as the foremost example of state influence over local decision taking. Its importance is in the attempt to tie all levels of decision taking within a single policy framework. Senate Bill 100, passed in 1983, aimed to protect from development sprawl the prime agricultural and forestry land crucial to the state's traditional economic pattern. The Bill was promoted in a legislature which still contained a strong farming influence, but at a time when there was a spreading environmental awareness in the state. At the same time the state was introducing requirements for deposits on glass bottles, regulating billboards, creating cycle paths and taking action to combat pollution. There was also a nagging worry that Oregon might be vulnerable to a huge incursion of population from California, as that state filled up, bringing with it pollution and other problems. Indeed that worry still persists in some quarters of the state. Oregon regards itself as something special, and the state planning system can be seen as a reflection of that self awareness. Three times the system itself has been the subject of a state-wide voters' initiative – a vote of confidence. Three times the system has emerged with majority support.

In fact that support was not universal. It was centred around the part of the state under greatest development pressure – Portland (the largest city), Salem (the state capital), and Eugene (a relatively sophisticated university city). These three cities are located along Interstate 5 that runs through the most fertile areas of the 2 million acre agricultural plain of the Willamette valley. The suburban spread of these cities and the pressures generated by building a high capacity road through the best farmland in the state were important elements in generating the need for the state system.

(i) The setting

Perhaps a few more facts would make it easier for the English reader to picture the state. A population of less than 3 million lives on a land area about the size of West Germany. Most live in the metropolitan areas of Portland, Salem and Eugene in the Willamette Valley. The valley is separated from a relatively undeveloped coast (cold water and cloudy climate) by the coastal range of mountains. To the east of the valley and running down the centre of the state is the Cascades range of mountains. Both coastal and Cascades ranges contain vast areas of prime forest land, much in public ownership; the combination of climate and soils makes the state an ideal place to grow trees. About 30 million acres (about half the state's land area) are used for this purpose.

Against this picture it may seem surprising that the state is concerned about growth problems; there is so much space to start with. But forest and farming practices are reckoned to become very much more expensive if the population begins to spread into the areas used for these prime industries. For example, grass seed production requires that straw and fields are burned thoroughly after harvest to kill weed seeds and burning is much more difficult with houses in the vicinity. Similarly in the forests, isolated second home cabins divert the attention of firefighters from saving trees to saving property. The need to protect the land for the farming and forestry industries against a background of local government disinterest in planning controls or the direction of development pressure was the primary motivation for the introduction of a state-wide system of control.

Figure 8.3 Inappropriate development on some of the most fertile land in the United States; burning the field in the foreground would put at severe risk the mobile homes in the background, built just before Oregon's state-wide planning system began to bite.

(ii) The development of the state planning system

Senate Bill 100 created a Land Conservation and Development Commission which was to prescribe planning goals and objectives to be followed by all state agencies and local governments throughout the state. A new state agency would then administer the implementation of the goals, for example by monitoring and approving the content of locally prepared plans. The importance of this approach was that the Legislature did not need to

167

concern itself with the detailed content of the goals, nor indeed with how those goals would be applied.

Once the state-wide goals had been adopted – a process that involved widespread public debate – every local government in the state was required to prepare and adopt a new comprehensive plan consistent with the state-wide goals. Their zoning, subdivision and other regulatory ordinances had to be amended so as to conform with the state approved plans. All these plans and ordinances were reviewed by the appointed state agency, a process that dragged on for over a decade. Targets for comprehensive plan approval proved susceptible to slippage, rather like the programme for the approval of structure plans in Britain during the late 1970s. In a parallel process, state agency plans had also to become consistent with both the goals set by the state and with the plans prepared by local government in conformity with those goals. With the entire process in place, the objective was to return routine decision making responsibility to local governments, who would be constrained by the provisions of their own ordinances and plans approved by the state. Enforcement would be a matter for locally affected people to pursue, resorting to law where necessary.

(iii) The planning goals   What of the goals themselves? These are set out, with a commentary of non-binding guidelines in a 24 page tabloid newspaper issued by the state[14]. They represent the full statement of state policies on land use, resource management, economic development, and citizen involvement. The full list of goals covers:

> **Citizen Involvement;**   the aim is to provide widespread citizen involvement in all phases of the planning process, including the communication to the public of technical information.

> **Land Use Planning;**   this goal requires the establishment of a comprehensive land-use planning process as a basis for all decisions and actions related to the use of land. City, county, state and federal agency plans and actions related to land use must be consistent with city and county comprehensive plans, which in turn must comply with the state-wide goals. The state's Land Conservation and Development Commission has the task of evaluating plans for compliance with the goals.

> **Agricultural Lands/Forest Lands;**   these two goals are relatively short and straightforward, and underline the main reasons for introducing the state-wide planning system. The aims are to preserve and maintain agricultural lands, and to conserve forest lands for forest uses. The mechanisms include the designation of exclusive farm use and exclusive forest zones, and the prohibition of sewer hook-ups for inappropriate development.

> **Open Spaces, Scenic and Historic Areas, and Natural Resources;**   this goal encourages programs to conserve open space and to protect natural and scenic resources.

> **Air, Water and Land Resources Quality;**   planning has to take account of the various pollution control regimes.

> **Areas Subject to Natural Disasters and Hazards;**   a goal to protect life and property.

Recreational Needs; although this goal is intended to satisfy the recreational needs of the citizens of the state and visitors, the main subject dealt with is the siting of so-called destination resorts. These are sites of at least 160 acres (except near the shore, where 40 acres is sufficient) providing visitor orientated accommodation and recreational facilities in a setting with high natural qualities. At least $2 million has to be spent on each, at least one third of this being devoted to recreational facilities. These are rather like off the shelf Special Development Order permissions, in the English sense.

Economy of the State; such a goal was important in the development of a state planning process which some saw as anti-growth. In fact, the state is anxious to diversify and improve its economy, which is still based very heavily on farming and forestry.

Housing; this goal too is very brief, and basically requires communities to ensure that their plans accommodate the needs of all Oregon households, and allow flexibility of location, type and density.

Public Facilities and Services; this goal is intended to require the development of infrastructure to go hand in hand with land use decisions, and its importance is that it applies to agencies in the state responsible for different aspects of infrastructure provision.

Transportation; this goal lays down the need for comprehensive planning of transport, both public and private, both for people and goods.

Energy Conservation; the allocation of land and the uses permitted on it should seek to minimise the depletion of non-renewable sources of energy.

Urbanization; the establishment of urban growth boundaries is one of the key elements to increasing the efficient use of land on the fringes of urban areas. In some ways, the boundaries resemble the green belt boundaries around London and other English cities.

Willamette Valley Greenway
Estuarine Resources
Coastal Shorelands
Beaches and Dunes
Ocean Resources
⎫
⎬ each deals in more detail with particular areas of environmental sensitivity
⎭

Each goal is set out with its guidelines on one page of tabloid size, but some are so lacking in specificity that they appear to be meaningless, or at least capable of easy manipulation. The distinction between the goals and the guidelines is that the text of the goals is mandatory and has the force of law; they are adopted as administrative rules in accordance with Oregon law. The guidelines contain suggested courses of action, but are not binding. This structure bears an uncanny resemblance to the content of British development plans; but the 19 goals are rather more general than development plan policies, and their force in law is rather stronger. The legal standing is significant in that they bind local and state agencies (provided that those bodies are concerned about the possibility of a legal challenge).

The way is open for a legal challenge if local government action can be shown to conflict with the goals. To handle the appeals that this structure generates the state has established a special land use court, the Land Use

Board of Appeals. It can consider appeals against both legislative acts (for example, plan adoption or zoning ordinance revision) and quasi-judicial decisions (judging whether a particular development proposal accords with the ordinances). It consists of three referees appointed by the state governor and confirmed by the state senate. Their decisions may be appealed further to the court of appeals and the state supreme court. Could this be a model for a different British mechanism to handle planning appeals (for it is no secret that the Department of the Environment's Planning Inspectorate would prefer to reduce the numbers of appeals received)? Probably not, but facets of the organisation of this Board of Appeals may well be of potential application.

Unlike the British Planning Inspectorate, LUBA does not hear a case from scratch. It takes the record already established at the local level, and considers the precise content of the appeal before it. It is therefore much more like an independent land use court, a sort of preliminary filter to prevent cases going unnecessarily to the courts proper. It is a specialised element of the judicial process, and indeed was set up to replace three separate review or challenge avenues. There had been uncertainty about the scope of each of the three previous methods, and therefore about which was the correct course for resolving any particular problem. The previous methods had also proved costly and slow, and had resulted in inconsistent decisions from the different judicial and administrative bodies involved. The objective in setting up LUBA was to expedite any necessary legal review in the land use process, and to provide greater consistency between decisions in a simplified process. The board should be seen as a replacement for the local circuit courts, with two major advantages. First, channelling all land use cases through one body should encourage greater consistency of decision taking. Second, making it a board rather than a court ensured that the state had control over the qualifications of the people appointed; a court would have required judges, and judges are elected in Oregon. Perhaps also it was more politically acceptable to have a specialist appointed body to override the decisions of locally elected officials, rather than a further elected tier.

The appeal process[15] is open to anyone who can show that they have 'standing'. This generally means anyone who has appeared before the local government or has delivered written testimony at the decision stage, *and* whose interests are adversely affected or who is aggrieved by a local land use decision. This is tantamount to saying that in Britain no-one could give evidence at a planning appeal who did not do so at the application stage. If there is more than one local stage, then it may be necessary to appear at each to preserve one's right of appeal. The second element of the above qualification formula has become less restrictive as it has been interpreted by the courts. The original limitation meant that it was necessary to demonstrate a realistic possibility of harm to use or enjoyment of property or to other personal interests. The position now is wider, but there are reports of impending attempts to narrow the scope to exclude third parties whose interests are not directly affected. This would make enforcement of state planning laws by interested individuals taking legal action harder to achieve.

The British reader should bear in mind that this concept of standing confines not only those entitled to appear and be heard by LUBA (rather like interested parties appearing before a planning inspector) but also those entitled to appeal; the right of appeal to LUBA extends to *third parties* aggrieved by a grant of permission, rather than being limited to aggrieved *applicants* as in Britain. However, the number of third party appeals appears to be kept down by three factors–the need to demonstrate clearly the alleged breach in the law, the appeal fee together with the risk of being faced with a fee for the applicant's legal costs, and in many parts of the state a simple reluctance of an individual to take action against both the local government and the neighbouring landowner.

The LUBA administrative processes include the making of a charge to hear an appeal (currently a flat rate fee of $50). In addition $150 is required as a deposit against awards of costs (a potentially attractive way of concentrating the minds of those contemplating a planning appeal). Written briefs may be supplemented by no more than half an hour of oral testimony from each party, and no-one may testify who has not submitted a written brief. Multi-day hearings are therefore unheard of, but the scope of the appeal is very much narrower than in the British planning appeal, being restricted to the alleged legal breach rather than the case being heard *de novo*. Rather like British High Court appeals, a successful challenge generally results only in the remission of the case back to the local government or state agency to reach a new decision. Appeals come from both those who have been denied a permit and from third parties, some supported by Oregon's citizens' advocacy body in the land use planning area–the 1000 Friends of Oregon.

Overall, there seem to be rather more similarities between LUBA and the legal stage of the British planning appeals process. But there may be some food for thought here for those who will continue to grapple with the problem of how to keep the number of planning appeals, especially minor ones, to a minimum, while continuing to maintain the Secretary of State's influence over decisions as a whole. For example:

(i)   there is a charge for justice dispensed (albeit small by comparison with the likely development value or even the legal costs of making the appeal);

(ii)   the board of appeals is bound by a statutory 77 day time limit (although that can be extended with the consent of the parties; and it is not clear what happens after a breach). In practice, despite the time limit, cases take far too long in the view of many participants, and that is because of the practice of referring cases up and down through the chain (the court of appeals might refer a case back to LUBA for reconsideration of the evidence, who may in turn refer the case back to the local government or appellant);

(iii)   the evidence taken at the local government level, in other words the record of the case to date, is taken as read;

(iv)   the grounds for the appeal have to be clearly stated, for example by reference to the planning goal breached, otherwise the board will refuse to consider it;

(v)   written and oral testimony are limited in length (I was greatly impressed by the efficacy of a flip board used by the Development Commission chairman, which read 'You only have 5 minutes left'!);

(vi)   participation is limited (although inevitably this has generated court cases to establish the exact boundaries of those limitations).

But in all this it should be remembered that the planning goals of the state have the force of law, and that there is thus a right and wrong answer in each case. Such a luxury is not permitted in the discretionary British development control system.

(iv) How effective has Oregon's land use planning programme been?

So much for the administrative framework itself, how effective a system operates within it? The difficulty of judging the effectiveness of any state wide programme such as this is knowing what would have happened in its absence. Just near the farm of Hector MacPherson, the former state senator responsible for originally pushing the legislation, is a mobile home park located on the extremely fertile flat farmland of the Willamette valley. It was approved by the local government concerned shortly before the time when the need to be consistent with state wide planning goals would probably have resulted in the refusal of the rezoning request. As it is the mobile home park hinders the farming process; for example it makes it much more difficult for farmers to carry out the field burning that is an essential component of the rye grass seed harvest. Most commentators in the state seem to believe that a major benefit of the state land use planning programme has been the establishment of extensive and relatively effective local planning where virtually none existed before away from the larger cities.

(v) The system in operation in the rural areas

The enforcement route available to interested citizens enables the challenge of local government decisions that do not accord with the state goals. For example[16], when Clackamas County approved a non-farm dwelling on land zoned for exclusive farm use, a neighbouring farmer was able to get that decision revoked by LUBA. The state law, reflected in the county comprehensive plan, prohibits buildings in such circumstances unless they pass some tough tests. For example, the person requesting permission for the house must prove that the land it will cover is unsuitable for farming; that the house is compatible with farm uses and will not seriously interfere with accepted farming practices; and that building the house will not materially alter the stability of the land use pattern of the area. The county was unable to demonstrate that it had been satisfied by the applicant on all counts, and the decision was therefore quashed by LUBA.

A more significant action was brought by a residents association in a farming area of Washington County (directly to the west of Portland and under great development pressure)[17]. They were able to satisfy a hearings officer (rather like a planning inspector in a case recovered for the Secretary of State's decision in England) appointed by the Land Conservation and Development Commission (the appointed state agency) that the county had engaged in a pattern or practice of decision taking which violated their comprehensive plan. The county had failed to provide evidence in support of all its findings when approving non-farm dwellings, and had failed to make findings where those were required by their own adopted rules. The remedy adopted by the Commission at their meeting of 29 July was to establish state oversight of the county's decisions in the offending category for a limited period. The extent to which this will concentrate the minds of other counties with a less than adequate standard of decision taking remains to be seen. Certainly the cost of state monitoring will be significant, and the state will be just as reluctant for the Commission to institute other monitoring arrangements as the English Department of the Environment is reluctant for the Secretary of State to call in individual planning applications for his decision.

Both of these cases illustrate the difficulty of leaving the administration of a comprehensive land use planning system in the hands of local governments not entirely convinced of the need for land use planning along the lines promulgated by the state. In some counties in Oregon the general attitude about the 'inalienable right' of the individual to do as he wishes with his land can lead to unpleasant consequences for the minority who might think of bringing an appeal against the approval of yet another non-farm dwelling. In small communities the number of neighbours is small and it is not always pleasant to take action which will prevent a neighbour perhaps raising the $20,000 he needs to sustain his basically unviable farm. In these counties there are few pressure groups willing to take a stand, and the 1000 Friends do not have the resources even to monitor and identify abuses, let alone bring them to the courts. They must concentrate on a handful of the most significant cases, augmented by a group of almost 100 co-operating lawyers prepared to take on one planning case a year *pro bono*.

Many of those who have been participants in the development of the state land use planning system believe that the major challenge now is to improve the political integrity of the elected commissioners who run the counties. Only three are elected for each county to administer the county services, and for this they earn more than state legislators. Perhaps this combination of circumstances makes them acutely aware of the needs of their electors. They are all too accessible to their constituent who is requesting just a small exception to the land use planning law. Just as with the Metropolitan Council for the Twin Cities Area, whether the administrators are elected or appointed is crucial. The accessibility of locally elected county commissioners who have no sympathy with the state planning process leads to an imbalance between the interests of the individual developer or landowner and the state wide interests.

The results can be seen from a steady stream of research studies. These have shown that the approval rate for non-farm dwellings in exclusive farm use zones, areas where farming uses are supposed to be protected by local zoning prohibiting non-farm uses, is around 90 per cent. One survey, carried out in 1980 for the 1000 Friends of Oregon, finding this level of approvals, also revealed that 80 per cent of the approved applications violated procedural standards for findings of facts and conclusions of law required to support such decisions.

So, although the state-wide planning system has succeeded in stemming the overflow of large suburban tracts onto fertile farmland, there remains a steady erosion of the resource zones. In an attempt to remedy this dripping tap, the Land Conservation and Development Commission considered a new subdivision of the resource lands into primary and secondary categories. In primary areas tougher rules would apply, perhaps even with powers removed from the county government and placed with a state agency (certainly there are those in the counties who would prefer that the state carry the can for decisions to refuse development). In secondary areas, 'hobby' farms and rural residences would be more readily acceptable. At the time of writing[18], the Commission had prepared proposed new zoning frameworks for the secondary areas, but had yet to decide exactly how these areas would be identified. It is conscious that, if left to their own devices, counties would designate rather more land as secondary than state agricultural and forestry economics would concede. At the same time it is necessary to increase development freedom in some areas as the political price of acquiring more control over others.

Whatever arrangements are ultimately settled, they will do little to ease the pressure to subdivide and build on farmland. Farmers, unlike developers who purchase land, cannot choose what zone their land lies in. They will always see their land as sufficiently different to warrant an exception. So there will always be a strong emotional appeal from those needing cash, perhaps to pay capital transfer tax, for an exception to be made in their case. It may be easier for a state agency to deny permission, but that decision will still need to be taken. The fundamental problem seems to be that county planning boards and elected commissioners are simply not convinced that a few exceptions in their area will undermine the whole purpose of introducing the state wide system. It is perhaps a failing of the system that it is perceived in some quarters as dominated by legal rules, while the purpose in relation to local land remains unclear. There is a clear need to sell the vision of the state that the system was designed to deliver.

To my mind, there is a problem too in the way that large lot sizes are used to distinguish the shape of development in rural residential zones (ie those rural areas not needing to be conserved as primary farm or forest land) from that within the urban boundaries. By specifying lot sizes of, for example, 5 acres, those developing in those areas are required to take more land per dwelling than the market would dictate if left to its own devices. As a result, more land is taken out of its previous interim use as farm or forest than is necessary to fulfil market demands. The argument for such large lot zoning is that it is necessary to distinguish between development in the serviced urban areas, which can and should take dense development, and that in the unserviced rural areas which it is necessary to protect from urban sprawl. But, that objective could be achieved while taking less farm land by abandoning minimum lot sizes but limiting the number of units over a particular area. Moreover, adding a clustering concept, or a transfer of development rights scheme could encourage the rural developments into easier to serve hamlets while keeping larger tracts of surrounding farmland intact. At present, practitioners see the land uses in black and white; thus the corollary of an exclusive farm use zone is almost that farming should not be supported or expected to take place in the other zones. In practice there are many small farms in those areas contributing to the state's economy, and the rigidity of the zoning principles may be forcing them out of business prematurely.

The state wide land use planning system was set up to protect the state's farm and forest lands from incursion because of the dependence of the state economy on those industries. Rural diversification might have the benefit of reducing that dependence, but the process funnels development into the urban areas.

(vi)   *The urban areas*

Not nearly so much research has been focussed on the urban areas, and yet it is in these areas that the state wide system has appeared to achieve almost more than was expected. The concept here was to draw urban growth boundaries to indicate the anticipated limits of urban development. Within these boundaries services could be provided more efficiently, and as a result there should be lower housing production costs and industrial overheads. Lower housing costs should feed through to lower prices, the argument went, and lower industrial overheads should attract inward investment to the state. In practice, the key element keeping down house prices appears to have been the precise goals set for greater densities in the major cities. One report[19] describes a reduction in average lot size from 12,800 to 8,280 sq ft, reducing the land cost element of a new home by $7,000. In addition, much more land was allocated for multi-family housing and the maximum number of buildable units increased from 129,000 to 301,000. This is in contrast to California, where housing developments also seem to be getting denser, but where the approval process is becoming slower and the number of available sites is decreasing, elements which must surely be contributing to the enormous increase in house purchase costs there.

Some say that the urban growth boundaries were drawn comparatively generously, and that their real effect in constraining development has yet to be seen. The fight to contain urban sprawl may yet spread from the rural counties to the city edges. Already, there are real estate firms prepared to take an option on land just outside the urban growth boundaries, at much lower cost than designated urban land, and expend energies to try to get the designation changed. The potential development profits are enormous. It is paradoxical that, the more firmly the local government defends the boundary, the greater are the potential gains to be made, for the firmer boundaries are marked by greater differentials in land value. This feature is not unique to Oregon, or indeed to the United States.

(vi) Other problems and achievements

Another problem is the extent to which the state agency, the Department of Land Conservation and Development, is limited by its drive and resources from delivering all that the goals require. The difficulty flows from conflicts with local governments. One instance in the early 1980s involved the City of Salem and Marion County. Each refused to amend its proposed comprehensive plans to cut down on the amount of development that would be permitted. Ultimately, through political pressure, the Commission conceded; its decision was subsequently overturned by the Court of Appeal. But there are plenty of other instances, according to the 1000 Friends of Oregon[20], where 'despite the judicial rebuke, again and again LCDC or its staff cut deals with recalcitrant local governments, allowing them to violate certain goals in whole or in part in exchange for obeying other goals.' Although the 1000 Friends have been active in pursuing legal remedies to these shortcomings, there is inevitably a limit to the resources that it can devote to enforcement, especially as enforcement can be seen as rather a negative activity. The 1000 Friends must also have regard to politics and choose carefully the arguments worth its time and money.

The state agency is also accused of not speaking out firmly enough, or not taking a strong stand in the implementation of the goals, which are legally binding. As a result, other local governments are encouraged to think that they too could get away without fully complying with the legal requirements. The state was not doing enough to counter what one former state senator termed[21] 'moral corruption arising out of susceptibility of county commissioners to flattery'. This problem will become more acute as the local governments take on more responsibility for operating the land use planning process themselves.

After problems with the operators of the system, most people involved with Oregon's land use planning process felt that legal and administrative complexities were the next most major obstacles[22]. Some thought that imaginative projects and innovative solutions to problems were being prevented by the rigidity of the land designation. The state attorney general, Dave Frohnmayer, is said to have characterised the process as 'too fossilized; too trivialized; too legalized'. The governor's environmental policy adviser was concerned to find ways of informing the local government process at an early stage so as to narrow the scope for appeals and references up and down the system. What she had in mind was state officials going out to give evidence at local government public hearings, so

Figure 8.4 Examples showing that, even 15 years into the state-wide planing era, Oregon continues to require positive action to deliver the original goals.

'Actions of the planning commission seem designed, first, to circumvent the law and second, to intimidate those who oppose illegal development . . . For instance, one developer freely admitted in an open hearing that he had engaged in [off the record] contact by providing private tours of the development site for planning commission members before the vote was taken.'

Robert Mason, Linn County farmland owner
Testimony to LCDC, December 17, 1987

'I am furious that this county takes extra effort to aid applicants that are applying for these illegal mini-farms rather than working to maintain the land as prescribed by the Oregon State Legislature. On a recent visit to the county planning office I overheard an applicant be advised as to how he should tailor his application so that it could be approved for a home site on a 5-acre parcel in an exclusive farm use zone.'

Russell Newcomer, Clackamas County farmland owner
Testimony to LCDC, February 17 1988

'During the fourteen months that I served on the Planning Commission *not a single application was denied*. Regardless of whether I invested a large amount of time in studying an application or whether I merely showed up to a meeting and voted, the effect was the same.'

Frank Conley, Wallowa County,
Letter of resignation from Wallowa County Planning Commission,
August 14, 1986

that a correct policy interpretation was established and put on the record at the first stage in the process.

On the other hand, if making the process more flexible means that it appears easy for developers to obtain exceptional permits or for local governments to change zoning provisions, that would undermine the certainty that the system is supposed to provide. That certainty has already attracted a great deal of high tech industry, confident that the state's strict environmental regime is more likely to secure the clean air and water that they need.

The final problem that emerged in my interviews with some of the key proponents of state land use planning was the problem of success. The more successful the system in determining strong growth and zoning boundaries, the greater the land value gradient across those boundaries, and therefore the greater the incentive for real estate developers to fight those boundaries or to invest speculatively on the hope of a future change. This difficulty is seen to apply particularly to land near good new roads, such as the Interstates and a new beltway being constructed into Washington County. This is a paradoxical effect that bears on all planning systems, and is to be found in Britain in the great pressure for development in the green belt adjacent to junctions on London's ring motorway.

(vii)   Conclusions

Most commentators regard Oregon's state land use planning system as a very good achievement of the original objectives of preserving farm and forestry resource lands from urban sprawl. Certainly, the urban achievements of denser development within properly defined boundaries have slowed down the loss of farmland on the edge of cities. But, in the rural areas the pressure to build new non-farm dwellings is great, and there is currently no effective enforcement mechanism (the 1000 Friends are promoting two solutions – the establishment of more local enforcement groups based on the county branch structure of the Council for the Protection of Rural England, and changes in the tax regime to prevent hobby farmers from obtaining property tax relief). The root of the problem is the people, and it remains a fact of life in all America that very many rural people see no role for regulations that interfere with their right to do what they wish with their land. Oregon has achieved a lot, but there is still much to do.

Vermont: state wide permitting in a vacuum reveals shortcomings

(i)   Development of Vermont's state land use control system

The state of Vermont enacted a land use and development law (Act 250) in 1970 in order to control and direct development. I set out the basic reason at the beginning of this Chapter. It established a special permit process for major developments, and was intended to lead ultimately to the preparation of a state land use plan. In practice, only the first objective was achieved, and even that permitting process proved inadequate to deal with the pressures of development in the state in the 1980s. The result was a new growth management law, known as Act 200, passed in 1988. It is too early to say how effective the new law will be, but the original permitting system itself is of some interest. After setting out below the way the process worked originally, an interesting question is to examine how it was perceived to be inadequate. Is there a chance that similar problems may arise in the parts of Britain under intense development pressure?

(ii)   What development is caught by the control?

Nine regional environmental commissions were appointed to grant special permits for all significant developments. The process controlled all residential construction of more than 10 units or residential subdivisions into more than 10 lots, commercial or industrial development involving more than 10 acres (where both zoning and subdivision bylaws have been adopted by the municipality) and commercial or industrial development involving more than 1 acre (where zoning and subdivision bylaws had not been adopted). In addition the controls extended over the construction of roads longer than 800 feet, or serving more than 5 parcels of land and all construction or improvements for commercial, industrial or residential uses above the 2,500 foot contour. Nearby related sites could be combined in considering a permit application.

(iii)   Who exercises control?

The environmental commissions comprise three residents appointed by the Governor and chosen for their general familiarity with local conditions, diversity of occupations, and, most importantly, common sense and sound judgement[23]. Seven co-ordinators within the 9 regions administer the hearings process. Otherwise data, personnel and facilities must be provided by the other state agencies. With the agreement of the parties concerned, one of the environmental commission members may himself act as a hearing officer and take a decision.

The process also incorporates an appeals procedure from the 9 environmental commissions to the Environmental Board of the State, a 9 member body with members appointed by the Governor and subject to confirmation by the State Senate. This body hears appeals from the commissions, has policy making responsibilities, sets procedures, and responds to petitions for declaratory rulings. It is independent of all other state agencies. Vermont is a state where there is great suspicion of government agencies – a state that is proud of its part time legislature, that allows representatives to pursue their occupations. Observers suggest that the appointment of lay boards, with an ultimate right of appeal to the courts, was important in gaining acceptance for the development review process.

(iv)   What are the procedures for control?

Having established with the district coordinator whether the project will need a special permit (a special procedure is available, including the possibility of a hearing before the State Environmental Board, in cases where there is dispute over the need for a permit), the applicant secures all other permits required for the development. He then makes a formal application, including detailed plans, information about the applicant's interest in the site, and the substantial interests of any others, a full list of the adjoining property owners and their addresses, and the application fee set at $1 per $1000 of estimated construction costs. The applicant must copy his application to the relevant municipality, and to the local and regional planning commissions. He must also post a notice in the local town hall, and publish it in a local newspaper. The coordinator ensures that any necessary state agencies are informed, and is required within 25 days to schedule a hearing within 40 days. There is an expedited process whereby the permit may be granted without a hearing if the coordinator gives notice and no-one objects. Pre-hearing conferences may be held to clarify issues of controversy, to identify witnesses and documents and to define the scope for the hearing. The outcome of such a conference will be recorded in an order which is binding on the parties.

Following an optional site visit by the commissioners, the quasi-judicial hearing takes place, at which those other than the main parties are limited to giving evidence on the relevant criteria (see below) that affect their own interests (ie neighbouring landowners may comment only on the criteria affecting their own properties, and interest groups on criteria relevant to their declared interests). The commission may summon witnesses in order to obtain the information it needs to reach a decision, and that decision, containing findings of fact and conclusions of law, must be issued within 20 days of the completion of the hearing. Conditional permits may be granted, including the posting of bonds to ensure that the applicant has the capacity to comply with the conditions imposed. Once a permit is granted, construction must start within a year and be completed within a period set by reference to the project concerned. Non-compliance with the timetable can lead to the revocation of the permit.

Any party recognised at the hearing may lodge an appeal within 30 days of the decision, but only in respect of the criteria on which they were entitled to give evidence at the hearing. Appeals are heard *de novo* on the criteria that were the subject of the appeal. Between two thirds and three quarters of the appeals are from the applicants, the reminder being from local governments or third parties.

(v)   The criteria employed in exercising control

The proposed project must satisfy all the following:

    i   – no undue water or air pollution will result

    ii   – adequate water supply must be available

    iii   – no unreasonable burden may be placed on any existing water supply

    iv   – no unreasonable increase in soil erosion or impact on soil stability

    v   – no unreasonable congestion or unsafe conditions with respect to transportation facilities

    vi   – no unreasonable burden on the ability of the municipality to provide educational services

    vii   – no unreasonable burden on the ability of the municipality to provide services such as the police, fire and road maintenance facilities

    viii   – no undue adverse effect on scenic or natural beauty, aesthetics, historic sites or rare and irreplaceable natural areas (although this is qualified to allow a project to proceed if the public benefits would outweigh the loss and the developer has no other suitable site in his ownership)

ix – demonstration of consideration of impact on:
   – the ability of the town and region to absorb the growth
   – reduction of agricultural potential
   – secondary agricultural and forestry soils
   – mineral and earth resources

There are also assessments of energy conservation in the project, of the utilities proposed to ensure they are compatible with the municipality's plans, of the wider impact on the community (a criterion used to resist out of town shopping malls because of the likely resultant effect on economic and social importance of the traditional town centre) and on public investment, and of the quality of the site plan in providing such features as clustering of houses where appropriate

x – conformity with plans and capital programs adopted by local government

Over the first 13 years of operation of the process 4,265 decisions by the regional bodies resulted in 3,902 approved permits (97.5%). There were 199 (4.7%) appeals from those decisions, some against permits granted. Permits were granted in about one half of the appeal cases, while most of the others were withdrawn or settled before a decision became necessary. Although the success rate of applicants seems high, it is important to remember that applications are tailored for the approval process and permits are frequently granted subject to conditions.

(vi) What were the results?

There has not been a drastic curb on growth; indeed some observers suggest that confidence that the environment is properly protected has actually encouraged investment in the state. The consensus is that the process has resulted in a significant improvement in the environment, although it has also thrown up a contrast with the effectiveness of some municipalities in dealing with the smaller projects not covered by the review process.

According to the Environmental Board's own report, the development control process has received sustained public approval and support from the political leadership of the state. It proved politically impossible, however, to introduce the final state land use plan that was intended to inform the process. The process therefore remained primarily reactive and only half complete. Local zoning decisions were taken on the basis of a local comprehensive plan, but there was no overall land use plan to form the basis for the state permitting process. The kind of problems identified with that system are best summed up in the following extract from the report of a policy analysis conference in 1987:

'With an overall strategy in place and local-regional-state plans to carry it out, it would not be necessary to judge whether individual developments were the best use for a particular site or whether they fitted the town's, the region's, or the state's long range goals, which is the process now. All that could be determined in advance. With a broad strategy to guide them, local communities, regional associations of local communities, and state agencies could plan together what development should take place, where, and when. The regulatory process could then be used as it was intended: to determine whether the proper steps were being taken to prevent environmental damage, alleviate traffic problems, and comply with the other standards spelled out in the law.'[24]

Landmark Legislation

On May 19, 1988, Governor Madeleine M. Kunin signed the Growth Management Act of 1988 (Act 200) into law. *The Act significantly strengthens the process of integrating plans at the local, regional and state agency levels.* It also increases the resources available to towns and regions for planning and provides substantial and sustained funding for the Housing and Conservation Trust Fund (to protect open land, valuable resource areas, and affordable housing). The Act authorizes communities to assess 'impact fees' and establishes two programs to help Vermont's farmers stay in business.

The following is a summary of the Act's key components:

Vermont's Planning Goals

The planning process will be guided by 32 planning goals. These goals must be followed by state agencies, regional planning commissions and towns in the development of comprehensive plans. The goals are broad and flexible–recognizing the unique character of Vermont communities– yet they will oblige decision-makers to consider all the values important to Vermonters (the goals are listed below).

Town Planning

Planning at the local level will remain optional, but towns that choose to adopt plans consistent with the Act will receive additional funds, technical assistance, and greater influence over state actions that affect their communities. *Most important, towns will gain control over their own future.* Beginning July 1, 1991, towns that adopt plans must make them consistent with the Vermont planning goals, and must follow a process that guarantees active citizen participation.

Regional Planning

In the late 1960's, the Legislature authorized the creation of regional planning commissions to provide coordinated planning throughout the state. *Until the passage of Act 200, towns had the option of participating in their regional planning commission. Now all towns are automatically members.* Towns will continue to appoint representatives to their commission's board of directors, and thus they will control decision-making. The commissions will provide technical assistance to communities and review town plans to ensure that they are consistent with the Vermont planning goals and with plans of neighboring municipalities. Commissions are also required to develop regional plans that follow the goals and are compatible with approved town plans in the region. The regional planning process must actively encourage citizen participation.

State Agency Planning

The agencies of state government that make decisions affecting land use–such as the Agency of Transportation and the Agency of Natural Resources–must adopt plans and take actions consistent with the Vermont goals and plans developed by regional planning commissions, municipalities and other state agencies. For example, if the Agency of Transportation plans to re-route part of a highway hrough Washington County, it must ensure that the project is consistent with the Central Vermont regional plan as well as the plans of the towns along the route. Because the construction of highways (as well as sewage treatment plants, transmission lines, etc.) plays a major role in channeling development, towns and regions will now have more control over where growth occurs. But remember, *towns and regions must have approved plans to influence state decisions.*

Council of Regional Commissions

On July 1, 1989, a Council of Regional Commissions will be created. The Council will be composed of a municipal representative from each of the regional planning commissions, along with three state agency or department heads and two members of the public appointed by the Governor. The group will review regional plans and the various state agency plans and ensure that they are compatible with each other and consistent with the Vermont Planning Goals. Through a three-member Regional Review Panel, the Council will also hear appeals of regional planning commission decisions.

Geographic Information System

Vermont has made a substantial commitment to the rapid development of a computerized geographic information system (GIS) to help in the planning process. A GIS transforms essential land-use data–such as soil types, groundwater locations, topographic conditions and population concentrations–into easily understood maps. *This technology will soon make it easy for communities and regions to base land-use decisions on comprehensive and up-to-date information.*

Housing and Conservation Trust Fund

The General Assembly in 1987 created the Trust Fund to preserve open land, protect important historic and environmental resources, and support affordable housing. The fund is administered by a nine-member board that reviews applications from towns, non-profit organizations and certain state agencies. Through Act 200, the Legislature committed $22.5 million to the Fund in fiscal year 1989 and more than $3 million per year thereafter.

Property Transfer Tax

To provide a continuous source of revenue to support town and regional planning as well as the Trust Fund, the Legislature increased the Property Transfer Tax from 0.5% to 1.25%. The first $100,000 of the value of principal residences and the entire value of working farms will be exempted from the increase. For example, if you buy a $105,000 house, you will pay 0.5% on the first $100,000 and 1.25% on $5,000.

Impact Fees

Municipalities with approved plans will now be able to charge developers impact fees to cover the cost of services required by the development. If a major residential project is built in a community, the town will be able to collect money from the developer to offset new municipal costs caused by the project–such as for new traffic lights, road improvements or school construction. The amount of the fee must be tied directly to the project's impact, and must be spent on the needed capital improvement.

Farm Programs

Agriculture is a critical component of Vermont's rural character, yet because of federal pricing policies, farmers are going out of business at an accelerating rate. To help farmers stay in business, the Legislature established two new programs through Act 200: the Dairy Income Stabilization Program and the Working Farm Tax Abatement Program.

The first is a one-year program that will provide immediate payments of up to $5,000 to dairy farmers who make more than 50% of their income from farming. The Tax Abatement program will pay 95% of the property taxes on open land and farm buildings for non-dairy farmers in the first year and for all farmers in future years.

Vermont's Planning Goals

• A coordinated, comprehensive planning process and policy framework shall guide decisions by municipalities, regional planning commissions and state agencies.

• Citizen participation shall be encouraged at all levels of the planning process, and decisions shall be made at the most local level possible commensurate with their impact.

• Consideration must be given to the use of resources and the consequences of growth and development, not only for the community, but for the region and the state.

• Whenever appropriate, municipalities shall be encouraged and helped to work creatively together to develop and implement plans.

• Important and economically viable agricultural and forest lands shall be protected by limiting alternate uses on those lands to low density uses designed to preserve the long viability of farm or forest use.

• Fragmentation of lands identified as important for agriculture and forestry shall be discouraged.

• The quality of air, water, wildlife and land resources shall be maintained or improved.

• Special resource areas shall be identified, development shall be planned so as to protect and preserve them and, when necessary, they should be placed in whatever form of public or private ownership that would best maintain and utilize their value to the public.

• Strategies to facilitate the appropriate extraction of earth resources and the proper restoration and preservation of the aesthetic qualities of the area shall be addressed.

• Energy conservation should be actively encouraged and wasteful practices discouraged.

• Public access to noncommercial outdoor recreational opportunities shall be identified, provided where feasible, and protected.

• Growth shall be planned to maintain and enhance recreational opportunities for Vermont residents and visitors.

• Those natural resources referred to in Act 250 should be planned for development and use consistent with the environmental principles found in Act 250.

• Public investments, including the construction or expansion of infrastructure, shall be made so as to support development in a locally designated growth area, and shall not be made so as to lead to development in important and economically viable agricultural or conservation areas.

• The rate of growth should not exceed the ability of the town and the area to provide facilities and services.

• The development and provision of government and public utility facilities and services should be based upon a projection of reasonably expected population increase and economic growth, and should recognize the limits of the state's human, financial, and natural resources.

• Development shall be planned so as to maintain the historic settlement pattern of compact village and urban centers separated by rural countryside.

• Economic growth shall be encouraged in locally designated growth areas, or employed to revitalize existing village or urban centers, or both.

• Intensive residential development shall be encouraged primarily in areas that are identified as village or urban centers, and strip development along highways shall be discouraged.

• Development should be permitted at reasonable population densities and reasonable rates of growth.

• Economic development should be pursued so as to provide maximum economic benefit with minimal environmental impact.

• Expansion of economic opportunities shall be addressed in areas with high unemployment or low per capita incomes.

• Access to educational and vocational training opportunities shall be addressed.

• Strategies to help the agricultural and forest industries remain viable shall be developed.

• The manufacture and marketing of value-added agricultural and forest products shall be addressed.

• The construction, expansion or provision of public facilities and services should be planned so as to not significantly reduce the resource value of important and economically viable adjoining agricultural or forestry lands.

• The housing requirement for Vermont's expanding resident population, particularly for those citizens of low or moderate income, must be met by the construction of new housing units and the rehabilitation of existing structures.

• Sites for multi-family and manufactured housing should be readily available in locations similar to those generally used for single-family conventional dwellings.

• There should be a reasonable diversity of housing types, and a choice between rental and ownership for all citizens in a variety of locations suitable for residential development and convenient to employment and commercial areas.

• Transportation systems should provide convenience and service commensurate with need, should respect the natural environment, and should be energy efficient. Public transportation shall be addressed.

• New construction or major reconstruction of highways should provide pedestrian paths when economically feasible and in the public interest.

• Development and expansion of governmental and public utility facilities and service should occur, where appropriate, within highway or public utility right-of-way corridors.

Figure 8.5　The State of Vermont's new planning legislation 1988

In other words, the aim was to encourage more enlightened decision taking at the local level, leaving the state agencies responsible for the specific environmental aspects. Act 250, while successful in improving the quality of development projects, was not effective in dealing with the effects of cumulative growth.

In the light of these and other conclusions, in 1988 the state enacted a new law (Act 200) to strengthen the process of integrating plans at the local, regional and state agency levels. It also increased the resources available to towns and regions for planning and provided new funding for the Housing and Conservation Trust Fund (to protect open land, valuable resource areas, and affordable housing). The Act also authorised local governments to extract impact fees from developers to pay for the new infrastructure demanded by their developments, and established new funds to underwrite the agricultural industry (Vermont regrets its rapid transition from a farming economy).

The enhanced plan preparation process will be guided by 32 planning goals, which must be followed by state agencies, regional planning commissions and towns in the preparation of plans. They are set out in Figure 8.5. The extent to which these will change the shape of development in the state remains to be seen. One part of the proposed 1988 legislative package was a proposed tax sharing measure, under which municipalities would share the increase in local revenue generated by new developments. The idea was to reduce the incentive of property tax enhancement for municipalities to promote any and all kinds of development without regard for the broader environmental consequences. This part of the package apparently failed to secure approval.

In many respects the Vermont development review process is similar to the procedures followed in Britain when there is a planning appeal to be determined by the Secretary of State. The following aspects may be of particular interest to those who administer the process:

   i   the statutory requirement, and accompanying expectation, that hearings will be held within a set time of lodging a formal application;

   ii   the binding nature of the pre-hearing conference

   iii   the deliberate appointment of a committee of people *from the region* to take decisions, but with appropriate input from officials and state agencies on the criteria

   iv   the limitation of evidence, especially that of neighbours and interest groups, to issues that are of direct concern to them

   v   the requirement for any appeal to the state level to relate to specific criteria

   vi   the significance of information about land ownership (for example, who are the neighbouring owners, what other land does the applicant own nearby, and what other sites does he own that might be suitable alternatives for the proposed development). The fact that Americans control land divisions and note land ownership changes so assiduously makes it difficult for an applicant to evade the review process by pursuing development proposals on a number of small adjacent sites vii a permit or certificate of compliance from another state or local agency on a particular criterion relating to the proposed development can create a rebuttable presumption that the criterion concerned has been satisfied

Of interest too is the method of determining the application fee by reference to the estimated construction cost, with the estimate being made by the applicant. Apparently[25] this leads to few problems, and there is a safeguard that the district co-ordinator can challenge the estimate on the basis of usual construction costs (average per square foot tables). The applicant can also be required to submit a post-construction affidavit on actual costs, and pay an additional fee if the estimate was way off. Such a scheme has the advantage that it is never necessary to increase planning application fees to keep pace with inflation.

There have been court cases on the rights of various parties to participate in the process, and about the scope of the review process in respect of particular proposed developments, but overall there seems to have been smooth operation of a process which, measured in terms of applications per head of population, would cover about 1 in 10 British applications, or about twice the number of major[26] applications.

New Jersey: the struggle for control in the most densely developed state

(i) The background to the development of a state plan

New Jersey is one of the latest states to be tussling seriously with these state planning ideas. By way of background the stimulus for the current state planning process in New Jersey arose from the third wave of outward migration from New York City. First there had been the suburban housing boom, to about a 30 mile distance from New York, further along the rail routes. All this development had been in the most northerly part of the state and was prompted by relatively easy access to the city by both public and private transport. Then the corporations moved out, setting up offices and some industry on the fringes of the suburban ring where relatively large green field sites were available, and where it was possible to employ a work force, who no longer needed to commute, at lower cost. Finally, the third phase was a simultaneous discovery of the attractions of being 50 miles from the city, on the main roads, by both a suburban population looking for more space, and companies looking for campus style office locations. Now, many of the employees in these offices and in the supporting businesses servicing them, drive daily from eastern Pennsylvania, a further 30 miles out from New York. A dramatic growth of development in the area and the resultant increasing traffic, combined with the low income housing crisis described in Chapter 11, led to the start of a state planning process.

The state planning system is not yet implemented at the time of writing, despite enabling legislation in 1985, and this is because of the sophistication of the process devised. Writing about a process that is in the preparation stage has certain shortcomings but sufficient progress has been made to see what shape the system will take. In a sense, as it should, the proposed system draws on the best of what has gone before. Having attended public meetings of the State Planning Commission responsible for drawing up the plan, I have been able to draw on material produced by that Commission in order to describe some of the features of state planning New Jersey style. The relevance of what is happening in that state to planning in South East England is apparent from a Commission answer to the question 'Why is a State Plan necessary?':

'New Jersey is not able to construct and maintain public facilities and services fast enough to meet the demands of new growth. As a result public services are deteriorating throughout the state because:

- growth is occurring in areas of the state in which public agencies had not planned to provide services; and,
- the public sector is reaching the limit of its ability to raise the additional public revenues necessary to construct, maintain and operate new and expanded facilities and services.

In the absence of adequate public services, the very amenities of the state which attract new residents and new businesses are rapidly disappearing. Many believe that if present trends continue, **the recent economic resurgence of New Jersey could grind to a halt, along with the traffic on most of its major arteries** (my emphasis). It is not the state plan that will inhibit growth – it is the absence of a plan.'

There are physical and economic parallels with the recent rapid growth in south east England leading to traffic congestion, tremendous pressure to develop, high house prices due to the market being unable to meet demand, and certain areas where residents are keen that no more development should take place once they have arrived (not in my back yard is becoming so common a statement that we shall soon all be calling our gardens yards!). The completion of the Channel Tunnel in 1993 will add further traffic congestion, even if no more growth is generated; in fact we shall probably have both. And there is another, more intriguing administrative parallel: in New Jersey, one of the main reasons for the emergence of the state planning process was the fragmentation of the local comprehensive planning process, with 567 municipalities each preparing their own plans in isolation. After the next English Planning Bill, the number of separate development plans in the growth areas of south east England may multiply, and may need the sort of the regional strategies that appear to be necessary in the state plan to coordinate planning efforts in New Jersey.

There are common elements that New Jersey shares with the experience of others coordinating planning regimes in the United States. For example, there is state concern with critical areas such as wetlands and unspoiled countryside, that economic development might damage the very aspects of the state that attract the development that is so necessary for economic well being, with infrastructure provision. There is a general desire to direct development to the inner urban areas where there is capacity and infrastructure is less stretched. The people taking part in the process share characteristics with their counterparts in other states. The New Jersey farmer is just as adamant as his Oregon counterpart that his land is there to be developed, and if the state wants to stop development on that land it should pay the full price (whatever that might be). It is the New Jersey communities which are suffering from growth that want controls, while those yet to come under the influence of suburban development do not see why they should be denied their share of the property tax ratables.

To put the rate of development into perspective, it is worth mentioning that some municipalities are growing at the rate of 10 per cent each year. This makes planning of schools, to take just one example, difficult to say the least. Loss of farmland is proceeding at a rate that implies there will be none left in 20 years without action. Aquifers have been pumped dry. Septic tanks, which are more frequent in areas of development on large lots which it is not economic to link to sewers, are beginning to damage ground and surface water supplies. Sewer systems are at full capacity, driving developers to install more septic tanks. Inner city employment dropped by one quarter over 12 years, while over the same period employment in the state as a whole increased by one quarter. Air pollution, much of it from car exhausts, means that the state fails the Federal Environmental Protection Agency standards. Traffic congestion is increasing, while the scope for building new roads to relieve it is reducing, especially when it is argued that such new roads would actually simply encourage more development along the major routes instead of in the cities. Where the metropolitan areas of Philadelphia and New York City overlap in the centre of the state near Princeton, a linear city is rapidly forming along the line of Route 1 (see Figure 1.2), the New Jersey Turnpike and the main railroad. Twelve million square feet of office space has been built in the open countryside since 1980, and the zoning in place will permit about the total volume of office space of Manhattan[27]. It is a city with no centre and no overall history and identity; students of urban design are fascinated.

(ii) How the state plan is evolving

In early 1989, the State Planning Commission embarked on its final lap, known as 'cross acceptance'. This is an interesting procedure. Over an 8 month period the counties will work with the municipalities (in New Jersey the whole state is covered by incorporated municipalities, with groups of municipalities falling into county areas, a system familiar in the English non-metropolitan areas) to compare the preliminary state plan with county and municipal plans and regulations. The idea is that inconsistencies, and there will be many (for otherwise there would have been no need for a state plan at all), should be removed either by amending local ordinances, or by amending the draft plan. The Commission will negotiate with the municipalities using the medium of the counties. Only when all the negotiation is over, and optimum compatibility is achieved, will the state plan proceed to final adoption. The Commission hopes to do this in 18 months – by mid 1990; in Oregon a similar process on much more general policies took 10 years, albeit from a less developed planning base in the state. Already in New Jersey it has been a much slower process than supporters of state planning had hoped. And at one stage more than 80 per cent of local mayors were on record as saying that planning should remain in local hands; only 6.5 per cent supported the plan[28].

What is much more interesting is the content of the plan. For it is far more detailed, and far more prescriptive than any American state plan that has gone before, and yet it does not require that local and county master plans conform. There is only what is termed for reasons of politics the 'bottom up' cross acceptance process. In addition, it is intended to be a truly comprehensive plan, rather than one addressed to achieve particular environmental objectives. The January 1988 working document totalled nearly 400 pages and the draft issued in early 1989 was accompanied by some very impressive material designed to present the significance of the plan to the interested public.

The plan divides the state into 7 tiers, on the basis of the existence, or planned extension, of public facilities and services. In this way the plan scenario has most of the projected population and employment growth in existing growing suburbs, major transportation corridors (the linear cities of the future), and towns and small villages, without impairing natural resources and environmental qualities. The declining urban areas of the state are to receive incentives and public spending to make development there more attractive. Housing densities are to be increased in order to protect the environment, while reducing land and infrastructure costs per

184

unit. In rural areas, agricultural areas and environmentally sensitive areas, development is to be restricted to the carrying capacities of the environment. The discouragement to development in these areas is not only through rules such as those mentioned in Chapter 5, limiting the densities of development served by septic tanks, limiting what can be built in stream corridors and so on, but also requiring the builder to pay the entire cost of the infrastructure his development will require – roads, schools, police, fire protection, sewers and water supplies. Of course, whether this will be a sufficient discouragement depends very much on the market; the result may not be a sufficient depression of rural land values to make farming a more attractive option. In addition, I suspect that New Jersey municipalities may behave in a similar fashion to the counties in Oregon which do not respect the state role in the process. New Jersey will clearly need a citizens' advocacy group like the 1000 Friends of Oregon to enforce against the worst offenders.

All state agencies will be supposed to take account of the plan in drawing up their own plans for infrastructure investment and service provision. In addition, state permits for those developments that need them will not be granted in the areas which the plan says are inappropriate for development. There is a clear intention to use the specific grant regime to enforce the plan for some local governments. As we have seen earlier in this report, grants for quite unconnected projects may be held back as the price for not respecting the state plan. So, in practice the enforcement will be diffuse, and often indirect rather than involving the courts. It will be hampered by a lack of specificity that some say has to creep in to the plan if the municipalities are to endorse it in broad terms at the end of the process and amend their plans accordingly.

As if by way of contingency, new direct controls over specific developments at the county level are planned quite separately of the state planning process. These will control access to main roads, will enable counties to review major projects, will enable special tax assessments to cover the cost of roads resulting from new development, and will enable a much wider transfer of development rights programme in the state. And with a change in state governor in 1989, it may be that the possibility of property tax revenue sharing, such as Minneapolis has got and Vermont wanted, can come back on to the agenda. In my view, the state plan is intended to put direction into the market to secure the environmental and economic outcomes desired. I think that the state will find that it needs to tackle the question of tax equalisation in order to bring some logic and direction into the process of chasing tax ratables.

Conclusions

In general in the United States, there is no separation between different tiers of government of development planning from development control, in the way that in much of Britain structure plans have until now been prepared by counties while development control is exercised by districts. On the contrary, many of the state enabling acts which authorise local government to control development by zoning and other means specifically require that process to be informed by properly prepared local master plans. The separation comes in the distinction in the American government structure between the legislature, the executive and the judiciary. So, in a typical municipality the elected township committee might endorse the master plan and zoning ordinances drawn up by the appointed planning board, while the separately appointed zoning board of appeals would interpret the ordinances in case of difficulty and consider applications for variances in cases of hardship.

However, that separation can do nothing to prevent the problems that emerge through local governments' lack of coordination. The fragmented structure of local government that has emerged, especially in states where annexation was stopped by suburban municipalities, has proved inadequate to cope with regional infrastructure problems (as with Minneapolis/St Paul), with massive growth and its effect on the environment (as in Florida, Vermont and New Jersey), with the need to protect land resources from inefficient development (as in Oregon), and with the need to take special steps in certain critical areas, such as coastal zones or the Pinelands of New Jersey. In these circumstances the politics become such that a majority in the state are willing to impose their will on local governments. (Incidentally, it is nearly always the states that have a Democratic background that have gone farthest into state controls).

So, the starting point is a general picture of local governments preparing their own plans locally, subject to varying degrees of restriction from state government on the way it is to be done, and through the range of mechanisms that are to be used in the state concerned. Regional associations of local governments seem usually to fail to deliver coordination of infrastructure and service provision, especially since their role in reviewing grant applications has been scaled back with the reducing level of Federal grants. To succeed, regional government needs to have a relevant range of powers over regional agencies that impact on development – for example over sewers, water supply, transportation, parks and airports.

Acute problems of growth or environmental problems, or both, can drive the states to act. In California and North Carolina the emphasis is on protecting particular coastal environments. In Oregon it is more on the protection of agricultural and forest resource lands. Vermont depends on its attractive character to sustain its all the year round tourist economy, among other things. In Minnesota, the legislature created a regional government with sufficient teeth to achieve infrastructure and pollution objectives while taking only a minimum of powers away from local and state government.

The states cannot afford their own development control systems for any but the most significant developments. So the balancing act is to shape local government actions by adopting general restraint powers, and then using combinations of fiscal arrangements, threats to withhold grants, and local non-profit groups to enforce the system. Inevitably, only the worst excesses of development are controlled. On the margin, it is always easier for a local government to approve a development contrary to the state rules, rather than one contrary to its own, which it might believe in to a greater degree. That is why the latest systems are tending to try to cajole local governments into conformity. Different methods for this have been used in Oregon, Florida, Vermont (especially in the latest system) and New Jersey.

What is particularly interesting is that the latest series of planning systems carry with them a more comprehensive system of control and infrastructure coordination than is to be found in the average English structure plan. Over the next few years we should see whether or not such comprehensive planning spreads to other states. It may be that, like English structure plans, detailed documents prepared by the non-implementing/non-permitting authority will prove to be too cumbersome and inflexible. In other words, in England the shift of emphasis from county structure plans and towards making districts responsible, in other words to a more American process, will be seen to be the right one. The sort of regional strategic coordination in the Twin Cities may be the future role for English counties – coordinating key infrastructure provision such as highways and public transport on a cost effective scale, and reviewing the most significant projects, all within the framework of metropolitan guidelines.

I cannot predict whether there will be one right answer, but the trend in America seems to be towards greater controls at regional and state levels. That is backed by a tradition of many more specific grants in America, rather than the general rate support grant in England, originally designed to preserve local democratic control decisions on expenditure priorities. We might watch carefully to see how long that increase in state controls, in the growth management movement of the 1980s, continues to bring more and more complexity into the development process. The right answers in New Jersey, the most densely populated state, and suffering some of the greatest growth, may have something to teach us in the south east, especially if local government expenditure controls in Britain force more local deals whereby developers provide infrastructure and more. That is the subject of the next chapter. Or it could be that without the race between English local authorities for tax rateables, we do not need to create such a cumbersome control mechanism. We share the same aims, to encourage redevelopment of redundant urban land before taking green field sites, and to encourage denser development, but against a background of a reluctance to accept development, rather than a race for certain types of tax rich offices, shops and large lot houses. But some of the control methods used themselves encourage profligate use of land – for example using minimum lot size zoning.

In addition, several of the state systems incorporate methods of referring cases between tiers of government, and administrative appeal procedures. In the text of this chapter I have pointed out what I regard as some of the interesting parallels and lessons for the English planning appeals system.

NOTES TO CHAPTER 8

1. Land, Growth and Politics by John M DeGrove, published by the American Planning Association (1984)

2. Political Change in the Metropolis by John J Harrigan, published by Little, Brown and Co. (1985).

3. The Zoning Game Revisited; Richard F. Babcock and Charles L. Siemon – Lincoln Institute of Land Policy (1985)

4. In the chapter, Land Development Regulation, of Local Government Law, published by Callaghan and Co. (1986).

5. The approach adopted by the state built on that used in the Meadowlands and in the 1971 Adirondack Park. (This is a six million acre state park established by New York State, in a wild and beautiful mountain area increasingly attracting second home development, given the accessibility to New York via improved roads. In much of the designated area, the zoning now only permits one dwelling per 640 acres.)

6. Hobart Gardner v New Jersey Pinelands Commission et al, decided by the Superior Court of New Jersey, July 8, 1988.

7. See note 2.

8. In an interview with the author, June 1988.

9. Construction of the first 3 million square feet is under way. The development will be by the same firm which developed the West Edmonton Mall in Canada, the world's largest shopping and leisure complex. (It will be the first development of this size in the United States and it is interesting to note that Bloomington was also the home of another related first in America – the first enclosed out-of-town shopping mall, at Southdale.)

10. Making One Community out of Many; Perspectives on the Metropolitan Council of the Twin Cities Area, by Professor Arthur Naftalin of the Hubert H. Humphrey Institute of Public Affairs, University of Minnesota, and published by the Metropolitan Council of the Twin Cities Area, September 1986.

11. The Future of Development Plans; (Cm 569) published by HMSO, January 1989.

12. My comments about the City of Minneapolis are drawn from an interview with city planners Ollie Byrum and Paul Anderson, June 1988.

13. See also 'Striking a Balance; Reflections on 10 years of managing the North Carolina Coast', published by the Division of Coastal Management, North Carolina Department of Natural Resources and Community Development (1985)

14. Oregon's Statewide Planning Goals, published by the Land Conservation and Development Commission (1985)

15. Information on the procedures for appealing to LUBA is largely drawn from 'A Citizens' Guide to Land Use Decision Taking' prepared by 1000 Friends of Oregon in July 1984.

16. Drawn from a case described in 'Landmark', a journal of 1000 Friends of Oregon (Fall 1987)

17. More details can be found in a paper dated July 20 1988 prepared by the Department of Land Conservation and Development.

18. August 1988

19. The Impacts of Oregon's Land Use Planning Program on Housing Opportunities in the Portland Metropolitan Region, published by the 1000 Friends of Oregon (1982)

20. See, for example, The Oregon Planning Experience: Repeating the Success and Avoiding the Mistakes, by Robert Liberty, a paper prepared for a conference on the Chesapeake Bay Critical Area Protection Program, sponsored by the University of Maryland School of Public Affairs, 24 June 1988.

21. Ted Hallock, in an interview with the author, August 1988.

22. More details are to be found in a short paper prepared by this author for the 1000 Friends of Oregon, entitled 'The state of land use planning in Oregon today and the Future Role of the 1000 Friends', 30 August 1988.

23. According to Managing Rural Growth; The Vermont Development Review Process, published by the Environmental Board, State of Vermont (1983).

24. Extracted from 'Growth in Vermont: Under Control?', the report of the thirteenth Grafton Conference November 1987, published by the Windham Foundation.

25. According to Leonard Wilson, Chair of the Environmental Board.

26. 'Major developments' in Britain are defined in Development Control Statistics: England published by the Government Statistical Service (1987)

27. According to Robert Guskind, in an article in Planning, June 1988, published by the American Planning Association.

28. According to a poll quoted in the Trenton Times, November 27, 1988, page A35.

9   The Price of Permission

Introduction

'Fire fighters want developer funds for Countryside project' ran a recent American local newspaper headline. To understand its meaning it is first necessary to know that Countryside is the name of a development project that is huge by British standards – 2,345 housing units on 339 acres of a rapidly growing municipality in New Jersey. If approved, the development will double, to about 10,000, the number of residents protected by the local fire service. The thrust of the headline is that the local volunteer fire company would not be able to function properly if the development went ahead without investment in fire station improvements, an additional pumper truck, and some paid manpower. A representative of the fire company is quoted as saying that large donations to fire companies in need of equipment are common. As the need for this investment would arise directly as a result of the new development, is it not right that the developer (and thus, the local political logic goes, ultimately the new residents) should pay for it? Why should the existing residents pay for the improvements that they do not need?

Of course, at this early stage the development contains no interested residents who might consider taking legal action against the planning board, should it require the developer to pay for the improved service. If there were, their action might allege that the payment would be improper in that it would result in double payment for the same service. One payment would be through the house purchase price, part of which would have gone via the developer to the municipality; and one through the local property tax applied evenly across the community and intended to cover part of the cost of a fire service, among other things.

In practice, equity probably demands that some contribution to the costs of the new infrastructure ought to be borne by the new development as a one off payment. But, that contribution should not amount to the full costs of that infrastructure, because some of the facilities will be shared with the existing residents and the new residents will also be paying local taxes to support the renewal of shared infrastructure.

The first difficulty is to establish the exact extra capital cost attributable to the new development. That task is easy in relation to the fire service, a public library requirement, or perhaps the need for a park; it is much more difficult in relation to the provision of water and sewerage infrastructure which is often shared between different areas, or where the development is just sufficient to require the installation of a major new pumping station or sewage works which will benefit many future newcomers; the task is well nigh impossible when it comes to identifying off-site improvements, for example, to roads or to low income housing needed to maintain balance of opportunity in an area.

Figure 9.1   Fire fighters parade in Princeton; how much should developers contribute?

Then there is the problem of subtracting the element in the local tax representing the servicing of the bond which paid for the existing infrastructure. The more new developments there are to share the new infrastructure, the more complex the apportionments and calculations become.

Terminology

The need to fund extra infrastructure to service new development is not a new one. But in recent years the rate of development in a few localities, the general reduction of Federal grant aid to the cities for infrastructure, and capping of local government income by state laws or by local referenda have together encouraged local governments to look to developers to finance such infrastructure. The terms used for such developer contributions are exactions, impact fees, special assessments, and linkage contributions.

A *development exaction* would result if, in the case described above, the municipality required the developer to provide a new firehouse as part of the development, whether on or off the development site. Alternatively, the municipality might establish a regime in a local taxation or zoning ordinance to require a contribution for each dwelling built towards the extra capital costs. Such payments would be called *impact fees*, because they would be designed to reduce the financial impact of the development on those living in the community at the time of the development. In some states the legislation permits more by way of exactions or impact fees than in others. But even in the more restrictive regimes developers may still make contributions, for example by dedicating land voluntarily to the school board in order that a permit is not withheld for lack of adequate educational infrastructure. The most extreme type of impact fee is to be found in *linkage* programmes in several large cities, where the developer of downtown offices is required to provide or finance low income housing provision elsewhere in the city.

All these options should be regarded as going further than is possible through what are known as *special assessments*. These are very local tax arrangements whereby the costs of particular items of infrastructure are spread among the properties that benefit directly from them. Examples of

190

such assessment schemes are charges for roads through an area that is being developed as an office park, or for street furniture that gives a shopping centre an overall identity. Legal constraints, usually in the enabling legislation, ensure that the funds collected are used for no other purpose, and often prescribe the method of taxation. For example, there is often a requirement that payments for benefits must relate directly to the precise benefit received. A road assessment might be charged on the basis of the length of frontage of the site. There may also be a need for a local vote among those to be taxed, with a majority needed before the tax can be levied. Once the tax stream is guaranteed, bonds can be raised to cover the capital expenditure. Special assessments are therefore rather like a collective mortgage. They are common, but generally so limited in their application that they are not used for other than easily identifiable and apportioned on-site infrastructure.

Exactions, impact fees, and linkage schemes go further. They can be regarded as a form of development tax, of varying specificity in terms of revenue application for infrastructure investment. Their importance is that they concentrate the minds of administrators, politicians and developers alike on the links between the development to be permitted and the cost of the construction of infrastructure to serve it. A significant side effect may be to encourage developers to look to redevelop land in areas already built up, to the benefit of the economy of some of the depressed urban areas. Locally, their attraction is that, if properly assessed, they can give a community long term benefits of development without the start up costs. But they can also force developers to operate in a market that reflects more sensibly the costs they impose on communities. Moreover, the spread of requirements for environmental impact reviews is improving the methodology for identifying the impacts which ought to be mitigated by investment in social infrastructure.

The evolution and extent of exactions and impact fees

(i) The origins

Exactions are not new. Some writers have traced examples in colonial ordinances and royal directives[1]. The modern history begins with the planning legislation of the 1920s. The Standard Planning Act of 1928 envisaged ordinances providing for the grant of subdivision permits, conditional on the provision and dedication to a public agency of streets and water and sewer lines. Before that, developers had frequently undertaken to construct on-site infrastructure such as roads and sewers with funds provided by the city concerned. Those funds would be raised by bonds, which would then be repaid by a special assessment on the homebuyers over the lifetime of the bond issue. Such arrangements helped to keep house prices lower, made funding the development easier, and ensured that the infrastructure was built to the desired standards. However, this method did not survive the crash in the bond market in the 1930s. From that point on, the trend has been for developers to carry more and more of the cost of the public infrastructure needed by their developments.

During the beginnings of the massive post-war suburban expansion, the developer's responsibility would often extend over the local streets, sidewalks and street lights on the development and to the water mains and sewers under the large sites developed. These requirements were imposed by local government exercise of control over subdivision of land. (In the English development control system, the parallel is with those things which might be reasonably required by condition on a planning permission). Schools, main roads, sewers, and parks were generally not the developer's responsibility, even on the largest sites.

At this time, Federal programs began to stimulate tremendous growth in the shape of large numbers of single family homes on vast green field development sites. Gradually, the problems of funding the local government share of the infrastructure costs led the developer to take on some of that share. Parks and school sites were typical elements covered in this expansion of the scope of development requirements. This shift could not have happened without the backing of the courts; indeed, the whole history of exactions and impact fees can be seen as local government constantly pushing up against the legal limits of what may be required.

The perceived need for developers to provide infrastructure in return for the freedom to proceed, set against the constant legal threat and the associated costs and delay, led to a spread of *voluntary contributions*. This phenomenon reflected the introduction of new zoning devices such as floating zones and planned unit developments. These zones existed in the ordinance but had no site specific location on the zoning map. Their conversion into development permits depended on the developers making the right offers of infrastructure provision. If a city made unofficial requirements (sometimes referred to as 'political' requirements[2]), the developer would often find it cheaper to comply than to challenge. This scenario will be familiar to British developers 'invited' to enter planning agreements, by local authorities looking to secure mitigation outside the scope of normal planning conditions attached to a permission. Voluntary offers have come to play a large part in development control in the United States today, despite the background of an as-of-right zoning system. Negotiation is a large element of a planner's job. Negotiated development exactions clearly remove the certainty which might be thought to characterise a zoning system, but they also permit flexibility in place of rigid design constraints.

(ii) The emergence of impact fees

The trend towards more flexibility also meant contributions in cash rather than in kind. For example, requiring a park of a certain size with each new development is all very well, but the community might be better served if there were fewer, larger parks. The answer was to produce mechanisms for collecting a fee, according to a properly defined or negotiated basis, and build up a fund for use in providing larger parks in more suitable places. But there was no reason why such cash contributions should have to be limited to use for the purchase of land. Local governments began to include the costs of infrastructure in such required contributions, and those contributions became known as *impact fees*. The fees were required to mitigate the impact of new development on the existing community. Combining the cash contributions concept with a spreading range of infrastructure covered opened up the way for local government in growth areas to impose impact fees covering a wide range of expenditure on both on- and off-site infrastructure, almost as a tax on that growth.

This trend was encouraged by the financial constraints that began to apply in the late 1970s. For example, by passing Proposition 13 the California electorate succeeded in capping the ability of local government to raise revenue. Under a phenomenon known as fiscal federalism, there has been a substantial reduction in the 1980s in the steady stream of Federal support for local government infrastructure programmes, such as sewer construction subsidies that did so much to encourage suburban growth in the 1950s and 1960s. Impact fees are just one response of municipal decision takers to the challenge to tap their own sources to address the demands of their areas[3]. They are backed by voters who regard impact fees as at least encouraging the newcomers to pay their own way, and at best discouraging growth altogether.

The 1970s and 1980s have also seen a rapid increase in environmental awareness, especially in areas of rapid growth and those with attractive qualities. It is not surprising that the areas where impact fees have been most prevalent include the San Francisco Bay area, Santa Monica, California and the Boulder area to the north of Denver, Colorado. For it is in these areas that the politics of the environmental movement have been reflected in municipal growth control exercises. The thrust of the local political argument is that if development cannot be prevented altogether, given the background of Constitutional rights, at least its negative effects should not be subsidised in any way by the existing community.

Now a few states are trying to trim back what can be required by way of exactions. They are prompted to do this by the increase in the cost of housing apparently resulting from widespread imposition of impact fees. Impact fees are alleged to exacerbate the problems of low and moderate income households. These problems become acute if the local community, realising that growth cannot be altogether halted, imposes high impact fees and infrastructure requirements in order to ensure that new developments house only the 'right' kind of people (see the section on exclusionary zoning in Chapter 4). On the other hand, in adopting legislation to deal with a few excessive demands, states are also legitimising the process, removing legal doubts and thus encouraging more local governments to extend their schemes to the limit of what is permitted.

Another factor likely to result in more caution in the imposition of impact fees is one of the US Supreme Court landmark judgements of 1987 – the *Nollan* case – mentioned in Chapter 5 above, and described in more detail later on in this chapter. It is too soon to see whether the effect of the Nollan judgement will be to stem the steady growth of the imposition of exactions over recent years, but it seems likely that the creativity of lawyers will be able to continue to deliver the effects that communities want.

(iii)   The incidence of impact fees and exactions today

Whether justified for financial reasons, or to impose fairness by reducing the externalities of new development on the existing community, or to ensure that infrastructure capacity keeps up with the pace of development, or simply to exclude altogether the wrong sort of development, the factual position seems to be as follows. In the late 1980s special assessments raised about 5 per cent of local government expenditure, excluding education, and impact fees and exactions together represent an extra cost to developers of as much as $1bn a year[4]. A survey published in 1987 in *Development Exactions*[5] demonstrated that the chances of a given development requiring dedication of land for roads, sewers, water lines and drainage seemed to be rather more than 50 per cent. Equally common were requirements for developers to build or install such facilities as part of their development. Such requirements are little different from planning conditions dictating the design of development and raise few eyebrows. By contrast, few communities required provision of schools, water and sewage treatment facilities, solid waste facilities, police or fire stations or housing for low and moderate income families, or land dedications for those uses. Nor was the survey successful in eliciting information distinguishing on-site from off-site exactions. It is probably rather difficult to quantify the scale of the exaction in the price to the developer of obtaining his permission to develop.

Cash payments or impact fees are somewhat less prevalent. The *Development Exactions* survey showed that only 58 per cent of local governments required cash payments as compared with nearly 90 per cent for land dedication or building requirements. The main purposes were again road provision, widening, or intersection improvement, sewers, water, and park provision. The majority of local governments responding to the survey believed that the way forward would involve stricter standards, more impact fees, and more costs for developers in other ways.

The book *Paying for Growth* contains information about average impact and other fees that would need to be paid in respect of detached single family houses with three bedrooms in Southern California. The houses are assumed to be constructed on a 100 unit, 25 acre site, with the developer paying for all on-site infrastructure. The average amounts per unit were as follows:

Roads	$1635
Schools	$1313
Parks	$1128
Water	$928
Sewer	$905
Flood control	$358
Other impact fees	$382
Fees for recording maps, zoning changes, environmental assessments, etc.	$92
Fees for building permit, plan check, building inspections etc.	$985
TOTAL	$7724

Despite the amount of writing on the economic and legal aspects, factual analyses of the incidence of impact fees and exactions seem thin on the ground. Perhaps it is easier for academics to develop theories and expose particular aspects than to set about a large scale collection of complex local data requiring judgements about negotiations and costs. An approach starting at the developer end, but not just a series of case studies, might be capable of more rigorous analysis. It might also be more reliable in that catching a set percentage of houses built would be more apposite than catching a set proportion of local governments (unless it was possible to ensure that the local governments surveyed were those where growth was occurring).

(iv)   Linkage; the phenomenon of the eighties

A most extreme type of exaction, known as *linkage*, is found in Boston and San Francisco, and a few other places. In this, the rules require developers wishing to build a major office or other significant commercial development[6] to pay a contribution per square foot of floor space into a fund used for the provision of social infrastructure. Boston's housing linkage program requires developers in the downtown area either to build housing for lower income households elsewhere in the city, or to contribute money to the City to provide it. The contribution for office buildings of over 100,000 square feet is set at $5 for every square foot of floor space. A 20 storey office building would generate about $2m worth of housing for lower income households. There is a further linkage programme, requiring contributions, for job training for lower income persons, of $1 per square foot for new office developments over 100,000 square feet. By

Figure 9.2 downtown Boston; do large office buildings genuinely create an impact requiring extra low income housing and job training for the disadvantaged?

January 1988 the housing linkage scheme had been applied in 35 projects and \$29.5m of contributions had been collected. This sum would increase to \$62m if all the projects in the approval process in January 1988 materialised. These funds are then used at the discretion of trust funds to produce low income housing or job training in various ways.

There is a second form of linkage in Boston, known as parcel to parcel linkage. This is removed from the development control process, in that it applies to development land controlled by the Boston Redevelopment Agency. Access to that land is limited to those developers prepared first to develop other publicly owned sites in other neighbourhoods in need of low income housing, job training, or social services. Furthermore, the programme requires the economic participation of local community development organisations, minority businesses and developers, and the neighbourhood residents themselves. The first project is to involve a \$400 million development. In this case the City pays the full price for the restrictions on developers it imposes, by accepting a lower price for the land, provided it does not grant itself a more generous zoning approval for the downtown land than it would have given if that land was not controlled by the City. It is as if the City of Birmingham could decide to sell a key city centre site it had acquired subject to a condition requiring purchasers to develop an East Birmingham site first in association with residents' groups there.

Linkage systems of this sort can only work where there is sufficient demand for development permits to force developers to pay the price; in other words if the market value of the offices developed is great enough to bear the development tax linkage represents and yet still provide an acceptable price to the landowner whose land is to be developed. They are designed to close the gap between those who benefit from growth and residents who are excluded. In other words they are a form of exaction for the provision of off-site social infrastructure.

They are therefore a kind of exaction that can only be imposed in buoyant local economies. It is this condition which restrains developers from

195

challenging such schemes. As Douglas Porter of the Urban Land Institute (a developer funded research organisation) has commented[7], many developers may reluctantly accept linkage requirements to get on with their projects, while privately resenting what they believe to be inequitable taxation. His article, on developers' attitudes to linkage, goes on to assume that it is the developer who bears the linkage fee, which is then recouped through higher rents (perhaps by 1 to 2 per cent in Boston, but by 4 to 5 per cent in San Francisco). However, there is another approach that says that an established and predictable linkage system would be reflected in land values, since the market will always tend to maximise the rents or sale proceeds that can be achieved. So, it is only the transitional period that should give developers difficulty, when the rules are changed while they are holding the land.

That points up the equity problem – a problem shared with the introduction of any form of standard impact fee or exactions scheme where none existed before; for new development is seen as being taxed, while that just completed is not. The subject continues to tease. Given the other variables in downtown office supply and demand, rate of growth and profitability, there seems little chance of any definitive rules emerging from only a few examples. It seems better to regard linkage as simply a special case of exactions. Yet the rational nexus that is needed to avoid linkage schemes from becoming unauthorised local taxation demands the demonstration of a link between the new development proposed and its impact.

How development exactions feature in the development control administrative process

Development exactions are generally applied as a condition imposed on some development approval. For example, Boston's linkage requirements are fully incorporated into its zoning code, so that what is required to achieve a development within the code can be clearly seen. Impact fees are set out in the local ordinances. In the United States there is no constraint on conditions such as is imposed by British Government circulars, backed by quasi-judicial appeals and case law, to exclude conditions involving work or actions on land outside the ownership or control of the applicant, or on exchanges of funds in return for permission.

Conditions involving development exactions may be applied at any of several stages of permitting – for example, at subdivision approval, at zoning approval, when the building permit is granted, or in connection with some environmental impact review procedure. In general, the requirements are imposed in connection with some discretionary approval by the local government rather than attached to more automatic procedures such as certifying compliance with a particular ordinance. So, exactions cannot be defined by reference to any one permitting procedure; they are any substantial requirement for some element of infrastructure to be dedicated to the public, and which would traditionally have been funded by the local government or other relevant agencies through general taxation or financial bonds. There is no clear dividing line between such an imposition and a simple condition, for example to install pavements or trees, or to locate power lines underground. Similarly, in the British equivalent, there is no clear line between those things that can invariably be required by simple condition, and those requiring the negotiation of some other agreement under Section 52 of the Town and Country Planning Act – so called 'planning gain'.

All conditions add costs to development, unless they reflect exactly what the developer would do in their absence. The question to be addressed in separating American planning conditions from exactions is how far the requirements for payment, land dedication or service provision directly and solely relate to the development to be permitted and can be regarded as a part of the development itself, albeit a part required by the ordinance. There is always a possibility that the existing community take advantage of their political position to set an entry fee for those wishing to join them. What distinguishes the exaction from the condition is that what is required is something generally funded in the community by general taxation. One distinction between the impact fee and the exaction is simply that the price is more easily recognised or calculated. This excites *economists* because it makes the sums easier. On the other hand, exactions seem to relate more frequently to questions of whether particular features are sufficiently linked to the development to be permitted. This makes them more exciting to *lawyers*. Here I consider each approach in turn.

The economic approach to exactions

(i)   Economic effects

It is generally not profitable to enter into discussion of just what land use planning is and is not. However, in the United States there is a reasonable expectation that planning should encourage orderly and efficient use of land and infrastructure. Moreover, the market approach demands that the starting point for achieving that objective is to ensure that benefits, goods or services are priced at their marginal cost. Any deviation from that is likely to lead to economic inefficiency. Where the public and private sectors are providing various elements necessary to create a home for which a series of buyers exists, there may need to be some pricing adjustments and other actions by the public sector, as part of its land use planning responsibilities, to ensure that the market delivers the optimum use of land and infrastructure. With sound economic advice in a theoretical world, it should be possible to determine a scale of impact fees to achieve that objective. However, by common consent, even where there are no legal constraints to a sound economic scheme, impact fees generally result in a distorted market. This is because the schemes for them are simply not drawn up in a sufficiently sensitive way, in their application to different types of development in different places, but tend to be straight per unit or per bedroom rates. In reality impact fees alone will never be sufficiently developed to provide a comprehensive development control mechanism based on an identification of the real cost to the community of developing particular sites as a way of achieving optimum efficiency in land use. Other cruder land use regulation tools will continue to be required.

(ii)   A critical view of the impact of development fees

In 1986, the Urban Land Institute published, in a book called *Paying for Growth*, the results of research[8] funded by the US Department of Housing and Urban Development to examine the potential economic impacts of development fees (in cash or in kind). The authors' main conclusions were that:

(i)   impact fees based on currently accepted legal doctrines are likely to produce undeserved windfall gains to established residents, amounting to the imposition of an entry fee for those wanting to come to the community concerned;

(ii)   impact fees can cause sale prices and rents to rise for existing as well as new housing in the area;

(iii)   private financing of infrastructure often results in undesirable distortions of the local budgetary process; and,

(iv) the method of implementation of impact fees largely prevents the improvement in the efficiency of land use decisions and the use of public facilities that proponents claim should result.

Development Exactions also contains a chapter about the economics of development exactions. The authors – Paul Downing and Thomas McCaleb – argue, as in the ULI report, that properly structured exactions are potentially an economically efficient means of funding the costs that growth imposes on the community. They also argue that in the steady state once a scheme has been introduced, incidence is likely to fall either wholly on the original landowner, or mainly on that landowner and partly on the consumer of the development. Developers will bear the costs only where they actually own land at the time that the exactions scheme is introduced or made more costly by the local government concerned.

(iii) Impact fees produce windfall gains for existing residents

The ULI authors analysed what residents would pay for infrastructure, provided on a relatively smooth incremental investment programme, in relation to its economic cost. They modelled how a growing city would meet infrastructure costs over time, and demonstrated how residents can pay less for infrastructure than the real cost of the facilities. This is because constant increases in population mean that more people share the cost of the facilities than at the time the investment was made. However, against this effect must be offset the capital cost of new facilities demanded by new residents, if this cost is to be publicly funded. The outcome will depend on the rate of growth, the life of the facilities installed, the cost of borrowing, and the financing period. Impact fees tend to shift the burden of payment for new facilities away from the public purse generally, and towards the new residents. To that extent they reduce the capital cost offset and thus the cost of infrastructure for existing residents, who can still rely on the taxes paid by the newcomers to help fund the original facilities. The authors concluded that only where the rate of development exceeded the real interest rate would exactions be justified for incremental infrastructure financing, and even then the amounts to secure equity would be small.

For lumpy investments such as reservoirs and new sewage treatment plants the position is different, because existing residents have to carry the costs of infrastructure in excess of their needs until growth catches up. The economic analysis shows that windfall gains to existing residents, such as with incremental investment, are quickly eroded if growth rates are more than nominal. The distribution of payments between established and future residents is difficult to quantify when expansion replacement and financing periods are all different. And yet, these lumpy investments needed for any growing community are exactly those which the authors conclude justify some form of exaction.

It is ironic that the legal constraints in devising development fee regimes tend to make it easier to demand the financing of incremental infrastructure such as roads, water mains and sewers. Lumpy investments such as treatment plants and schools are more likely to warrant special schemes if the aim is equal treatment, in economic terms, of existing and new residents.

(iv) Impact fees increase all house prices in the area

There is widespread concern in the United States about the shortage of affordable housing. Against this background the authors of *Paying for*

Growth suggest that local policy makers should be cautious about impact fees that raise the capital costs of existing housing, and hence the rents of existing tenants in the area. The argument runs as follows. The fee is initially charged to the developer. Unless the imposition was an unexpected one, the developer will have budgeted to pass it on. On the analysis that the burden is passed on rather than being reflected in the developer's purchase price for the land, depressing the realisation of the original seller, the buyer of the new home will find himself being asked to pay perhaps 10 per cent more. This may be through a higher purchase price, or perhaps partly through a special levy payable to a building authority over a period of typically 15 years. However, it is not only the new house buyer who pays extra; as a substantial pool of housing on the market in a rapidly developing area is likely to be new, the higher prices for the new units will also be reflected in the second hand market. The burden therefore falls on those who are seeking housing rather than others in the community, and in particular on those who are moving into the area from an area where development fees are not charged.

However, this picture only applies in markets where there is a high demand for housing, and increasing the price does not adversely affect that demand, or in markets where all the municipalities levy fees at about the same rate. If that is not the case, it is likely that the market will adjust by slowing down production. This flows from sales of land to developers slowing down because the price offered is not enough, or because the developer foresees difficulties in marketing the units at the price he would have to charge to make his profit. The developer may seek other ways of economising. First, he may consider building in a neighbouring community where fees are not charged. Second, he may look to build on smaller plots if that is possible within the zoning in force, or reduce the quality of the units by installing cheaper fittings, or by using cheaper materials. Incidentally, the last course itself is a hidden way of passing on the development fee to the purchaser, who will face higher maintenance costs sooner. Alternatively, the developer may concentrate on higher value units, where the incidence of fees will represent a smaller element of the sale price.

So, in short, on this analysis impact fees increase house prices to the extent that the market will bear, and disadvantage lower income people intending to move into the area. The communities that seek to impose them are generally reacting to rapid and costly growth, itself driven by the attraction of the community. The result is a greater polarisation between communities. One particular element of the population which may suffer is those who happen to be renting existing property in an area where impact fees are charged on new development, and whose rents increase to reflect the increased value of the property they occupy. Impact fees that do more than bring the burdens for existing and new development into balance can therefore be seen as a kind of tax, applicable only in attractive, growing areas, but being borne by more than simply those who purchase the new houses. The extent to which the tax may be levied depends on the attractiveness of the area, and its imposition may well achieve another objective of those living in the area – that of slowing down incoming development, of growth management.

(v) Distortion of the local budgeting process and land use locational decisions

Some commentators suspect that with the developer perceived to be paying for new facilities, local governments might be tempted to invest in unjustifiably high excess capacity, or in facilities with an unreasonably high quality, designed to minimise running costs borne by the community's local tax base. Inflexibility also results from fees being channelled into specially earmarked budgets. The community may well end up with more parks than it would otherwise afford, simply because the dedicated fee had earlier been set at a higher than necessary level. Impact fees will not improve the efficiency of land use by directing development to areas where infrastructure costs are less, everything else being equal, unless the fee structure is carefully structured and varies locally according to the cost of providing infrastructure at different locations for different types of development. By influencing decisions on the type of units built, development fees imposed on the basis of acreage, number of bedrooms, lot frontage, or even number of units, distort the market and lead to inefficiency in supply. And development charges do not promote efficiency in the use of infrastructure, given that so much of it is shared with other users who do not pay for them, and given that house purchasers have little say in the negotiations that lead to certain services being provided.

There is also a salutary warning in the ULI report for local governments adopting a substantial development impact fee regime. The longer that schemes exist, especially if the fees are increased with rising costs, the more permanent they are likely to become, because of the enormous tax increase that would be needed to revert to general funding of infrastructure costs. In turn it may lead local governments to encourage growth that is not in their best interests, merely to sustain their income from impact fees. This serves to illustrate the scale of windfall benefit an impact fee scheme can deliver if the amounts are not restricted to a modest scale.

(vi)   A more positive approach

The economics argument in *Development Exactions* emphasises the importance that impact fees should reflect the marginal costs of providing services to new development, varying with the distance from the centre of public service provision[9]. If exactions are calculated on this basis there is a much better chance of an efficient market. Certainly, they say, without an exactions scheme existing residents fund a proportion of the costs of new development in their area. Carefully designed exactions are a means of imposing on beneficiaries the central capacity and location costs, both on and off site. Dedications of land are in the authors' view less likely to fulfill this objective, and yet are more legally feasible. Legal constraints and administrative complexity, on the other hand, may deter the structuring of impact fees in such a way as to deliver the most efficient land use decisions. The authors concede that even the more sophisticated fiscal impact fees lack the attributes of efficient exactions.

The legal approach to exactions

(i)   Legal constraints

The development of the imposition of exactions and impact fees has continually pressed against the boundaries of legality. The main problem is to design a development fee structure that does not amount to an unauthorised tax. (The Boston linkage program was successfully challenged in the courts on these grounds, but the program continues following the enactment of state legislation to permit the city to tax in this way.) If no specific legislation exists, it is necessary to rely on the police power. This allows actions to protect public health, safety, morals and general welfare, provided that the constitutional requirements of due process, equal protection and no takings without just compensation are met. The courts have generally settled now on a test called 'rational nexus' to help decide the acceptability of exactions.

Figure 9.3 dedication of nearby open space for public use was the price for this development in San Luis Obispo, California

The *rational nexus* test comprises three requirements. First, it is necessary to demonstrate that the development, to which the exaction scheme is to apply, itself creates the need for the public infrastructure or facility to which the exaction is linked. Although the mere existence of state legislation authorising the levy of exactions has been held to be sufficient to show that a need exists (after all, the state would surely not have legislated if there was not a need), generally more site specific examination of the attribution of the need to the infrastructure or facility is also needed. For example, it may be necessary to consider who else will use a road, or what other sites might benefit from the installation of a new sewer. Even so, the existence of a shared demand does not itself need to rule out the funding of facilities to which the rest of the community will have access. The general requirement is that there should be at least a rational relationship to a reasonably related public interest.

Moreover, and this is the second requirement of the rational nexus test, the relationship of the exaction to the public need should not be dispro-portionate. Examining such relationships can become extremely complicated if accurate calculations of apportioned costs are to take into account the condition and thus value of existing infrastructure; this is relevant in considering the appropriate allocation of costs when the new development triggers the need for a major new facility. The complications multiply when the availability of other funding sources (eg taxes that have traditionally financed infrastructure) is taken into account.

The final requirement is to demonstrate a reasonable relationship between the expenditure of the funds collected and the needs attributable to the development. This requirement is generally satisfied by separate accounting arrangements.

(ii) A Supreme Court examination

In 1987, in an unusual degree of activity on the land use front, the US Supreme Court ruled on three cases where it was alleged that the action

201

of a public authority had substantially reduced the value of property. The third of them, the *Nollan* case[10], gave strong indications of the Court's views on exactions and the continuing relevance of the rational nexus test. In particular, this was the first Supreme Court consideration of requiring land dedication as a condition of granting a zoning permit. In the case, such dedications had been required as a condition of a permit for a house to replace a small bungalow, directly on the California shore. The Coastal Commission had the power to refuse a permit, but instead chose to grant permission subject to the owners granting an easement for public access along the seaward side of the property's beach wall. The Commission sought this easement as a less intrusive way (than refusal) of ensuring visual access to the ocean, a public value of recognised and significant importance. The Supreme Court could find no link between that objective and the condition imposed:

> 'It is quite impossible to understand how a requirement that people already on the public beaches be able to walk across the Nollans' property reduces any obstacles to viewing the beach created by the new house.'

A viewing platform on the property, accessible from the front of the house would have been a different matter, the judgement continued.

There is debate about the implications of the case for the practice of imposing exactions. The Court introduced the concept that exactions should 'substantially advance a state interest'; this approach seemed more stringent than the normal presumption that the local government has acted in good faith (usually it only needs to be shown that they 'could rationally have decided' that the regulation achieves the public purpose). But the decision also indicated that there was no reason to suggest that different standards should apply to exactions than to other uses of the police power.

A commentary in Land Use Law and Zoning Digest[11] interprets the judgement as confirming that a rational nexus between a condition and a legitimate public objective is all that is necessary to sustain an exaction. The authors suggest:

> '. . . if the Supreme Court were presented a less extreme set of facts, it would hold:

> • that a development condition involving a concession of property rights (a concession that would otherwise constitute a compensational taking), need only bear a 'rational' or 'reasonable' relationship to the public interest that is intended to be served;

> • that only those exactions that 'utterly fail' to relate to the stated purpose will be invalid.'

and later,

> 'If an exaction is a 'substantially advancing alternative' to a regulatory limitation of equal or greater economic impact on the landowner that itself is not otherwise a taking by depriving landowners of 'all' use, then the exaction is likely to be sustained.'

They conclude that needs driven impact fees, where the cost can be computed of the development's share of the infrastructure needed before a development can proceed, are likely to fit within the test implied by the court. This would be because the development could not otherwise proceed, and the mitigation represented by the impact fee would accord with the public interest that is to be served.

In another analysis of the decision, in *Development Exactions*, Fred Bosselman and Nancy Stroud summarise their view of the important legal implications as:

(i) increasing responsibility for regulators to substantiate the purpose and amount of the exaction;

(ii) backing for the decisions of some state courts that the exaction must be limited to purposes directly benefiting the development concerned;

(iii) clearer requirements for the cumulative impact of developments to be taken into account in designing an exaction scheme. The burden of exactions should not bear on the development alone if it is reasonable for others to share it. On the other hand, the burden could rest on one individual development if that was sufficient to tip the balance and require some mitigation;

(iv) discouragement of unnecessarily harsh regulations designed to facilitate individual bargaining over the terms for breaching those regulations. Such devices seem widespread to an outside observer, but it may be that it is difficult to prove that downzoning, for example, is deliberately intended to create a discretionary development control process, against the background of a reasonable presumption of good faith; and,

(v) reinforcement for the rational nexus test, examining the relationship between the needs generated by the new development, the element of resultant expenditure attributed to those needs, and the benefit accruing to the development.

(iii) How exactions compare with British 'planning gain'

Discussion of such fine legal points seems to matter more in the United States than in Britain, where fewer cases turn on a decision of the courts. The government minister, the Secretary of State, has wide discretion in reaching a decision while acting in a quasi-judicial role in deciding appeals against local government decisions. He, or in most cases a civil servant acting in his name, must consider each case on its merits, and must act reasonably in reaching a decision. Unreasonable decisions are susceptible to being quashed by the courts. In this quasi-judicial process, which must be followed through (where the applicant for permission is dissatisfied with the local authority decision) before any High Court challenge, there is no binding effect imposed by earlier decisions, and an array of legal precedents does not generally feature in the public presentations made at a planning appeal inquiry. Argument concentrates on the case in hand and the planning issues raised.

Having said that, there are general constraints on the decision process, not the least being the guidance of the Secretary of State in government circulars. These documents are one of the material considerations which local government and the Secretary of State are bound to take into consideration in reaching development control decisions. Such circulars advise against making development approvals conditional on works being carried out on land belonging to others (because enforcement action could not subsequently be taken if those works were not carried out), against conditions requiring the dedication of land (not a proper purpose of the planning system), and against conditions resulting in payment of sums of money in return for a planning permission.

The closest the formal British development control system comes to exactions is in so-called Grampian conditions. These are named after a Scottish court judgment. The form of such conditions is to require that a development to be permitted should not proceed until some event such as infrastructure provision has occurred. There has to be a reasonable prospect of such provision taking shape within a reasonable time, but there is no bar on a developer reaching a separate agreement with, say, the utility company to encourage them to reorder their priorities in return for a sum of money.

Where planning conditions cannot be framed within the scope of the advice in the circulars, developers and local authorities may resort to a special type of such agreements. These are called Section 52 agreements after the section of the Town and Country Planning Act which authorises them. Planning Policy Guidance Note 1[12] explains these agreements, otherwise known as 'planning gain':

> '[such] agreements can assist towards securing the best use of land and a properly planned environment. But the planning authority is not entitled to use the mechanism and the applicant's need for planning permission as an opportunity to exact a payment for the benefit of ratepayers at large. The obligation of landowners and users to pay tax on development profits is met through the general arrangements for the taxation of individuals and companies.

> 'The terms of such agreements are likely to be reasonable if they meet the following three tests:

> - whether what is required
>   - is needed to enable the development to proceed, for example alterations to road access or additional sewerage; or
>   - is a financial payment towards the costs of those works; or
>   - is otherwise so directly related to the development or its subsequent use that permission should not be given without it, for example the provision of car-parking or open space, or a financial contribution towards its provision by others; or
>   - is designed to secure an acceptable balance of planning uses on the site

> - whether what is sought is fairly and reasonably related in scale and kind to the proposed development

> - whether what the developer is being asked to provide or help to finance represents in itself a reasonable charge on the developer as distinct from being financed by national or local taxation or other means, for example, by a charge on users of facilities to be provided or financed by the developer under the terms of the agreement.

'The essential principle is that the facilities to be provided or financed should be directly related to the development in question or the use of the land after development. Agreements should not be used to impose matters which would be unacceptable in a planning condition against the tests . . . above, apart from that of enforceability.'

The tests on conditions referred to are that a condition must be necessary, relevant to land use planning, relevant to the development to be permitted, enforceable, precise and reasonable in all other respects:

Need: the authority should ask itself whether, in the absence of the condition, permission would have to be refused. If not, the need for the condition would require very special justification. In particular, conditions should be tailored to tackle specific problems and should not go wider than the resolution of the problem identified.

Relevant to planning: the condition imposed must relate to the regulation of development and the use of land in the public interest. In particular conditions may not relate to matters that are the subject of a separate control regime, or which are separate functions of the local authority. This makes it *ultra vires* to require that some proportion of a residential development must be set aside for people nominated by the local authority's housing department, for example. Similarly, the planning system cannot be used to require a particular type of resident or tenure in a completed development, for example, that the housing be rented, or that the tenants be moderate income. (In Britain there seems a rather narrower view of the proper scope of planning than in the States, but there has been some recent flexibility in respect of low income housing need in rural areas).

Relevant to the development to be permitted: it is not sufficient that the condition is related to planning objectives, it must also be called for by the nature of the development permitted or its effect on its surroundings. For example, if permission were being granted for the extension of a factory building, it would be wrong to impose conditions requiring additional parking facilities simply to rectify a problem with the existing building. Similarly, it would be wrong to require the improvement of the appearance of a neighbouring part of the site simply because it was untidy and congested. But it would be proper to impose conditions on other parts of the site in the control of the applicant to mitigate the effects of the new development. In this way sound proofing of other units on the site might be needed to protect the occupants from the noise from the altered building nearby.

Enforceability and Precision: the need for these will be apparent to lawyers, but as tests they are worth spelling out. It is necessary to ask who is to do what and by when, and indeed whether the action envisaged is within the control of the applicant.

Reasonable in all other respects: this catch-all concept flows out of a key English legal case, and lawyers sometimes call it 'Wednesbury reasonable' after the case. Put simply, in this context it means that conditions may not be imposed that would bear so harshly on a proposal as to be tantamount to a refusal.

There is an important legal distinction to be drawn between requirements on developers imposed by conditions attached to planning consents, and requirements incorporated into Section 52 agreements. The former are open to challenge by the developer on appeal to the Secretary of State–a process for which no fee is payable, and which is relatively informal. (This course is nevertheless costly in the delay it imposes on the development, and the developer must decide whether to challenge a local decision, by setting the costs of delay against the cost of compliance with the condition). By contrast, Section 52 agreements do not form part of the planning consent; they are separate contracts in which the planning authority undertakes to grant a consent in return for certain undertakings voluntarily entered into by the developer. Any legal challenge to such undertakings would have to be direct to the courts. But, since the contracts are voluntarily entered into, the parties themselves are unlikely to initiate a challenge. On the other hand, third parties would find it costly to mount a challenge in the courts, even if information about the terms of an agreement was easily come by. There is not usually any possibility of the Secretary of State's guidance in Circulars giving grounds for such an challenge, unless it can be shown that the Circular was a material consideration in the *planning permission*, as distinct from the Section 52 agreement, and was not properly taken into account.

In practice, in Britain there are very few cases where a local government is taken to court for either misdirected planning decisions or agreements, because it is very hard to prove unreasonable behaviour in a field that contains so many discretions. In addition, there is very little empirical evidence of the values in the trades of money or infrastructure in return for permissions. The Secretary of State's guidance is all too easily set aside, when the local authority and developer are in agreement, and the opportunity for supervision through the appeal system does not arise.

One English case of planning gain, reported in the Daily Telegraph of 31 December, gives a good illustration of the stakes. Just as in the United States, financial constraints encourage enterprising initiatives by local government. Local authorities have similar powers to the American redevelopment cycle of declaring an area to be blighted, then compulsorily acquiring land, and finally selling off the assembled site to a developer. In Bromley, an outer London borough,

'The Glades Centre . . . will provide up to 60 shops . . . 400,000 square feet of shopping space . . . and 2,000 parking spaces.

Under the [planning] agreement, . . . the council will receive the equivalent of £90 million in cash and property.

The council spent nearly £14 million on compulsorily purchasing the land. In return for a 125 year lease with the developers it will receive £57.75 million in cash. It will get another £5.5 million when the development is complete in about three years.

The council will also receive, at no cost, more than 1,450 parking spaces, a leisure centre with a swimming pool, housing, two churches and an extension to the town centre gardens.

Mr Dennis Barkway, council leader, said 'The net value of this deal is £90 million. With this money, the council will replace will replace what will be lost from the fall in the Government's rate support grant."

With financial deals like this it is hard for third parties to be certain that the planning decision was properly reached, or for that matter that the exaction of cash and property was reasonable.

The legal problem is the same on either side of the Atlantic. How far is it legitimate to go in asking developers to pay their own way and a little more? Whether that legitimacy is tested depends on the markets. To reduce the arguments to simple terms, one can use the example of a new development requiring car parking space, but having inadequate land within the development site on which to locate it. In both Britain and America the local authority would be justified in seeking a fee towards provision of a car park if the development proposed would demand more parking capacity in the town. The spaces to be funded should be no more than the extra demanded by the development, and it would be improper to attempt to rectify an existing shortage of parking in the area. Extra spaces would have to be built; the development should not be tapped to pay for any surplus of spaces already built. Excessive quality (perhaps the use of a cobbled surface) could not be funded unless that is what the authority would normally provide. And finally, the car park would have to be built within a reasonable time. But although the rational nexus and planning gain tests might be met, there is still the equity point. Why should new shops pay for the spaces they require, as well as make a contribution through their taxes to the overall municipal parking budget attributable to car parking generally that is of benefit to their competitors? Legally, on both sides of the Atlantic, it is possible to charge developers more than an economically fair price. Developers may sign up for the high costs of linkage because of the even higher costs of delay that would accompany a challenge, itself inevitably costly because each party pays its own legal costs irrespective of who wins the case. But often the boundaries of the law remain untested because a challenge would not suit the developer concerned.

As a footnote to this description of the British context, it is interesting to note that the Water Act 1989 extended the scope for impact fees to be paid in respect of water and sewerage infrastructure. As well as paving the way for privatising the public sector water and sewerage authorities, the Act extended the amounts payable by developers demanding new water and sewerage infrastructure. In future the sums would be calculated to cover off-site average costs of such facilities as treatment works which new developments eventually demand. The amounts payable differed for each of the 10 water and sewerage companies, and are subject to approval by the Director General of Water Services – the economic regulator for the newly privatised industry.

Developer attitudes

Impact fees and exactions do have the potential to impinge significantly on the development process. There may be effects on the type or design of the development, or on the location of that development, or it may be that the development will simply not proceed. These effects, however, apply only when the development process is under way when the exactions scheme is introduced, or when negotiations lead to rather different exactions than were originally predicted. This is because the costs of an exactions scheme which is in place and certain before the development process starts will generally be reflected in the purchase price for the land. In his calculations, the developer starts from the market price he estimates that the completed development will command, and deducts expenses including impact fees and exactions and profit to obtain the price he is willing to pay for the basic site.

In some places, knowledge of the exactions scheme in place can so depress land values and discourage firms from the burdens of progressing an application, that development proceeds instead in neighbouring communities. This was the experience of Ramapo Township, in New York State, about 30 miles north west of New York City. The town suddenly became attractive to developers because land was available and much less expensive than in nearby prime Westchester County. The local government imposed strict requirements on developers as a way of controlling growth that the local residents did not welcome[13]. The method used was an 18 year capital improvements programme designed to facilitate full build out of the Township. Permits for individual tracts would not be available until the programme reached the sites concerned. If they wished to develop faster, developers would have to pay the full infrastructure costs. Developers reacted by looking to develop elsewhere, and a real estate recession in the mid-1970s also affected the community. Ultimately, in 1983, the Township withdrew its scheme. It had found that by restricting house building, it had also restricted retail and commercial development, and that had meant inadequate local property tax revenue to provide local services. One of the legal milestones in growth control proved ultimately to be an economic failure.

Overall, development fees, like zoning, are a regulatory system where knowledge of exactly what will be permitted and required reduces uncertainty for the developer. Such collective certainty among developers ought to have the effect of reducing the margin set aside to cover risk of adverse zoning decisions, and either:

(i)   increase the developer's profit; or,

(ii)   result in a narrower gap between the values of developed and undeveloped land. In the latter case the benefits may be shared between the selling landowner who can command a slightly higher price, and the purchaser who may, for example, get more housing for his money.

However, the difficulty in achieving certainty, just as with zoning itself, is covering all the possibilities in a comprehensive ordinance. Mistakes of omission can be politically costly if they lead to development of a kind that the local community does not want, or development rights that can be purchased only at high cost to the community. For this reason, administrators prefer to try to retain elements of discretionary approval in the development control process, as well as openings for negotiation in the exactions process.

The way forward may be towards negotiated agreements and away from formal requirements, despite the trend towards more and more complex requirements in local zoning and subdivision ordinances. The Fort Collins method (see Chapter 5) seems to give an example of this approach. Little is permitted on sites as of right. Individual agreements are then reached on what can be built on individual sites. Generally that is very much more than the base zoning would have permitted. How much more depends on how far the developer can shape his proposals to score the necessary points on the City's guidance scale for greater density in return for contributions to community infrastructure. The Fort Collins method of development control grew out of a formal joint report of the City and developers on the issue of development exactions.

Conclusions

In economics terms, impact fees look like a political tax imposed in order to slow down growth or at least satisfy existing constituents that new growth pays its own way. Not many of those constituents will appreciate or be motivated by the windfall benefits they may gain. Nor will they generally be concerned that the fees themselves are likely to distort development decisions and result in less than best use of infrastructure. Exactions are also a way of satisfying constituents convinced of the inevitability of development that a developer is paying a reasonable price in mitigation of the adverse effects of development.

In terms of equity, the newcomers have little influence over the requirements of the existing community. Their representative is the developer, who knows that if too great a burden is placed on the development in mid stream, he will have difficulty selling the houses. So long as most developing communities in an area charge fees in one way or another, the developer seems unlikely to resist the existing community's demands for the standards which the newcomers may pay for. In practice the initial landowner, rather than the developer or the consumer, may well bear most of the burden, through accepting a lower price when disposing of his land. This is because developers generally sell at the maximum the market will bear. (Only when the rules change while the developer is holding the land can the developer truly be seen to be paying the 'tax' imposed.) In itself such a system does not seem too unfair, so long as fees are carefully matched to the costs that new development imposes. The landowner who sells development tracts will realise something closer to the net gain through the prospective change to a more profitable use, rather than capitalising also on the externalities imposed on the community.

On the legal front, it seems likely that as individual states introduce legislation, the practice of imposing exactions will continue to consolidate at around the existing level, although the number of authorities adopting schemes may increase, encouraged by the certainty that the legislation will provide. But, because there are wide local variations in what a fair scheme should provide, fairness will not be easily legislated for. In other words it will remain reasonably easy to create a market distortion if that is the local political demand.

For both lawyers and economists in local government, impact fees and exactions will continue to concentrate the minds of local administrators on the links between the development and its effects on the existing community and infrastructure. The spread of environmental impact reviews is making the spread of these links, and their costs, ever clearer. Negotiated exactions in particular are softening the hard edge of certainty inherent in traditional subdivision and zoning ordinances. But they do permit flexibility in place of rigid design constraints intended as safeguards against overdevelopment.

The science of exactions is still developing, but linkage – its latest manifestation – seems like a bridge too far. Only the most buoyant economies can tax new developments to the extent of Boston and San Francisco. Acceptance of such taxation levels reflects the cost to the developer of *not* being able to proceed in those markets. Challenging linkage seems unlikely to be worth the legal cost, and more significantly, the cost of delaying a development in one of the most profitable locations in the United States.

The subject of exactions seems to be uniquely attractive on the conference agendas of planners on the one hand and developers on the other (after all the developers have to learn to cope). The subject is attractive both because it is on the boundaries of what is constitutionally feasible, deciding what amount of taking can be legitimate; and because there is a challenge to economists who see the scope for a new economic approach to land use planning in the shape of negotiated economically efficient arrangements for securing compensation for the community suffering the impacts of development.

NOTES TO CHAPTER 9

1. Judicial Limitations on Mandatory Subdivision Regulations by Ferguson and Rasnic in 13 Real Estate Law Journal 1984, pages 250/252.

2. For example in Paying for Growth (see below)

3. America's Urban Challenge: Fiscal Crisis or Entrepreneurial Opportunity, by Robert Duckworth and John Simmons, in Cities, November 1986.

4. Exactions put to the test, by William Fulton, in Planning, December 1987.

5. See chapter 6 of Development Exactions, edited by James Frank and Robert Rhodes, published by the American Planning Association Planners Press (1987).

6. In Boston the scheme is voluntary to the extent that contributions are only required when a rezoning or variance is needed for construction, but in practice the base zoning is so low, and the extra floor space permitted through discretionary permits so high, that building within the code is not financially worthwhile.

7. In an article called 'Pain before gain: developer views on housing linkage programs' in the Winter 1988 issue of New York Affairs.

8. Paying for Growth: Using Development Fees to Finance Infrastructure, by Thomas Snyder and Michael Stegman, published by the Urban Land Institute (1986)

9. Detailed investigations of this are currently being pursued by a group in Chicago.

10. Nollan v California Coastal Commission, [__US__]107 S.Ct. 3141.

11. Exactions and Takings After Nollan, by Charles Siemon and Wendy Larsen, in Land Use Law and Zoning Digest, September 1987.

12. Planning Policy Guidance: General Policy and Principles, published by the Department of the Environment, London, January 1988.

13. See Planners' Notebook, Volume 4 Number 5, published by the American Institute.

10 Development by Right or Discretion?

Introduction

New York City is frequently identified as the place where it all started. There was zoning in other cities before New York, but that city was the first to divide itself, in a comprehensive way, into districts within which different uses and development standards could apply. The zoning concept was slow to take off at first, but after endorsement by the courts, the New York process became the model for other cities. In particular, the New York procedures influenced those who prepared the 1926 Standard State Zoning Enabling Act. Most states adopted or adapted this model Act, action which facilitated the spread of zoning across the country. It is therefore appropriate to focus on the agonising that was going on in New York City 60 years on, concerning the operation of their zoning permit process. The key question was whether there is now too much discretion, and thus scope for abuse in the permitting process.

Zoning bonuses in particular can illustrate the tension between certainty and discretion. This and other systems, such as transfer of development rights programs, can amount to the creation of markets in which trading of development rights for socially desirable public goods takes place using a specially created zoning currency. They draw attention to a major problem of zoning as an as-of-right system within the American constitutional context – that is the cost of buying out people whose land has acquired value as a result of earlier decisions that are now not appropriate, or simply as a result of reasonable expectations. These problems are of more than academic interest to those involved in planning in Britain. Here, the introduction of the Simplified Planning Zone legislation reflected the perceived need for more certainty in the system through permitted development rights akin to zoning in the United States. This chapter examines how far the British might go towards a more certain process before encountering the disadvantages of the American regime.

The Origins of Zoning

Three major constituencies can be identified as motivating the introduction of zoning in the first place. First, there was concern about the effect on public light and air at the street level when steel framed construction methods and elevators first began to permit the construction of very tall buildings in the financial district, where land was scarce (being bounded on three sides by water) and demand from the rapidly developing corporate America was great. The Equitable Building of 1915, which covers the whole of its site and rises without setbacks for 42 stories, is quoted as the building around which pressure for control crystallised. A second group demanded the protection that separating incompatible uses of property would provide. These were the store owners and residents on the most desirable stretch of Fifth Avenue, under pressure from garment manufacturing concerns attracted by new fireproof buildings and the proximity to retail outlets. Finally, development standards would protect the neighbourhoods of those who had moved into the suburban areas of the city, and who viewed with

Figure 10.1 the Equitable Building of 1915, 42 stories of street wall dominating Broadway on this side and Nassau Street on the other; one of the catalysts for zoning in New York City, itself the model for the nation

concern the very dense development destined for the later waves of people following in a constant flow out from the city. The original zoning can therefore be seen as a reaction to extreme examples of bulk and height, to inappropriate mixes of uses, and to unduly dense development threatening those who had already moved to less dense areas to improve their lifestyle. Its primary aim was to protect property values of existing occupiers of land, but it stemmed too from concern about the effects of private development on adjacent publicly owned space.

The zoning that was developed as a result of these pressures comprised a clear set of rules defining exactly what could be developed and where. Since 1916, New York City has relied primarily on such rules to shape its urban development. In particular, the City has never had a comprehensive plan for development, preferring to rely on the regulations alone to reflect its urban design aims. In time the rules have become more complex, often in response to the specific demands of individual developers. Moreover, the system has become more characterised by negotiations over development so that by the 1980s the city had become an ideal place to examine the advantages and disadvantages of an as-of-right system.

Incentive zoning

The tensions between as-of-right and discretionary development control systems are most apparent in the development of what is termed 'incentive zoning'. In an as-of-right system, reading the appropriate ordinance should give a firm answer whether a development is permissible, and it should be very difficult to change the rules or to develop in breach of them. Otherwise the as-of-right system will become in effect a discretionary system, where an elected or appointed body is free to decide individual applications on the merits of the case put before them. At first glance, an as-of-right system gives certainty but no flexibility, and a discretionary one flexibility but no certainty.

Incentive zoning was one reaction to the inflexibility of the original 1916 as-of-right zoning ordinance. Developers had begun in the 1950s to demand changes of rules to enable them to put up buildings that were different from the 'wedding cake' design effectively prescribed through set-back provisions in the original ordinance. These new buildings stood out and were perceived to have architectural merit; one reason was the dedication of parts of the site to what have become known as plazas (which Europeans should not confuse with large squares at which streets converge and where there might be markets or other pedestrian activity). Architects could use plazas to show off the buildings better. The community could benefit from the creation of extra open space at the street level. The Seagram (see Figure 4.5) and Lever buildings set an example, and the public envisaged plazas like the open space in the Rockefeller Center on 5th Avenue with its gardens and ice rink (effectively provided *pro bono* because that family could afford not to fill the entire zoning envelope).

However, the city did not move to *require* such plazas by the zoning ordinance. Perhaps at that time such an exaction would have been at undue risk of legal challenge. Instead, they adopted on a wide scale a concept which had first appeared a few years earlier in a 1957 comprehensive revision of the Chicago zoning ordinance. The principle was simple – any developer choosing to incorporate a plaza within his development would be entitled, as-of-right, to a bonus in the shape of extra floor space over and above what the ordinance would otherwise permit. There was a clear link between public concession of what might be termed the 'integrity' of the zoning, and public benefit. Zoning had been concerned with light and air at the street level from the very start, and the loss of air and light caused by extra bulk could be offset by well designed plazas bringing extra open space at the street level. There was therefore some discretion for the developer, and an implied acceptance that more than one zoning envelope might be right for a particular site.

Incentives as compensation for downzoning

Plaza bonuses did not arrive simply out of a public desire to secure more open space in the city. They were also a major mitigation in a package of proposals amounting to a major downzoning of the city. Until 1961, when the plaza bonus scheme was introduced, there had been no limit to the height of buildings; towers were restricted to 25 per cent of the ground covered by the building, but their height in this part was determined by the developer, economics, and the influence of the architect. A clear example of a 25% tower on a base incorporating set backs can be seen on the cover photo. The 1961 ordinance brought the City the concept of floor area ratio (FAR) – an expression for the maximum floor area permissible as a simple multiple of the site area. The FARs in the new ordinance represented a severe curtailment of existing zoning rights, by as much as 50 per cent in some cases[1]. Plaza bonuses, and an increase from 25 to 40 per cent in the site area that the tower portion of a building could cover, were sweeteners

Figure 10.2 an example of a building incorporating a public plaza; the General Motors Plaza at Fifth Avenue and 58th Street. The tower itself is set back on the left from Fifth Avenue in the centre of the picture.

for developers to offset against the reduction in permitted development rights. According to the City's Chief Urban Designer, Lauren Otis[2], there was thus a significant upzoning in what was permitted only on the Avenues, the City's main north-south roads, and a substantial downzoning elsewhere. The result was a dramatic switch in the locational interests of developers.

The new ordinance resulted in a large number of offices with plazas. (Clearly, the cost of plaza provision was rather less than the return to the developer from the extra floor space a plaza could generate.) One study[3] suggested that so much extra office space was produced by the incentive that rent levels and tax receipts were adversely affected. To the extent that reduced tax receipts were not offset by the tax revenue generated by the bonus floor space, residents of the city might even have been paying for private plazas through housing attracting a greater share of the total tax bill, as well as through having less light at the ground level beneath bulkier buildings. Nevertheless, spurred on by the early success of the incentive bonus scheme in getting a public benefit at no apparent public cost, other incentive schemes began to appear, often limited to special districts defined in the zoning ordinance.

The spreading scope of bonuses

The plaza concept was adapted for buildings in areas where plazas would not be appropriate. Interior plazas and covered pedestrian arcades in return for FAR bonuses were introduced for 5th Avenue where traditional plazas would break up the character of the street and devalue its retail coherence. The 20 per cent bonus for an interior plaza could be compounded by a further 20 per cent if the ground floor and two others could be secured for use as a department store or series of boutiques. This bonus was designed to secure the public benefit of maintaining shopping on 5th Avenue, against the pressures turning the stores over to uses such as airline offices.

These can be seen as variations on a theme, retaining the original link between the breach of original ordinance permitted and the public amenity acquired. But meanwhile a much more significant initiative had led to the creation of the Theater Special District. The developer of a site on Times Square was seeking a special permit to allow the tower element of the development to exceed the 40 per cent site coverage limit. The City Planning Commission suggested that if the developer were to include a legitimate theatre within the development, the larger building would be easier to approve. It was not that the redevelopment site already contained a theatre; it was simply the first opportunity on a prominent site to respond to concern about a potential invasion of the traditional Manhattan theatre district by office towers. As Barnett puts it in his book, *An Introduction to Urban Design*, 'After negotiation, the Planning Commission determined that a 20 per cent larger tower was a legitimate form of compensation for the costs of building a theater – costs that could not be paid for out of the income the theater would generate'[4]. The developer achieved a 55 per cent floor plate.

The regulations for the special district subsequently created to facilitate this sort of exchange, of floorspace for cultural provision, are also significant. They were an attempt to codify the deal made with one developer, so that others could apply for it too. But, they also required each case to be negotiated with the developer; it was simply too difficult to define the exact circumstances in which the bonus could be applied. And of course, the creation of a new theatre could do nothing to protect existing theatres on other sites in the neighbourhood: that would require separate action.

In other special districts other bonuses were offered. In one[5], an extra 20 per cent of FAR was made available around the perimeter of a mainly residential area if the developer renovated housing within the site. The amount of FAR bonus would be determined by the number of rooms improved, and be conditional on there being no net increase in number, and on rents being limited, and on the developer agreeing to contribute to park maintenance. This has never been utilised, however. Opposite Central Park it was seen as important to maintain the street wall, rather than allow it to be punctuated by plazas. So bonus FAR became available in return for a contribution to a fund used for park maintenance and improvements. As a result about $800,000 was raised and used mainly to plant flowers along 5th Avenue[6]. This is viewed now as a dubious approach, not to be duplicated. On part of Sixth Avenue, greater FAR was available to developers who guaranteed the preservation of light manufacturing uses in the adjacent manufacturing zones. In other areas, if subway entrances were incorporated in a new building so that the pavement outside became less cluttered, or if pedestrian walkways or arcades or through block parking facilities were provided, bonus floor space was the reward. This has now become a mandated requirement in many districts. In one case[7], 16 trees in Greenwich Village were worth 488 sq ft of offices in the bonus zoning currency.

The effects of bonus schemes in directing development

Such zoning bonuses can be presented as contributing to what one commentator, Melville Branch, has termed 'misguided densification in large US cities'[8]. He suggests that pressure from land owners wanting to maximise the value of their assets originally led to zoning for apartment and commercial use in much wider areas than market demands would justify for a long time. As a consequence development has spread over cities in a more random manner than efficiency in the provision of infrastructure would ideally demand. Density bonuses, he argues, only exacerbate that effect.

However, Branch seems to ignore the background thrust, of attempting to correct the original overzoning. No-one originally conceived that some parts of the city would begin to be developed to the maximum that the ordinance permitted – in a 'build-out' of the ordinance. The 1961 ordinance was a major step to reduce the amount of development most sites could take, and subsequent revisions have continued the trend. For example, pressure in certain areas on the east side of the midtown area of the city, around Grand Central station and on 5th Avenue, and the need to spread that pressure, led to another incentive bonus scheme, and a substantial modification of the existing one. On the east side some of the plaza and other bonus mechanisms were consolidated into the zoning regulations to become mandatory requirements, while on the west side the FAR available was increased, for a 6 year period, from 15 to 20. The result was to entice development into an area with more infrastructure capacity and good access to the subway system at Times Square. The FAR incentive in this case was compounded by a second incentive in that there was no guarantee that it would continue at the end of the limited period. Indeed, at the time of writing it seemed unlikely to do so. Another screwing down of the overall density of development in the city will have been accomplished, at the same time as a spread of the benefits of development within the midtown section of Manhattan. But bonuses were not an essential ingredient, only a useful sweetener, in achieving this step.

One of the biggest surprises to a stranger coming to New York City is the large number of sites occupied by surface car parks, or modest old buildings in an apparently poor state of repair, in close proximity to gleaming towers with some of the highest rents in the world. One reason for this is the long time and careful steps needed to accumulate sites for major development. When only 25 per cent of a site could be used for the tower element, a large basic plot was needed to ensure that the tower floors were of sufficient area once the service shafts and lobbies had been subtracted. Acquiring control over a whole block was the aim. The 40 per cent coverage figure improved the economics of medium sized sites, so part blocks are now more likely to be developed. Reducing FARs may make the tower a less important component of many developments. Perhaps the downzoning trend will ultimately encourage more building on currently under-used smaller sites, at a scale consistent with tight transportation capacity. It may also reduce the stakes in 'hold outs' (where owners of small lots can obstruct development of whole blocks by refusing to sell or asking very high prices of those who are carefully accumulating holdings of land to develop). To the extent that bonuses have made the downzoning process politically palatable, they may well be encouraging more even, better quality development of land in the city.

On the other hand, bonuses and other encouragements to development in Manhattan are seen by some as undermining efforts to increase investment in more needy areas[9]. It is hard to quantify this, but to the extent that zoning bonuses allow more floor space on a site than would otherwise be permitted, they are contributing more to satisfying the total office demand in New York City. What cannot be estimated is whether fewer bonuses, or more downzoning, would encourage development in the other boroughs, or drive it further out to more attractive suburban locations in New Jersey or Connecticut.

The attractiveness and usefulness of facilities encouraged

Zoning bonuses have not proved popular with the citizens whose light and air has been exchanged for plazas and street arcades. For example, a report by Civitas[10] suggests the elimination of bonuses for residential plazas and other amenities:

> 'The use of bonuses has been a major factor in making a mockery of the FAR limits of the existing regulations. Not only have the bonuses been used to construct buildings that are larger than the FAR limits were intended to allow, but in most cases the 'amenity' for which a bonus was granted has proven to be only cosmetic and not an improvement of real value to the neighborhood.'

Elsewhere, the plazas seemed to emphasise the separation of buildings from their surroundings or from neighbouring buildings, an effect that can be seen clearly on Sixth Avenue where a number of buildings with rather bleak plazas have arrived and are not regarded as contributing to the urban design quality of the city. Urban design has suffered because the 1961 ordinance was founded on the premise that the entire city would be rebuilt on the new pattern. In practice, the redevelopment process has proved to be much slower, leaving the city with a mixture of styles and a rather more disjointed consistency. Small wonder that some people were pressing for a return to the style they now discovered they rather liked, the wedding cakes of the 1916 ordinance. Others have welcomed the best designed plazas and open spaces. The introduction of regulations defining more clearly the siting, furnishing and maintenance of commercial and some residential plazas has gone some way to reduce criticisms, but illustrates the complexity of regulation that results from using as-of-right rules to stimulate good urban design.

Other benefits such as the extra flowers in Fifth Avenue, the preservation of manufacturing jobs, or the retention of Fifth Avenue retail space, can be seen to be a 'good thing' by most constituents of the city, both physically and in terms of maintaining desirable aspects of social structure. The wider question here, therefore, is not the benefit itself, but whether the bonus scheme is the most appropriate way to achieve it.

The administrative effect of zoning bonuses

Another effect of selective incentives is the sheer volume of ordinance which results, both from the need to set out exactly what is permitted and required, and through the ever increasing complexity of the coverage of the city, with the creation of many special districts in which unique bonus schemes may apply. The result is a mass of paper which it is difficult for both city planners and developers to interpret. The current resolution contains almost 1,000 pages of legal size (larger than A4) paper, covered with small print, and another volume of maps. In the 10 years from 1961 to 1971 alone, the ordinance grew from 937 to 2131 sections, and during the same period there were 1200 map changes. No wonder the developer of an apartment block on E 96th Street could reasonably claim to have been misled by the maps into building an apartment block 13 stories too high, an action which led to an interesting enforcement dilemma[11].

Negotiations, mitigations and amenities

One effect of the responsiveness of the city to suggested bonus schemes and special districts to contain them was to encourage negotiation and thus undermine the authority of the as-of-right zoning system. Developers came to see how the zoning ordinance might be individually crafted to fit their own requirements; they offered amenities and mitigations in return for the breaches they required to maximise their returns. This practice of offering amenities and mitigations gathered momentum as a result of the environmental impact statements, required by state legislation and city mayoral directives, for major private sector developments (complementing the federal requirement for statements for all major public sector developments; the statements expose the adverse effects of development and lead to pressure for mitigations as a condition of approval). But, as these complications have increased delay into the developments that need a special permit, re-zoning or variance, the attractiveness of as-of-right schemes has increased, because they can proceed quickly.

In the Midtown Special Zoning District, only 13 out of 34 buildings proceeded as of right between 1977 and 1982. In the following 5 years, 28 out of 35 buildings received as-of-right permits–an increase from 38% to 80% of the major projects proceeding[12]. Elsewhere, the proposed $11.5m Riverview Chateau and another block of 393 flats in the Astoria area of Queens[13] are examples of how other areas of New York City can benefit from the delays and complexity of developing in Manhattan. (They also show how the outer boroughs are helping to house those who are excluded from the suburbs on one hand, and from Manhattan on the other.)

The latest review

The increasing sophistication of the community boards that, rather like parish councils in England, have a statutory right to be consulted about proposed developments, led them to start to try to extract amenities and mitigations from developers. In return, they then undertook to endorse developers' proposals in comments to the Planning Commission. This bargaining by bodies with no absolute power over the application caused political problems at a time when the Commission was attempting to scale down the extent of negotiation and to relate amenities and mitigations more clearly to the problems identified. (The equivalent English issue would be if parish councils attempted to conclude agreements with developers, whose applications would be supported if they agreed to make contributions to the local community, in the shape of a sports centre for example).

The Mayor issued draft guidelines[14], and asked the New York City Bar Association to carry out a public review. The Association looked at the possibility of requiring both developers and community boards to disclose any agreements, so that the Planning Commission would not be misled, but it also made clear, by its approach, its intent to make recommendations about the role of negotiation and bonuses. Some developers pressed for a return to the simplicity of the 1916 ordinance[15].

The Committee's report was published in June 1988. It suggested that, despite the need in New York City for public projects, taxing developers to provide the city's needs was the wrong approach when those needs were unrelated to the project proposed. Such taxes were not levied in an even-handed way on the basis of neutral principles, but were *ad hoc* and cast city government in an unjust and untenable role. They distorted decision taking and 'corrode the integrity of city government and its zoning and land use laws'. (So, although the provision of unrelated amenities might seem to reflect an economic bargaining process, the committee thought that the bargaining ought to be on the basis of city wide rules).

The solution, the report said, would be to bar every body in the city government process from requiring unrelated amenities. Local community boards ought to be able to obtain guidance from the City Planning Commission about the amenities that might be considered related. The committee's recommended definition of a project related amenity was one which either addressed a need directly arising from the project, ie with a nexus to the project, and identified during the environmental review process, or one otherwise specified by law. Enforcement of the new requirements would be through a public record being kept at every stage of the review process of agreements and understandings between developers and governmental bodies or community organisations, involving any kind of amenities or gifts which developers have offered or given. Making these disclosure statements public would allow members of the public to enforce fair play, through civil remedies if necessary, with the back-up of criminal sanctions if disclosure was not made in full.

The parallel approach in the English system would involve a disclosure statement put on the record with the planning decision in every case where a local authority approved or considered a planning application involving a Section 52 agreement (see Chapter 9). In this way adequately funded individuals and community groups could make an input to the decision process and consider a High Court challenge where it might appear that the authority had acted unreasonably.

Is incentive zoning efficient in economic terms?

It is difficult to assess whether it is entirely proper for theatres, to take just one example, to be subsidised by the sale of development rights held by the city. One view might be that the most efficient use of the land and infrastructure will flow in a free market, where it is open for the City to trade the property rights it holds by virtue of its zoning regulation for benefits offered by any developer willing to trade. Maximisation of public benefits in such a trading system ought to occur in the scenario where the City required a discretionary permit for every development, however small, and granted development rights to those prepared to offer the most while still remaining in the realm of local community acceptance. (For this postulation one has also to assume that the City fairly represents its constituents). The development size would then be set at the level where no amount of extra benefit could offset the adverse effect for the average community member of any more floor space, or whatever.

Even setting aside the constitutional concern of whether such an action would amount to a taking, some would say that setting the zoning provisions at such a low level would create an extreme workload and result in great uncertainty for the developer. But the British development control system sets permitted development rights at this level. The fact that in Britain there is usually no 'auction' of the sort described flows from two main factors. First, the circumstances in which conditions may be imposed on a development to compensate for adverse impact are relatively limited, especially where they would involve action away from the development site or would not clearly relate to the development to be permitted. Second, the British local authority always has to have an eye open to how the Secretary of State, constrained by the courts, might approach the application for permission if an appeal resulted from its decision. But, this kind of bargaining is occasionally seen in the field of 'planning gain' (see Chapter 9), which is largely immune from interference by the Secretary of State. Moreover, despite the limited freedoms to develop, the British local planning office appears to be no more swamped by applications than its American counterpart. Perhaps it is always the case that the more minor applications caught in the net absorb comparatively little time, thus leaving officials on both sides of the Atlantic to concentrate on the major cases.

The opposite approach would be to set the permitted development rights in the zoning regulation at the maximum level possible without unduly damaging the health, welfare and safety of the population. Such a level ought not be too far removed from the expectations reflected in the value of the land because the certainty would permit little scope for speculation. It might be termed a purist approach. In theory most developments ought to proceed with only a minor variance, if any. Indeed the city concerned would have to take a very hard line against variances. Such an approach might be adopted by a 'pure' planning agency, interested only on what is appropriate for a site, and not concerned with the wider issues of, for example, the need to promote economic development. Under such a system there would be little scope for any bonus scheme, except where there was a clear link between the damage to amenity conceded and the public benefit gained.

Defining the maximum permitted development rights in this way would be practically impossible. Considering and setting out all the variations that might be acceptable on a given site, let alone in a whole area, would be an administrative nightmare. The larger the zone, the less likely it is that the general provisions that apply truly represent the maximum that could be permitted on any one site within that zone. Moreover, the nature of developers seems always to push up against whatever limits have been set. It might perhaps be argued that there is a minimum amount of zoning activity that will always be generated by those trying their hand at squeezing a little more value from the site. Finally, there is the political reality; within this it is necessary, as a sort of safety precaution, to set relatively cautious limits to permit intervention in anything likely to be controversial.

In practice, neither the market nor the purist approach can exist in the United States. The level at which the zoning is set probably could not be shifted down to the British level without running foul of the Constitution on the grounds of amounting to a taking. On the other hand equal treatment of land holdings within a zone, and the requirement not to 'spot zone', as well as practical reasons, rule out zoning for the various maximum developments that might be acceptable. Some cities, such as Boston, clearly keep down the zoning ceiling to facilitate individual negotiation followed by a very high chance of obtaining a variance. That can be seen by deriving the building size likely from the value of land, and comparing it with what the as-of-right zoning would permit. The City of Boston should not be so surprised that so many more applications for variances are received in that city than in New York[16]. It is simply a statement of the relative interference with the market that the zoning code represents. Because the zoning code permits less, the solutions in Boston are more likely to be individually bargained, and the outcomes might be expected to be more economically efficient. By offering less scope for bargaining New York City can in theory run a quicker system with more certainty to developers; the overlay of bonuses can be seen as offering more choice to the developer, and the economic efficiency need not necessarily suffer if the bonus scheme is carefully crafted.

Whether the bonus scheme is carefully crafted, however, is another problem. Bonus schemes, rather like zoning itself, apply over a delineated area, sometimes quite small, sometimes extensive. In order to succeed in acting as an incentive, the bonus has to be large enough to tempt the developer into providing the public facility in the majority of sites in the area. That inevitably means that the city is giving away more than it needs to in a good many other parts of the area. A through block walkway may require a set concession of extra floor space on one site, while elsewhere in the special district developers may be prepared to deliver an equivalent benefit for half the concession. But the bonus scheme, through certainty rather than negotiation, rewards the developer with more than was needed to secure the public benefit. What the City needs to do is to carry out a detailed examination of the currency of exchange, measuring how various benefits translate into FAR on a geographical basis. Only then could the city assure itself that it is giving away no more of the public property right than necessary to obtain the benefits it desires.

This research would need to be backed up by information on how the citizens who suffer the extra floor space and benefit from the amenities would value the exchanges. For another element in the economic analysis is the assumption that the decisions of the regulators reflect those that the individuals in the community would themselves make in some collective bargaining process. The evidence points against that being the case. For example, if Civitas and the local Community Board are to be believed, the average resident of the Upper East Side would not be prepared to purchase plazas at a 1 per cent FAR bonus, let alone at the 20 per cent price that applies. There also seems to be doubt whether citizens are prepared to pay the real cost of subsidizing theatre. If the market demand were there, the theatres would surely be provided by developers or the sleazier cinemas in 42nd Street might be converted without the need for an incentive. If people are prepared to accept an extra 20 per cent FAR, with loss of light and other consequences, in return for a subsidised theatre, that simply seems to suggest that the baseline represented by the zoning ordinance has been set too low. Overall, the current system seems to be operating at some distance from a market where the inhabitants would bargain with the developer to establish the point where they are prepared to pay more to stop the extra floor than the developer would gain in return by building it.

The success of the plaza bonus in encouraging extra offices seems to indicate that the 20 per cent FAR bonus might have been more than was needed to generate the desired plaza. Most of the bonus schemes allow an extra 20 per cent, suggesting that the economic calculations by the City have been relatively crude. Just as the combination of zoning and due process leads to uniform limitations on wide areas (when individual sites could probably take more development) and thus encourages urban sprawl, so bonuses must give away more than is needed in most cases to ensure a reasonable response. Perhaps that is the meaning of an 'incentive', but there is no doubt that incentives cost the city in terms of light and air which zoning is there to protect. A more cost effective way to produce the plazas, or other necessary amenities, would involve individual negotiations of the sum needed in each case. That is done in Boston, where pro formas have to be furnished. The difficulty is that for payment to be made in

FAR, if the citizens prefer that currency to cash from their taxes, individually negotiated settlements may offend constitutional principles. But, individual negotiations outside the zoning system could allow amenities not adjacent to the development site; if it were dealing in real money, the City's priorities might be to tackle needs and problems in Brooklyn before those in Manhattan. That would call for a development tax, rather than a bonus scheme, possibly along the lines of Boston's linkage scheme with each commercial development in the downtown area providing funds for low income housing elsewhere in the city[17].

Future of incentive zoning   Incentive zoning, therefore, has played its part in sweetening the downzoning process, in directing development towards the most sensible areas, and in achieving public amenities and uneconomic uses that would not otherwise have been achieved. But it has generated paper and public discontent, it has encouraged unwanted discretion into the process, and has obscured decisions about the most efficient provision of public facilities. It is not surprising that over the last 8 years New York City has gradually drawn away from incentive bonuses[18]. It is possible to perceive a cycle. First, a bonus scheme is introduced for some element of urban design that appears desirable. Depending on its attractiveness, that special optional element can be fine tuned and incorporated into the general requirements or withdrawn. For example, the plaza bonus scheme was introduced, then defined more precisely, then withdrawn in some areas and reduced in others from 15 to 1 FAR in value. Other bonus eligible items, for example relocation of subway entrances to buildings from the streets, have gone from being optional items to mandated requirements.

But it would be wrong to say that incentive bonus schemes have had their day. The preparation of new bonus experiments continues; on the Upper East Side it is proposed to allow 20 per cent more residential floor area in developments on parts of 5th and Park Avenues in return for provision of low income housing nearby. Just as with the provision encouraging legitimate theatres, it is not clear whether the scheme will result in a net increase of a desired commodity. Some are saying that the scheme will encourage developers to buy up nearby parts of the city and thus displace more low income families than are provided for under the bonus scheme. However, there would be a stronger link between bonus and conceded zoning integrity than the Central Park maintenance bonus which it would replace[19].

Other cites have embraced the bonus concept. For example, a 20 per cent bonus is available to all new buildings in Coral Gables, Florida, provided that they are constructed in accordance with the provisions of a design guide mandating 'Mediterranean' architectural style[20]. In New Jersey, many of the new housing developments are built with the benefit of a density bonus to facilitate the financing of low and moderate income housing. Elsewhere in that state, density bonuses are available around the fringes of the Pinelands area; the aim of the bonuses is to facilitate the transfer of development rights from the core preservation area, where virtually no development is permitted, to the edge of the area where development is more acceptable.

In many of these areas a first step in introducing bonuses is to tighten up the base zoning. Such downzoning is a deliberate step taken so as to facilitate delivery of bonuses. As Barnett puts it in his book, incentive zoning 'depends on the usual allowable limits being pitched to create smaller buildings than the market would otherwise permit.' Whether this is entirely fair to those who want to use their land to the maximum effect while not adversely affecting public health, safety or welfare, is open to question. At some point the courts may rule on this practice, in a case where some more generous provisions were quite reasonable, but withdrawn in order to extract some exaction.

Unless downzoning is invalidated, zoning bonuses will continue to lead towards more complicated controls, setting out the options for particular areas. These controls are more likely to have a discretionary element given the difficulty of defining public benefits in urban design terms. This begs the question whether it would not be better to move openly to a discretionary approach and adopt a system of specific consideration of each development proposal, which would be considered on its merits against the objectives of the local master plan. To go this far is not an option as the Constitution stands, because it would amount to a taking of private property and would probably be difficult to reconcile with equal treatment.

Although zoning controls cannot reduce private property rights that far, it is necessary to make a significant area-wide reduction if the bonuses are to act as a successful incentive. Such downzoning is also necessary in the case of other initiatives in the zoning field where trades of development rights are set up in some market created by local governments.

Other trading mechanisms in the zoning field

Other examples of trading systems involve transfers of air rights over landmark buildings, and transfers, often over quite long distances, of the right to build dwellings. Such transfers can be voluntary, where for example a farmer can choose either to build on his land at a density of one unit per 25 acres, or to transfer his development rights elsewhere where they might be applied at a greater density. The aim of such systems, rather like the zoning bonus, is to encourage but not necessarily compel, some desirable social objective such as farmland preservation. Alternatively the transfers may be compulsory, where the public asset to be secured is irreplaceable, and the transfer of development rights scheme is a mechanism to avoid a constitutional taking that would go so far as effectively to require public purchase of the land.

(i) Transfer of air rights

It is not necessary to go outside New York City to find the first of these types of trading systems. For a long time the city was regarded as a frenetic place, where buildings seemed hardly to be completed before being torn down to make way for some newer and more profitable use. Only relatively recently has preservation of the historic heritage become a key element of the City Planning Department's work. Together with the Landmarks Commission, the department has worked to preserve as many structures of distinction as possible. One of the most famous is Grand Central station.

It is famous in land use planning circles because it was the subject of legal action in the United States Supreme Court[21]. The Penn Central Transportation Company alleged a taking arose from the designation of Grand Central station as a landmark, action that prevented the Company from realising substantial profit from the construction of a 55 storey office building over the architectural masterpiece. The importance of the issue for New Yorkers can be deduced from the fact that demolition of the even grander Pennsylvania Railroad terminal to make way for the Madison Square Garden complex in the early 1960s was a key event in the creation of the Landmarks Commission. The popular battle before the Supreme Court over Grand Central is entertainingly described in Babcock and Siemon's *The Zoning Game Revisited*[22]. The significance in this chapter is that the ability to the private owner to transfer air development rights to neighbouring properties was one element contributing to the decision of the court to uphold the action to preserve the station.

In a transfer of air rights the owner simply takes the net extra volume of construction that would have been permitted by the zoning ordinance, were it not for the landmarks designation, and transfers it to a neighbouring site. There have been several redefinitions of what the limitations on the neighbouring constraint means – whether to an adjacent site on the same block, or across the street, or more recently by following a chain of ownership through a block. The general rule is that the transfer can be made to where the influence and benefit of the transfer remain essentially local, and where there is an interaction between the new development and the landmark. This limitation, of course, does nothing to save the setting of a landmark building. The transfers from Grand Central station could not be located far enough away to prevent it being swamped by neighbouring tower blocks. (Dick Babcock speculates about how long it will be before another attempt is made to demolish the building, although there are more recent plans that should result in better exploitation of its assets. Meanwhile the building that replaced the Pennsylvania Terminal, Madison Square Garden, looks unlikely to last 30 years; there are already plans to replace it with a more profitable office use, while transferring the Garden's activities to a new building on a less valuable site near the new Jacob Javits Convention Center by the Hudson River.)

The essential points to note are that a trade in development rights takes place, in this case a straight transfer of building volume, and that the need for the trade arises because of the value of the rights previously vested by virtue of the zoning ordinance. Had there been no vested rights other than to operate a railway station, the question of a taking would not have arisen. Moreover, the enormous value of those air rights was more than sufficient to rule out the option of a straight cash purchase by the City; the cost in damage to amenity nearby was apparently one that the citizens were more ready to bear.

(ii) Farmland preservation through transfer of development rights

Montgomery County, Maryland lies to the north west of Washington D.C. and is one of the suburbanising areas of the United States currently wrestling with the problems of how to manage growth. That growth has followed the traditional pattern described above in Chapter 2; small towns on the rail lines have merged in the motor car age into bedroom communities serving Washington, and more recently commercial development has followed the housing out. There is much pressure to develop, and at the same time concern from the inhabitants to see growth properly managed. The County has used a range of tools in a sophisticated way, perhaps reflecting on its relative size and thus its ability to organise professional resources. One of those tools is a transfer of development rights system devised to retain more land in agricultural use than would be the case if the market were left to itself. It is aimed at securing green wedges of open space between the developing corridors.

A task force set up by the Montgomery County Planning Commission examined the prospects for agriculture in an area under great pressure. The value of land was high, so an agricultural profit was insufficient to service the costs of ownership. But selling off parcels for subdivision and development would leave a smaller and less viable unit, more vulnerable to further piecemeal development. Nor did such development accord with the planning objectives for the area. The fundamental problem was that too much value had been granted through earlier zoning regulations. The task force examined three options for reducing that value, so that agriculture would again become the highest and best use of land in an area where that would also be the general aim of the population. Those options were:

(i) to buy out the land, a very expensive process;

(ii) to downzone it substantially, which would have been politically unacceptable to the farming constituency and likely to constitute a taking for which payment might have had to be made; or,

(iii) to secure a partial downzoning with compensation available through a sale of the publicly owned development rights in the corridors of the county where development was to be encouraged.

The third option, of a voluntary transfer of development rights scheme, was adopted. It has been used widely by farmers to realise some of the capital locked into their land, sometimes to expand their holding sizes and hence their efficiency of operation. At the receiving end, developers have purchased development credits from the farmers to increase the density, and hence profitability, of residential developments. The base zoning density for the agricultural land was set at one unit per 25 acres, with a maximum lot size of 40,000 sq ft (not so large by American standards as by British) and with clustering of the units. But development credits were available on the basis of one unit per 5 acres, to be applied as an increase over the otherwise maximum density in the receiving areas. The difference between the two values was calculated to be a sufficient incentive for trading of development credits to take place.

The scheme started to work in that trades took place on a scale not seen in earlier attempts to operate transfers of development rights to secure farmland. But, for simple operation it was designed in a somewhat crude way. As the original underlying values of farms in the sending areas would have varied with factors such as the availability of services, distance from Washington and so on, so the uniform rate of credit per acre gives disproportionate compensation for the downzoning to those whose land was under least pressure to start with. Once again the need to create uniformity results in a scheme that cost more than it needed to for efficiency of trades, by granting more density bonuses than the inhabitants of the developing areas needed to suffer. The fact that the scheme is perceived to be largely acceptable in such areas (developers are increasing densities and still making sales, while the other programmes of the County ensure that service provision is adequate) seems to indicate that the base zoning density in the receiving areas could in practice be higher than its established level. Another way of putting this is to assert that the receiving areas as well as the sending areas have been downzoned in order to create a currency in the public domain that can then be traded.

Transfer of development rights in the Pinelands area of New Jersey

The crudeness of the currency of Montgomery County contrasts with a little more sophistication in the scheme devised to safeguard the core of the Pinelands area of New Jersey. This little known rural area covers 1 million acres, about a quarter of New Jersey (Chapter 8 gives more details of the special planning agency set up to secure the fragile ecology of the area). Here a development credit scheme was set up reflecting to a limited extent the prior values of the land in the sensitive core. Credits of one housing unit in the fringe areas designated for development were made available for each 4.9 acres of farmland, 9.8 acres of pineland, or 48.8 acres of wetland. No reflection was made, however, of the actual values that previously existed in the land as a result of the disparate zoning practices of the local governments before the Pinelands Commission was created. Again, as in Maryland, the aim was to avoid paying for takings by ensuring some residual value in the land. But here, the market did not need to be so carefully devised, as the transfer would be compulsory, there being effectively no residual development rights (apart perhaps from apiary). That fewer trades have taken place in the Pinelands area does not detract from its success in stemming the tide of development in the area. Perhaps farmers now have no need to rush in to cash their development credits in the same way as when the zoning regulations were clearly about to change rapidly to their disadvantage.

Conclusions

It is possible to demonstrate that incentive zoning and transfer of development rights schemes are very successful mechanisms in directing development to the areas that can best absorb it, and in achieving public amenities and securing uneconomic uses that would otherwise not be available. I am sure that such schemes will continue to spread rapidly in the United States. But the element that all these schemes seem to have in common is the need to buy out development rights. Such development rights represent the unused development potential of a parcel of land; they exist as a result of rights vested by the Constitution or of earlier actions of the local government body responsible for creating a comprehensive zoning ordinance. New York's bonuses were largely created as a result of a need to downzone; its transfer of air rights results from a need to prevent permitted development in the interests of conservation; the farmland and pineland preservation schemes were only necessary because of what the original development rights allowed.

The Constitutional starting point guarantees the owner of land the right to make economic use of it if he can, with the police power intervening only to the extent necessary to protect the health, safety and welfare of the community. But many zoning ordinances were drawn up in a comparatively generous way, and, just as New York City's, without any conception that all the development and uses permitted would emerge in a build out of the ordinance. Indeed such generous treatment of the existing landowners may have been part of the price for getting the ordinance passed in the first place. Now, with greater environmental awareness, and different values emerging in the newly suburbanising and more environmentally sensitive areas, the community is faced with a need to buy back the development rights previously granted.

The most cost effective way of doing this is not to use real money, but to create some new artificial currency by downzoning, in a way that would not otherwise be justified, in areas capable of taking development, and then inventing development credits that can be applied in those developing areas to increase the density of development permitted, perhaps only to what it might have been before. The relative inflexibility, of creating values which are then costly to buy back, is the most telling indictment of the as-of-right zoning system. Moreover there is always the possibility in the wings that the downzoning necessary to create a trading climate might be subject to a successful legal challenge on the grounds that a taking requiring financial compensation was involved. Transfer of development rights schemes can only be sustained on the basis that small reductions in property rights can be achieved in the public interest without a substantial financial penalty.

Apart from the disadvantages of trading with development rights rather than with dollars, incentive zoning turns out to have administrative disadvantages. Incorporating bonus schemes into zoning ordinances, or providing for transfers of development rights, result in extremely complex regulations. Yet, the choice offered to developers may not be popular among the local population. In particular, the bonus cannot be tailored uniquely to variations in what development land will take, any more than the zone itself can define the maximum development envelope for each piece of land. Each plot is different, even where the streets are laid out on a regular grid pattern, and each might potentially take a little more, or a little less, than the zoning ordinance or bonus provide in their lumpy way. The ideal would be a kind of infinite bonus scheme, where nothing is permitted in the base system, but anything might be permitted on a discretionary basis on an application from a developer, who might offer mitigations and compensations in return for a favourable decision. The economists would love such a trading system. Such a scheme would resemble British development control, except that there are few circumstances where a developer is obliged to deliver anything by way of mitigations in return for his permission (planning gain is relatively rare).

Lessons for Britain?

Most British development rights were effectively nationalised by the Town and Country Planning Act 1947. With only a few exceptions (where, for example a specific planning permission has been granted and is still extant), development value in land exists only in a speculative sense. A development plan policy indication that land might be suitable for conversion from agricultural to housing use will create extra value by comparison with land in an area where open countryside policies can be expected to prevail. No compensation is payable if, even given the favourable plan position, planning permission is denied. Nor would there be any entitlement to compensation if the policies in the plan were to be changed at the next revision. So, trading systems of the sort described above do not appear to be needed.

But that is not to say that the American model has nothing to offer to planning in Britain. The Special Midtown Zoning District was created with the aim of achieving balanced growth, by stabilising the East Side core while encouraging development in West Midtown. A key element was making the special zoning bonuses subject to a 'sunset' provision, so that after 6 years they would no longer be available. This appears to have been successful. According to the Department of City Planning, nearly 60 per cent of new development in the Midtown area between 1982 and 1987 has been in the area designated for growth, a substantial shift by comparison with earlier periods. In the last year of the temporary inducement, there has been a rush of developers ensuring that their projects are started before the sunset provision applies. Some sought an extension of the programme, but the City was resolute in sticking to the deadline, in particular because to concede would reduce the effectiveness of future incentives of this sort.

Developers look for certainty, and so do local authorities in attempting to secure economic regeneration of their areas. By offering as-of-right permissions slightly in excess of what would normally be available, for a limited period only, New York City created temporarily higher values for developers to capitalise on, and without the delays that the discretionary nature of that size of project would normally bring. This is exactly the concept of the Simplified Planning Zone initiative which the British Government made available through the Housing and Planning Act 1986. As the 1984 consultation paper[23] put it:

> 'Instead of subjecting all development proposals to the uncertainty and delay of discretionary planning control, the SPZ scheme would specify types of development . . . allowed in the zone and the conditions and limitations attached. Insofar as local planning authorities stated their objectives and requirements in advance, developers would thus be offered greater speed and certainty. Local authorities would be able to pursue a more positive approach than is possible with traditional development control.'

The Government envisages that SPZ permissions will remain extant for 10 years. The Midtown incentive has lasted 6 years, during some of which there was doubt about the outcome of a legal challenge. Government advice on SPZs[24] suggests keeping conditions and limitations to a minimum, but descriptions of the complexity of zoning throughout this paper seem to suggest that such hopes will be difficult to realise for an SPZ of significant scope. Many cities in the United States have found that prescribing urban design through as-of-right documentation cannot be achieved with few words. It is rather like simplifying the planning system by using the General Development Order to grant more general permissions; the Order seems to increase in volume along an exponential curve, with each new simplification imported.

Moreover there have been criticisms of the hurdles through which a proposed SPZ scheme must go[25], and suggestions that it might be more worthwhile for local development plans (which share the same basic procedures) to grant planning permission for types of development specified in the plan, subject to whatever limitations and conditions the local authority thinks necessary. That would have the secondary advantage of increasing public interest in the preparation of the plan. New York City manages with only one document, the zoning resolution itself, though the stages it needs to go through to get to that stage can be protracted indeed. Nevertheless, the New York experience with temporary bonuses should encourage local authorities in England with areas in need of development that are in close proximity to areas of development pressure.

Development by right or discretion?

This chapter points up the contrast between the starting points of the British and American development control systems. Britain starts with discretion and imports some certainty, but no guarantees, by ensuring that the development plan influences decisions, and by providing an appeal process to help achieve consistency of decisions. In the United States, zoning started by designating precisely what could be done on land – certainty if ever there was any. But there were pressures to bend that certainty to provide alternative approaches for particular types of site, and to use the system itself as an incentive for particular types of development. In other words, the system became more than a regulation of what the citizens would accept by way of development on land; it became a positive tool to encourage particularly desirable developments to the exclusion of others.

Zoning bonuses, transfer of development rights schemes, exactions schemes and other related mechanisms are all designed to create a development market, in which development rights become a currency created by the city and used for trades. However, when developers began to exploit the system, by creating black market deals with community boards, New York City took fright and looked to revert to a more simple, more open as-of-right process. But in the more certain process, bonuses apply more widely than they strictly need to; the public concedes more than is necessary to achieve the particular features of a development they want to see, such as a subway access from a new office building. Zoning bonuses, like zoning itself, hand out development rights in discrete chunks which are applied on a uniform basis over quite wide areas. In practice, better development of land demands a more flexible approach, a little more volume here, a little less height here. For those reasons I conclude that it would be undesirable for Britain to go further into zoning than the relatively straightforward examples of simplified planning zones in areas where uniform standards can be applied because little of value needs to be respected, and of general development order permissions which apply nationwide and are already criticised as offering too much freedom in some circumstances and too little than others. My personal answer to the question in the sub-heading is 'development by discretion every time', especially if some of the ideas of Chapter 9 could be used to create a market in which developers and the local community can trade mitigations on a fairer basis without the need to resort to appeals to the Secretary of State.

NOTES TO CHAPTER 10

1. An Introduction to Urban Design, by Jonathan Barnett, published by Harper and Row (1982) p.72.

2. In an interview with the author.

3. Incentive Zoning in New York City: a Cost-Benefit Analysis, by Jerold Kayden, published by the Lincoln Institute of Land Policy (1979).

4. An Introduction to Urban Design, see Note 1.

5. The Clinton Special District.

6. Mixed Reviews for Upper East Side Rezoning, in the New York Times, Thursday December 10th 1987, page B5.

7. Quoted in Babcock and Weaver's City Zoning; the Once and Future Frontier

8. Don't Call it City Planning, by Melville C Branch, in Cities Vol 3 No 4 November 1986.

9. This point was pressed frequently at public hearings in January 1988 when developer amenities and mitigations were under scrutiny as part of a review prompted by Mayor Koch.

10. No More Tall Stories: A Study of Upper East Side Avenues, a Planning Study by Civitas (1986). Civitas is a not-for-profit citizen organisation concerned with maintaining and improving the quality of life on the Upper East Side.

11. Beheading a Tower to Make it Legal, in the New York Times, Real Estate Section, Sunday February 28, 1988.

12. Midtown Development Review, published by the New York City Department of City Planning, July 1987.

13. Astoria Housing Features a River View, in the New York Times, Friday March 4th, 1988.

14. In a letter of June 1, 1987 addressed to the Community Boards.

15. The point was made, for example, by Seymour Durst, of the Durst Organization at the hearing on January 21, 1988.

16. In 'Downtown Zoning', published in 1987 by the City of Boston and the Boston Redevelopment Authority, it is stated that in 1984 the number of variance applications had risen to 712 (from 363 in 1964) and that this was four times the number in New York City for that year.

17. Incentive Zoning, by Robert S Cook Jr., in Land Use Law and Zoning Digest, September 1982, reviews the alternatives to incentive zoning. He concludes that there may be a place for imaginatively applied incentive zoning, but only if there is no alternative applicable.

18. According to Lauren Otis, Deputy Director of the Manhattan Office of the City Planning Department.

19. Mixed Reviews for Upper East Side Rezoning, in the New York Times, December 10th, 1987, page B5.

20. According to Richard Roddewig of the American Bar Association Section of Urban, State and Local Government Law.

21. Penn Central Transportation Co v New York City, 438 US 104 (1977).

22. The Zoning Game Revisited (1985) by Richard F Babcock and Charles M Siemon published by Oelgeschlager, Gunn & Hain in association with the Lincoln Institute of Land Policy.

23. Simplified Planning Zones, published by the Department of the Environment, London (1984)

24. Planning Policy Guidance Note 5; Simplified Planning Zones, published by the Department of the Environment (January 1988).

25. Extracted from 'Growth in Vermont: Under Control?', the report of the thirteenth Grafton Conference, November 1987, published by the Windham Foundation.

11 Planning for Affordable Housing: the Mount Laurel saga and others

It comes as quite a surprise, in the United States, where ownership of land and the right to develop it are almost sacrosanct, to discover an increasing use of land use planning mechanisms to determine who shall be entitled to own particular pieces. The aim is to attempt to deliver affordable housing and to limit its ownership or tenancy to less well off households This use of the planning system is much more sophisticated than simply relying on subdivision and zoning density rules to determine lot size, and thus the type of occupier by house type and price. Increasingly, developers are being asked to incorporate low income housing at affordable prices (subsidised by the original landowner, the developer or his other customers), and to deed restrict that housing so that only low income households will be entitled to purchase.

To set out the background and provide a commentary on current developments in this policy area there seems no better place to start than Mount Laurel. Despite having tripled its population in the last 25 years, the township of Mount Laurel in southern New Jersey is still a relatively small outer suburb of Philadelphia. But its name is familiar to many in the state, and to others outside it concerned with land use planning issues. 'Mount Laurel' housing has come to be used as a term to describe a certain type of affordable housing, following a court decision that this township's restrictive zoning regulations were in breach of constitutional rights of equal protection. The regulations were held to be unconstitutional because they effectively excluded the poor, the young, and the old. Over nearly 20 years the case has led to two State Supreme Court judgements, millions of dollars spent on the fees of lawyers and planning professionals, legislation establishing an administrative process to oversee the delivery of affordable housing, and perhaps the beginning of the creation of a more balanced housing stock in the suburban communities of New Jersey.

Yet, can this extraordinary New Jersey saga possibly provide lessons for land use planning in England? In England there are no constitutional rights of equal housing opportunity. There is nowhere near the same flow of people ever outward from the cities, nor the fear that the next wave of outward migration will be black. English provision of housing for low income needy households has been traditionally through public housing, run by local authorities or housing associations, which amounts to over one quarter of the housing stock, as compared with only a few per cent in the United States. British planning conditions could not normally demand conditions of developers such as I described at the end of the first paragraph. It is not generally regarded as a proper function of the British land use planning system to control the type of person who may occupy housing, by reference to their income or to the type of tenure. This is because the ownership of land is generally regarded as being irrelevant to whether development is to be permitted: if there are no sound, convincing and clear cut reasons for preventing the development proposed from going ahead, then permission should be granted notwithstanding who is to carry out the development, or what type of person is ultimately to own it.

However there are some lessons. For example the aftermath of Mount Laurel provides a salutary warning against trying to deliver broad objectives through over-technical means. (Arguments as to how to show the existence of a 5 year supply of housing land, occurring frequently in English planning appeals, are as elementary arithmetic by comparison with the methodologies for calculating how many affordable housing units a municipality must zone for.)

There are parallels too between the State of New Jersey and the South East of England outside London. Each shares an affordable housing shortage in the suburban areas, arising from similar locational reasons. New Jersey contains substantial commuting populations who work in New York City at the north end of the state. The same effect can be seen in relation to Philadelphia at the southern end of the state. Development is therefore substantially influenced by factors outside the borders, rather as the pressures in the south-east of England are largely influenced by the London's economy. People, and subsequently employment, have been moving out from New York and Philadelphia. The pressure to build new homes in the rural band between these cities, and to establish office parks and out of town shopping centres along the main routes is immense. The same pressures as are found in south-east England, especially close to the M25 orbital and other motorways such as the M11 to Cambridge and the M4 linking Heathrow Airport to the West of England and South Wales.

Limitations of infrastructure in New Jersey are putting only a small brake on the rate of development. Nor are there the same restrictions on development that the English planning system imposes, with green belts, and restrictions on development outside existing urban areas. But, the operation of the basic zoning process by the many small municipalities often restricts housing to larger lots than the builders would prefer. Using up more development land in this way leads to higher land values and house prices just as does tight planning control in the south east of England. In turn there is an increasing shortage in central New Jersey of affordable housing for craftsmen, clerical staff, and for those in the more poorly paid professions such as teaching and social work.

The same phenomenon can be seen in south-east England, where high house prices discourage the unemployed from other regions from coming to take up vacant positions. Against a background of much reduced public house building, and local planning authority resistance to both high-density infill developments in established residential areas and development outside existing developed areas, there is a major social problem resulting from a lack of affordable housing. Couples are having to work longer and delay starting a family because they need two incomes in order to buy their first flat. Single people are having to club together to purchase. There is relatively little private or public rental housing available.

The New Jersey solution is aimed at providing a reasonable pool of housing for such low and moderate income households, typically by reserving 20 per cent of new housing in developing communities for that category, and requiring the market units to subsidise that pool. Deed restrictions ensure that when units change hands in the future the new owners or tenants are also low or moderate income qualifiers. Other states have been taking other steps, though not to the same degree, to achieve similar objectives. Would this sort of planning solution, bringing tenure or type of occupant into the process as a material consideration, fit the problem in south east England? This chapter considers that question.

Background history: the legal stages

A detailed account of the so-called Mount Laurel I and II court cases is set out in an anecdotal way in Babcock and Siemon's *The Zoning Game Revisited*[1]. But it is worth outlining the development of the story here, as an illustration for the English reader of just how land use policy can develop in a system where the courts play such a significant role, and where there is strong resistance to any State intervention in the affairs delegated to local governments.

Zoning as a system of land-use planning is inevitably exclusionary to a degree. Indeed the 1926 landmark ruling in which the Supreme Court finally decided whether the principle of zoning was constitutional included the statement:

> 'under these circumstances, apartment houses, which in a different environment would be not only entirely unobjectionable but highly desirable, come very near to being nuisances.'[2]

Once an activity is justifiably regarded as a nuisance, it is proper to regard it as coming within the police power functions of government, aimed at protecting health, safety and morals. But, from distinguishing between apartment houses and single family houses in one part of a municipality, it is not a very great step to introduce a zoning ordinance for a whole municipality that has the effect of permitting only development likely to be occupied by certain classes of people. The question is how far a municipality can go in using zoning to protect their neighborhoods from unwanted incursion. Examples of methods used are zoning for excessive minimum lot sizes, requiring minimum house sizes or excessive setbacks from the highway, or simply not providing on the zoning map for apartments or mobile homes (the first home for rather more people in the United States than in England).

Mount Laurel I

The New Jersey State Constitution contains the statement:

> 'All persons are by nature free and independent, and have certain natural and inalienable rights, among which are those of enjoying and defending life and liberty, of acquiring, possessing, and protecting property, and of pursuing and obtaining safety and happiness.'[3]

In a dissent in an earlier judgement (in 1962[4]) one of the State Supreme Court justices had expressed his reservations about exclusionary zoning. By 1971, those concerned with equal rights in the state judged that the make up of the State Supreme Court had changed in such a way as to be receptive to an argument that exclusionary zoning was unconstitutional. An action was therefore brought against the Mount Laurel Township by the local branch of the National Association for the Advancement of Coloured People. The charge was that the Township's zoning ordinance was drawn up in such a restrictive way that the poor, young and old were excluded from the area, and that this breached the constitutional rights of those groups.

The case was decided by the New Jersey Supreme Court in 1975. They ruled that all 'developing communities' in the state should take positive steps to include realistic opportunities in their zoning ordinances for the construction of their 'fair share' of the state's present and prospective need for housing for low and moderate income people. There was a presumptive obligation for each developing municipality affirmatively to plan and provide by its land use regulations a reasonable opportunity for an appropriate variety and choice of housing. This would include low and moderate income housing by way of multi-family dwellings, townhouses, mobile homes, small houses on small lots and so on, to meet the needs, desires and resources of all classes of people who wished to live within its boundaries. The ruling was quite clear:

> 'In sum, we are satisfied beyond any doubt that, by reason of the basic importance of appropriate housing and the long standing pressing need for it, especially in the low and moderate cost category, and of the exclusionary zoning practices of so many municipalities, conditions have changed . . . to require . . . a broader view of the general welfare and the presumptive obligation on the part of developing municipalities at least to afford the opportunity by land use regulations for appropriate housing for all.'[5]

But, the ruling did not prove clear enough. It was intended to apply only in developing communities, so as to leave untouched those small towns that were not in the path of the spread of population from the big cities. There was also an exception where threats would otherwise be posed to New Jersey's ecology, which, despite the smutty image of the state held by many, is sensitive in a good part of its area. Municipalities argued in the courts that they were not 'developing' or that their land was environmentally sensitive, or simply delayed action until others had determined what the terms 'fair share' and 'least cost' meant. In the end the decision simply did not get implemented as the Court had intended.

Mount Laurel II

In view of the lack of action and the amount of litigation, in 1978 the New Jersey Supreme Court consolidated six of the outstanding cases arising from the first decision, with the intention of reviewing that decision in the light of the problems it had caused. After written statements and oral argument it was not until January 1983 that a new judgement issued. This judgement has become known as Mount Laurel II[6], and it caused widespread consternation. It was intended to strengthen and clarify the earlier decision, and to make it easier for public officials, including judges, to implement. In this way the Court provided the means by which low and moderate income housing would actually be built.

In short, if a municipality did not provide a realistic opportunity for the needs of a defined share of the poor, then it would be vulnerable to suffer what is known as a 'builders remedy'. This is a means by which a court can overrule a municipality, and allow a proposed development to go ahead. In the Mount Laurel context, development would be likely to be permitted by the court if the builder undertook to set aside for low and moderate households at least 20 per cent of the units to be built. The defined share of the poor allotted to individual municipalities turned out to be quite large in some instances, but it was the combination of that with the leverage ratio of 20 per cent affordable to 80 per cent market housing that caused the controversy. If the municipality could not show how their planning process would deliver their share, a developer could go over their heads and obtain permission from the courts to build 5 times as many dwellings in total (with 4 market priced units subsidising each unit intended for a low or moderate income household). For example, in Lawrence Township the Court approved fair share was 2,408 housing units to be built over the 10 year period from 1980 to 1990. On a 1 to 4 subsidised to market unit ratio such development would have meant around 12,000 new houses – quite extraordinary growth in a district of only 7,500 houses. Similarly in Cranbury Township, which has just over 800 dwellings, the court ordered permission for 816 below-market units, implying that another 3,250 market rate units might be permitted if an application for a builders remedy were made.

The aftermath of the Court decision

Not surprisingly, many municipalities did not like the implications of this decision. Nor did the Governor of the State, who called it 'communistic', inferring an objective of the Court to make each municipality a carbon copy of the next. Nor were the developers particularly happy with the outcome. They were worried that it might prove difficult to reduce the price of the subsidised units sufficiently to attract low and moderate income buyers, without pricing up the market units so much that potential purchasers would be discouraged. But the immediate consequence of the decision was an enormous amount of litigation as municipalities tried to avoid, or at least postpone, the effects of the decision, and as developers proceeded to seek builders' remedies as the Court had provided. According to *The Zoning Game Revisited*, by February 1985 there were more than 135 lawsuits in process against municipalities by developers seeking a builder's remedy.

Some municipalities settled out of court, others were judged to be in compliance with the Court ruling, and some developments incorporating 'Mount Laurel' housing got under way. It was clear that this controversial and litigation-packed approach was not the best way to proceed; but equally, no-one was prepared to take a clear lead towards resolution. As John Selig neatly puts it in his *Report on Implementing Mount Laurel*[7], few suburban lawmakers wanted to enrage their constituents by embracing the Mount Laurel concept, while representatives from the poorer urban centres had too few votes to enact appropriate legislation, and saw too little benefit for their constituents to want to make a name through forging legislation in this particular policy area.

Ultimately in the run-up to the 1985 election for state governor, a political climate emerged that drove the Legislature to action, not only on this subject but also in a linked sphere of growth management and the need for a more comprehensive state planning process. I described this process in Chapter 8.

The Fair Housing Act

In June 1985 the State Senate and Assembly passed the Act which has transferred most, but not all, of the argument about fair shares from the courts to the executive arm of government. The Act established a Council on Affordable Housing which had the task of dividing the state into housing regions, estimating the present and future need for low and moderate housing in each region, and assigning fair share obligations to each municipality. The Council must also administer municipalities' compliance with the obligations (certification that they are proceeding in compliance with the Act provides municipalities with immunity from builders' remedies).

The Act also introduced a new concept by which municipalities were entitled to agree, subject to the approval of the Council, to transfer up to 50 per cent of their affordable housing obligation to urban municipalities within the same housing region. The aim of this was twofold: to allow the most effective use of funds to create affordable housing in the older urban areas where rehabilitation of existing substandard housing was desirable and cheaper per unit created; and to provide suburban municipalities with some relief in circumstances where they could more than satisfy their indigenous need, but did not wish to accept all the remaining allocation of the region's need. Effectively, it amounts to a redistribution of housing resources within the region. The 'sending' authority must still raise funds for low income housing: but it can choose to transfer those funds to areas poorer in terms of local tax base to fund the creation of rehabilitated housing there. Those funds might be found through local taxation (for example Princeton Borough sold $6m municipal bonds), but most municipalities are choosing to levy special fees on housing, or even other development.

For example, in December 1987 Princeton Township approved an affordable housing program. It required developers either to construct low-cost housing, or to donate 10 per cent of their land to the township, or to contribute to an affordable housing trust fund a fee of $42,700 per affordable unit required (equivalent to a contribution of $17,080 per acre of the complete site). The contribution would then help the Township pay nearby urban Trenton to provide units there which will cost only between $20,000 and $27,500 per unit. In return for his contribution the developer will be entitled to a 25 per cent increase in permitted zoning density (ie 1.6 acre lots instead of 2 acres per house). But, the ordinance also reduced the overall base densities of housing development permitted. Looked at in these terms, the program does not look very different to a type of development tax, and of course, the developers affected look likely to challenge it in the courts. There is pressure to pass legislation to authorise such developers' impact fees, in order to protect municipalities from such challenges.

In the absence of such legislation, voluntary contributions are proceeding apace. In Wall Township, a developer has offered to contribute $7m to a housing trust fund for use in rehabilitations in nearby Neptune and Long Branch. This voluntary payment would be made only if the developer should happen to be able to proceed with a particular type of valuable development on one site, development that would not be permitted under the present zoning ordinance. In essence, the municipality can be seen to be selling a part of its zoning integrity, that part of the property rights it holds, to raise the money to house low income people in the state, but outside Wall. As in the context of other zoning practices involving similar exchanges, the question remains whether the original zoning was a fair reflection of what sound land use control demanded. The Township could be said to be fortunate that they had kept their zoning sufficiently restrictive to have such rights available to sell without conceding too much extra damage to the community. It almost amounts to a reward for the exclusionary zoning practices of the past.

The Fair Housing Act also provided State funds to help the provision of affordable housing. The New Jersey Department of Community Affairs (the department responsible for housing policy) and the New Jersey Housing and Mortgage Finance Agency together received $17m. A further $8m per annum was expected to be raised by an increase in the realty transfer tax for real estate valued in excess of $150,000 (the tax rate was increased by 1.5%).

Mount Laurel emasculated?

The State Supreme Court, in its Mount Laurel judgement, had clearly intended that individual municipalities in the growth areas designated by the State should make provision not only for its own indigenous poor, but also for a fair share of the region's present and likely low and moderate income households. Regional Contribution Agreements, the major change from the Court's solution, meant that municipalities could now discharge their responsibilities outside their own boundaries. The legislators had taken the court's mechanism, designed to secure integration through better opportunity for poor households, and turned it into half a housing programme, designed to improve the urban housing stock, rather than increase the supply of housing. Moreover, the mechanisms devised make it less likely that the more needy urban areas of the state will receive a fair share of housing funds. By requiring that transfers be confined to regions, the poor areas in the wealthier regions do better than cities such as Newark, where the problems are so great as to defy resolution simply by placing it in a region with even the richest suburbs. Regional Contribution Agreements may allow eradication of sub-standard housing in Long Branch and Neptune, while leaving relatively untouched the needs of the most needy cities. In this the legislation bears a clear political stamp, by contrast with the court's decision.

So, the idea that developing communities should contain a balance of housing opportunity had been substantially eroded. On the other hand, the result could be more rehabilitated units in the urban areas most in need of them. That may help to stem the flow of the lower middle class households from the urban areas, and thus make those areas more stable. However desirable that objective may be, it can be criticised as exclusionary if the result is a narrower range of opportunity for such households: the previous wave of urban households to move out will be seen as having successfully defended their new back yards against those left behind. One of the judges administering settlements in the municipalities with outstanding court actions commented that he believed the transfer of cash in place of an obligation to provide in the municipality would perpetuate urban segregation, and could be tantamount to exclusionary zoning, while the sums transferred were modest and unlikely to stem the tide of urban housing decay[8]. Against that, there may be a hidden benefit to the urban poor in that the encouragement to move out to financial difficulty and social isolation in the suburban communities will not be so great. Although taxes may be lower in the suburbs, many other costs are higher – in particular the costs of greater mobility in the shape of an extra car needed to get to the shops or friends.

John Selig's *Report on Implementing Mount Laurel* tells how housing advocates believe that the Act, rather than codifying the Court judgement, has emerged as a housing policy *per se*. They are concerned because the Act itself is far from comprehensive in addressing the housing needs of the less well off. The calculations are quite complicated, but it is generally acknowledged that Mount Laurel housing is accessible only to households with incomes of between 40 and 50 per cent, or between 65 and 80 per cent of the regional median. These are relatively narrow bands. The households initially benefitting in the suburban areas will be those already living, or perhaps working in those areas. Princeton wants to earmark some of its Mount Laurel housing for graduate students at the University; in other areas it is the elderly or those who have already acquired a job in the area, or the children of existing residents that will benefit. Some of the latter may well have moderate incomes for only a short time at the start of their careers, but continue to benefit from the subsidised housing until such time as they choose to leave. None of these people are likely to be poor inner city minority residents.

Regional Contribution Agreements should eventually benefit the urban poor. However, if the transfer of funds must await the collection of fees from incoming developers, who in turn are anxious to hear the courts' views on such arrangements, it seems likely to be some time before the full impact of urban rehabilitation resulting from this program will be seen. Enforcement of the law under the new administrative arrangements depends, as did enforcement of the second Mount Laurel decision, on the willingness of developers to institute builder's remedy actions, and on the extent to which municipalities prevaricate. It has been suggested that the new option of a Regional Contribution Agreement will attract some municipalities where the potential threat of builders' remedies is less, and that as a result more units overall will be built in the state. However, the option of agreements may well reduce the scale of the developer's perceived benefit and thus the effectiveness of the builder's remedy in producing housing in urban areas. Nevertheless, in due course some funds should become available in urban areas, and governments in those areas welcome any addition to what they see as inadequate funds for housing available to them at present. Federal monies for affordable housing have sharply reduced in recent years; the State has not found sufficient resources to fill the gap; and local taxes cannot be raised without further discouraging inward investment by new businesses.

However, if the legislature has acted because of a combination of pressure from poorer urban areas for adequate housing and from suburban employers concerned about a growing shortage of affordable housing, there could be frustration in time. For, in the suburban areas it is the indigenous households that will take priority, and many of these will be either the elderly, or the young professionals, and not the work force for which the employers had been looking to provide. Many of the local poor who need low cost housing are not the employees whom local businesses seek. And in the towns there will be some delay before significant effects are felt; meanwhile the very existence of the Mount Laurel program will tend to put off the day when other housing programs need to be devised.

The practical consequences of the current policy

In an October 1987 update of an earlier report[9] the MSM Regional Council, an independent non-profit regional planning and research organisation, reported on the implementation of the Mount Laurel program in the central New Jersey area. This is the most pressured area of the state: in 5 years between 1980 and 1985, employment grew at a rate 50% faster than in the state as a whole, and housing starts increased at twice the average state rate. Nevertheless, the Council point out, there is still an acute shortage of affordable housing in the area. They report that of the MSM region's fair share of 10,000 or so 'Mount Laurel' units, some 5,000 had been incorporated into formal programs prepared over the 4 years since the Supreme Court decision. Of these, 485 were already occupied, 549 were

Figure 11.1 Mount Laurel affordable housing is incorporated in this development, but one cannot readily identify the units concerned from outside; all share the communal swimming pool, for example.

under construction, and 2,254 had received preliminary zoning approval. These figures compared with the total of about 225,000 dwellings in the region, a figure which might rapidly increase under current zoning provisions and with current growth rates, by a further 100,000 units.

Some housing units are now under construction in the urban areas too. The New York Times reported[10] the start of construction of a 1,100 unit housing development in inner city Newark, in the area that suffered severe riots in 1967. Some 15 per cent of the homes will be subsidised for low and moderate income buyers with money from suburban municipalities under Regional Contribution Agreements. Market priced units would sell for between $58,000 (one bedroom apartment) and $98,000 (three bedroom townhouse), but for those earning less than $30,800 the price would be reduced to $35–45,000 and for those earning less than $19,000 prices between $25,000 and $30,000 were likely. The element of subsidy in these prices was effectively determined by a constraint that, to be regarded as affordable, mortgage repayments should not exceed 28 per cent of household income (itself constrained to bands of less than 50 or less than 80 per cent of median income for the region).

Most of the units in the suburban MSM area are to be located in 'inclusionary developments', where affordable and market units are interspersed. Overall development densities might be between 3.5 and 10 units per acre, depending on location. The qualities of the affordable and market units are different, but this generally shows on the inside where air conditioning, fireplaces, trim additions and a second bathroom might be omitted. One major developer's 2 bedroom affordable units have only 900 sq ft of floor space, compared with 1100 sq ft in the market units. No wonder that Governor Kean called the Mount Laurel scheme communistic: these schemes sit at odds with such often quoted tenets of American society, that hard work is rewarded by a good house in a good neighbourhood, and that people have the right to choose their neighbours.

The local newspapers need only to report the possibility of Mount Laurel type housing becoming available and the municipality concerned is immediately swamped with applications. There is no doubt that the demand for the affordable units is very great. However, the MSM Report[11] outlined the types of reason that meant that many applicants were ineligible. Many applicants had incomes that were just too much – ie incomes over 80% of the median for the region. Others fell foul of the distribution of households, mandated by some court settlements, into low and moderate bands of 40–50% and 65–80% of median income. Even then, there was another financial constraint: households needed to find a 10% downpayment plus $3,000 for the incidental costs of purchase (savings of some $8,000 to $15,000 were therefore required), and they needed to obtain a mortgage. Finally, others were apparently discouraged by deed restrictions preventing them from keeping pets, from installing air conditioners, or most significantly, from reselling later at market prices.

Even so, there were plenty of takers for most of the housing being built, with the financial difficulties of applicants being overcome in one instance by assistance from the State. Early surveys of occupants[12] revealed the following breakdown:

craftsmen, operatives, non-farm labourers	26%
sales, clerical, service employees	34%
professions (teachers, social workers, dental assistants etc)	25%
retired or not working	9%

The surveys also showed that almost 60 per cent of the heads of household were under 35, probably indicating a large proportion of first time buyers, but contained no information about the previous residence of those surveyed. It was therefore not possible to see whether the Mount Laurel program was succeeding in its aim of widening housing opportunity for less well off urban dwellers. Nor did the surveys give an indication of the integration of the newcomers into the community, or the political consequences of the compulsory diversification in that community.

An illustration of the complexity

Not all the municipalities in the state have decided to transfer to the administrative agency, the Council on Affordable Housing, in order to obtain the necessary endorsement of their Mount Laurel affordable housing programs. Some have opted to remain with the courts, in which case they remain vulnerable to builder's remedy challenges. Consideration of the position of one such municipality serves to demonstrate the extreme complexity of the methodologies involved. In this municipality, the court appointed a master to help clarify the issues. Figure 11.2 outlines the main areas of difficulty identified in the master's report, before an imminent court hearing brought a more realistic stance by the township concerned. Overall, it is difficult to comprehend the precision that is required in some parts of the calculation when there is such a great risk that things will not turn out as planned. One fundamental problem arises because it is possible to exercise fairly tight control over a development using zoning ordinances, but it is simply impossible to force the owner of the land to start his development. (In discussing the likelihood of the scrapyard becoming available for development, the density to which it would have to be zoned in order to stimulate a housing project was a subject for speculation.) It is incongruous that there can be detailed arguments about the precise numbers of houses to be built, or the size of the obligation to be transferred, based on speculation about the likely pace of development. And yet the process itself is designed for such a crudely defined section of the population, raising the question of whether the constitutional rights of others excluded are being abused.

- a difference of 100 units (in a total of about 800) in the overall size of the program for the period to 1992. The reasons for the difference were in the assumptions about the number of housing units that were likely to be demolished, about the likelihood that units would become available to low and moderate income households when existing occupiers moved on up the market, about the likely number of sub-divisions of large houses into apartments, and about the possibility that the private sector would, without public subsidy, rehabilitate units for low income tenants. In each case the predictions seemed speculative and it was difficult to see how any satisfactory resolution of the differences could be achieved. There were also difficulties over the extent to which the township might claim credit for rehabilitations already completed and mobile homes established since 1980, likely but not guaranteed to be occupied by low income households, and over the application of an adjustment designed to encourage the provision of rental housing (to meet the needs of those who cannot qualify for a mortgage, even on the subsidised units).

- the Township's claim of a credit for grant aided rehabilitations they intended to carry out, when there was no evidence to suggest that there are such units in need of rehabilitation.

- the inclusion in the program of inclusionary developments unlikely to be built because of the unsuitability of the sites in the view of the master. One was a scrapyard where the owner had shown no interest in redevelopment (such businesses are notoriously difficult to relocate). The other was a former sand and gravel pit, which seemed to present substantial difficulties to construction.

- the Township had been slow to negotiate a proposed Regional Contribution with its neighbours and there was doubt about the feasibility or likelihood of development on the sites expected to generate the funds, through builders' impact fees, to pay for the transfer of the obligation.

- defects in the Township's ordinance intended to control the sale and future transfers of the subsidised units

- the timetable for the program, which the master considered to be unrealistically optimistic.

Planning for affordable housing in other states

The most frequent use of planning powers to secure low income housing in other states is through inclusive zoning. This means that the zoning ordinance itself will condition new housing development approvals so as to secure that a set proportion of the units provided are maintained, effectively in perpetuity for low and middle income families. A few places have developed this idea further, in linkage schemes, so that commercial development is conditioned to require either the provision of affordable housing somewhere in the city, or the provisions of funds to underwrite such housing. These types of zoning measure are tantamount to exactions of items for the public benefit, items which more traditionally the public sector would have been expected to secure in one way or another. In order to work, there often has to be some kind of trade of zoning rights, as we saw in Chapters 9 and 10.

In neighbouring New York State, a recent court case[13] along the same lines as Mount Laurel failed to achieve the aims of those who brought it. Legal commentators suggested that the New York Courts were looking out for an opportunity to clarify the proper roles of planning and zoning in the provision of housing for 'all citizens', but that the facts and handling of the particular case did not provide them with a basis for so doing. In particular the courts seemed very wary of the type of Mount Laurel case, which might be regarded as the judiciary stepping over the line into the area of responsibility of the legislature.

However, there are other steps being taken in other areas to attempt to use or improve the planning system in order to deliver more affordable housing. In Chapter 7 above, I described the work of New York City's Office of Housing Coordination, established in 1986 by Mayor Koch to speed socially desirable housing projects through the City's complicated regulatory system. Its aims include:

241

- coordinating approvals for projects in the City's own housing program;

- coordinating approvals for a 3,000 unit program that developers are implementing on a non-profit basis for the City, itself a novel idea;

- streamlining the construction process by implementing a whole catalogue of measures recommended by two of the Mayor's committees.

These are daunting tasks for an office of only 6 staff. In an interview with the New York Times[14], the director of the office said that their best results had been obtained by bringing development problems to the attention of high ranking staff in the regulatory agencies concerned, or by bringing together representatives from several agencies that have conflicting requirements. In implementing reforms, the role of the Office is to ensure that the appropriate decision makers consider the various regulations and act on the legislative issues involved. In this area no big successes have been achieved, but many small processing improvements have been implemented.

However, the extent to which this Office can achieve a major improvement in the provision of affordable housing is limited. In the same article, a development company president who is a former president of the City's Public Development Corporation is quoted as saying 'The Mayor has a strong commitment to affordable housing without, unfortunately, a clear concept of how to get it built.' Another developer suggested that the affordable housing shortage would have to get very much more severe before the City responded: 'Nobody is about to make any changes in this misdirection until there is a realisation how bad it is. We didn't do anything about the war until we had a Pearl Harbor. We need a Pearl Harbor in housing'. Perhaps he meant a Mount Laurel?

The land use planning recommendations of one of the reports that led to the establishment of the office were relatively minor. In the main the recommendations of the Mayor's Panel on Affordable Housing[15] are directed towards improving city processes, liberalising building code requirements, eliminating restrictive labour practices, providing city subsidies for housing and establishing a housing trust fund. One of the major zoning difficulties is that apartment buildings can be built on only a restricted element of the building plot. This means that large sites have to be accumulated before the tower cross section is sufficient to incorporate the common services such as elevators and fire escapes as well as a reasonable number of apartments. Once this has been achieved, the economics of construction demand high rise buildings incorporating expensive materials. Smaller developers cannot fund such buildings and are thus excluded from the market. The Panel suggested increasing the proportion of the site coverage permitted, and lower blockier buildings are beginning to appear. Other suggestions were to increase the number of families to be permitted in more traditional houses, so that many more districts would become 3 family, and to allow suitable basements to be converted. The difficulty about these proposals would be the effect on parking; as the Panel pointed out, insufficient parking can adversely affect neighbourhood character, and yet increasing household density is as sure a way as any of increasing the amount of parking required. Making on-site parking a requirement for new development reduces the very affordability which the Panel wished to enhance.

It is in considering other measures that the scope for improving the supply of affordable housing begins to look difficult. For example, the Panel recommended that licensed professionals could self-certify their compliance with the City's building code requirements in respect of all buildings not exceeding 4 storeys. The reason for this recommendation was the delay that many small builders experience in obtaining a certificate of occupancy. Allowing anyone to occupy a building without such a certificate can lead to a fine, and to get the certificate it is necessary to get the appropriate Buildings Department inspections carried out at the right time. Shortages of City staff, and a hint of corruption, make this difficult for the smaller operator. Yet the registered architects and professional engineers do not want self certification, because it would increase their insurance costs. Liability would be transferred to them from the City for problems that escape the inspection. It would mean increased pressure on them to sign off buildings in false circumstances.

If that reform is elusive, what chance does the City itself have in producing affordable housing, when the labour regulations insist on an electrician being present on site whenever a light is to be switched on, and prevent plumbers filling small holes?

Nevertheless, the City is allocating significantly more to its own housing construction and refurbishment programs, as the following shows:

1985	1986	1987	1988
$25m	$50m	$147m	$400/450m

There have been some difficulties in spending the money on schedule, partly because the agency responsible has had to make a transition from being a conduit and monitoring agency for Federal funds to a construction agency, as Federal grants have been reduced under the Reagan presidency. But producing 66,000 units by City construction and renovation over a 10 year period will not adequately address the shortage of affordable housing. The New York Times article concludes that the real problem is the disappearance of very many small builders who used to construct affordable housing. They have been discouraged by regulatory red tape, including the zoning process.

The City finds it hard to move its own projects in the 10 year programme through the planning stages. In a recent example there was substantial opposition from the residents of Kingsbridge and Riverdale in the Bronx to a plan to build a 1,000 unit project on a 10 acre site nearby. The proposed housing, intended for middle income families, was part of a no profit demonstration scheme sponsored by city developers. In the end Mayor Koch had to make substantial concessions, in particular to guarantee the Manhattan Borough President a similar project in Harlem. Eventually, a 750 unit development was approved by the City's Board of Estimate. With a $25,000 direct subsidy for each apartment and City guaranteed low interest rates, final sale prices would be $110,000 for a 2 bedroom apartment for families with incomes between $25,000 and $48,000.

An approach likely to be no more effective in producing new affordable housing in the City, and with some environmental cost to the neighbourhood concerned, is a proposal to rezone parts of the City (in upper Fifth and Park Avenues in South Harlem). It would offer a bonus of bigger and taller apartment buildings to developers of luxury housing who provide low income housing as well. An article in the New York Times[16] explains the

243

effect of the proposed change on a site on Fifth Avenue. Instead of 19 stories, the developer would be entitled to go to 26 stories comprising 180 units over 192,000 sq ft of floor space. But to obtain the extra 7 floors, he would need to build 21 apartments to let at $300 a month on a nearby site. But no-one takes account of how many low income properties are demolished to make way for the new towers. Local community board representatives are opposed to the proposed bonuses because they believe that the effect may be to stimulate speculative purchase of the area by developers, forcing households out of reasonable housing to make way for luxury redevelopment, the uglier side of gentrification.

At the same time as this proposed bonus scheme was being prepared the City Board of Estimate were endorsing a change in the zoning laws that would make it more difficult for developers to demolish habitable single family houses in order to construct higher density housing. The amendment had been sought by residents of the Borough of Queens, and would also apply in parts of Brooklyn. The device applied was to prohibit demolition on blocks where 75 per cent of the houses remained in single or two family occupation, thus partially repealing a 1973 ordinance permitting more dense development on vacant lots in 'predominantly built up areas' zoned for one or two family houses.

Developers are reported as preparing a legal challenge to the new ordinance, on the grounds that it did not go through all the necessary procedures before being adopted. If the challenge fails and the new zoning stands, it will become more difficult to build affordable housing in the City. The justification for the action was the increasing demolition in established areas of the City along with the need to build at a greater density because of increasing land values. If infill developments are not now permitted, the demand for other developable areas will go up, and it is likely that the shortage of new housing opportunities will result in an increase in house prices down the scale too.

Another housing saga in the New York area also impinged on planning, and is a good example of the power of the judiciary over the administration procedures of local government. In Yonkers, which is a city in Westchester County adjoining New York City, the courts had decided in 1985 that the City was guilty of intentional discrimination in education and housing, and had been so over a period of 4 decades. By late 1987 there was still no apparent action on the housing front to provide 200 public housing units (in a city of 50,000 units overall) for low income families in the predominantly white eastern and northern neighborhoods of the city. The low income families concerned were likely to be from the mostly black south eastern part of the city. The Federal judge therefore decided to bar the city from offering incentives to any private developers until action on the public housing front had been taken. Moreover, the City was threatened with an order preventing it from taking any action in respect of most of their zoning ordinance, special exemption, tax abatement and other real estate functions. Effectively the judge was dictating to the City what the priorities of their planning staff should be, and he threatened to impose penalties that would double each day until the City conformed or until they were bankrupt. He also appointed a housing consultant to 'help' the City to identify the necessary sites for the public housing. (In January 1988, the City submitted, despite the hostility of the unwelcoming inhabitants, and plans were initiated for about 10 sites in the city capable of accommodating the housing for minorities but the saga continued throughout 1988.)

The Jersey City approach

One common strand running through all this Chapter is the susceptibility to legal challenge. Developers are challenging impact fees where these are intended to finance Regional Contribution Agreements, as well as taking action where municipalities seem not to have an adequate Mount Laurel housing program. On the other hand, implementation of the Mount Laurel policy throughout the state of New Jersey seems to depend on the willingness of developers to keep up their challenges against the laggardly municipalities. It is therefore refreshing to study the City of Jersey City's draft 'experimental housing policy'[17], which is 'based on the use of guidelines rather than ordinances'. The aim is similar to so-called 'linkage' programs which San Francisco and Boston[18] have adopted, to tap the profitability of market rate housing, commercial and office development in order to subsidise inner city affordable housing.

The difference is the voluntary nature of the scheme. The policy document sets out three mechanisms for the creation of affordable housing, by direct construction, by funding of a project elsewhere in the city, or by contributing to a trust fund used to sponsor affordable housing. There is a detailed linkage formula which requires one new unit of affordable housing for each 2,163 sq ft of office space over 100,000 sq ft. However there is no mechanism designed to enforce compliance. The policy appears to represent guidelines that will influence other City decisions – for example when the City Planning Commission is required to approve some development in a blight area where a redevelopment plan has superceded the zoning ordinance. There is evidence too, in another earlier document[19], that zoning ordinances are to be drawn up in such a way as to assure the economic viability of inclusionary developments incorporating affordable housing. That document also suggests that special handling through all the various approval processes will be given to any proposal in conformity with the Fair Share Plan. At a time when the City is under tremendous pressure from developers, that is a valuable advantage. Moreover, it would be difficult to allege that the City had acted less than expeditiously when considering proposals not conforming with the plan. After all, such proposals would need much more scrutiny of their impact!

Summary of American approach to affordable housing provision as represented by Mount Laurel and its aftermath

Spurred on by various special interest groups, and in some cases by the courts, many states are pursuing planning policies directly designed to achieve the provision in new developments, where it would not otherwise be provided, of subsidised owner occupied and rental housing for those who could otherwise not afford it. Some states are using the taxpayers' money, enhanced by some remaining Federal subsidies. Others are effectively taxing those who buy new houses in a developing area, or those who occupy commercial property in nearby areas, or perhaps the landowner who can no longer command quite the same price from the developer, if the developer is having to subsidise affordable housing at the same time as producing a marketable product in a competitive situation. To the extent that lower land prices cannot be achieved, perhaps where the developer already has ownership, there may be some increase in the price of the market houses. Alternatively, the tax taken may be a simple deduction of extra value granted through a zoning density bonus for the site.

All of this might in turn make house purchase more difficult for those who do not qualify for subsidised housing. There may be a wider gap between those dragged upscale into owner occupation and those left behind. It is not yet clear, and it may never be clear, what the full effect of New Jersey's most fundamental approach will be, despite a good deal of academic interest.

In their social analysis[20] of the Mount Laurel policy Mark Hughes and Peter Vandoren suggested that the court had four major objectives;

    i   the provision of affordable decent housing for every citizen in the state

    ii   the provision of access to acceptable levels of local public goods (local public services such as education as well as access to other benefits such as a better physical or cultural environment)

    iii   the provision of access to expanding employment opportunities to every worker in the state;

    iv   the socioeconomic integration of the municipalities in the state so that each municipality contains a distribution of household incomes approximating the state's income distribution.

They concluded that, with some amendment, the Regional Contribution Agreement overlay on the original court decision had the valuable potential to redistribute resources from the suburbs to the urban areas, where there were people in need of assistance. They argued that amendments were necessary to ensure that the suburban municipalities paid the maximum amount to transfer their responsibilities, and thus secure maximum benefit to the urban areas. Part of their conclusion was that it is acceptable for a municipality to pursue an exclusionary zoning policy, provided that they pay the market price for doing so. It is rather like breaching zoning envelope determined by the community as appropriate in a particular area, justified only on the basis of the sum on offer from the developer by way of compensatory benefit to the community. This may be the market solution to acquiring optimum community facilities as that community develops. But it does seem to put at risk the whole integrity of the planning process. Who is to determine whether the baseline – the as-of-right zoning provision – is properly designed if it is no more than an artificially low opening offer for the bargaining process?

Mount Laurel and many of the other mechanisms for using the planning system to deliver affordable housing do have the potential to produce results. Affordable housing is being built today on a scale rather greater than previously. The mechanisms can be seen to work, although the extent to which they achieve the social objectives outlined by Hughes and Vandoren remains to be seen. However, the scope for widespread application is limited to regions where there is strong growth. For, it is only where there is growth that there is development to tap, or perhaps tax. This shows the futility of trying to solve a major social problem that goes much wider than land use – the integration of minorities – by using mechanical formulae, without a properly directed public subsidy adjunct, and assuming a different criterion for those in need (income) than the true nature of the target population (colour). Moreover, the initial attempt to meet *integration* objectives has been watered down on the basis that the potential resources the judicial solution generated would be better employed in pursuance of *housing* objectives in the urban areas, objectives which arguably ought to have been the subject of separate state action at an earlier stage.

Could elements of the policy be adopted in an English housing policy?

Looking at the objectives of the Mount Laurel judgement, set out above, suggests that the lessons are of more limited interest to those concerned with the British planning system than might have appeared to be the case from my introduction to this chapter. That reflects my own approach to this subject; I was originally encouraged and excited to think that compulsory set asides in return for greater density might work well in Britain to overcome some of the housing difficulties of the south east, but as I learned more, the scheme seemed to have less relevance.

Certainly, no-one could disagree with that first objective set out above, the provision of decent affordable housing for every citizen; indeed, it calls to mind the sort of statement that usually appears in political manifestos. But direct forced subsidisation within private developments does not generally feature in the mechanisms to deliver that objective in Britain. The only examples that come to mind are where a developer has undertaken as part of an agreement incidental to a planning permission to construct public housing and hand it over to the local authority granting the permission.

The second objective is one shared in England by central government grants, which by complicated formulae are intended to ensure that Central Government's substantial contribution to the funding of local government takes account of the differing circumstances of individual authorities. So, despite different total rateable and potential community charge resources, local authorities should be put into a position to spend up to the Government's assessment of what they need to provide a standard level of service.

The third objective, of achieving wider employment opportunities for workers, is the most relevant. There is a substantial variation in unemployment rates in Britain between north and south. Local variations are not so significant. In the south there are unfilled vacancies to which the qualified unemployed from the north have only restricted access because of a contrast in house values (perhaps by as much as a 4:1 ratio). It is in addressing problems such as this that the setting aside of affordable housing in new developments may have a part to play. One could envisage a pool of affordable housing available in towns in south east England intended as a stepping stone for families from the north. In time, with promotion and accrued savings, those families could afford to transfer to market units.

In other words the units would not be intended for those on low or moderate incomes, but for those whose physical location results in their lack of capital and hence mobility. The disadvantages of such an approach are that without more land or denser development standards (and there is not the same scope for either as there is in New Jersey) it could reduce the number of new houses available in the market. The shortage would increase the prices of market units and could widen the gap between north and south, and increase difficulties for other young households already in the south and trying to establish themselves in a home of their own. It would also tend to work against any more general objective of encouraging new employment generating development in the regions where a workforce is more readily available.

Perhaps the only scope for something along these lines might be by a parallel scheme to that designed to provide low cost housing in rural areas of England. In an announcement on 3 February 1989, the Secretary of State for the Environment clarified government planning policy in order to encourage low cost housing for local people in rural areas where house prices have been forced up by factors such as second home buying. Provision of extra housing over and above the general totals provided for in development plans could be justified given adequate safeguards outside the development control process to restrict occupancy by reference to income and origin of the tenant or owner. Covenants and planning agreements under Section 52 of the 1971 Act were given as examples of acceptable restrictions. It may be that in the south east a similar exception to the general planning provision could be made for families in the special position of moving from the north to a vacant position in the south. Equally, it may be better to leave employers to initiate such action on their own behalf if that made economic sense to them.

Finally, returning to the objectives above, the fourth, of spatial socioeconomic integration, is not one that would be recognised in Britain, where objectors to dense housing development are generally concerned about dense development *per se*. They do not tend to act out of some motivation to exclude poorer people, or people who would make a disproportionate demand on local services and hence lead to tax increases. The greater concern is about traffic and on-street parking, and about the claustrophobic effect of ever denser development in urban areas. Where development is proposed on the fringes of towns, it is the loss of open space as a public amenity, or the loss of character as the village becomes dominated by 'little boxes'. Perhaps the most hostility towards types of occupiers of new housing comes when new public housing is proposed. This may be based on perceptions of older estates elsewhere, especially larger ones. However the emphasis of housing policy in Britain is changing; financial constraints, the rapid growth of housing associations, and the need to allocate priority to the refurbishment of existing housing make large public housing developments increasingly rare. The perception of estates is changing too, as substantial numbers of houses are sold to tenants. So, exclusionary zoning is not an issue, and there is no great thrust by groups analogous to those in New Jersey and elsewhere working for greater integration.

As the Mount Laurel saga progressed, and the legislation emerged that incorporated the Regional Contribution Agreement concept, the focus of the solution moved away from the need to incorporate an element of affordable housing in every development in the suburbs. The shift was towards the solution of a different problem – how to provide decent housing for the less well off households in the state, located in urban areas with a much greater proportion of substandard housing stock than the suburbs. It was this shift that takes the solution away from being of so much interest in south east England. There is a much greater contrast in New Jersey between areas in need of substantial housing improvement and the higher class suburbs. The need to set up a scheme whereby, say, suburban towns agreed to fund the rehabilitation of housing in certain London Boroughs seems limited. First, there is not such a wide range of housing condition than in New Jersey. Second, the capital value of property in most parts of London and the availability of improvement grants ought to have the effect of rehabilitating private housing in all areas. But more fundamentally, if there is a problem of inadequate affordable housing in the outer suburbs, it will not be resolved by authorities in those areas providing more affordable housing in central London. And finally, Britain has traditionally had broad mechanisms that go some way to compensate for the difference in local fiscal resources in different local government areas, and less hypothecation of taxes.

Conclusions

The main conclusion in all this is to warn against relying on the planning system to stand in the place of a properly constructed housing policy. Much better for the State of New Jersey to have a comprehensive program of housing assistance for all its residents in need. This may mean interfering with the zoning freedom of municipalities, if the normal categorical grant mechanisms such as matching funds raised locally will not work.

The idea that better off households, affording to move into an area, can afford to contribute to the needs of the less well off in the area, might be much better codified as a tax regime, than hidden for negotiation between individual municipalities and developers. After all the $30,000 or so contribution by the developer per new dwelling in Princeton under their new policy could quite easily be made more open to the purchaser as an overt tax. But why should only those moving into new housing pay for the needs of those less well off than themselves? The answer is that they probably do not: except in a booming market it seems unlikely that higher prices will be paid for the market houses on inclusionary developments, compared with the position without Mount Laurel in place, when the market in second hand houses has not been affected. Land values are the floating factor in most equations such as this, and landowners who sell to developers are probably also bearing a share of the cost through lower receipts, as are the existing inhabitants who suffer reductions in the capital value of their assets as a result of selling off an element of their environmental integrity, as represented by the zoning that is waived.

Still keeping the transfer of funds within the housing market, it might be considered fairer for a real estate transfer tax to bear the entire burden. Certainly, rather less than $30,000 per dwelling would raise the same amount for subsidised housing. But then, why tax only those who have to move, for whatever reason, while leaving alone others lucky enough to live in valuable housing in a more permanent way, and whose representatives were responsible for the exclusionary zoning (although not for the need that suddenly has been allocated to them)? Perhaps the real obligation to provide for the housing needs of the less well off should be spread across the State by means of a local property tax assessed on a standardised basis – perhaps one that only bites on assessed capital value of more than $100,000. That would mean a much greater role for the State in the redistribution of resources to those municipalities most in need. The redistribution would no doubt be on the basis of a complex formula, and a very political process – rather like the British Government's grants to local government – but applicable to housing needs alone. And it would need to be combined with a statutory obligation for municipalities to act in the provision of suitable housing. By comparison with Hughes and Vandoren's concept of a market in the redistribution of resources such a scheme might seem bureaucratic and subject to political manipulation. But it would not depend on development pressure to enforce compliance, and it would make provision of land for affordable housing a component, rather than the driving force in the planning process of the state. And it would be no more bureaucratic than Mount Laurel has proved. Moreover, an overt housing policy of this sort might be more likely to be targeted on the most needy areas, as compared with the distortions introduced by the regional constraints in the Regional Contribution Agreements administration.

Such an idea could only be pursued in the United States, where the political structure leads to the wholesale hypothecation of tax receipts. It is generally only possible to increase a state or local tax when there is a specific expenditure line which requires funding. New Jersey's state income tax was introduced only as a result of a court case requiring a more even distribution of the wealth of the state to education; petrol tax increases tend to be linked to road improvements. British taxes are rarely hypothecated in this way, and that makes potential New Jersey solutions involving amendments to the real estate tax of little interest in Britain. Our own stamp duty on transfers of property is imposed at a higher rate on more expensive property; but that is not perceived as an important redistributive element in the housing market because the application of stamp duty receipts is not applied to a particular service but goes to the Exchequer for use on general expenditure needs determined by government ministers collectively. Greater linkage between taxes and spending might help the creation of more efficient redistribution of resources in discrete markets, but is rather beyond the relevance of this report. Indeed I sense that I am getting to the point where the parallels between America and Britain have been exhausted, and we are getting to some of the perpendiculars as I called them in my title–the main ones being our different altitude to development generally, the financial independence of American local governments, and the absence (bar a few exceptions) of specific grants from British central government to local authorities and hypothecation of tax revenue streams in this county.

So, to return briefly to Mount Laurel, I see the main lesson for the British planning system as a warning against over-complexity in any attempt to deliver very broad objectives. Most of all there is the incongruous contrast between the precision of the calculations for the program of each municipality and the risk that the predicted development will simply not materialise. But generally, although the problem and the solutions are interesting, the read across of the mechanisms described here to the British planning system seems limited. A more interventionist government, pursuing social ownership of the land, might quickly achieve more affordable housing in Britain by changing the policy on planning conditions to allow conditions relating to the income of the occupier. Mount Laurel solutions of leveraging affordable housing by allowing greater numbers of market houses to be built would not be necessary, as the starting point would not be constrained by the Constitution. . .

NOTES TO CHAPTER 11

1. The Zoning Game Revisited (1985) by Richard F Babcock and Charles M Siemon published by Oelgeschlager, Gunn & Hain in association with the Lincoln Institute of Land Policy.

2. Village of Euclid v. Ambler Realty Co., 272 US (1926)

3. New Jersey State Constitution, Article 1, paragraph 1.

4. Vickers v. Gloucester Township Committee, 181 A.2d 129(1962)

5. Southern Burlington County NAACP v. Mount Laurel, 336 A.2d (1975)

6. Southern Burlington County NAACP v. Mount Laurel, 456 A.2d (1983)

7. A Report on Implementing Mount Laurel (draft of Sept 22, 1987) by John M. Selig; Woodrow Wilson School of Public and International Affairs, Princeton University

8. Judge Serpentelli at Ocean County Court, Toms River, 21 March 1988.

9. Affordable Housing in Central New Jersey: 1987. The Consequences of Mount Laurel II and the Fair Housing Act. Prepared by MSM Regional Council staff (October 29, 1987)

10. The New York Times, Monday December 7 1987, page B2

11. Op cit pp.35–37

12. MSM Regional Council generated a sample size of 355 households by combining three separate surveys, one by Alan Mallach, a long time advocate for affordable housing, and two by the large developer, K. Hovnanian.

13. Suffolk Housing Services v. Town of Brookhaven, Court of Appeals of New York No. 150, June 11, 1987, reported in Land Use Law and Zoning Digest, September 1987.

14. The New York Times, Real Estate section, November 14, 1987

15. Report by the Mayor's Panel on Affordable Housing, published April 1986, by the City of New York, Office of the Mayor.

16. Mixed Reviews for Upper East Side Rezoning; The New York Times, December 10, 1987

17. Experimental Housing Policy for Jersey City: undated, but obtained from the City in December 1987

18. See chapter 9 above.

19. Proposed Fair Share Plan: Jersey City, New Jersey, February 16, 1987

20. Social Policy Through Land Reform: New Jersey's Mount Laurel Controversy (draft). Mark Alan Hughes and Peter M Vandoren, Woodrow Wilson School, Princeton University, October 1987.

12 Summing up

Introduction

What then does all this add up to? What lessons are there for the British practitioner? Do the American and British development control systems share sufficient common threads to suggest that some American ideas might fit a British framework? Or are the starting points too widely separated to make the consideration of such potential worthwhile? Many aspects of American development control are necessarily very different than in Britain. But I believe it is still possible to set aside differences and discover some useful read-across. This chapter pulls together some personal thoughts resulting from my year living American planning.

In a chapter entitled 'What the United States can learn from the British', Harvard lawyer Charles Haar[1] writes that the primary value of foreign exploration lies not so much in the discovery of readily transferable concepts, technologies or techniques that can be packaged up, imported duty free and unwrapped to delight policy makers. The benefits, he says, are in the stimulus of insightful reflection of culture and experiences.

The early chapters of this paper provide some indications of how cultural evolution and the vast amount of space have contributed to the wide difference in development control systems between the United States and Britain. Despite that difference, there are tantalising parallels. As often as not where there are parallels the American and British processes seem recently to be headed in precisely opposite directions – for example, America towards more discretionary control, and Britain in the late 1980s towards deregulation and some zoning. There are no right answers; no-one can say that either one or other direction is the right one, on either side. All I can hope to do in a paper such as this is to explain how American processes work (or at least to set out my perceptions of how they work) and explore the development control issues that have interested me; other aspects will interest other readers.

This is not the sort of report that has findings of fact, conclusions and recommendations. For that reason this chapter does not purport to contain conclusions, but is merely entitled 'summing up'.

Dick Babcock advised me to 'tell it how it is'; in this chapter I lead the reader along my personal choice of trails through the administrative tangle of development control – the methods used by planners and others to shape development on the ground and achieve their wider planning objectives. The trail leads through the size of local governments; and the size and nature of the decision making bodies and the extent to which they are open to public influence. Then there is local government financial self sufficiency, a key factor which leads some communities to sell the integrity of their zoning protection in exchange for community benefits such as low income housing, public plazas, and preservation of farmland for open space reasons. Such sales may risk distorting the planning process, or they may simply represent a trend towards a more market based approach to decision taking, more likely to deliver economically efficient outcomes. That they are more frequently found in the United States reflects the status of local governments almost as independent local public service businesses.

The trail then leads us to consider zoning itself, its positive attributes and its shortcomings. It emerges that zoning is not sufficient to meet the demands of today's appointed and elected officials at the various levels of authority in local and state government. Its lack of flexibility and restrictions on its application are leading to new control mechanisms which supplement and supplant it. Some of the new mechanisms are simple extensions of traditional controls over actions such as the sub-division of land. Some are additional environmental controls; the most sophisticated result from state wide comprehensive planning processes influencing local decision taking. Various aspects of these new controls suggest ways in which British mechanisms might be reviewed.

Some new controls amount to social engineering on a grand scale. Chapter 11, for example, explained the requirement on New Jersey housing developers to set aside and subsidise one fifth of houses built on new estates for low income households. Could this be a way of securing housing availability for all society in a market economy at a time when public housing is out of favour? The policy goes further than one would expect to see in Britain's planning system just now. But there are interesting questions to pose in this general scrutiny of American development control and others more specialised than me will want to think about the possibilities. I simply hope that reading this paper will have stimulated the reader to exclaim 'Well, I never thought *that* would be a workable proposition!'

The scale of local government

With the 1974 and 1980 local government reorganisations in Britain affecting the scale and responsibilities of local government, with the abolition of the metropolitan counties and the Greater London Council, and with prospective changes in the tier of local government to be responsible for development plan preparation, it is interesting to compare planning administration in different American local governments. The range is spectacularly wide, from New York City, covering a population of 7 million with its single City Planning Commission and relatively powerless community boards, to the smallest municipalities with populations of less than a thousand, responsible for preparing their own master plan and zoning ordinances (by employing contract professionals or a neighbouring local government). There are arrangements such as those in Jacksonville Florida, where the city and surrounding county have merged so that the city and most of its economically related hinterland can be planned for as one entity. There are cities such as Philadelphia, Boston and San Francisco where the suburbs managed to stop the expansion of boundaries at such an early stage that the city is only a small and relatively old core to a region of fragmented local government. There are counties which cover huge areas of the American heartland where there are no municipalities to provide urban services – just the county to do the minimum necessary for law and order and to protect the health, safety and general welfare of the rural inhabitants.

The sophistication of the planning mechanisms employed is much greater in the relatively few counties of Maryland, where there are virtually no municipalities, than in most of the 567 municipalities of New Jersey where the counties seem relatively weak. Fragmentation leads to competition between local governments to grab the development projects that will bring in the most rateable value for the least demand on services. Often there is no co-ordination between neighbouring authorities. It is no accident, in my view, that three of the states currently developing state-wide planning systems – Florida, New Jersey and Vermont – have traditional combinations of very small jurisdictions and clear localist views. Oregon's state plan was introduced to control development in farming and forested areas – again where small cities are surrounded by vast spaces with only a farming and forestry community. Minnesota developed the Twin Cities' metropolitan council to overcome regional fragmentation in infrastructure provision. I conclude that autonomous local government on a small scale is not a model for delivering the right decisions when strategic planning is needed, even if that strategic planning is in the interest of the local communities concerned, as was the case in rural Oregon.

However, if larger bodies are better at regional planning, and more likely to be able to sustain a substantial professional input, there are clear advantages to localism too. Foremost among these is more responsive government. Where planners are exposed on a regular basis to gatherings of interested and vociferous local people, decisions are more likely to reflect local wishes. Not that these decisions are necessarily in the best interests of the region or the state; they are local decisions and local people must live with the results. Equally, more local bodies may well take a more pragmatic approach to their residents who cannot abide by the ordinances. One only has to imagine how planning decisions and enforcement would change in Britain if parish rather than district councils were responsible.

Local government structure in the United States evolves only very slowly and usually in response to local popular demand in that annexation often needs the consent of those to be annexed. Reorganisations combining two neighbouring boroughs would often need the endorsement of the local electorates in a vote. Wholesale change imposed by the state as in Britain in 1974 is quite out of the question. Maryland's arrangements cannot be instantly introduced to New Jersey. The scale of Jacksonville's planning could not easily be brought to the Boston conurbation. This fragmentation and the difficulty in overcoming it reflects ideals flowing directly from the original colonies' desire for self determination. People remain suspicious of outside bodies being entitled to interfere in local responsibilities and boundaries. Outside the relatively few big city and county planning agencies, the dominant picture is local government on the Jeffersonian scale, with many small jurisdictions covering relatively small areas. And in these areas the fact that the planning system is basic probably does not matter, because there is so much space to start with.

In a US Department of Housing and Urban Development report[2] designed to improve the availability of affordable housing there is a good summing up of the community attitude to planning, reflected in every local government planning action:

> 'In many communities, changes in land use and building regulations will be necessary if such market adjustments are to occur. Citizens support zoning and building controls that they believe will preserve or enhance the livability of their neighborhoods and the value of their properties. They oppose changes that threaten to reduce such values. Every local elected official knows and understands this. But a problem arises when local policies inhibit the market adjustments that must occur if the people of this Nation are to be decently housed at reasonable prices.'

The difficulty of the Federal task in overcoming local prejudice is enormous. For the very steps that might deliver new housing at much lower cost are those which will undermine the market value of existing houses and alienate local voters.

I came away from the United States more satisfied that, in terms of size of population covered and assignment of responsibilities, the English two tier local government system in the rural areas delivers planning administration reasonably well. It is a local process, constrained by county policies, within a national framework. It is almost the structure that New Jersey is trying to establish for its 567 municipalities, on average with a smaller population than the English district. Chapter 8 described the process there bringing the state planning structure into place. Compare the Federal controls, which apply only occasionally to local decisions, to the regulation in Britain as a result of European Community action, and one can see a significant parallel between environmental control arrangements in Britain and in America's densest state.

In urban areas the English metropolitan boroughs are also reasonably responsive and accessible in terms of their planning functions, compared with the extreme example of New York City. And they are more effective by comparison with other examples where the centre city is surrounded by over 100 small suburban units such as in Pittsburgh. Successful cities with a single local government unit covering a large area, such as Denver and San Francisco, seem to have much more drive in representing a single unit, and a responsibility for planning for the city as a whole, than British cities containing many local government units (perhaps this is Leeds compared with Manchester). But in Philadelphia the amount of thought and investment in the planning of the central core seemed to ignore the all too visible need for action in the surrounding depressed neighbourhoods. In America as in Britain there are inner city development areas where normal planning procedures have not worked and need to be suspended, although in the American example the control is usually transferred to a development agency appointed by the city itself; it may even be the city planning board taking responsibility back from normally devolved decision making. Full deregulation, as in enterprise zones in Britain, has not yet been tried in the United States. Responsive local government created the regulations and would not see relinquishing control as an option.

The decision taking arrangements
(i) the planning committees

Over and above the different sizes of jurisdictions in terms of population and area, there are interesting questions of the composition of governing bodies, and of the arrangements made to despatch their land use planning responsibilities. In general, American city and county governments seem to have fewer elected members than their British counterparts. Even in the largest cities, the number of councillors is rarely more than fifteen. A more typical number is seven or nine, and in some areas elected commissioners can be effectively planning czars. Similar domination can arise, area by area, in those cities where ward based councillors predominate.

Cities and counties with so few elected officials need other appointed or elected bodies to support them if sufficient time is to be devoted to proper administration. State legislation controlling local government often requires appointed planning boards to take decisions on different aspects of land use. Sometimes arrangements are made to separate the quasi-legislative functions of plan making from the quasi-executive functions relating to decisions on applications or appeals. But *appointed* bodies are the norm. This flows perhaps from the local government reform movements of the early part of this century; the theory was that efficient local government, free of corruption, demanded business-like elected boards, who would delegate tasks requiring experts to appointed committees of experts. Planning boards often comprise those in the locality who are most likely to be qualified to act in a professional manner – the architect, real estate agent or academic perhaps. Selection standards can be very tough, as for example with New York City's Planning Commission. Elsewhere, volunteers might be sought. Curiously, selection does not appear a particularly political process; a change of local government does not often lead to a wholesale change in appointed members. And yet one of the problems of the appointment process arises when elected council and appointed board are out of sympathy. The board could not be seen as effective if it devised plans which the council would not implement in its political decisions.

Such problems are capable of resolution by formal reporting lines. What is noteworthy is that the planning committee is more likely to comprise 'experts' than is the case in Britain, provided that experts can be found in the community. It is likely to comprise fewer members – perhaps 7 with two alternates or reserves. These appointed boards sit on the dais, perhaps in the local courtroom, making their fortnightly or monthly decisions in full public view. They comprise sufficiently few members to be able to devise and stick to the strategies they wish to pursue. If led and advised well, and given clear political direction, they can be very effective, given the constraints of the tools available to them. And in bigger cities they may be advised well because political appointees stretch much further down all government hierarchies than in Britain. Mayors will have cabinets and aides; the planning officer and his team of assistants may well serve at the pleasure of the political masters.

But it is not in the relative dominance of political appointees, but in the size of committees, where I think British planning committees can learn by observation of American experience. Perhaps smaller planning committees would become more effective teams. Larger constituencies might allow councillors to be less parochial, defending their own patches less. Such committees might be more likely to work as a team with the appointed professionals, especially if one of those professionals was a formal committee member (or would such a proposition be anathema in Britain where the dividing line between political and public servants is traditionally so clearly drawn?)

In most places the American planning board is less likely to be influenced by ward based interests than its British counterpart, which might comprise one of the three councillors elected for each of the perhaps twenty wards of the district or borough. I cannot judge the extent to which smaller boards elected at large might lead to better or worse decisions in the United States. But I heard the view expressed in many places that a city as an economic entity was more likely to be prosperous if there were fewer councillors in total, with about half elected on an at-large rather than a ward based system. So, the antidote to local planning decisions weighted too much to local interests might be for planning decisions to be taken by small boards of experts, elected or selected on a district wide basis, but with a few ward based representatives of the local community.

(ii) Responsibility for decisions

Another important element to bear in mind is that American local government's planning decisions carry no right of appeal except to the courts on a point of law. Local governments are often able, by their ordinances or decisions, to refuse development they do not want. But they also bear a much greater responsibility for their own economic destinies. The buck stops with the municipality, and local government must live with its own decisions. But those local decision taking responsibilities are balanced by the financial independence of American local government; no development means no extra property tax income. So, smaller committees not based on ward elections would not be the only elements that might encourage more responsible decision taking in England. There needs to be greater accountability for the consequences of preventing development – a theme to which I return in a moment.

If too many small local governments are left to take decisions in a growth area, the effect of local responsiveness can be regional inefficiency in the use of land and infrastructure. America has so much land that this is not a crucial factor; that is one reason why effective regional government has been so slow to emerge. But this American experience of fragmentation might be relevant to planning in the shire counties when development plans become district based; it may also be relevant to co-ordination arrangements between London boroughs. There are no direct parallels here with Britain, because of the Secretary of State's role in development plan preparation and appeals. British local government's decisions are constrained, in the interests of national and regional co-ordination, by more than the threat of court action. The American lesson points to the main benefit of the Secretary of State's role in planning in Britain.

(iii) Open government

I was particularly impressed by the apparently open nature of much of American local government in the planning arena. Hundreds of local people attended some of the planning board meetings I observed, eager to see their community representatives question the developer about his proposal, and then take their own turn. Hundreds too attended the meetings of the State Planning Commission, held in various hotel conference rooms up and down the state. All the various local planning consultants would discuss matters of mutual interest over the free coffee and doughnuts provided, while inside the meeting the official sessions always ended with time for questions from the floor. Even weekend retreats of such bodies had to be open to the public under the state's sunshine laws. There is no doubt that planning out in the open is more difficult. It is challenging for appointed officials to have to stand and explain their policies to a sceptical public. Public pressure groups flourish in America, nurtured by the accessibility of the politicians – of which there are a lot given that so many posts are elected (even the judges are elected in some states). The public nature of the planning process seems healthy, even though inevitably some of the process does take place behind closed doors; developers do not willingly negotiate in public.

The public do not easily forget what they see as the primary purpose of zoning – the protection of their property rights and values. This factor is no less important in the United States than in Britain, so it could be said that the public interest in planning is equally narrow on either side of the Atlantic. But in fact it is recognised as a legitimate purpose of zoning to protect property rights, if that is a way of protecting the local tax base, and thus the means to protect the health, safety and public welfare of the citizens.

In Britain, I wonder how much interest the local public might take, even if the system were more open, for example by questioning development proposals at planning meetings. In the main the British attitude might well be more reserved and more lethargic; perhaps we trust our planning officials to do a better job in protecting our interests than our respective American counterparts. We would be equally interested in protecting our property values no doubt. In any case, planning committee agendas are already too full; how could any time be made available for the public to ask questions? The developer himself is often not permitted to make a presentation. That is where greater delegation would be needed of minor decisions to officials, perhaps in accordance with guidelines, or by locally variable development orders which would give more certainty to applicants just as zoning does in the United States. Greater delegation of minor cases would mean more time for proper public debate and consideration of the major ones.

(iv) Public influence: Initiatives and referendums

To an English observer, one of the most extraordinary aspects of open and responsive local government in the United States must be the facility to put individual issues to the vote. Local people can use initiative and referendum powers to impose decisions on their local government representatives. California is the state where these powers seem to be most prominent, and issues may be 'put on the ballot'. In Walnut Creek in that state, I saw the last new office building following a city initiative that imposed a moratorium on development until the traffic levels at all the key intersections in the town had been reduced by a specified percentage. In practice, there is little chance of reversing congestion. So the voters halted development in a partially completed city that was expected to become a major commercial and residential satellite of San Francisco.

As I said in Chapter 3 above, it is not so much the number of planning questions balloted, because very few are, but the risk of a ballot that is constantly at the back of planning officials' minds. Ballots can be seen as a vote of no confidence in planning department actions. At best they lead to more responsive local government; at worst, at a local level they encourage rampant parochialism. At the state level the best known example is Proposition 13, which froze property assessments in California in an attempt to reign in public expenditure. More recently San Francisco's growth cap initiative, putting major restrictions on the developments to be permitted, was of great political importance. There are certainly no parallels between our two systems in this topic.

Local government finance

A major factor which can distort decision taking is the local fiscal structure. In a nutshell, local governments nearly always believe that they are strapped for cash; their constituents want lower taxes without spending less on services. The main way to achieve this is by attracting particular types of development. Since neighbouring local governments share the very same objective, there is a race to see who can secure the most profitable development the fastest. In this local governments can be seen as competing local businesses all anxious to make the best return on capital employed. In Colorado, the sales tax is made available in the area where it is paid; the result is fierce competition for shopping centres. In New Jersey and many other states dependence on property tax encourages attraction of offices and shops, which provide local employment and local tax income without straining local services. The local government that is slowest off the mark gets the poorest housing or mobile home parks, with service costs disproportionate to extra tax revenue, or else simply misses out on development, leaving its residents with higher taxes and poorer services.

(In the long term, I am not personally convinced that this local government will do so badly; its undeveloped assets may ultimately become rather more valuable).

Local financial constraints are leading local governments to be more entrepreneurial in their approach to revenue raising. One reflection of this is the rapid spread of charges for the right to develop. Especially in the west, impact fees amount to as much as $10,000 per dwelling unit, partly because that is the only way, with other budgetary constraints in place, that some localities can fund the necessary infrastructure; but there is also an element of taxing development. That can be seen in the linkage schemes of Boston and San Francisco, where contributions towards low income housing provision are demanded as the price for some large development permissions.

Payment for permission In Chapter 9 I examined this trend towards requiring developers to pay an impact fee, or to contribute some amenity as the price for obtaining a permit to proceed. Some impact fees are designed to be lump sum hook-up charges per unit. But such fees distort developers' decisions and lead to less efficient use of infrastructure (to encourage efficient sewer investment it is necessary to minimise length of sewer per unit dwelling; if the fee is unrelated to the distance from the existing main drain, then the developer will have no incentive to build close to that drain, and the same is true of roads and other public facilities). A flat rate impact fee scheme also risks inequity among citizens, because it is difficult to separate out the costs properly attributable to the development, and tempting for the community to adopt gold plated investment standards as the norm once developers are perceived or required to pay all the costs of new infrastructure.

However, if investment standards can be set objectively, and the calculations of the impact of each relevant development properly apportioned, there seems a good case for making the development pay. Some would suggest that such a scheme would increase house prices. I disagree. In most cases there is a sufficient float of second hand houses and property for that to set the market price. So, the developer would not be able to pass the fee on. But neither in practice would he bear it himself, unless he happened to be unlucky enough to own the land at the time the scheme was introduced. This is because in the main, a developer's calculation starts with the price he thinks the finished product will raise, which depends on the type of development and the market for it. From this he simply subtracts his profit and all the costs necessary to convert the raw land into a finished product. So, he would negotiate for the price of any sewer, school or park fee to come out of the original landowner's proceeds on selling the land. In this way, an impact fee is properly regarded as being a price payable from the enhanced land value which can only be realised if the infrastructure is installed.

This is a policy area where the United States does have something to tell; the relationship between land use planning and infrastructure seems to me a neglected one in Britain, due to the narrow scope of what is regarded as relevant to development control. The aim would be to create a more flexible development market, where land conversions more accurately pay their own way, and communities could perhaps even compete for new development of the kind they wanted on the basis of what different developers had to offer. There seems to be scope for developers in Britain to do more to sell the attractions of their proposed development by making clear how they would mitigate the environmental disadvantages that are usually prominent, in a society that is rather more anti-development than the United States.

Development rights as a currency

Impact fees and exactions are examples of developers and local communities deciding on the price of a development permit. In this way the developer is encouraged to pay for the public infrastructure the development demands. Another way of encouraging the developer to provide public benefits is through zoning bonuses, which I described more fully in Chapter 10. The process of establishing such a scheme may sometimes involve a general reduction of zoning rights. Striking examples of this are to be found in New Jersey, flowing out of the Mount Laurel court cases described in Chapter 11. Here, a zoning density bonus may be granted provided the developer agrees to set aside a proportion of units for low and moderate income households. Municipalities wishing to escape their obligation to provide for low income housing are establishing methods of securing substantial sums from developers as the price for the right to develop more intensively than the zoning ordinance would otherwise permit. Those contributions to various low income housing funds are then used to rehabilitate housing in the inner urban areas, which have an insufficient tax base to fund an adequate programme for themselves. One reason for their inadequate tax base is the scale of tax exemptions the inner cities have had to grant in order to attract development against the competition that the suburbs offer in their race for rateables. One way of ensuring that developers apply for the bonus is to start by reducing the permissible density, before increasing it in return for a payment.

Setting the as-of-right permitted development rights at a lower level than the community might reasonably expect, if it planned purely on the basis of what each site could take by way of maximum development, facilitates trading of zoning rights. The local community is minting a local currency. Extra development permits created in this way can be used to buy locally desirable projects and investments. Having downzoned, developers can be allowed to breach the limits, up to the envelope permitted before the downzoning, provided they contribute to the community. The trades might be of air rights to save a landmark building, or of development rights to preserve farmland in the suburbs, or areas of outstanding natural importance. Or it may be to facilitate the granting of a bonus, where extra floor area is exchanged for subsidies for loss making theatres.

There is no doubt that in America these are all extremely successful methods of bending the course of development. Provided that a reasonable number of competitor local governments are operating the same sort of systems, the developer has little choice but to play the game. But these bonus schemes are ponderous; better economic analysis of the developers' options would often enable cities to obtain the same gains without conceding zoning rights to the same extent. The sorts of mechanisms that operate in Fort Collins Colorado, as Chapter 7 explained, are much more subtle and capable of relatively easy modification.

In all these cases, just as with the low income housing provision, the community is effectively creating a cheaper way of securing its environmental and social objectives than paying for them with straight cash. Why must it find these resources? Basically because in the United States there is much more value tied up in land than in Britain, where the development value attached to a piece of land was effectively nationalised in 1948. It is almost impossible for a local government to zone land for agricultural use merely as a way of preserving it as open space. Where agricultural zoning does apply, in states such as California and Oregon, it is justified for economic reasons, because of the fertility of the land. The risk of zoning for agricultural use for amenity reasons alone is that such an action could amount to a constitutional taking in respect of which compensation would be payable. That is one reason that the American National Parks are publicly owned; using development control methods as in Britain would be either ineffective or costly. The Pinelands area of New Jersey, the nation's first (and only) national reserve, is an interesting experiment towards British national park methods, in that the land is partly in private ownership with controls preserving the landscape. Yet it relies on a development rights transfer scheme to compensate the landowners in the most sensitive areas for their loss of development rights; and the Executive Director believes that land purchase will be necessary to create long term security.

Constitutional factors are also in play when it comes to protecting historic landmarks; it is impossible to pick out landmarks and treat them individually in the zoning ordinance while all the surrounding sites have development rights. So, mechanisms such as the transfer of air rights between sites have to be used for protection. The disadvantage of this is that without initial downzoning of the whole area, the nearby sites become redeveloped to an even more intense degree, thus dwarfing the landmark that is to be protected.

Can the nation afford to have so much zoning currency in circulation?

So zoning for no development can be rather more expensive than in Britain because of the compensation payable if a constitutional taking results. One reason why there is so much development value in the land in the first place is the zoning itself. Localities tended not to adopt their first zoning ordinances until there was some kind of development pressure on them. Once that pressure was there, the constituents could see the potential value of their land increasing. So, although there was a need for a more formal plan, that had to be produced against a background of not taking too much potential value away from the influential landowning class. The net result was zoning that was too generous in the largest cities and in the most rural backwaters. For example, in 1946 Los Angeles adopted its first city-wide zoning ordinance incorporating a theoretical population of 10 million, compared with the master plan estimate of 4.2 million population at build out. To put the planning and zoning on to the same basis has meant a recent downzoning of 200,000 parcels of land – no mean feat, and one accomplished only under severe pressure from the courts. Much the same considerations lie behind New Jersey's new State Development and Redevelopment Plan.

It is pointless to suggest that the United States need only follow Britain's 1947 Act model, nationalise development rights, and all its development control problems would be solved. In any case the American development culture and frontier spirit would simply not permit such a proposition to become a political reality. Yet, although overnight nationalisation of development rights in land is inconceivable in the United States, nationalisation is the precise direction in which development control is going, by a cumulative process. In reviewing their ordinances, cities and suburbs are generally reducing the amount of development that is permitted as-of-right. The motivation may be to secure more discretionary review powers, or to make sure that bonus schemes work without destroying the local amenity, or to fund trading systems. The fact is that it is happening.

The problem with such downzoning is making it go far enough to create the control that sound land use planning demands in the absence of economic forces that would deliver the same result. If there is a given market for single family houses in the suburbs, downzoning from one dwelling per acre to one dwelling per two, in order to keep down the demand on services, will result in more land being used up by more spread out development. Devices can be used to cluster the units and preserve larger tracts of open space around the housing. But the end result will still be an evenly distributed population and relatively little relief within quite large but relatively sparsely populated suburbs. Some would see no problem in this continuing until such time as the market prices of housing and agricultural land reached a balance, especially if through impact fees the developers were paying for the externalities of dispersed development. But the problem is that even greater dependence on the motor car is fostered by such spread; public transport is simply not feasible without clearly focussed patterns of travel. Less dense development also tends to make other services more expensive to provide and denies the urban dweller open countryside for his enjoyment. In any case, such development resembles nothing like the small town character that so many Americans would like to share in. Downzoning is not enough; positive action has to be taken to encourage denser development where it makes sense–around railway stations in commuter areas, around neighbourhood shopping centres, and along well serviced transportation corridors. Yet so often local politics prevent it.

Zoning as a land use planning tool

Zoning ought to be able to deliver this denser development as islands in greener landscapes. It is a forward looking process, identifying uses for all potentially developable land. But, the difficulty is the starting point–the generous zoning or development rights already in place. Here is a major contrast with the clean sheet start available in much of Britain. A cursory study of the American landscape demonstrates an absence of structure. Developments are scattered widely in a way that is expensive to service. Private motor transport is essential for access. Those unable or unwilling to use a car suffer more by the separation of uses that is a direct consequence of zoning.

(i) two major problems

There seem to be two main problems inherent in zoning itself. First, zoning does not adapt easily to the encouragement of mixed use centres. It is almost impossible to draw up a zoning map that would result in the balance of activities and uses that has emerged in the villages and small towns on the east coast that predate strict separation of uses, or in the traditional older neighbourhoods of the larger cities. In Denver, Colorado an attempt is being made to achieve that impossibility. The central Platte Valley area comprises 430 acres in need of urgent redevelopment comprising abandoned railroad yards and low value trucking industry very close to the downtown area. After two years work a 44 page zoning resolution covering an 84 page zoning regulation was produced. Anything less and the developers would not have had the confidence to invest in the changed uses proposed. The whole development is mapped out as a completely integrated series of uses, representing a complete community with jobs, housing and shops, all adjacent to Denver's downtown. I doubt whether British simplified planning zone schemes will become as complicated.

Second, just as in Britain, the system itself does little to make development happen or phase it over time. Conversion of plans into reality depends in both countries on the developer seeing that the time is right, that he has the right site, and the right return and so on, to start the development process. The difference between the British and American systems is that the British control can be used to phase development so that it can be serviced in an orderly way, and so that attractive landscapes are not

262

developed until the need is pressing. But in America, once the zoning map establishes a potential land use pattern, the developer may proceed anywhere on that map, and the mobility of society encourages developments to spread. The result is the creation of a patchwork quilt of development. Only recently have state plans such as in New Jersey and Florida started to come to grips with this temporal aspect of development, by insisting that development permits do not race ahead of infrastructure provision.

In any case, zoning can only be as useful as the use that is made of it. The mechanism itself cannot take the blame if local governments create ordinances which imply substantial imbalances between the number of homes and the number of jobs in any area, or between manual and professional workers' homes.

(ii) Flexibility and certainty

On the other hand zoning has its positive attributes. Willard Rouse, a major developer in Philadelphia, was asked[3] what he thought was the most attractive feature of the American planning process, the one from which other countries could benefit most. His response was the single word, 'flexibility'. He could not work, he said, in a system where government could come in and designate private land as green belt, not to be developed and there was an end to the matter. By flexibility he meant the freedom to act within the various zoning constraints, or to seek to change them; and the freedom to choose from a wide range of sites designated for development and on which he had a guaranteed right to proceed, and indeed to choose from a wide choice of local governments.

It is a different flexibility to that which English developers enjoy, of being free to propose whatever type of development they choose, arranged on the site in whatever way they choose, and of knowing that the local planning authority has the freedom to agree to proposals on a discretionary basis. Of course, what is perceived as local authority inflexibility in considering the case before it can lead to demands for more certainty. But, experience in the American system suggests that more certainty of what can be developed requires there to be less flexibility when an exception is proposed. In both systems, there is tension between flexibility and certainty.

The American flexibility is predicated on there being plenty of land available for development, and the lack of a phasing control in most zoning ordinances ensures such a choice. But, at the same time, zoning ordinances can prescribe uniformity of certain design aspects that represent a constraint on flexibility, justified perhaps only by the need for certainty for the adjoining owners, and perhaps by the distrust of local government action if total discretion were in its hands. The list I set out in Chapter 7, of model measures intended to deliver affordable housing, demonstrates how much land can be used up by rigidity in the zoning ordinance. Standard set-backs, yard sizes, frontage lengths and so on mean that more land is used per dwelling than the developer would otherwise choose for his design. In these circumstances, planned unit developments some way from traditional zoning mechanisms can provide the flexibility needed; whether they provide certainty depends on the local government ordinance concerned.

Another aspect of certainty in zoning arises because the master plan tends to be drawn up by the same local government as is responsible for the zoning ordinance. The two ought to conform, with the zoning map representing the concrete outcome expected if the policies set out in the master plan come to fruition. In California, state law *requires* the two to conform, and if they do not the local government concerned can find itself in court, challenged by either developers or residents, according to the nature of the inconsistency. Perhaps this underlines that more certainty should emerge from the proposed change in England that will give districts that decide applications more responsibility for preparing development plans.

(iii) zoning as a positive incentive

One of the most effective applications of zoning certainty that I observed was the temporary density bonus available on the west side of Midtown Manhattan. By making clear that the bonus provision would be available only to developments started in the six years before a 'sunset' applied, and sticking to its original intentions rather than wavering and extending the scheme, New York City refocussed growth from an area under pressure to a nearby location where there was rather more public transport capacity. The scheme worked because of its precision and the temporary certainty that it created. It was clear how the developers' sums would work out with and without the scheme.

Because in Britain there is little certainty about how much development a site could take in the base case, it is difficult to see how this type of initiative could be applied. But if it were possible to persuade developers that what a simplified planning zone scheme permitted was rather more than the scale of development that would be permitted after expiry of the scheme, then a similar positive effect might be seen. It is towards the end of their time limits that the general permissions of simplified planning zones may prove to have real value as positive tools in addition to their functions of removing bureacratic applications.

(iv) Innovative zoning

In Chapter 4 I outlined a whole series of special types of zoning that had emerged in response to the limitations of zoning itself. In particular, floating zones and mixed use districts underline the realisation that the separation of uses and types of housing, in the way that zoning without frills does, is not the most appropriate way of meeting social and environmental needs. Zoning bonuses and incentive zoning represent overlays to try to bend the zoning process to the benefit of the community. Planned unit development arrangements reflect that on any site of significant size, traditional zoning rules will not deliver the best solution. The examples of unnecessary constraints, in Chapter 5, demonstrate some of the particular elements of a zoning mechanism which bring certainty, but certainty that developers would prefer to do without.

The tension between as-of-right and discretionary processes is brought out in Chapter 10. I concluded that the constitutional constraints over zoning were what created the tensions. Without those constraints, there would have been no need for the many devices that have been invented. An as-of-right answer turns out to be exceedingly complex, if it is not to be unduly crude. As long as 1947 Act principles remain in Britain we do not need as-of-right development control mechanisms – just a predictable relationship between development plans and development control decisions.

(v) zoning and design

The extent of development control varies widely between different places in the United States. I quoted examples to demonstrate this in Chapters 1 and 5, where I also reported my efforts to try to measure the different extent of control. It seems that, in terms of applications per head of population, there is perhaps only one eighth the degree of discretionary control in the United States as in Britain. But that does not mean that development control is that much less stringent. The effect of zoning is to constrain all developments according to the rules in place, so although no discretionary decision is needed, development is very definitely shaped by the ordinance. This can lead to uniformity of shape of design that is unnecessary - for example in the lot layouts of vast areas of suburbia, or in the wedding cake architecture of New York City effectively demanded by the 1916 ordinance there. This is an area of subjective judgement, but I cannot help feel that the discretionary approach suits urban design in Britain better, given that we all live so much closer to each other. America may be home to some important modern architecture, but I would hazard a guess that not much of it took place without the need for variances or discretionary approvals; the zoning envelope does not necessarily give the architect freedom, and in some cities that freedom is further constrained by design commissions (intended to prevent the architects' clients demanding dull buildings!)

The latest innovation is now towards more traditional mixes of uses, often on a grid layout rather than on curvilinear cul-de-sacs. Picket fences, compulsory porches, requirements for buildings to come close to the street in walkable towns and use of traditional materials all seem likely. Planned unit development rules may start to deliver what is seen as the traditional shape of American small towns again. At last zoning is being used as a tool to improve design, rather than as a functional control that obstructs good design.

(vi) zoning bites through the life of a building

One major advantage of zoning is that it continues to apply after the construction phase is over. The setback for the zone continues to apply to any subsequent extension during the life of the building. No house in a zone with a maximum floor area can be extended to exceed that constraint, except with a variance related to hardship (perhaps an unexpectedly dependent relative). Thus the original permission sets the maximum development that can ever be permitted, and only development within that envelope is acceptable. This has a considerable advantage over the British process where the local authority looks at the application in hand on the merits of the development proposal. Normally the 25 per cent floor area house extensions that the General Development Order permits, usually without any further opportunity for local government intervention should not be a material consideration. But it is hard to ignore, and either the initial review leads to smaller houses being permitted, to allow for some leeway for later extensions, or the local government must seek to impose conditions taking away basic rights – conditions frowned upon by central government at appeals.

(vii) Doing without zoning

Of course it should not be assumed that zoning is the only development control mechanism. Usually it is applied in combination with some other controls. In Houston, Texas it is notable by its absence, and other controls go a long way to ensure that new development is properly planned. Some say that the lack of zoning there shows in the poor living quality in some neighbourhoods; others believe that the extra freedom has benefited the local economy. By making it easier for poor people to set up businesses, Houston has generated extra resources for purposes such as infrastructure construction.

The ideas of Fort Collins and Breckenridge in quantification as an aid to decision taking are interesting. Councillors are being asked to rank and quantify their objectives. The Fort Collins process seems to be designed to ensure that most developments are considered on an *ad hoc* discretionary basis, with the zoning code as a residual safety net – not permitting much compared with what can be obtained by the alternative of what amounts to a highly developed planned unit development process backed by exactions. The result is an attractive and well planned city making efficient use of land within the built up area – based on orderly negotiation. It is an example worth studying, and most developers in those places choose it in preference to zoning.

The eclipse of zoning

For all its advantages and disadvantages, zoning is not the same comprehensive land use planning mechanism as in the past. It is not becoming less used; on the contrary, it is only a few cities that can do without. And state planning initiatives are bringing planning and zoning to many rural areas that until recently saw no need for it. It is simply that Americans are becoming much more environmentally aware. Recycling schemes are spreading at a rapid rate as the cost of landfill in the relatively few acceptable sites rises. Nuclear power stations are almost impossible to commission. There is increasing concern about the development of wetlands, groundwater recharge areas, wildlife preserves, air and ground pollution, and the despoliation of coastlines. This increasing awareness is being reflected at state and Federal levels in new pollution legislation and new regulation. The growth of regulation has been so great that some states have had to establish special commissions to try to ensure some efficiency in the exercise of control. This new regulation is not so concerned with the defence of property values against the effects of marauding developers or inappropriate neighbours. It seems to reflect a wider environmental concern about the cumulative effects of development, especially in the less inhabited areas – even farmland – over which urban Americans are increasingly coming to believe that they have a right to determine use.

That all of these new systems, including the state planning initiatives, have been set up outside the traditional method of controlling land use – zoning – might be regarded as an indictment of that method of control. One reason for this phenomenon of incremental extension is that zoning is one of the main powers of local governments and is jealously guarded by local politicians. Any new state power limiting a power of local governments is controversial indeed. The response of the states seems to be to find other, more effective ways themselves to secure development control objectives. Another reason for the proliferation of control systems is that it is easier to set up a new and comparatively confined process for avoiding past difficulties, rather than trying to reshape existing systems. If there is a state wide problem of one kind or another it is easier for the state to set up a new specific regulatory system, than to try to coordinate local government action against a problem that may not have arisen locally. In Arizona it is now necessary to demonstrate a 100 year supply of water before development proceeds. New Jersey's draft state plan seems to presage a whole range of new measures designed to prevent the profligate use of green field sites and stream corridors when serviced infrastructure exists elsewhere. Other states have implemented procedurally complex environmental impact reviews, extending the requirement under Federal law to other than Federal developments. All of these control mechanisms by-pass zoning, which therefore becomes less significant among the hurdles that a developer faces.

Despite the efforts of environmental efficiency commissions and permit co-ordinators, development seems likely to continue to become more beset by bureaucracy. Lack of co-ordination of planning between neighbouring communities is leading to state efforts to achieve some structure for the regional planning process and consistency between authorities. But there is also little co-ordination between different state permitting departments.

Balancing advantages and disadvantages of development proposals is difficult enough where the end result is one permit, let alone the number that are sometimes necessary from different local and state government departments. Figure 4.1 gave an indication of the burdens that developers must increasingly bear.

Local communities are supplementing zoning with more sophisticated subdivision controls and site review procedures. And the rules that apply in one community are bound to be different to those in the next. So is the extent to which any of the rules are enforced by communities.

Zoning conclusions

All this means that, by comparison with Britain there is a great deal of complexity in the development control processes. One recent trend in Britain has been to deregulate wherever possible, including in the planning field. The government is able to make some inroads, because it sets the rules in the General Development Order and the Use Classes Order, which apply to all local governments. There is no prospect of the centre in America taking a similar approach to try to improve the national economy by streamlining rules. Even the states have little influence over the way in which local governments create and administer their development control systems. In such circumstances, it is the competition between local governments to attract the right kind of development that keeps the permitting process reasonably fast. And developers often have access to the system by the importance of political financial contributions.

By now the reader will have deduced that with few exceptions (such as the model code produced by Andres Duany and Elizabeth Plater-Zyberk), zoning has to be highly complex if it is to succeed as an effective development control tool. Yet such complication is the last thing the developer wants. By creating certainty about the potential use of land it does create development value in land and thus helps to narrow the initial scope for negotiation over proposals between the developer and the local government. But that same value created is a huge obstacle to proper planning when priorities change. I have become a firm believer in discretionary control as against as of right zoning, despite the views of Willard Rouse, provided that the discretion is properly informed by a proper plan to ensure consistency of decision taking. And in Britain we should also value the capability of the planning system to take on board a wide range of material considerations, avoiding the need for a whole raft of incremental specific approvals from other public agencies.

Efficiency of operation

With 10,000 planning authorities operating within at least 50 different legal structures, and with no clear boundary defining which uses of the police power are genuine land use planning matters, it is perhaps not surprising that comprehensive data about the operation of the planning system are practically non-existent. There can be little doubt that the costs of the development control system are high. The stages and delays that a development must pass through adds to financing costs. Some of the affordable housing demonstration projects show that quite straightforward procedural initiatives could cut $2,000 from the price of a house, although whether that would benefit the purchaser or developer is not clear.

However, there seems little interest in attempting to collect comprehensive data about delays, even on a state wide basis. So, no-one can say with certainty whether the delays of environmental reviews in New York City are driving development to Connecticut, where procedures might be quicker. No-one knows how quick anyone else is; the only evidence is anecdotal. Developers point out that they would rather have a process of certain speed, even if that speed was slow, than tax incentives for a project of unknown timing. Nor does anyone know what a 'normal delay' is; in the light of one of the 1987 US Supreme Court cases anything more than a normal delay by a local government might give rise to a liability to pay compensation for a temporary taking. Nor can anyone start to measure whether the extent of controls in different places yields a better quality environment; if developments of a certain type are always allowed, then there seems little purpose to that control in the first place. Yet there seems to be little comparison done.

I attempted to collect some data through questionnaires to about 100 local governments. There seemed no great resistance to providing information, some of which is reproduced in this report. I am grateful to all those who helped. It helped me to compare the extent of American controls and to investigate the speed of the American process. But much more time is needed than I had available to bring information about different development control systems to a standard basis. Meaningful comparative information about the operation of the local development control system is a subject that a body with the resources of the American Planning Association ought to tackle. I suspect that research on management measures is simply not as attractive as investigating the latest innovations in trading development rights. But published data on the time taken to obtain permits in different places might just influence developers in their choice of location in a competitive field. I believe comparative competition has a role to play in the local government marketplace

The Federal role in land use planning is slight; there is therefore little role for the deregulatory thrust that has been behind recent central government planning initiatives in Britain. It is generally for local government to be accountable to its electorate and to the state courts – constrained by the rules set in state legislation. Against that background there seems little scope for any general acceleration of the process, although there will always be a proportion of local governments concerned enough to take action themselves.

Other administrative aspects

In looking, in Chapter 7, at the efficiency of the American planning process, I suggested a number of measures that might be of interest to those administering planning processes in England. Perhaps the most interesting idea is the use of hearings examiners, which are rather like planning inspectors. Because the Constitution seems to encourage more public participation in American local government procedures, hearings examiners are an effective way of making the process more efficient by focussing and depoliticising the debate. A prerequisite is that the local plan should be properly drawn up and kept up to date; indeed, it might encourage more interest in the preparation of local plans if local decisions were more clearly bound by them. American experience suggests that English local authorities could spend more time on the preparation of development plans if they delegated more of their development control decisions to appointed individuals, perhaps to the planning officer with a right of appeal to a local planning committee hearing. If more time was spent on the preparation of the local plans, those plans would be more up to date, and would lead to more consistent decision taking by the appointed official. Similarly at the appeal level, a hearings examiner might be appointed by the Secretary of State locally, operating rather like a small claims court in hearing all appeals for the county, once a month, except those called in for a full public inquiry.

Experience with the state environmental permitting process in Vermont provided some other interesting parallels with the planning appeal administration in England. For example, the hearings are statutorily required to be held within a specified time of the appeal, and any party in difficulty will presumably simply hire the expert resources it needs to abide by that timetable. Pre-hearing conferences are binding on the parties, appeals must relate to specified criteria, and parties may give evidence only if they can show a legitimate interest in the development proposed. The fees charged for reviews are based on a percentage of the construction costs certified by an appropriate professional; that avoids the need for updates to reflect inflation.

Concluding thoughts and some suppressed prejudices

In Chapter 1 I wondered whether there was a yawning gap between American and British development control systems. I concluded that there were some parallels and some areas where practices seemed to be so different to defy comparison. I hope that by following up some of the more interesting parallels, I have shown that American experience does have something to offer. I hope too that I have shed some light on some common misconceptions; I do not know how common, but at least I held them before embarking on a year of adventure. American practice is far more complicated, far more diverse, and far more bureaucratic than I had expected. In some cases the controls are far more stringent than in Britain – for example in regulating changes in the ownership and division of land. My illusions about the certainty of zoning were rudely shattered. If developers have certainty that they are going to get their permission, that is generally not because of the zoning, but because there is competition between local governments which need the development to sustain their tax revenues. The social engineering of the Mount Laurel housing process, described in Chapter 11, goes much further than we would envisage in Britain.

The processing of applications involves the same types of actors, but the tools used are very different. Even so, the negotiations are often similar, especially when it comes to planning gain. In most of America, there is a greater acceptance that development is right, but increasing numbers of areas are deciding that they have had enough, and that leads them towards the attitudes to development that are more prevalent in Britain. Developers, they suggest, should at least pay their own way. Here is a major parallel between our two countries, worthy of further examination.

Perhaps, at this late stage, I can admit to two prejudices. I never ceased to be amazed at what Americans will put up with in the shape of advertisement hoardings along motorways and main roads. Vermont has strict controls to prevent this, but no other state has gone so far. There are some Federal rules, which have had the effect of moving the signs further back from Interstate highways, to distances where they need to be even larger and illuminated by a power supply from the nearest farm to be effective. It is eerie to travel through the pitch black of rural Virginia, every so often passing illuminated billboards advertising the attractions at the next truckstop. It seems criminal to obliterate the wonderful South Dakota landscape between signs for Wall Drug and other tourist 'attractions'. Billboards and utility poles clutter urban and rural America, but during this report I have resisted the temptation to ask why. The planning system delivers what the local people want and can afford against the risk of a constitutional taking that might cost them a fortune. It is not for me, in an examination of how development is controlled, to criticise the starting point.

Similarly, I decided not to include in this report any description of the latest forms of growth – the developments which are catching on and might arrive in Britain any day soon. Thirty years ago, the out-of-town shopping center was about to turn American cities inside out. Today, mixed developments may be about to recreate new self sufficient villages of activity. Nearly every city seems to be finding a warehouse district, or a part of old downtown, onto which can be crafted boutiques with high profit businesses set to attract people back from the anonymous malls on the outskirts. Pollution, or rather strict Federal pollution controls are forcing some cities to invest in new public transport, such as the light rail system in Portland, Oregon. Developers like the solid and permanent nature of trolley routes, which cannot be diverted like buses, and land values are paying back some of the infrastructure costs. Urban design guidelines imposed by developers to enhance the value of their product might be about to take the place of local zoning codes, as in the case of Seaside, Florida which even featured on Prince Charles' television programme about livable cities. Who can tell what the future might hold, and what of it might be transferred to this side of the Atlantic. I preferred to observe the latest manifestations of this mobile, development minded culture, than to speculate about where they might lead and whether they might translate into Britain.

What I did observe was a very mixed set of local governments, in terms of size, style of administration and influence. Particular characteristics were the open nature, and the local financial and political accountability. Particular constraints were the Constitution and the inability to reform, except from within. As a result of the characteristics of local government, America has gone a long way towards methods of making the developer pay the costs he imposes on the local community, and perhaps more (and this may be inequitable). Similar mechanisms allow development rights to be traded for contributions to the public sector – whether in cash or in kind. Many development rights are granted by the zoning system, although not necessarily the right ones to allow for creative urban design and the most efficient land uses. But zoning does grant a degree of certainty alongside its inflexibility. When zoning becomes more flexible, it can become less certain. In any case, its shortcomings are leading to the development of other control methods which both build on and supplement the zoning. Efficiency and deregulation come a long way down the American agenda; but that does not mean a lack of innovation in planning administration – innovation driven by comparative competition and by pride in the discipline. We can learn from that innovation, perhaps if only to broaden the scope of ideas worth pursuing. I look forward to doing just that in my future career in the Department of the Environment.

In America, I found much to wonder at, in both senses of the word. Whether it was a distaste for billboards, or a surprising affection for tall buildings as part of urban design, or just total amazement at the amount of space, I thank America for making me think, by showing me parallels and paradoxes and examples of how different things might be.

NOTES TO CHAPTER 12

1. In *Cities, Law, and Social Policy*, published in 1984 by D C Heath and Co, Professor Charles Haar brings together nine chapters about different aspects of planning in Britain, presented by specialists in each field. He then distills some of the lessons for American practice that emerged in discussions at a conference in London that brought those specialists together with an international cross section of administrators, city planners, developers and officials.

2. Affordable Housing: How Local Regulatory Improvements Can Help, by Stevenson Weitz, published by US Department of Housing and Urban Development Office of Policy Development and Research, September 1982.

3. At the American Bar Association Mid-Year Meeting in Philadelphia, January 1988.

Index

Printed in the United Kingdom for HMSO
Dd292565 3/90 C15 G443 10170